Teaching Literature and Medicine

Modern Language Association of America
Options for Teaching

Joseph Gibaldi, Series Editor

Teaching Literature and Medicine

Edited by
Anne Hunsaker Hawkins
Marilyn Chandler McEntyre

The Modern Language Association
New York   2000

For information about obtaining permission to reprint material from MLA book publications, send your request by mail (see address below), e-mail (permissions@mla.org), or fax (212 477-9863).

"Song for Pythagoras," from *White Coat, Purple Coat,* by Dannie Abse, is reprinted by permission of Persea Books. © 1991 by Dannie Abse.

Library of Congress Cataloging-in-Publication Data

Teaching literature and medicine / edited by Anne Hunsaker Hawkins and
    Marilyn Chandler McEntyre.
      p.   cm.
    Includes bibliographical references and index.
    ISBN 0-87352-356-3. — ISBN 0-87352-357-1 (pbk.)
    1. Literature and medicine. 2. Literature—Study and teaching.
    3. Medicine—Study and teaching. 4. Medicine in literature.
    I. Hawkins, Anne Hunsaker, 1944– . II. McEntyre, Marilyn
    Chandler, 1949– .
    PN56.M38T43 1999
    809—dc21   99-43455

Cover illustration of the paperback edition: Andreas Vesalius, *De humani corporis fabrica* (Basel, 1543): book 2, plate 25.

Printed on recycled paper

Published by the Modern Language Association of America
10 Astor Place, New York, New York 10003-6981

Contents

Part II: Texts, Authors, Genres

Part III: Literature in Medical Education
              and Medical Practice

Part IV: Resources for Teachers and Scholars in Literature and Medicine

Anne Hunsaker Hawkins
and Marilyn Chandler McEntyre

Introduction: Teaching Literature and Medicine: A Retrospective and a Rationale

Literature and medicine have a long history of cross-pollination. From biblical and classical accounts of plagues and healings to humoral theory in the works of Robert Burton and Shakespeare and from the ubiquitous consumptives of the Victorian novel to the psychopathologies and malignancies of contemporary fiction, drama, and film, medical themes in literature abound. Works such as Thomas Mann's *The Magic Mountain* and major authors who are also physicians, such as Anton Chekhov and William Carlos Williams, are recent examples of this recurrent preoccupation with both the actualities and the metaphorical possibilities of illness and medicine.

It is no surprise, then, that courses in literature and medicine should be flourishing in undergraduate curricula, at medical schools, and in continuing-education programs throughout the United States and Canada; it is perhaps surprising only that they do not have a longer history in medical education. Yet in a sense they do. The fragmentation of the arts and sciences into the present array of

1

disciplines and subdisciplines that appear in course catalogs is fairly recent. Historically, training in medicine, as in the other professions, commonly included reading in the domain of "philosophy"—a category that comprised most of what we now call the humanities. Current widespread, systematic reintroduction of literature courses into premedical and medical education programs suggests a shared recognition that responsible and balanced medical education is not only enhanced by but also requires study of the humanities as well as the sciences.

Our intent in this volume is to present a variety of approaches to teaching literature and medicine—approaches that differ in subject and scope but that are all rigorous and methodologically grounded. To this end, the volume features descriptions of courses that bring the methods and skills of literary studies to bear on cultural, ethical, social, political, and psychological dimensions of medical practice, health, and illness. The intended audience is academic professionals —literary scholars and physicians, whether in colleges and universities, medical schools, or professional settings—who teach literature and medicine or who are interested in enriching courses in either discipline by introducing interdisciplinary dimensions.

Literature and Medicine as an Interdisciplinary Field

There is a great deal of reciprocity in the relation between medicine and the various cultural mythologies about illness, suffering, death, and grief embodied so often in literature. On the one hand, the tendency in recent literary and cultural studies to dissolve reality into subjective perception or ideological construct must take into account the hard and sobering factuality of the body, the materiality of our mortal flesh. Literary interpretation becomes daily more abstract and conceptual, while medicine—for all its scientific advances —remains grounded in concrete experiences of sickness and pain and in the pragmatic strategies of healing. On the other hand, as Kathryn Montgomery Hunter has convincingly argued in *Doctors' Stories*, medical practice is not, strictly speaking, a science. It is interpretive and not simply fact based, and the capacity to empathize and intuit can be as important in diagnosis and treatment as are scientific data and logical deduction. Moreover, medicine, like much of literature, is concerned with persons and their stories and participates both tacitly and explicitly in cultural values, assumptions, and ideologies. The methods of analysis that literary critics have learned to apply in their field can usefully be applied to medicine as well.

Teachers and scholars in literature and medicine have worked over the years to develop a theoretical framework specific to the field (see Banks; Hunter, "Literature," "Toward"; Rousseau, "Literature and Medicine: The State," "Literature and Medicine: Towards a Simultaneity"). Literature and medicine today is perhaps best understood not as a fusion of the literary and the medical but as a genuinely interdisciplinary (some would prefer cross-disciplinary) field, a dialogue rather than a merger. While recognizing the connections between literature and medicine, it is important not to ignore the deep-lying differences and resultant tensions between them. Humanists especially are tempted by what one might term the rhetoric of reconciliation, characterized by such phrases as "achieving a synthesis of the literary and the medical" or "reconciling the two cultures." There are dangers, conceptual and pedagogical, in adopting even tacitly such a synthetic goal. An interdisciplinary course is more challenging in every sense if it acknowledges tensions, points out contrasts, and encourages controversy than if it tries to establish a harmonious complementarity or subordinates one discipline to the other. For example, one such tension is that between constructivist and reductionist notions of illness. Few would argue that illness experience, like medical practice, is not in some way shaped by cultural values and assumptions. But it seems clear that the degree of social constructedness varies widely between a disease that has a definable pathogen, such as tuberculosis, and one that seems to derive from cultural norms and values, such as anorexia.

The recent appearance of courses in literature and medicine can be traced back to the educational reforms of the 1960s, which led to the introduction of humanities programs in medical school curricula.[1] Humanities courses were intended to remedy an imbalance in medical education (and practice) in which too much emphasis was placed on the technological aspects of health care and too little on the human aspects of medicine and caregiving, an imbalance that may have resulted from bedazzlement with new technologies from x rays to MRI scanners and with antibiotics and miracle drugs that seemed to succeed whether administered with compassion or not.

Literature and medicine first emerged in its present form as an academic discipline in 1972, when Joanne Trautmann (Banks) was appointed to a position in literature at the Pennsylvania State University College of Medicine. Ten years later, the discipline began to occupy a recognized place in scholarship with the advent of the Johns Hopkins journal *Literature and Medicine*. Since then the field has continued to expand to the extent that by 1995 courses in literature were being taught in one-third of all medical schools in the United States. Literature and medicine is thus now an academic discipline with its own heuristic strategies, methodologies, and research agendas (see Charon et al., "Literature and Medicine"; Hunter et al.).

Faculty members who teach literature courses in the medical curriculum have for years worked together closely through participation in annual meetings of the Society for Health and Human Values, through involvement with the journal *Literature and Medicine*, and through MLA special sessions.[2] Though literature faculty members in medical schools know of one another's work through professional meetings and scholarship, there may not be the same sense of community among those in undergraduate programs. Indeed there seem to be two groups of scholar-teachers in this field—those in medical schools and those in colleges and universities—and little dialogue between the two. A major goal in producing this volume is to bring about a scholarly community and further collaboration among all those who teach and write about literature and medicine.

Teaching Literature and Medicine in the Medical School Setting

Literature and medicine is now taught in medical schools at all levels: in first- and second-year courses; in clinical clerkships for third-

and fourth-year students; in ethics seminars and rounds; and in chaplaincy programs, residency training, and seminars for faculty physicians. Sometimes literary texts and skills are incorporated into courses in medical interviewing and in the basic sciences. A fair number of medical school courses, programs, and projects now require students to write about patients as individual persons: a salient example of such teaching is Rita Charon's innovative and much copied practice of asking students to write about illness from the perspective of the patient ("To Render").

The reasons for including courses in literature and writing in the already crowded medical school curriculum are, broadly speaking, threefold. The first concerns the patient: such courses teach physicians how to listen more discerningly to their patients' stories. They emphasize the importance of understanding the patient's and family members' points of view on the experience of illness and treatment, foster empathy for patients and family members, and help physicians hone the communication skills so important to establishing a therapeutic alliance. Recognizing that a text may have multiple meanings helps physicians better tolerate the multiple and sometimes contradictory responses that patients and their families may bring to an illness experience.

The second reason concerns the physician: reading and then discussing and reflecting on literature inevitably brings one face to face with one's assumptions, biases, and preconceptions and alerts one to the extent to which these can determine how a text—or a patient's story—is interpreted. Reading literature thus heightens personal awareness and fosters the habit of self-scrutiny.

The third concerns ethics: literature and literary skills enable physicians to think both critically and empathetically about moral issues in medicine. In ancient Greek culture, where both Western medicine and Western philosophy originated, literature was recognized as an important source of moral teaching. Today ethical theory has become the preserve of professional philosophers. However, poets, novelists, and playwrights continue to explore—and explore from different perspectives—the tensions and conflicts of the moral life in ways that are often relevant for medical practice. Robert

Coles, among others, has become well known for his success in teaching medical ethics through novels, and more recently narrative literature and narrative ways of knowing—what Rita Charon calls "narrative competence" ("Narrative Road")—have become widely accepted as offering a valuable, perhaps necessary, complement to the principle-based approach to medical ethics that derives from analytic philosophy.

When first introduced into the medical curriculum in the early 1970s, literature was considered important because it offered readers an imaginative grasp of other lives and other experiences, sensitizing readers to the vagaries of the human condition and, it was hoped, encouraging and fostering empathy. Courses in literature at that time tended to focus on images and roles of physicians or on patients' experiences. Such courses used traditional literary works—especially short fiction—that portrayed illness, dying, and medical encounters with the aim of motivating the student to attend to the patient as well as the disease. Gradually, and with the help of such movements as multiculturalism and feminism, courses in literature and medicine have come to address issues of socioeconomic context and cultural background along with issues of race, ethnicity, and gender. As the discipline developed, concerns about textuality encouraged instructors to approach literature not as a depiction of real-life persons and events but as a reconstruction inviting questions about genre, point of view, frame, narrative voice, and so on.

Over time various genres—autobiography, medical writings, poetry, and plays—have been introduced into the curriculum, and explicit attention has been paid to genre as significant in itself. Patient narratives, or "pathographies," prove especially useful because they directly introduce students to the many nonmedical concerns of patients and their families. Moreover, as autobiographies that interpret and transform the experiences they record, these narratives eloquently demonstrate the importance of the physician's understanding how patients give meaning to their experiences. Poetry is used extensively in medical school teaching for both practical and pedagogical reasons: because poems are often short, and because the analytic and imaginative act of reading poetry develops interpretive skills in listening and increases tolerance for ambiguity. Physicians now have less time with their patients than ever before, but the same skills of careful listening and accurate interpretation are required of them. It may be that the brief poem, utilizing metaphor and symbol and packed with overt and covert meaning, is closer in length to the now much abbreviated patient interview than is the more leisurely story. Moreover, a brief poem is often the best way to defamiliarize an ordinary routine or represent what is epiphanic in some inarticulate mood or commonplace event.

Stories, biographies, and autobiographies that focus on medical training, as well as those that focus on the experience of patients, cast light on the moral dilemmas that are the staple of medical work. Learning to address literary questions about narrative stance, point of view, dramatic irony, tone, resonance, and framing that arise in reading such texts, or even in viewing films like *The Doctor, Awakenings,* or *Whose Life Is It, Anyway?,* trains students to raise crucial questions about the clinical encounter, the institutional pressures on practitioners, the sources and uses of medical authority, and the complexity of medical discourse.

It is now not uncommon to find medical theater groups as well as exercises in role-playing and sometimes even in playwriting at teaching hospitals. The essay by Elizabeth Homan and Sidney Homan in this volume describes how theater is integrated into the curriculum at the University of Florida. Several schools have developed medical theater courses and programs based on the innovative Readers' Theater at the University of North Carolina Medical School, Chapel Hill. At the Pennsylvania State University College of Medicine, for example, readers' theater has been combined with a statewide playwriting contest on a designated medical theme.[3] Drama is superbly equipped to draw medical personnel (as actors) and laypersons (as audience) into an encounter that generates spirited discussion and genuine exchange of views.

Most courses in literature and medicine in medical school settings have not kept pace with scholarship in the field in finding ways to incorporate the various theoretical approaches that derive from structuralism and deconstruction. In part this is because students often come to medical school with only minimal experience in serious literary study. Because of the competitiveness of the medical school selection process, undergraduate science majors frequently avoid literature courses, in which they cannot be certain of receiving an A; moreover, premedicine programs tend to be packed with required science courses and leave little room for electives. But most undergraduate programs have distribution requirements, and most medical school admissions committees prefer applicants who have taken courses in the humanities. It is our hope that rigorous courses in literature and medicine will become widely available to undergraduates across the nation. If they do, literature can be discussed in the medical school setting in more sophisticated ways.

How, in the crowded medical curriculum, can a course in literature and medicine succeed? There is no formula for success, especially given the ongoing and extensive changes in medical curricula across the country. Perhaps the most important factor is support from clinical and basic science departments, deans, and program and course directors—and this varies widely from school to school.

There are special problems in offering literature and medicine courses in a medical school curriculum, and success depends on recognizing and then dealing with these problems creatively and constructively. One difficulty is that such courses tend to attract a heterogenous group of students that includes those with extensive undergraduate training in literature as well as those with no background in literature at all. The instructor alert to this discrepancy can make provisions for the less literarily trained students, perhaps providing an extra class or handouts.

Other problems tend to cluster around differences between the first two years of medical school training, when students are immersed in studying basic science, and the last two years, which are devoted to learning clinical medicine. Beginning students are overwhelmingly occupied with the heavy demands of science courses; moreover, they have little experience with patients or with the culture of medicine to draw on and bring to their readings. Courses in literature and medicine at this point may succeed best if linked to existing courses, as essays by LaVera Crawley and Douglas Reifler demonstrate. Students in their clinical years have had experience with patients and with the medical system and there is more flexibility in their schedules; the problem is that their various clerkships frequently send them to other sites. Literature and medicine courses for these students can be successful as minicourses directly attached to particular clerkships (which might last from three to eight weeks) and incorporated in the students' clerkship schedules, as suggested in the essay by Joseph Cady. There is good reason to offer freestanding courses in literature and medicine late in students' medical training when they have time for lengthy and challenging readings and, after three years of scientific and clinical training, welcome a new perspective on their work. Success in teaching at any level is enhanced when instructors adopt realistic reading and writing assignments, show sensitivity to students' schedules, and limit class size so that discussion is possible.

Also, in planning a literature and medicine course, it is important to allow for recent—and ongoing—changes affecting medical curricula across the nation. Changes include the move in medical schools toward problem-based learning, with its "case-based approach" and essay rather than multiple-choice exams; the increasing emphasis on primary care, with earlier and more extensive patient contact and community involvement; the need, greatly enhanced by a consumer-driven health-care market, to train physicians who can communicate well with patients; and the changing demographics in the United States, requiring physicians to be responsive to patients with differing cultural values and expectations. These developments suggest increased need and increased opportunities for innovative interdisciplinary teaching.

Teaching Literature and Medicine in the Undergraduate Setting

Introduced into undergraduate education somewhat later than into medical schools, courses in literature and medicine are now flourishing in many colleges and universities. But the literature and medicine course is not automatically self-justifying in the world of undergraduate liberal arts and sciences. Not every curriculum committee leaps at the chance to offer a new interdisciplinary course. Not every English department is eager to cater to the needs of literature-resistant premeds. And it is the rare premedicine program that is looking for a way to enhance its protégés' literary skills and poetic aptitude—the MCAT does not measure negative capability.

Three distinct groups of undergraduates stand to benefit most from a course in literature and medicine: premeds; students who are considering medicine as well as other careers in the health professions; and students majoring in fine arts or the humanities, particularly in literature or history. For premeds, such a course serves many of the purposes outlined above: fostering in students an awareness of narrative as an epistemology and mode of ethical reasoning; opening up aspects of medical ethics for discussion; training students in methods of interpretation of text and story; and sensitizing students to the multilayered nature of language and discourse so as to make them more skilled listeners and communicators. A literature and medicine course in the undergraduate years helps establish a frame and context for students' later medical school education, providing perspective on the intense, sometimes overwhelming, immersion in the scientific, technical, and pragmatic aspects of medicine.

Undergraduates (despite what many of them seem to think) are under less immediate pressure than are medical students to sacrifice time for reflection to the demands of classroom, lab, and clinic. In the undergraduate years there is curricular time for a rigorous and well-conceived course, study time for reading long and challenging texts, and classroom time for the instructor to introduce the basics of literary analysis as well as some of the subtleties of new theoretical approaches. Undergraduates are required to take classes outside their major, so interdisciplinary dialogue is easier to achieve and sustain here than in medical school. Regular contact between students in science and those in the humanities and fine arts, especially in classes that bring them together purposefully, can help test their assumptions by raising questions from outside the immediate frames of reference provided by disciplinary training.

For students attracted to health professions other than medicine, courses in literature and medicine can help open up exciting ways of thinking about nursing, hospice work, public health administration, health counseling, health education, and other careers. Such courses can also model adventurous ways of bringing together apparently disparate interests and skills and thus be of interest to the many students who find that their aptitudes do not fit traditional academic categories.

For students majoring in literature, history, social sciences, or fine arts, a literature and medicine course invites new practical and imaginative applications of their training and engages them in dialogue with sciences they might otherwise strenuously avoid. The "two cultures" problem identified decades ago by C. P. Snow—the polarization of sciences and humanities—endures in higher education; "math anxiety" is rife among those who identify themselves with the artists and literati on campus, and, similarly, lab-coated chemistry and biology majors suffer from "poetry anxiety" in epidemic numbers. The demystification that may result from such a course can encourage students to venture outside their most comfortable intellectual territories and experiment with different styles of thinking.

In short, a course in literature and medicine can fulfill the deepest purposes of liberal arts education, enabling students to consider their frames of reference and question their assumptions. It may enlarge their understanding of the texts and phenomena they study in terms of complex cause and effect; whole process; and the dialectics of institutions, belief systems, and behavior. It may also help them acknowledge that total objectivity is not a human possibility but that subjectivity can be reckoned with responsibly, ethically, and even fruitfully. Students who leave college having learned to pose the kinds of questions interdisciplinary work raises take with them a valuable set of skills and an approach to problems likely to enrich colleagues and enhance patient care.

A number of discrete arguments may be made to justify a course in literature and medicine to curriculum committees, English departments, and foreign language departments and programs, as well as to premed students, liberal arts majors, trustees, health professionals, and slightly grudging colleagues who are waiting their turn at the coveted "special topics" course. The purposes served by the under-graduate literature and medicine course are manifold, as are the shapes such a course might take. Here we suggest six distinct pur-poses of such a course—some of which may also extend to the med-ical school setting.

1. Offered as an elective or even a requirement in the premed program, such a course may broaden and sophisticate the ways stu-dents preparing for medical school think about health, illness, med-icine, and medical careers. Lynn Payer's *Medicine and Culture* and Ted Kaptchuk's *The Healing Arts* are useful and readable texts that introduce students to cultural variables in medical practice. Both jolt readers out of parochial assumptions about medical norms by cata-loging astonishing variations from one country to the next in med-icalization thresholds, dosages, integration of alternative therapies, uses of medical authority, and attitudes about the body. Confronting the idea that medicine participates tacitly and explicitly in cultural mythologies and values—that French Cartesianism, English empiri-cism, German Romanticism, and American pragmatism have helped significantly to shape and define medical practice—exposes stu-dents' unexamined assumptions. This exposure sets the stage for students to practice the pluralism to which the arts and literature in-vite us—that is to say, a healthy pluralism, very akin to humility, the recognition that the way we do things in American medicine is one among a number of possible ways, and not necessarily always the best.

2. As a distribution requirement or general education course, literature and medicine may provide a model for interdisciplinary study and initiate interdisciplinary dialogue on campus. Not all col-leges and universities are hospitable to courses that cross discipline boundaries. In campus cultures where such courses remain slightly suspect and are relegated to the realm of the dilettante elective—a dessert on the academic smorgasbord—a course in literature and medicine may build the long bridge between the humanities and sci-ences by focusing directly on their epistemological and pedagogical differences. When half the students in a class are humanities majors

and the other half premeds, opportunities abound for students to raise their awareness of the discourses and methods of the disciplines they regard as home ground while demystifying those disciplines they may have regarded as either intimidating or irrelevant. Students from both the sciences and the humanities learn something about their own styles of thinking that deepens self-respect, curiosity, and confidence in bridging disciplinary differences.

3. A literature and medicine course organized by genre may focus students' awareness of literary genres as ways of knowing. One may move from nonfiction to short stories to drama to poetry, interspersing medical essays and journal articles along the way. With each shift in genre, the instructor might ask how that genre by its nature shapes and frames what we notice. Sometimes looking at the same general experience represented in different forms helps elaborate this question. Reading about AIDS, for instance, one might move from the intensely personal pathos of Paul Monette's autobiographical *Borrowed Time* to the gentle ironies of "Slim," a short story by Adam Mars-Jones, to Larry Kramer's explosive, darkly humorous play *The Normal Heart*, to any of a variety of poems that articulate the loneliness, anger, alienation, and changed time frames of those who write from what Monette calls the front lines of the war. An emphasis on the relation of genre and epistemology may bring students to a more complicated understanding not only of how narrative or poetry or autobiography shapes, and indeed constitutes, experience but also of the ways the lab report or case history limits, predetermines, and organizes language in the clinic or hospital setting.

4. Other forms of course organization can build very different interdisciplinary bridges. A literature and medicine course organized as a historical survey, for instance, can reframe students' idea of history by foregrounding issues of medical practice, public-health issues, and attitudes toward the body instead of the political and economic issues usually emphasized in history texts. Certainly to map world history by plagues, epidemics, medical breakthroughs, and changes in institutionalized care for the sick is to help students recognize new historiographical options and different ways of thinking

about civilization, progress, and community. Such mapping also raises important questions for American students at present, who will have to deal with the immensely complicated issues inherent in managed care, hospital administration, public health organization, research funding, and medical technologies.

5. Ethical issues raised in stories, plays, and poetry can introduce students to narrative as a mode of ethical reasoning. Besides complicating the discrete ethical issues a doctor or nurse might face, stories invoke the imagination as a crucial tool in medical understanding. Short stories like William Carlos Williams's "The Use of Force," Lynne Sharon Schwartz's "The Wrath-Bearing Tree," and Richard Selzer's "Mercy," to name a few, are apt vehicles for considering how ethical issues can be better understood over time and in the context of multiple points of view. Learning to read stories with an appreciation for the relation between narrative and ethics can prepare students to better listen to their patients.

6. A course in literature and medicine can train the empathetic imagination. All literature courses ought to do this. All medical training ought to include this. Literature teaches us in unique ways to imagine the other, to use the imagination as an instrument of compassion, to tolerate ambiguity, to dwell in paradox, to consider multiple points of view, and to recognize that the truth about any human experience is, as Mark Van Doren puts it, that "there is no single way it can be told" (228). Texts chosen from different cultural settings; stories told from different age, gender, professional, or religious perspectives; and poems that give us images for pain we haven't felt all stretch our capacities for empathy. Empathy might well serve as an organizing idea for a course that allows us to consider literature and medicine as complementary ways of knowing, both inviting us to the highest uses of the imagination.

Contents and Contributors

It is our hope that this volume will reflect the vitality and variety of the relatively new field of literature and medicine. Indeed, as editors we were surprised—and somewhat daunted—when we received an overwhelming number of essay proposals for the volume. Because of limitations of space we could not pursue a number of excellent proposals on important texts and significant topics. In any case, there is no way we could include discussion of all literature relevant to medicine and medical practice. For example, this collection does not feature courses on popular culture or on film and other visual media (though readers will be gratified to learn that recent volumes of *Literature and Medicine* have focused on these subjects).

There are three areas that deserve special mention but that are not foregrounded in this volume, since they have been treated extensively (and well) in recent scholarship: medical texts, narrative, and clinical ethics. In recent years literary scholars have attended carefully to the literary dimensions of contemporary medical texts of various sorts, from multiauthored hospital charts to full case histories and from students' case presentations to specialists' case conferences.[4] These scholars begin with the observation that medical writings may be understood as interpretations and not simply as records of reality. Like fiction, case histories involve authorial subjectivity, in that material is selected and arranged with the aim of achieving coherence and intelligibility. Studies of medical texts have yielded an increased understanding of how clinical knowledge is arrived at and transferred and of the extent to which the patient's point of view is included. The "clinical tale," a term Oliver Sacks uses to describe his rewritings of medical case histories as stories, is now a widely published subgenre in which reflection, interpretation, speculation, subjective point of view, and felt reaction may all be embedded.

Narrative theory has recently inspired a number of excellent essays on the narrative dimensions of the medical encounter and of medical knowledge.[5] Such studies have been invaluable in helping students and physicians alike focus on the "story"—in its full literary meaning—that a patient tells. A narrative approach requires the reader to recognize metaphorical and symbolic systems; tolerate ambiguity and accept the polysemous nature of a story; adopt different and sometimes uncomfortable points of view; and attend to motivation, narrative voice, and narrative frame.

Not surprisingly, narrative concepts have begun to be seen as especially relevant to clinical ethics.[6] Carol Gilligan, Mary Belenky et al., Stanley Hauerwas, and others have elaborated from various disciplinary perspectives the notion that narrative is an irreducible form of moral reasoning. Margaret Mohrmann's recent *Medicine as Ministry* testifies to the necessity of understanding patients' situations as story in order properly to confront the ethical decisions medical practice so often poses. A narrative approach to ethics places moral dilemmas within the framework of a particular individual's life and culture rather than within a system of abstract principles and includes emotion and intuition as valid and informing responses to moral situations. A narrative approach can not only help physicians to practice ethical medicine but also enable ethicists to understand better how preconceptions and assumptions affect the construction of an ethics case (Chambers, "The Bioethicist," "From the Ethicist's," "Dax").

———

The authors of the essays included in this volume represent a cross section of instructors in the diverse field of literature and medicine. They hail from universities and colleges in all parts of the United States (one is Canadian). Some are senior professors and some are still completing their graduate training. Some teach in medical schools and some in undergraduate settings. One author is a registered nurse with a graduate degree in English literature. Eight have medical degrees, and of these all but one have done graduate work in literature.

Our aim was to put together a volume of essays that would be genuinely useful in teaching. Thus we asked authors to avoid abstractions and generalizations and to concentrate on how they teach a text or how they present a particular theoretical approach. The resulting collection is intended to reflect the range of teaching in this field. Some essays are highly theoretical (Jan Marta's, for example); some, such as Janice Willms's, adopt a fairly straightforward and practical thematic approach. In selecting essays, we attempted to include a variety of texts, genres, and approaches. We considered each essay's potential applicability across teaching settings and the degree to which the author's approach has been tested, honed, and proved in the classroom.

Each of the essays in part 1 describes a model course in such a way as to reveal the course's theoretical foundation and show its relevance to medicine. The aim is to present a broad cross section of different kinds of courses and different theoretical perspectives. Essays in part 2 concern specific texts, authors, or genres. The introductory essay to part 2 surveys readings so widely taught as to have become standard reference points or touchstones in literature and medicine courses. It discusses the purposes those texts have served and how other texts might be used to complement the points of view and approaches to medical and ethical problems they represent. Part 3 includes a discussion of texts and approaches with specific application to medical settings. This section directly addresses the experiences and events of medical education and the practice of medicine. A final section includes bibliographic material, information about relevant academic meetings and societies, and instructions from Felice Aull, general editor of the widely used online *Literature, Arts, and Medicine Database,* on ways to access and share bibliographic and other resources. This online database, updated bimonthly, has become an invaluable instrument in building community among academics and medical practitioners. We also include a selective bibliography of important primary and secondary works in the history of medicine, reflecting medical thinking and medical practice from classical antiquity through the eighteenth century.

The essays in this volume differ widely in emphasis. Some outline theoretical, historical, or pedagogical perspectives, while others focus on particular issues. It may be useful to reflect on how essays with similar foci complement one another. To that end we suggest the following as an alternative arrangement of the essays that may make this a more convenient sourcebook for some readers.

Focus on Theory

Several essays describe ways in which particular tools and approaches from literary theory may enhance not only the reading of literary and medical texts, but also the practice of clinical medicine. Rita Charon, a physician herself, shows how concepts like "genre, narrative stance, reader response, subtext, metatext, and imagery" can become tools for medical practice that may enable clinicians to hear and see their patients in terms of story and suffering. Correspondingly, Charon claims, the "diagnostic gaze" clinicians learn can inform and enrich the reading of texts. Jan Marta, a psychiatrist, similarly focuses on the appropriation and application of particular literary metaphors and mythic figures in clinical psychology and considers how those figures become vehicles for defining and understanding disease. Both essays establish a strong relation between literary and clinical competencies.

Dieter Boxmann, taking an alternative point of departure, considers the "rhetorical dimensions of medical practice," using texts from the Hippocratic oath to Hans-Georg Gadamer's *The Enigma of Health* and Ken Kesey's *One Flew over the Cuckoo's Nest*. His course focuses on rhetorical strategies by which medicine makes implicit its claims to authority, establishes protocols for decision making, and justifies its means and ends. Jonathan Metzl, a psychiatrist, also considers medical strategies through a literary lens, taking a deconstructionist approach to the "symbolic functions of [. . .] medication" and bringing together theories of psychosomatic medicine and semiotics in an analysis of factors in clinical efficacy.

Iliana Semmler describes a course that brings narrative theory to bear on both the Hippocratic oath and contemporary poetry. She asks students to consider the linguistic contexts of ethical knowledge and the malleability and multifaceted nature of *story*. Michelle Bollard Toby also foregrounds questions about the nature and function of story in her reading of Willa Cather's "Paul's Case," a story about closeted and unrecognized homosexuality. She shows how the story "illuminates the limitations of any one interpretive approach to Paul's trouble" and "impresses on the reader the historical contingency of our various models of interpretation," thus opening the paths of new historicism and hermeneutic pluralism to readers who might too reductively consign behaviors to social or clinical categories. G. Thomas Couser's essay suggests a multidimensional approach to illness narratives, or pathographies, that considers metaphor as an organizational device, the enabling functions of particular narrative conventions, and the relation between text and body.

Focus on History and Culture

Stephanie Browner's "Illness in America" and Lilian Furst's "Medical History and Literary Texts" provide richly suggestive models of courses focused on medical history as an axis of cultural understanding. In both courses, medical history is taught through literary texts that reflect medical issues and controversies and the changing relationships between doctors and patients in the nineteenth and twentieth centuries.

Suzanne Poirier's course on women's health draws on feminist research and theory, using literary texts to examine womens' roles in health care and gender dimensions of medical issues such as hysteria and depression, pregnancy, abortion, and childbirth. Like Furst's and Browner's courses, hers is focused primarily on nineteenth-and twentieth-century texts and covers a historical trajectory of development in both medical treatment and professionalization of women.

The course Kendrick Prewitt describes historicizes conceptions of the body with its "wealth of cultural, religious, and political baggage." Starting in the sixteenth century with Vesalius and Rabelais and moving on chronologically through Donne, Swift, and Whitman to O'Connor and Auden, the course gives an ambitious overview of notions about body, mind, and soul that have undergone surprising shifts, both linguistic and theological.

Paul Child subjects eighteenth-century medical texts to literary scrutiny, claiming that at least for that period, the division between literary and scientific texts is a false dichotomy and that the century's own definition of literature "comprehended all books and all writing." Child immerses students in the medical-literary culture of the time and asks them to examine the forms, rhetorical strategies, narrative techniques, plots, character types, themes, imagery, symbols, and styles of medical texts in terms of their application to medical authority, practice, and norms. H. Bruce Franklin's essay on *Frankenstein* takes up where Child's leaves off, examining the ways that this story represents the medical issues of the emerging industrial age and focusing for us a rather wild moment in medical history, with its new claims, expectations, and fallacies. Carol Donley and Sheryl Buckley's course on the "tyranny of the normal" takes a similarly critical look at the often uncritical and therefore problematic application of the term "normal" in medicine and popular culture of our own time.

Focus on Medical Issues and Diseases

Martin Donohoe, a physician, writes the only essay in the collection that represents a course focused entirely on public health issues, though many courses are taught in which plagues and epidemics are the primary theme. Donohoe combines literary texts with contemporaneous medical articles to consider the changing contexts of public health policy making.

Janice Willms (also a physician) traces madness and suicide as themes in Western literature, in a course whose focus is both historical and, ultimately, evaluative: students are encouraged to consider critically "society's role in evaluating and caring for those who are mad or suicidal."

Elizabeth Willingham's course approaches a number of themes in Spanish and Latin American literary texts that invite reflection on the cultural settings of disease and treatment. The topics include mental health, substance abuse, sexually transmitted diseases, family planning, pregnancy and birth, aging, and death and dying.

Many of the essays in part 2 focus on works that feature particular illnesses or medical issues, ranging from Bryon Grigsby's reflections on plague in *Piers Plowman* to the ethnic-cultural contexts of illness in Deborah Grayson's essay on African American women writers. Included are essays on death in *Hamlet* and in Sharon Olds's poetry, encephalitis lethargica in Pinter's *A Kind of Alaska*, tuberculosis in Kafka's stories, cholera in Mann's *Death in Venice*, and hysteria and suicide in Flaubert's *Madame Bovary*. Paul Delaney's essay on the hospital poetry of U. A. Fanthorpe, and, in part 3, Rhonda Soricelli and David Flood's essay on gender issues in medicine focus more broadly on representations of institutional issues and ethics.

Focus on Pedagogy

The essays in part 3 focus on the possible uses of literature in medical school settings. Thus Kathryn Montgomery (Hunter) uses Sherlock Holmes stories to reflect on clinical reasoning, and Joseph Cady suggests ways to work with poetry in the limited time of a short course or workshop.

LaVera Crawley takes a backward glance at her own medical training, contrasting how medical students are taught to see the body with ways of seeing and understanding the body made available by literature. Anne Hunsaker Hawkins, describing her course for practicing physicians, suggests a wide range of literary texts, from biblical and classical to contemporary, that are likely to spark lively discussion about practical and ethical issues in medicine.

Focus on Writing

Many of the courses represented in this volume include both expository and creative writing assignments that encourage students to make connections between clinical experience, personal experience, popular culture, history, and literary texts. A few courses focus specifically on writing. Lois Spatz and Kathleen Welch's essay outlines a writing course that takes "being human" as its theme. Using Camus's *The Plague* as a focal text, students responded to the issues it raises with a range of writing: personal essays, research papers, persuasive essays, and imaginative essays.

Cortney Davis, herself a nurse, describes the content and character of the poetry that nurses write about their work. Davis discusses the function of writing in the lives of professional caregivers, exploring the significant differences in perspective represented in nurses' poems and narratives and those of physicians.

It is our hope that this volume may be useful as a sourcebook, that the courses and readings described may serve as points of departure for developing new avenues of interdisciplinary research and dialogue. Courses designed for medical school may, with some adjustments, be easily adapted to undergraduate settings and vice versa; the short courses and workshops described in Cady's essay might also serve as usable models for continuing medical education programs. We encourage readers to continue exploring the possibilities and purposes of interdisciplinary dialogue at both the undergraduate and graduate levels, as well as in various venues of adult education.

It should be clear from the variety of approaches represented here that just as literature and literary theory and critical methods may open up creative and effective new ways to approach clinical practice, so also familiarity with basic medical concepts, terms, and paradigms must inevitably produce readers who are reflective about the relation between the life of the body and the life of the mind and about how particular concepts of health, illness, medical authority, and healing shape and reflect culture.[7]

Notes

1. The first medical schools to have humanities departments were the Pennsylvania State University College of Medicine (in 1967) and Southern Illinois University School of Medicine (in 1969) (McElhinney x–xiv).
2. The Society for Health and Human Values, now called the American Society of Bioethics and Humanities, is the academic society for humanists of various backgrounds who are affiliated with medical schools or involved in other venues of medical education.
3. See Hawkins and Ballard, who provide texts of three original plays about issues that patients, families, and medical caregivers confront in dealing with dying; suggestions for performing the plays as staged

readings and leading after-play discussions; and information about living wills and other advance directives.

4. See Hillman; Charon, "Doctor-Patient," "To Render"; Poirier and Brauner, "Ethics," "Voices"; Donnelly; Hunter, *Doctors' Stories*; Poirier et al.; Banks and Hawkins; Flood and Soricelli; and Hawkins. For a history of case history writing, see Epstein.

5. See Jones, "Literary Value," "Literature"; Miles and Hunter; Hunter, *Doctors' Stories*, "Toward the Cultural Interpretation"; Crawford; Charon, "Medical Interpretation," "Narrative Road"; Charon et al., "Literature and Ethical Medicine."

6. See Jones, "Literary Value," "Darren's Case"; Charon, "Narrative Contributions"; Chambers, "Bioethicist," "Dax," "From the Ethicist's Point of View"; Hunter, "Narrative"; Charon et al., "Literature and Ethical Medicine"; Nelson.

7. Given the number of essays in this volume, we encouraged authors to exercise brevity. Readers who wish additional information about texts or courses may write the essay author directly or care of Hawkins or McEntyre.

Works Cited

Banks, Joanne Trautmann. "Can We Resurrect Apollo?" *Literature and Medicine* 1 (1982): 1–17.

Banks, Joanne Trautmann, and Anne Hunsaker Hawkins, eds. *The Art of the Case History*. Spec. issue of *Literature and Medicine* 11 (1992): vii–182.

Belenky, Mary, et al. *Women's Ways of Knowing: The Development of Self, Voice, and Mind*. New York: Basic, 1986.

Chambers, Tod S. "The Bioethicist as Author: The Medical Ethics Case as Rhetorical Device." *Literature and Medicine* 13 (1994): 60–78.

———. "Dax Redacted: The Economies of Truth in Bioethics." *Journal of Medicine and Philosophy* 21 (1996): 287–302.

———. "From the Ethicist's Point of View: The Literary Nature of Ethical Inquiry." *Hastings Center Report* 21.1 (1996): 25–32.

Charon, Rita. "Doctor-Patient / Reader-Writer: Learning to Find the Text." *Soundings* 72.1 (1989): 137–52.

———. "Medical Interpretation: Implications of Literary Theory of Narrative for Clinical Work." *Journal of Narrative and Life History* 3.1 (1993): 79–97.

———. "Narrative Contributions to Medical Ethics." *A Matter of Principles? Ferment in U.S. Bioethics*. Ed. E.R. Dubose et al. Valley Forge: Trinity, 1994. 260–83.

———. "The Narrative Road to Empathy." *Empathy and the Practice of Medicine*. Ed. H. Spiro et al. New Haven: Yale UP, 1993. 147–59.

———. "To Render the Lives of Patients." *Literature and Medicine* 5 (1986): 58–74.

Charon, Rita, et al. "Literature and Ethical Medicine: Five Cases from Common Practice." *Journal of Medicine and Philosophy* 21 (1996): 243–65

———. "Literature and Medicine: Contributions to Clinical Practice." *Annals of Internal Medicine* 122 (1995): 599–606.

Coles, Robert. *The Call of Stories: Teaching and the Moral Imagination.* Boston: Houghton, 1989.

Crawford, T. Hugh. "The Politics of Narrative Form." Banks and Hawkins 147–62.

Donnelly, William J. "Righting the Medical Record: Transforming Chronicle into Story." *Journal of the American Medical Association* 260 (1988): 823–25

Epstein, Julia. "Historiography, Diagnosis, and Poetics." Banks and Hawkins 23–44.

Flood, David H., and Rhonda L. Soricelli. "Development of the Physician's Narrative Voice in the Medical Case History." Banks and Hawkins 64–83.

Gilligan, Carol. *In a Different Voice: Psychological Theory and Women's Development.* Cambridge: Harvard UP, 1982.

Hauerwas, Stanley, ed. *Why Narrative? Readings in Narrative Theology.* Grand Rapids: Eerdmans, 1989.

Hawkins, Anne Hunsaker. "Oliver Sacks's *Awakenings*: Reshaping Clinical Discourse." *Configurations* 2 (1993): 229–45.

Hawkins, Anne Hunsaker, and James O. Ballard, eds. *Time To Go: Three Plays on Death and Dying, with Commentary on End-of-Life Issues.* Philadelphia: U of Pennsylvania P, 1995.

Hillman, James, "The Fiction of Case History: A Round." *Religion as Story.* Ed. James B. Wiggins. New York: Harper, 1975. 123–75.

Hunter, Kathryn Montgomery. *Doctors' Stories: The Narrative Structure of Medical Knowledge.* Princeton: Princeton UP, 1991.

———. "Literature and Medicine: Standards for Applied Literature." *Applying the Humanities.* Ed. Daniel Callahan et al. New York: Plenum, 1985. 289–304.

———. "Narrative, Literature, and the Clinical Exercise of Practical Reason." *Journal of Medicine and Philosophy* 21 (1996): 303–20.

———. "Toward the Cultural Interpretation of Medicine." *Literature and Medicine* 10 (1991): 1–17.

Hunter, Kathryn Montgomery, et al. "The Study of Literature in Medical Education." *Academic Medicine* 70 (1995): 787–94.

Jones, Anne Hudson. "Darren's Case: Narrative Ethics in Perri Klass's *Other Women's Children.*" *Journal of Medicine and Philosophy* 21 (1996): 267–86.

———."Literary Value: The Lesson of Medical Ethics." *Neohelicon* 14 (1987): 383–92.

————."Literature and Medicine: Narrative Ethics." *Lancet* 349 (1997): 1243–46.

Kaptchuk, Ted. *The Healing Arts: Exploring the Medical Ways of the World.* New York: Summit, 1987.

Kramer, Larry. *The Normal Heart.* New York: New American, 1985.

Mars-Jones, Adam. "Slim." *The Darker Proof: Stories from a Crisis.* Ed. Mars-Jones and Edmund White. London: Faber, 1987. 3–13.

McElhinney, Thomas K. *Human Values Teaching Programs for Health Professionals.* Ardmore: Whitmore, 1981.

Miles, Stephen H., and Kathryn Montgomery Hunter. "Case Stories." *Second Opinion* 15 (1990): 54–69.

Mohrmann, Margaret. *Medicine as Ministry: Reflections on Suffering, Ethics, and Hope.* New York: Pilgrim, 1996.

Monette, Paul. *Borrowed Time.* New York: Avon, 1988.

Nelson, Hilde Lindemann, ed. *Stories and Their Limits: Narrative Approaches to Bioethics.* New York: Routledge, 1997.

Payer, Lynn. *Medicine and Culture: Varieties of Treatment in the United States, England, West Germany, and France.* 1988. New York: Henry Holt, 1996.

Poirier, Suzanne, and Daniel J. Brauner. "Ethics, Language, and the Daily Discourse of Clinical Medicine." *Hastings Center Report* 18.4 (1988): 5–9.

————. "The Voices of the Medical Record." *Theoretical Medicine* 11 (1990): 29–39.

Poirier, Suzanne, et al. "Charting the Chart: An Exercise in Interpretation(s)." Banks and Hawkins 1–22.

Rousseau, George S. "Literature and Medicine: The State of the Field." *Isis* 72 (1981): 406–24.

————. "Literature and Medicine: Towards a Simultaneity of Theory and Practice." *Literature and Medicine* 5 (1986): 152–81.

Sacks, Oliver. *"The Man Who Mistook His Wife for a Hat" and Other Clinical Tales.* New York: Summit, 1985.

Schwartz, Lynne Sharon. "The Wrath-Bearing Tree." *"Acquainted with the Night" and Other Stories.* New York: Harper, 1984.

Selzer, Richard. "Mercy." *Letters to a Young Doctor.* New York: Simon, 1983. 70–74.

Snow, C. P. *The Two Cultures.* Cambridge: Cambridge UP, 1993.

Van Doren, Mark. "Sonnet XXV." *Collected Poems of Mark Van Doren.* New York: Henry Holt, 1939. 227–28.

Williams, William Carlos. "The Use of Force." *The Doctor Stories.* Comp. Robert Coles. New York: New Directions, 1962. 56–60.

Part I

Model Courses

Rita Charon

Literary Concepts for Medical Readers: Frame, Time, Plot, Desire

Literature and medicine has emerged from its disciplinary prologue. No longer an intellectual surprise and therefore no longer able to get along by virtue of novelty, the field now propels itself through honest cognitive work that leads to clinical and creative discoveries unavailable except through the disposition of literary methods onto medical texts and practices, on the one hand, and the transposition of the diagnostic gaze onto literary texts and traditions, on the other. The more closely the relations between literature and medicine are scrutinized, the better the deep structures of both are understood.

Teaching literature to doctors and medical students fulfills embarrassingly instrumental goals at the same time that it allows wild conceptual play. Instrumentally, training in such literary concepts as genre, narrative stance, reader response, subtext, metatext, and imagery can provide medical students and doctors with skills that their elders did not have, never got, and did without. Patients have suffered long enough the consequences of a medicine practiced by doctors without these skills—doctors who cannot follow a narrative thread; who cannot adopt an alien perspective; who become unreliable narrators of other peoples' stories; who are deaf to voice and image; and who do not always include in their regard human motives, yearnings, symbols, and the fellowship born of a common language. Literature thinks it can help medicine accurately interpret the stories of sickness and courageously recognize—and thereby soften—human suffering.

Conceptually, medicine offers the scholar a family of narratives generated by illness—the sickness itself as inscribed on and in the body, the patient's autobiographical account, the account as transformed by the doctor's cataloging mind (trained to be both arrogant and afraid of chaos) and written down, and the course of the illness itself—that exposes uncanny and telling relations among language, soma, self, and time. In the wake of Jacques Lacan's suggestion that "*the unconscious is structured like a language*" (20), the field of literature and medicine has considered disease and health, too, to be structured like languages.[1] Michel Foucault's observations on the semantic emergence of the prose of the world implicitly support this consideration and its thought-provoking converse, that language is structured like a disease:

> Language exists first of all, in its raw and primitive being, in the simple, material form of writing, a stigma upon things, a mark imprinted across the world which is part of its most ineffaceable forms. [. . .] [T]his is why nature and the word can intertwine with one another to infinity, forming, for those who can read it, one vast single text. (42, 44)

If disease is structured like a language, one needs an ear for its inflections to decode its signs, and one needs fluency with which to transmit and receive messages among its native speakers.

Combining the instrumental and conceptual natures of this enterprise, a literature teacher wants to educate medical students in the methods of unearthing meaning from language, including in the term *language* everything from grammar and metaphor to stigmata and scar. Such an education must provide students with the skills needed to read and translate medicine's texts, not only those that doctors write for one another but also those that the deep structures of the languages of diseases themselves convey. Along with linguistic skills, students must absorb the transcendent tongued knowledge— part creative, part empathic, part shamanistic—needed to hear both the disease and the patient afflicted with it. As an often overlooked dividend, this education in language and text simultaneously teaches about the body in pain.

Beginning with such elementary literary concepts as narrative frame, time, plot, and desire can help structure a course in literature and medicine toward its broad goals.[2] Training medical students to examine these specific elements of whatever text they study prepares them for disciplined readings of the chaotic texts of medicine, be they hospital charts, diagnostic images, stories that patients tell, physical examinations of patients' bodies, or clinical courses of illnesses. Reading the texts of medicine is not unlike reading, say, a chest x ray. A medical student learns to proceed through a drill— identical in sequence and detail in all academic medical centers in the country—not only in reporting the result of a chest x ray but also in the very looking at it: "This is a well-penetrated, nonrotated film. The inspiration is good. The bony structures are unremarkable. The mediastinum and heart size are within normal limits, and the pulmonary vessels are normal. There are no infiltrates or effusions." In like manner, when listening to a clinical story, the medical student ought to notice—as a matter of routine—the narrative frame, the temporal dimensions, the plot, and the desire (and absence) inherent in the text. The remainder of this essay describes a seminar structured to convey these four literary concepts. Fulfilling a humanities requirement for second-year medical students at the College of Physicians and Surgeons of Columbia University, the seminar assigned British and American twentieth-century short stories as primary texts and examined medical texts alongside the literary ones.

Teaching Narrative Frame

On opening a book, the reader first identifies the narrative frame into which he or she is situated by the act of reading and then endorses the contract implied by that frame. Only the most naive reader will not note who is telling whom about what happened and what that teller might want in return for his or her act of narration. Because all texts are simultaneously narrative and discourse, readers have to attend to both the told and the telling. As Gérard Genette reports, a text, "as narrative, [. . .] lives by its relationship to the story that it recounts; as discourse, it lives by its relationship to the narrating that utters it" (29). Even readers who have not mastered Genettian taxonomies recognize believable and unbelievable narrators and can identify multiple tellings nested within one another or multiple perspectives revealed in one story. By inspecting a text's narrative frame, one acknowledges, if not always answers, many questions: How are the teller and listener related? What license does the teller take? How reliable might teller and listener be? Whose narrative vision is intercepted by the reader?

In the preface to *The Awkward Age*, Henry James writes of "the neat figure of a circle consisting of a number of small rounds disposed at equal distance about a central object. The central object was my situation, my subject in itself, to which the thing would owe its title, and the small rounds represented so many distinct lamps, as I liked to call them, the function of each of which would be to light with all due intensity one of its aspects" (xvi). The skilled reader cannot do without the ability to inhabit the meaning-making position of another—or a series of others or a series of conflicting others—and must realize that any central situation is unknowable except as a series of distinctly lit aspects.

Medical narratives, too, are framed, often with frames as complex and submerged as those of James. However effaced and omniscient the medical narrator may try to be, the teller inhabits his or her own set of motives, fears, and hopes and is limited by his or her angle of vision. One cannot intelligently decipher a progress note written in a hospital chart by an intern in July without taking into account the depth of guilt of the newly minted doctor and without filling in the subtext written by inexperience, arrogance of first authority, and unaccustomed sleepless terror. Neither can one interpret a medical interview without identifying the gradient of authority against which the teller-patient's words must climb in disagreeing with the listener-doctor. Achieving multiple points of view—seeing events from the nonmedical, suffering perspectives of patient and family member or from the nonmedical, professional perspectives of nurse and social worker—is perhaps the most critical skill for a doctor to achieve, and this skill is achieved only through explicit and demanding training.

The literary texts chosen to exercise seminar participants' ability to identify narrative frame and point of view included Ernest Hemingway's "Indian Camp," Flannery O'Connor's "The Lame Shall Enter First," and Alice Munro's "The Wilderness Station." These stories were chosen for their layered narrators, the irreconcilable differences among their multiple tellers, and the characteristics—the young age of Hemingway's Nick, the unrelenting judgment of O'Connor's Sheppard, the allegedly altered mental status of Munro's Annie Herron—that mark the narrators' worldviews. These texts provide good narrative problems for students who must decide who the teller is, how many tellings there are and how they conflict, how the tellers are limited in vision, how many aspects of the situation are "lit," and where to sit as reader. Beginning the seminar with these problems ensures that subsequent readings proceed on the basis of such narrative reckonings.

Such medical texts as an ethics consultation note or an "attending rounds" presentation of a case might complete this section of the seminar, giving the students explicit crossover of their narrative skills into the medical setting. As listeners or readers and, later, retellers or rewriters of clinical stories, students need to pay exquisite attention to framing, getting used to asking questions about once- and twice-removed accounts of someone else's story. Such attention arms them with the requisite skepticism to question the angles from which medical stories are told, understanding that only one aspect of a situation might be seen from any one round.

Teaching Narrative Time

The temporal dimensions of a literary text enable it to represent and reconfigure human action in narrative terms. In the words of Paul Ricoeur, "Between the activity of narrating a story and the temporal character of human experience there exists a correlation that is not merely accidental but that presents a transcultural form of necessity" (52). That postmodern texts now attempt to reverse or defy chronology only attests to the necessary hold of temporal order over narrative. To read a story requires the reader to enter, respect, and identify the temporal flow of the narrative—structured as it may be in flashbacks, premonitions, backward tellings, and the like—and to discriminate between how the events occurred and how one learns about them in text. Inexperienced readers may need to recognize explicitly the folding and refolding of time within a story before they are able to interpret its meaning.

Medical actions are built on the body's temporal workings: witness five-year survival data, so-called developmental abnormalities, or bradycardia. The incessant staging undertaken by medicine and the unfolding and maturing that the body undergoes—and that diseases are endowed with—emphasize the critical role that time plays in both professional and lay conceptions of health and disease. Medical narratives, as a result, are built with complex temporal scaffoldings: the history of present illness prefaces the past medical history; a woman's medical history is bracketed between menarche and menopause; and acronyms have come into universal usage for such phrases as "prior to admission," "postoperative day X," and "usual state of health" (meaning up until now). Like any autobiography, the medical history is told by a narrator about a protagonist who is his or her younger self, and the tension inherent in the genre stems, in part, from the confrontation of these selves, dissimilar because separated in time.

Some literary texts, read closely, generate a heightened awareness of narrative temporal dimensions. Virginia Woolf's "Ancestors," a sketch for *Mrs. Dalloway*, reveals the protagonist's inner experience of the simultaneity of past and present and the manner in which the past trumps the present in her search for meaning. John Berger's "An Independent Woman" and Tillie Olsen's "I Stand Here Ironing" similarly require the reader to track, meticulously, past events into the present; to identify multiple middle distances in time; and to acknowledge the part that memory plays in life.

A medical school seminar could companion such short fictions with tape-recorded and transcribed medical interviews, available in published linguistic and sociological collections if not from a willing physician with a tape recorder and the permission of his or her patients (see Cassell, Mishler, West). Transcribed medical conversations, even the most routine transactions, reveal the obsession with time demanded by disease and by health care. Such transcripts reveal as well the asymmetry between time as experienced by the patient and as recorded by the doctor. If, as the phenomenologists of illness have taught us, the conflict between chronological time and lived time is one of the major burdens of suffering, then medical students and doctors schooled to respect the multivalence of temporality will not make the mistake made by the doctor in this medical interview:

Doctor. How long have you been drinking that heavily?
Patient. Since I've been married.
Doctor. How long is that?   (Mishler 85)

Teaching for the Plot

Inexperienced readers are sometimes chided for reading for the plot, and yet the most skilled readers read so too, for plot constitutes not just what happens but also the heart of what words do. If, since Aristotle's *Poetics*, plot has been understood as the action of the narrative, then plotting requires that events, character, motive, and desire culminate in consequences. Not only do narratives record action, but they also bring it about, as Jean-Paul Sartre suggests: "To speak is to act; anything which one names is already no longer quite the same" (36). Although some fictions present their plots in plain sight, others defy the reader in search of the plot: unseen events power the action; random acausal correlation replaces naturalistic or deterministic unfolding of consequences. Similar, perhaps, to real life and certainly to the events of disease, fictions that conceal their actions can most forcefully teach the reader about finding the plot. Never uncontested, plot is sought by ordering events so as to make them mean something, and yet the finest and most parsimonious order cannot banish the indeterminacy, inexhaustibility, and uncertainty of the text.

The plot of the patient's presentation is what the doctor seeks in the act of diagnosis. Assigning the name of a disease or pathophysiological process to a set of symptoms and findings gives shape to the patient's otherwise meaningless account, thereby both reporting and bringing about action. Random occurrence vies with organic determinism for the physician and the storyteller alike. Most medical students listen to a patient to find out "what happened," and they are stymied when the patient's account does not yield an orderly and causally connected sequence of events. Students do not realize that they are, in fact, in search of the plot and that it is their responsibility, not the patient's, to find the action within the narrative.

Short stories that help train readers to discuss plot are innumerable. Some texts that have been assigned in the second-year seminar include James's "The Beast in the Jungle," Charlotte Perkins Gilman's "The Yellow Wallpaper," and Sandra Cisneros's "Woman Hollering Creek." In James's masterpiece, the psychological interiority of events befalling John Marcher and their mediation through delusion and rumination baffle the student in search of what happens. Although Gilman's story is often included in literature and medicine courses for its depiction of madness, here it is used because the protagonist's plot conflicts with the husband-doctor's plot, generating irreducible tension over what, literally, goes on. And Cisneros's engaging young narrator tells what happens to her through the intertextual layering of *telenovelas* ("soap operas"), Bayer aspirin commercials, and a "ribbon of laughter, like water" (56).

This section of the literature seminar might be enriched by taking the students to see a patient—in the emergency room, perhaps, or the walk-in clinic—to take a history and to demonstrate how many plots might be "found" and how one chooses the best plot in diagnosing the ailment. Both plot-making enterprises, then, medicine and literature, rely on an Aristotelian understanding of that which moves human action and a Sartrean awareness of the power of words themselves to change the world. Teaching medical students to discern plot endows them with an attentiveness to the irresistible drive to plot otherwise random events, and such training may even demonstrate to them the great peril with which a doctor overplots a patient's narrative.

Teaching Desire

The desire that swamps medicine is the same desire that swamps literature: the hunger to tell, the yearning to hear, the longing to read to the end, and the drive to search beyond the ending. "Narrative," suggests Roland Barthes, "is determined not by a desire to narrate but by a desire to exchange" (*S/Z* 90). Bodily and sensuous, the actions of readers and writers are by nature consensual and fluid, and they occur on medicine's stage, Barthes says, for "the pleasure of the text is that moment when my body pursues its own ideas—for my body does not have the same ideas I do. [. . .] The text you write must prove to me *that it desires me*. This proof exists: it is writing. Writing is: the science of the various blisses of language" (*Pleasure* 17, 6).

As soon, however, as one finds desire, one finds absence, for the "text of bliss [is] the text that imposes a state of loss. [. . .] What pleasure wants is the site of a loss, the seam, the cut, the deflation, the *dissolve* which seizes the subject in the midst of bliss" (Barthes, *Pleasure* 14, 7).[3] Death, then, cannot but be beside desire, just as desire is consanguineous with both reading and writing. Jacques Derrida, having adopted the obituary as his most public literary genre in recent years, writes on the occasion of Louis Marin's death that "death is not one example of absence among others; it speaks to us of absence itself. [. . .] All work is also the work of mourning [. . .] and [. . .] mourning is interminable" (183, 172). Acts of reading and writing bring readers and writers, through desire, to the side of death.

Medical education and medical practice relentlessly draw the doctor's attention away from desire and passion. The body, it would seem, loses its passion in proportion that it accretes disease. Students report revulsion toward bodies they must behold. And yet are not doctors among the most privileged of readers, having intimate knowledge and sensate understanding of death, this lining of desire, if only they can reclaim the pleasure of the *mise en corps?* Doctors can second Walter Benjamin's observation about nineteenth-century fiction, that "what draws the reader to the novel is the hope of warming his shivering life with a death he reads about" (101). What draws doctors, unknowing, to the bedside is the hope of warming their lives with the deaths over which they preside, yearning to grasp—and able to ease—that which befalls us all.

Few fictions, on inspection, do not treat death. The short stories chosen for the second-year seminar to introduce readers to both the desire inherent in language and the inevitable destination of that desire in death are D. H. Lawrence's "The Odour of Chrysanthemums," James Joyce's "The Dead," and James's story "The Middle Years."[4] Each of these great stories centers both on corporeal desire as it is manifest in the desire to tell and on the ultimate resolution of that corporeal desire in death. In "The Odour of Chrysanthemums," Walter Bates's corpse exposes Elizabeth's hunger not only for his body but also for her soul; in "The Dead," Gabriel comes to understand, through Gretta's mourning, that death cannot overpower desire, just as desire cannot overpower death. In "The Middle Years," Dencombe's final words to Dr. Hugh merge his own passion to write and read with his eternal longing for life: "We work in the dark—we do what we can—we give what we have. Our doubt is our passion and our passion is our task. The rest is the madness of art" (105).

Reading hospital death summaries—oddly, they are formally called discharge summaries, as if the hospital extended an arm into the afterlife—with this selection of stories can reveal, if only by virtue of the breathtaking passivity of the prose, the traces of loss experienced by even the most perfunctory dictating physician. Accompanying Elizabeth and Gabriel and Dr. Hugh on their journeys alongside death can give students the power to then find and grasp and own their fellow doctors' submerged but readable passions in the face of loss. Perhaps by returning the pleasure of the text to the education of the doctor, one can recouple the joy of telling to the mourning that is the fate of us all. Derrida recalls that it is "the undeniable anticipation of mourning that constitutes friendship" (181), describing, without having meant to, the special friendship between doctor and patient.

The hope of such a literature seminar taught to clinically inexperienced medical students is that, when faced with a human being in some predicament of pain or suffering or when reading or listening to another's account of such a human being, students will have the skill and insight to ask themselves a series of questions about their relation to the teller, the transparency of time and memory in the life being lived or relived, the ways in which the story's actions change the world, and the thirst and hunger expressed by the rustle of language. When our students learn to approach the clinical stories that they write and read and hear with responsible literary practices, their knowledge of patients and of disease grows in accuracy and depth. As a dividend to themselves that is also a bonus to their patients, they grow in self-knowledge. Because they become good readers, they become good doctors.

Course Readings

Narrative Frame
Hemingway, "Indian Camp"
O'Connor, "The Lame Shall Enter First"
Munro, "The Wilderness Station"
Attending rounds presentation

Narrative Time
Woolf, "Ancestors"
Berger, "An Independent Woman"
Olsen, "I Stand Here Ironing"
Transcription of routine medical interview

Plot
James, "The Beast in the Jungle"
Gilman, "The Yellow Wallpaper"
Cisneros, "Woman Hollering Creek"
Interview with a patient in clinic

Narrative Desire (Absence)
Lawrence, "The Odour of Chrysanthemums"

Joyce, "The Dead"
James, "The Middle Years"
Discharge summary for patient who died in the hospital

Notes

1. See Charon and Taylor for an introductory application of Lacan's notion to medicine.
2. For a discussion of these four literary concepts in the making of medical ethical decisions, see Charon, Brody, Clark, Davis, Martinez, and Nelson.
3. I am indebted to Katherine Hawkins for her comments regarding absence on a preliminary draft of this paper read at the Teaching Literature and Medicine session at the December 1996 MLA convention in Washington.
4. "The Middle Years," it is true, was written in 1893. I beg the readers' indulgence in allowing me to include the story with twentieth-century works. My students were grateful for the inclusion.

Works Cited

Barthes, Roland. *The Pleasure of the Text.* Trans. Richard Miller. New York: Hill, 1975.

———. *S/Z.* Trans. Richard Miller. New York: Hill, 1974.

Benjamin, Walter. "The Storyteller." *Illuminations.* Trans. Harry Zohn. New York: Schocken, 1985. 83–109.

Berger, John. "An Independent Woman." *Pig Earth.* New York: Vintage, 1992. 23–33.

Cassell, Eric. *Talking with Patients.* 2 vols. Cambridge: MIT P, 1985.

Charon, Rita, Howard Brody, Mary Williams Clark, Dwight Davis, Richard Martinez, and Robert M. Nelson. "Literature and Ethical Medicine: Five Cases from Common Practice." *Journal of Medicine and Philosophy* 21 (1996): 237–41.

Charon, Rita, and Nancy Dew Taylor. "The Unruly *Mise en Corps:* Body, Text, and Healing. " *Literature and Medicine* 16 (1997): vii–xi.

Cisneros, Sandra. "Woman Hollering Creek." *"Woman Hollering Creek" and Other Stories.* New York: Random, 1991. 43–56.

Derrida, Jacques. "By Force of Mourning." *Critical Inquiry* 22 (1996): 171–92.

Foucault, Michel. *The Order of Things: An Archaeology of the Human Sciences.* Trans. Foucault. New York: Random, 1973. Trans. of *Les mots et les choses.*

Genette, Gérard, *Narrative Discourse: An Essay in Method.* Trans. Jane E. Lewin. Ithaca: Cornell UP, 1980.

Gilman, Charlotte Perkins. "The Yellow Wallpaper." *"The Yellow Wall-*

paper" and Other Writings. Ed. Lynne Sharon Schwartz. New York: Bantam, 1989. 1–20.

Hemingway, Ernest. "Indian Camp." *The Nick Adams Stories*. New York: Scribner's, 1972. 16–21.

James, Henry. Preface. *The Awkward Age*. James, *Novels* 9: v–xxiv.

———. "The Beast in the Jungle." James, *Novels* 17: 61–127.

———. "The Middle Years." James, *Novels* 16: 77–106.

———. *The Novels and Tales of Henry James: The New York Edition*. 26 vols. New York: Scribner's, 1909.

Joyce, James. "The Dead." *Dubliners*. New York: Viking, 1968. 175–224.

Lacan, Jacques. *The Four Fundamental Concepts of Psychoanalysis*. Trans. Alan Sheridan. New York: Norton, 1981.

Lawrence, D. H. "The Odour of Chrysanthemums." *Complete Short Stories*. Vol. 2. New York: Penguin, 1962. 283–302.

Mishler, Elliot. *The Discourse of Medicine: Dialectics of Medical Interviews*. Norwood: Ablex, 1984.

Munro, Alice. "The Wilderness Station." *Open Secrets*. New York: Knopf, 1994. 190–225.

O'Connor, Flannery. "The Lame Shall Enter First." *Everything That Rises Must Converge*. New York: Noonday, 1965. 143–90.

Olsen, Tillie. "I Stand Here Ironing." *"Tell Me a Riddle" and Other Stories*. New York: Bantam, 1956. 1–12.

Ricoeur, Paul. *Time and Narrative*. Trans. Kathleen McLaughlin and David Pellauer. Vol. 1. Chicago: U of Chicago P, 1984.

Sartre, Jean-Paul. "What Is Literature?" *"What Is Literature" and Other Essays*. Cambridge: Harvard UP, 1988. 21–245.

West, Candace. *Routine Complications: Troubles with Talk between Doctors and Patients*. Bloomington: Indiana UP, 1984.

Woolf, Virginia. "Ancestors." *The Complete Shorter Fiction of Virginia Woolf*. Ed. Susan Dick. New York: Harcourt, 1985. 175–77.

Stephanie P. Browner

Illness in America

Illness in America is an interdisciplinary course for upper-division undergraduates, though it might also be suitable in a medical school curriculum. The course examines representations of illness in a variety of discourses and suggests that all such representations reveal a culture at work negotiating philosophical, ethical, and political questions about the body. We begin by noting that every historical period is marked by a preoccupation with specific diseases—smallpox, yellow fever, cholera, tuberculosis, polio, neuraesthenia, cancer, chronic fatigue syndrome, AIDS—and we acknowledge that each disease has an undeniable physical reality. The course focuses, however, on how we know a disease primarily through our metaphoric descriptions of it, our characterizations of those who contract it, and our visions of what cures it. Chronologically organized readings survey dramatic shifts in both popular and medical views of illness and consequently survey important shifts in American culture. Throughout the course, we also look for connections between a particular view of illness in a text and current habits of thought about illness.

The course invites students to understand illness in a rich cultural context and to understand that the stories we tell about illness are often improvisations on stories told in the past.

Theoretical Issues

The theoretical underpinnings of the course come from recent developments in cultural studies, science studies, literary studies, and history that suggest all discourses, including medical discourse, are part of a network of cultural practices. The course often raises big questions, but the methodology—close analysis of individual texts—encourages students to resist drawing broad generalizations about our culture or others and to consider instead how each text offers a glimpse of illness as it was understood at a specific historical moment by persons living at the intersection of competing cultural habits and conventions.

Although theoretical issues are primarily left implicit in the course, I find it useful to begin with a discussion of terms and methods. Arthur Kleinman's distinction between illness and disease—illness is the patient's experience and disease is medicine's focus—is useful because it foregrounds a fundamental issue in the cultural study of medicine. The terms, at first glance, seem to distinguish between the subjective experience of illness and the biological reality of disease. Representations of illness, students usually accept, negotiate a complex ensemble of beliefs and cultural habits. Discourse about disease, however, can seem to be simply a matter of scientific facts—pathogens, cells, immune systems, and so on. Either you have tuberculosis or you don't, as a student pointed out in class one day. But, in fact, it isn't that simple, as Charles Rosenberg makes clear in his essay "Framing Disease: Illness, Society, and History." Rosenberg's commitment to a rich, cultural understanding of medicine makes the essay a good first reading assignment. He describes clearly the forces that shape our understanding of disease—patients' accounts; medical language; the history and current concerns of medical institutions; public policies; popular beliefs; presumptions about gender, race, class, and sexuality—yet he avoids the polemics that often accompany arguments about the social construction of illness. Rosenberg's concluding call for more attention to "the influence of culture on definitions of disease and of disease in the creation of culture" offers a succinct statement of one goal of the course, and it is a statement we return to again and again in class discussion (318).

Rosenberg's essay is also useful for one of the most challenging tasks in the course—teaching students to do readings of medical texts. Analysis of medical texts is difficult for even a trained cultural historian. Medical language, like all scientific discourse, seems transparent. With work, however, students learn to "listen" carefully to medical texts, to examine structure, language, metaphor, tone, ideology, politics, and implicit and explicit beliefs. Rosenberg's essay analyzes the connections between medicine and culture, identifying distinct disease models that have had currency at different moments in the history of medicine. Drawing on James J. Bono's work, I also point out that science does not exist in a vacuum. Scientists speak not only to other scientists; their language is formed and lives in a broader cultural context. Inevitably, as Bono notes, "scientific metaphors adapt themselves to a larger ecology of contesting social and cultural values, interests, and ideologies" (81).[1] In a course committed to the cultural study of illness, it is important both to acknowledge the real achievements of science and medicine and to hold on to an understanding of medicine as a cultural practice.

Although we study a range of texts in Illness in America—medical articles, religious treatises, films, news reports, and popular television shows—the course undoubtedly privileges literature. It does so in part because cultural analysis draws on terms and methods from literary studies. Indeed, practice with a cultural analysis of a literary text often makes students better readers of medical texts. But this is not the only reason I teach literary texts in this course. Studying literature, as Stephen Greenblatt suggests, is a particularly effective way to study culture:

> The world is full of texts, most of which are virtually incomprehensible when they are removed from their immediate surroundings. [...] Works of art by contrast contain directly or by implication much of this situation within

themselves. [. . .] Careful reading of a work of literature will lead to a heightened understanding of the culture within which it was produced. (227)

Specifically, literary texts are useful in this course because they are a rich source for some of the tropes and metaphors that inform stories about illness. Literary texts also provide a voice outside medicine, articulating critiques, evaluations, praise, and complex representations of how medical discourse, practice, and institutions respond to and shape the experience of illness.

Course Outline, Readings, and Assignments

The course is organized chronologically and falls loosely into five units, each intended not only to cover a particular historical era but also to identify an "illness story" that was once current and that may still shape contemporary habits of thought. A long tradition in Judeo-Christian culture links religion and medicine, and in the first unit, "Illness as God's Punishment," we focus on Puritan and early nineteenth-century texts. In colonial America, clergymen often served as doctors, and illness was commonly understood as part of God's plan, either as a general punishment for original sin or as a specific punishment to warn a person who had fallen from righteous living. Michael Wigglesworth's poem "God's Controversy with New England" (1662) is a powerful jeremiad calling on the colonists to realize their errant ways and to understand as God's warning the drought of 1661–62 and the attendant diseases. Similarly, William R. Alger's sermon *Inferences from the Pestilence and the Fast* is a religious response to the cholera epidemic of 1849. In "The Angel of Bethesda" (1724), Cotton Mather offers a range of medical theory and practical advice ("Selections"). Mather, a clergyman and devotee of science, was perhaps the preeminent medical thinker in colonial New England, and in several works he sought to reconcile religious and scientific thought.[2] In "The Angel of Bethesda," Mather moves readily between medical and religious language and issues, and in class we examine the significance of his free use of metaphors from both discourses.

Students may be inclined to reject the religious concerns that motivate all three texts and, in particular, to label Mather's work as unscientific. "The Angel of Bethesda" includes remedies that seem outrageous and beliefs that are now termed superstitions. Thus it is particularly important in this unit to remind students that the course is not concerned with the scientific validity of medical texts. Rather, the focus is on discovering how medical works deploy metaphors and narrative techniques and consequently how medicine participates in the construction of particular stories about illness. I ask students to resist the tendency to feel superior to Wigglesworth's, Alger's, or Mather's interpretations of illness, and I ask them to write about the ways in which religious responses to illness are evident or important in their own thinking about illness. It can be useful to have a student report to the class on current issues regarding religion and illness, for example the Christian Science movement.

The second unit, "Illness as Contagion," examines the fear of contagion that marks many discussions of disease. Contagion is both a fact about some diseases and a metaphor that has been used to ostracize particular groups. In Charles Brockden Brown's novel *Arthur Mervyn* (1800) and Edgar Allan Poe's short story "The Masque of the Red Death" (1842), contagion is a medical reality and a metaphor for moral issues. Brown knew firsthand the dangers of yellow fever. In 1798 Brown lived with a man who died of yellow fever as well as with a doctor who worked with its victims, and Brown himself contracted the disease. In his novel, Brown uses this knowledge to draw a vivid, realistic portrait of a city during an epidemic, and he uses the epidemic as a metaphor to characterize the city as a place of corruption and immorality. Poe's story also plays on nineteenth-century anxieties about epidemics, making metaphoric use of bubonic plague to tell a Gothic tale of the folly of trying to escape death, time, and disease.

In this unit we examine two medical texts: David Hosack's "Observations on Febrile Contagion, and on the Means of Improving the Medical Police of the City of New York" (1820) and Henry G. Pickering's digest of American sanitary law in *Public Hygiene in America* (1877).[3] These were landmark works in the emergence of public health as a discipline in the nineteenth century, and they offer an opportunity for students to examine the roles the medical profession and medical discourse — medical language and habits of thought—play in shaping policies that regulate individual lives and public spaces in significant ways. For historical context, we read selected chapters in *The Cholera Years*, Charles Rosenberg's analysis of religious, medical, and popular responses to the epidemics of 1832, 1849, and 1866; we also read Martin S. Pernick's "Politics, Parties, and Pestilence: Epidemic Yellow Fever in Philadelphia and the Rise of the First Party System." To make contemporary connections, I ask students to consider how "contagion anxiety," the term we coined in one class, shapes individual behavior and social policy regarding AIDS.

Both the third and fourth units focus on illness as a marker of individuality. We note in class that with the emergence of individualism in the nineteenth century, social contexts for understanding illness give way to an emphasis on the individual. In the third unit, "Illness as Ennobling Affliction," we examine Harriet Beecher Stowe's representation of the illness and death of Little Eva in *Uncle Tom's Cabin* (1852) and Louisa May Alcott's depiction of Beth's death in *Little Women* (1869). These are useful examples of death scenes in sentimental nineteenth-century fiction, and we note similar scenes in contemporary Hollywood films. We then read Susan Sontag's *Illness as Metaphor* and *AIDS and Its Metaphors* for her criticism of popular myths about the heightened sensitivity and spirituality of the dying patient and for her critique of metaphoric thinking about illness in general. I use Henry James's novel *The Wings of the Dove* (1902) to complicate Sontag's argument. Sontag suggests that James participates in the same kinds of misleading metaphoric uses of illness as Stowe and Alcott do. James's novel, I suggest, does indeed use illness as a metaphor, but as an open-ended metaphor and as a way to investigate the limits of medical responses to illness. Though long and difficult, James's novel is worth the effort because it dramatizes the shift in nineteenth-century medicine from an understanding of illness as a consequence of imbalances in a complex system of mind, body, and environment to a search for specific, somatic etiologies. In a bold gesture, James refuses to diagnose the central character's illness. The game of guessing Milly Theale's problem is popular with students and critics alike, but clearly James asks us to consider why we seek such certainty and what is gained by naming an illness.

In the fourth unit, "Illness as a Failure of Nerves," we read Charlotte Perkins Gilman's short story "The Yellow Wallpaper" (1892) because it raises two important issues: the gender politics of medicine and the validity of illnesses with unidentified etiologies. Students usually enjoy Gilman's story, the history of her treatment by S. Weir Mitchell, and her resolve to "convince him of the error of his ways" (Gilman, *Living* 121). Critical commentary is abundant on this topic (see Hedges), and the issues often make for good student research projects. Nervous ills were a locus for nineteenth-century debates about gender, sexuality, urbanization, and many other issues, and we turn to George Beard's medical treatise *American Nervousness* (1881) as a pivotal text. With a little work it yields many riches, offering insight into nineteenth-century views of illness and a historical frame for late-twentieth-century interest in stress-related illnesses. S. Weir Mitchell's medical works are densely scientific, but they too can be useful for studying nineteenth-century presumptions about gender and illness (see, e.g., *Gunshot Wounds*). His fiction is also a good source for a study of one doctor's view of the cultural implications of nervous ailments (see, e.g., "The Case").[4] For historical context, I turn to works by Carroll Smith-Rosenberg and by Tom Lutz on nervous ailments, gender, and nineteenth-century medicine. For contemporary examples of polemical literature on medicine, students might be referred to short stories or plays about AIDS, literary works that, like Gilman's story, explore and often critique medical responses to illness.[5]

The last unit, "Illness as a Consequence of Lifestyle," examines representations of illness that indict both the individual and society. Eugene O'Neill's play *Long Day's Journey into Night* (1956) investigates the psychological causes and consequences, as well as the philosophical implications, of illness by focusing on a mother's drug addiction and a son's tuberculosis. The play asks a difficult question about illness: Who or what is to blame? This question is evident in Wigglesworth's seventeenth-century poem and underlies many of the texts and issues considered in this course. The question of blame is intelligently addressed in Judith Wilson Ross's philosophical investigation of the language we use to discuss AIDS. We also read Don DeLillo's novel *White Noise* (1985), a darkly comic indictment of modern technology. *White Noise* depicts a society on the brink of disaster and suggests that it is modernity itself—the white noise of the media, a toxic chemical spill, and high-tech medicine—that threatens the physical, emotional, and spiritual health of individuals and the very fabric of society. I often use contemporary movies, television dramas, and news reports as texts, and we read reports from the surgeon general and recent articles in such journals as *New England Journal of Medicine* and *Journal of the American Medical Association.*

There are, of course, many other texts that would be appropriate, and I name only a few here. A course not limited to United States culture might include Tolstoy's "The Death of Ivan Illych," Camus's *The Plague,* and Thomas Mann's *The Magic Mountain.* For representations of mental illness, Ken Kesey's *One Flew over the Cuckoo's Nest* or Virginia Woolf's *Mrs. Dalloway* are possibilities. There are also many autobiographical accounts of illness: John Donne, Anatole Broyard, Oliver Sacks, Gerda Lerner, Audre Lorde, and many others have used their literary talents to write about illness.

My writing assignments ask students to work closely with a text, drawing on the theoretical, historical, and social contexts discussed in class. A sample assignment is as follows:

> Choose a text—a movie, story, or novel—and analyze how it represents illness. Your essay should make a strong statement about what attitude the text has toward illness. You might, for example, argue that in *Little Women* Alcott romanticizes illness in her depiction of Beth's final days; or you might argue that although Alcott deploys the traditional romantic metaphors associated with tuberculosis, she

never really valorizes illness as do many nineteenth-century European writers and that instead she values such middle-class stalwart virtues as good health and physical vitality. You might argue that a writer (such as Gilman) uses illness to make her or his social commentary; or you might argue that the representation of AIDS in the film *Philadelphia* unwittingly endorses (or, alternatively, is an attempt to combat) the stereotypes and myths associated with AIDS.

I encourage students to have an opinion, to decide if the text offers an enlightened or troubling representation of illness. In the final exam I ask students to identify the philosophical and historical arguments of such thinkers as Sontag, Rosenberg, and Ross and to understand medical and literary texts as participants in the same discussion.

Inevitably, class discussion will veer from illness to medicine. Students like to discuss the medical profession; tell stories of encounters with the medical profession; and focus on representations of healers, cures, and medical institutions in the texts we read. Evil doctors, good doctors, lay practitioners, hospitals, clinics, and emergency rooms are often vivid and concrete images, and discussions of these images can be fruitful and relevant. Studying representations of illness can seem a more amorphous task, but a discussion of doctors can become a discussion of illness if students consider how our stereotypes and representations of healers reveal something about how we understand illness. An examination of those who have claimed, or who have been given, the authority and privilege to attend to the body is an important part of any cultural study of illness.

The primary goal of the course is critical thinking, and I ask students to move from critical thinking about texts to critical thinking about history, about their own culture, and about the power of representation. The course presumes that all participants have a stake in thinking about these issues—as citizens who may shape public policy; as individuals who will be sick and who will care for others who are sick; and as participants in the construction of contemporary stories, images, and metaphors about illness and about healing. The course does not suggest, as Sontag does, that we should avoid

metaphoric thinking about illness. Indeed, I believe that such puri-
fied thinking is impossible. But the course borrows from Sontag's
argument, suggesting that we must pay careful attention to the
metaphors and narratives by which we know illness.

Course Readings

Introduction
Rosenberg, "Framing Disease"

Illness as God's Punishment
Wigglesworth, "God's Controversy with New England"
Mather, "Selections from 'The Angel' "
Alger, *Inferences from the Pestilence and the Fast*
Secondary sources: Beall and Shyrock, *Cotton Mather;* Blake, "The
    Inoculation Controversy in Boston, 1721–1722"

Illness as Contagion
Brown, *Arthur Mervyn*
Poe, "The Masque of the Red Death"
Hosack, "Observations on Febrile Contagion . . ."
Pickering, "Digest of American Sanitary Law"
Secondary sources: Rosenberg, *The Cholera Years;* Pernick, "Politics,
    Parties, and Pestilence"

Illness as Ennobling Affliction
Stowe, selections from *Uncle Tom's Cabin*
Alcott, selections from *Little Women*
James, *The Wings of the Dove*
Appropriate contemporary Hollywood film or television show
Secondary sources: Sontag, *Illness as Metaphor* and *AIDS and Its
    Metaphors*

Illness as a Failure of Nerves
Beard, *American Nervousness*
Gilman, "The Yellow Wallpaper"
Mitchell, selections from *Gunshot Wounds*
Secondary sources: Smith-Rosenberg, "The Hysterical Woman";
    Lutz, *American Nervousness, 1903*

Illness as a Consequence of Lifestyle
O'Neill, *Long Day's Journey into Night*

DeLillo, *White Noise*
Surgeon general reports
Articles in the *New England Journal of Medicine* and the *Journal of the American Medical Association*
Secondary source: Ross, "Ethics and the Language of AIDS"

Notes

1. This view of science is controversial, and students interested in the debate on the validity of science studies might be referred to the discussion that followed the physicist Alan Sokal's publication of a counterfeit study in *Social Text*, a respected journal of cultural studies. Responses to the hoax appeared between June 1996 and January 1997 in national newspapers and magazines as well as in scholarly journals.
2. See Beall and Shyrock for a study of Mather's medical thought. For historical context I assign Blake's study of inoculation in eighteenth-century Boston.
3. Many important medical texts have been reprinted by Arno Press in the Medicine and Society in America series.
4. See Golden for a reading of Gilman's short story against Mitchell's fiction.
5. For a reading of two AIDS plays, see Cady and Hunter.

Works Cited

Alcott, Louisa May. *Little Women.* 1869. New York: Bantam, 1983.

Alger, William R. *Inferences from the Pestilence and the Fast: A Discourse Preached in the Mount Pleasant Congregational Church, Roxbury, Mass., August 3, 1849.* Boston: Crosby, 1849.

Beall, Otho T., Jr., and Richard H. Shyrock. *Cotton Mather: First Significant Figure in American Medicine.* Baltimore: Johns Hopkins UP, 1954.

Beard, George. *American Nervousness.* 1881. Salem: Ayer, 1981.

Blake, John B. "The Inoculation Controversy in Boston, 1721–1722." Leavitt and Numbers 347–55.

Bono, James J. "Science, Discourse, and Literature: The Role/Rule of Metaphor in Science." *Literature and Science: Theory and Practice.* Ed. Stuart Peterfreund. Boston: Northeastern UP, 1990. 59–89.

Brown, Charles Brockden. *Arthur Mervyn.* 1800. Schenectady: New Coll. and UP, 1992.

Cady, Joseph, and Kathryn Hunter. "Making Contact: The AIDS Plays." Juengst and Koenig 42–49.

DeLillo, Don. *White Noise.* New York: Viking, 1985.

Gilman, Charlotte Perkins. *The Living of Charlotte Perkins Gilman: An Autobiography.* 1935. Madison: U of Wisconsin P, 1991.

———. "The Yellow Wallpaper." 1892. *"The Yellow Wallpaper" and Other Writings.* Ed. Lynne Sharon Schwartz. New York: Bantam, 1989. 1–20.

Golden, Catherine. " 'Overwriting' the Rest Cure: Charlotte Perkins Gilman's Literary Escape from S. Weir Mitchell's Fictionalization of Women." Karpinski 144–58.

Greenblatt, Stephen. "Culture." *Critical Terms for Literary Study.* Ed. Frank Lentricchia and Thomas McLaughlin. Chicago: U of Chicago P, 1990. 225–32.

Hedges, Elaine R. " 'Out at Last'? 'The Yellow Wallpaper' after Two Decades of Feminist Criticism." Karpinski 222–33.

Hosack, David. "Observations on Febrile Contagion, and on the Means of Improving the Medical Police of the City of New York." 1820. *Origins of Public Health in America: Selected Essays, 1820–1855.* Ed. Charles E. Rosenberg. Medicine and Soc. in Amer. New York: Arno, 1972. 59–79.

James, Henry. *The Wings of the Dove.* 1902. Columbus: Merrill, 1970.

Juengst, Eric T., and Barbara A. Koenig, eds. *The Meaning of AIDS: Implications for Medical Science, Clinical Practice, and Public Health Policy.* New York: Praeger, 1989.

Karpinski, Joanne B., ed. *Critical Essays on Charlotte Perkins Gilman.* New York: Hall, 1992.

Kleinman, Arthur. *The Illness Narratives: Suffering, Healing, and the Human Condition.* New York: Basic, 1988.

Leavitt, Judith Walzer, and Ronald L. Numbers, eds. *Sickness and Health in America: Readings in the History of Medicine and Public Health.* 2nd ed. Madison: U of Wisconsin P, 1985.

Lutz, Tom. *American Nervousness, 1903: An Anecdotal History.* Ithaca: Cornell UP, 1991.

Mather, Cotton. "Selections from 'The Angel.' " Beall and Shyrock 127–234.

Mitchell, S. Weir. "The Case of George Dedlow." *Atlantic Monthly* July 1866: 1–11. Rpt. in *"The Autobiography of a Quack" and Other Short Stories.* By Mitchell. New York: Century, 1915. 83–109.

———. *Gunshot Wounds and Other Injuries of the Nerves.* Philadelphia: Lippincott, 1864.

O'Neill, Eugene. *Long Day's Journey into Night.* 1956. New Haven: Yale UP, 1989.

Pernick, Martin S. "Politics, Parties, and Pestilence: Epidemic Yellow Fever in Philadelphia and the Rise of the First Party System." Leavitt and Numbers 356–71.

Pickering, Henry G. "Appendix IV: Digest of American Sanitary Law." *Public Hygiene in America.* By Henry Bowditch. 1877. Ed. Charles E. Rosenberg. Medicine and Soc. in Amer. New York: Arno, 1972. 299–440.

Poe, Edgar Allan. "The Masque of the Red Death." 1842. *Great Short Works of Edgar Allan Poe.* New York: Harper, 1970. 359–66.

Rosenberg, Charles. *The Cholera Years: The United States in 1832, 1849, and 1866.* Chicago: U of Chicago P, 1962.

———. "Framing Disease: Illness, Society, and History." *Explaining Epidemics and Other Studies in the History of Medicine.* Cambridge: Cambridge UP, 1992. 305–18.

Ross, Judith Wilson. "Ethics and the Language of AIDS." Juengst and Koenig 30–41.

Smith-Rosenberg, Carroll. "The Hysterical Woman: Sex Roles and Role Conflict in Nineteenth-Century America." *Disorderly Conduct: Visions of Gender in Victorian America.* New York: Oxford UP, 1985. 197–216.

Sokal, Alan. "Transgressing the Boundaries: Toward a Transformative Hermeneutics of Quantum Gravity." *Social Text* 46–47 (1996): 217–52.

Sontag, Susan. Illness as Metaphor *and* AIDS and Its Metaphors. New York: Anchor-Doubleday, 1990.

Stowe, Harriet Beecher. *Uncle Tom's Cabin.* 1852. New York: Macmillan, 1994.

Wigglesworth, Michael. "God's Controversy with New England." 1662. *Early American Poetry: Selections from Bradstreet, Taylor, Dwight, Freneau, and Bryant.* Ed. Jane Donahue Eberwein. Madison: U of Wisconsin P, 1978. 323–38.

Lilian R. Furst

Medical History and Literary Texts

This course offers an understanding of the ways in which scientific advances have affected the day-to-day practice of medicine. Current controversial issues such as assisted suicide, abortion, and allocation of donated organs are avoided in favor of factors such as power, compassion, and technology in the routine interactions between physicians and patients. Since the course grew out of my research into the changing balance of power between doctors and patients, this theme forms a unifying, though not exclusive, focus.

The scope of the course is roughly from the mid-nineteenth century to the late 1980s. This period spans the momentous introduction of a spate of diagnostic instruments—from the stethoscope and the thermometer to x rays and CAT scans—as well as a fundamental shift in the locus of medical practice from the patient's home to the doctor's office and the hospital. The implications of these changes for both doctor and patient are explored; the obviously positive aspects such as the enormous improvements in therapeutics are juxtaposed with the negative ones of an increasing impersonality, in part the price of specialization. Social factors, notably the rise in the doctor's standing (and income), and how such factors impinge on relationships with patients are considered too.

The course has so far been offered three times under the aegis of the Honors Program and the Curriculum of Comparative Literature; enrollment is limited to fifteen to allow a seminar format. It has attracted particularly bright undergraduates, many of whom plan to head for medical school and some of whom have already gained experience in the field through volunteer work, internships, or summer positions as research assistants. Although some freshmen have successfully taken the class, most students are more advanced. The numbers of men and women have been almost equal. An unusually high proportion of the students is working toward a dual major, combining a science (most frequently biology or chemistry) with a humanities option. They have been exceptionally enterprising, eager groups. The cross-fertilization of science and humanities cultures prompted by this course is especially rewarding, although it has also given rise to one difficulty: the science majors have tended to complain about the reading load so that I have had to reduce it.

The class, which meets twice weekly for seventy-five minutes, is structured into a mixture of lectures, oral reports by students, and discussion. This organization lends variety to the longish meetings and above all stimulates students' active participation. I introduce each reading by speaking about the author and providing information about the historical context. For instance, I explain the distinction between a physician and a surgeon in the nineteenth century, and I elucidate the problems encountered by women when they tried to gain admission to medical schools in the latter part of the nineteenth century. While there are no prerequisites for students other than a serious commitment to attentive reading and an interest in medicine, past and present, the instructor has to command a good knowledge of medical history as well as subtle reading skills. For the oral reports, a list of suggested topics, varying from two to five for each book, is handed out at the beginning of the semester. Students are required to contribute two reports and may, with the instructor's permission, address topics of their own choice. Volunteers are solicited in advance, generally from week to week. These reports, which normally run from ten to fifteen minutes each, are primarily intended to involve students by serving as a start for discussions. Often a lively exchange of ideas takes place. The exams, both midterm and final, are take-homes, and again students may write on subjects of their own choice following consultation with the instructor.

To provide an overview and facilitate comments on the course's rationale and methodology, I list here the works for 1997, in the order in which they were read: Erwin Ackerknecht, *A Short History of Medicine*; Anthony Trollope, *Doctor Thorne* (1858); Sarah Orne Jewett, *A Country Doctor* (1884); Arthur Conan Doyle, "The Doctors of Hoyland" (1894); Paul de Kruif, *Microbe Hunters* (1926); Sinclair Lewis, *Arrowsmith* (1925); Sherwin B. Nuland, *Doctors: The Biography of Medicine* (1988); Melvin Konner, *Becoming a Doctor* (1987); Oliver Sacks, *Awakenings* (1973); Abraham Verghese, *My Own Country* (1994). (With the exception of "The Doctors of Hoyland," these texts were all available in paperback in 1997.)

This list represents the outcome of a number of changes made during the planning stage and after the course was first taught in 1996. The most important rearrangement is the alternation of medical histories and literary texts. I had originally envisaged starting off with the three historical works (Ackerknecht; de Kruif; Nuland) to lay a foundational knowledge of the main developments in medicine in the nineteenth and twentieth centuries. However, I realized early on that it would be more fruitful to integrate the medical histories with literary texts that illustrate the various phases of medical progress, in order to show the essential complementarity of nonfiction and fiction. This strategy lends itself more readily to de Kruif and Nuland than to Ackerknecht, whose *Short History of Medicine* is a broadly sweeping survey. Ackerknecht's encyclopedic catalog is admittedly the weakest part of the course, and I warn students that they may find the reading tedious. Yet Ackerknecht conveys necessary information about the rapid and radical advances and discoveries in medicine. I endeavor to make this reading more palatable by contextualizing it with a lecture on pre-nineteenth-century medicine, focusing on the humoral theories prevalent since Galen and the conceptualization of the doctor's role as missionary to the bedside and confidential friend before reliable diagnostic tools and effective therapeutic means became available.

This early function of the doctor is made much more graphic and immediate in the literary texts than in the histories of medicine. The fictions give flesh, as it were, to the skeletal outlines provided by the historical accounts and are therefore essential to the students' understanding of situations alien to their own experiences. Trollope's Doctor Thorne and Jewett's Dr. Leslie in *A Country Doctor* both befriend their patients and negotiate treatment with them. (The arrogance of wealthy and aristocratic patients is clearly apparent in *Doctor Thorne*, where the paying clients claim the right to tyrannize and dismiss a doctor whose advice is uncongenial.) *Doctor Thorne* also illustrates competition among doctors for a patient's favor as well as a range of personal styles. The value of humane empathy—as opposed to technology—dominated discussion of both *Doctor Thorne* and *A Country Doctor*, a rather straightforward, idealized portrayal of cordial relations between doctor and patients in rural New England.

A Country Doctor also affords the opportunity to begin consideration of women doctors in the nineteenth century. In the novel, Nan, Dr. Leslie's ward, aspires to follow in his footsteps. At this point in the course a lecture provides an outline of women's struggles to be admitted to medical schools. The history of the long and violent resistance to women in the medical profession elicited astonishment from my students. The portrait of Nan, the beginner, is complemented by that of Dr. Verrinder Smith, the already qualified, highly successful woman doctor in Doyle's "Doctors of Hoyland," a short, satiric story about male physicians' prejudice against women in "their" profession. This ironic tale provides an amusing but still significant interlude after heavy reading.

The middle segment of the course is devoted to de Kruif's *Microbe Hunters* and Lewis's *Arrowsmith*, which are linked by their common concentration on bacteriology. From *Microbe Hunters* the two chapters on Pasteur and the one on Koch are read. *Arrowsmith* is daunting to some students on account of its length, but it is vital to the course for its insights into various types of medical practice (country doctor, public health, exclusive clinic, research laboratory) in the United States in the early years of the twentieth century.

The third historical work, Nuland's *Doctors*, is instrumental in making the transition to modern medicine. Chapters on the stethoscope, the origins of general anesthesia, and antiseptic surgery are assigned. The three historical works are not only used as sources of information but also explored as examples of different ways of writing medical history. Since this course is offered in the comparative literature curriculum, the same reading strategies are applied to both the historical and the literary texts. Students are taught to look at such narrative factors as perspective, point of view, voice, incidence of dialogue, and metaphor. Ackerknecht's dry history, with its overload of facts, names, and dates and its dearth of explanation, was deemed useful primarily as a reference guide. In de Kruif and Nuland we examined the interplay of fact and fictionalization. Although many students were enthralled by de Kruif's lively, folksy presentation of real figures and their successes and failures, his recourse to invented dialogue and his imaginative penetration into his subjects' minds were recognized as an attractive but questionable historical methodology. Nuland is best able to appeal to readers with his sound balance of vivid portraits and rigorous adherence to historical documentation. He is also skilled at explaining the importance of specific advances and at establishing connections between past discoveries and present practice.

The course's final segment is devoted to recent writings. Konner's evocation of his journey through the third year of medical school prompted a strong response, especially from those students planning to go into medicine. His criticisms of the system attracted greater attention than did his acknowledgment of its good points. The surprise flop in the course was Sacks's *Awakenings*, which had not been included in 1996. Students were asked to read Sacks's general reflections on patient care and a couple of the cases. The readings were found to be somewhat confusing and too technical (despite the appended glossary). Partly, I suspect, students were simply tired toward the end of the semester. To minimize the pressure, I dropped Arthur Kleinman's *Illness Narratives*; I had wanted students to read parts of this sensitive analysis of the problems attendant for physician and patient alike in handling chronic disease.

The course closed on a high note with tremendous enthusiasm for Verghese's *My Own Country*, which was introduced by an interview with the author taped from the PBS *Soundings* program.[1] From 1985 to 1989, Verghese practiced as an infectious diseases specialist in Johnson City, at the junction of Tennessee, Virginia, and North Carolina. A Christian Indian brought up in Africa by missionary parents, Verghese writes with understanding about his encounter with southern and gay cultures as the AIDS epidemic hits this remote and conservative area. Students were interested in the multicultural aspect of this autobiographical account, and its temporal and spatial proximity to their own world made it easy for them to become absorbed in the text. This last reading completed the circle of the course by showing a contemporary doctor who draws on all the resources of advanced technology but at the same time acts as his patients' confidential friend and even as a missionary to the bedside, visiting their homes and getting to know their families. Several major themes of the course—power, compassion, and technology—could be reviewed in discussion of this text. As a fictionalized autobiography incorporating remembered conversations, Verghese's work also raises once more the issue of the fusion of fact and fiction that preoccupied us in dealing with the medical history texts.

Between the first and the second version of the course a number of changes were made. The reading load was reduced by cutting portions of Ackerknecht's *Short History of Medicine* and by requiring only the opening 160 pages of *Doctor Thorne*. Although I do not normally use excerpts from long works, this seemed a reasonable compromise because the relevant parts about doctors occur at the beginning of the novel, and its ensuing, complicated marital plots are of minor interest in this context. A. J. Cronin's *The Citadel*, a graphic and not-too-long British novel about a doctor's picaresque experiences, was dropped, since it seemed redundant with *Arrowsmith* and required a great deal of explanation to American students. Two other books had to be eliminated because they went out of print: Perri Klass's *A Not Entirely Benign Procedure* and Robert Klitzman's *Year-Long Night*. Both are autobiographies of medical training that formed a fine cluster with Konner's *Becoming a Doctor*. Klass emphasizes her status as a woman, while Klitzman focuses on his internship. Sacks's *Awakenings* and Kleinman's *Illness Narratives* were substituted to exemplify different modes of current practice.

In the future I plan to experiment with a couple of the cases in Sacks's *An Anthropologist on Mars*. They are probably easier to grasp than those in *Awakenings* because each chapter is self-contained, but this change entails sacrificing Sacks's thoughtful reflections on his approach in *Awakenings*. I am also wondering whether to replace *A Country Doctor* with Elizabeth Stuart Phelps's *Dr. Zay* (1882), which has recently been reissued in paperback. *Dr. Zay* superbly illustrates the surprise of a young man from Boston at the competence of the woman doctor who cares for him following an accident in rural Maine. Unfortunately, the plot degenerates into romance as doctor and patient fall in love and decide to marry. I regret having to exclude from the earlier period Elizabeth Gaskell's *Wives and Daughters* and George Eliot's *Middlemarch*, both of which offer excellent realistic portrayals of the lives and difficulties of mid-nineteenth-century country surgeons. However, their length is prohibitive.

Along with the course outline and the report topics, I give students three lists of suggestions for further study: nineteenth- and twentieth-century literary texts on the topic, movies with medical themes available on video, and studies on various aspects of medical history. I realize that students do not have the time for extra work during the semester, although they might watch a video. But I also know that some of them do continue to read later on, often beginning with those books of which we read only parts (e.g., Nuland; de Kruif). So the course has an afterlife.

To literary scholars who may wish to teach such a course, I suggest the following books as good starting points. Stanley Joel Reiser's *Medicine and the Reign of Technology* charts the technological advances that are central to the development of modern medicine.

Charles E. Rosenberg's *The Care of Strangers* is a fine history of the evolution of the hospital from a dying place for the indigent into the fulcrum of late-twentieth-century medicine. The most authoritative historical study of women in medicine is Regina M. Morantz-Sanchez's *Science and Sympathy: Women Physicians in America*. My study *Between Doctors and Patients: The Changing Balance of Power* covers most of the historical and literary material in the course.

Under a new endowment at the University of North Carolina, the course has just been awarded a grant for the incorporation of a service learning component. Students will have the option of volunteering in a health science setting three to five hours per week for ten weeks. Placement and supervision will be handled by the office of student affairs. I plan to ask each student to keep a brief weekly journal of experiences and impressions and, late in the semester, to give class reports on what the student has learned. I have no doubt that this addition will enrich both the course and the participants by linking college study to the practical world beyond the classroom, helping hesitant students to choose a career, and bringing a new dimension—and dynamism—into the classroom.

What do the students learn from such a course? The anonymous evaluations at the end of the semester have been extraordinarily enthusiastic; several students have described the course as the best they have taken and as a turning point in their lives. They endorse the value of the interdisciplinary method, they enjoy most of the readings, and they are excited by the energy of the class discussions. Above all, perhaps, they are astonished at the changes in medical practice and in relationships between doctors and patients in the past 150 years. While some had taken courses in the history of science, none realized the relatively recent and fundamentally new departures in medicine. Not least important to me as a teacher of literature, the course helps turn the students into more discerning readers. In this way it affords an opportunity for humanists to reach out to scientists.

Course Readings

History of Medicine
Ackerknecht, *A Short History of Medicine*, 145–74
de Kruif, *Microbe Hunters*, 33–177
Nuland, *Doctors: The Biography of Medicine*, 200–37, 263–385

Literary Narratives
Trollope, *Dr. Thorne*, 1–176
Jewett, *A Country Doctor*
Doyle, "The Doctors of Hoyland"
Lewis, *Arrowsmith*

Autobiographies of Medical Work
Konner, *Becoming A Doctor*
Sacks, *Awakenings*, 1–86, 188–201, 202–57, 274–79
Kleinman, *The Illness Narratives*, 56–74, 88–99, 121–69, 209–26
Verghese, *My Own Country*

Note

1. Tapes are available for about five dollars from the Natl. Humanities Center, 7 Alexander Dr., PO Box 12256, Research Triangle Park, NC 27709-2567; 919 549-0661; fax 919 990-8535.

Works Cited

Ackerknecht, Erwin H. *A Short History of Medicine*. 1958. Rev. ed. Baltimore: Johns Hopkins UP, 1982.

Cronin, A. J. *The Citadel*. Boston: Little, 1937.

de Kruif, Paul. *Microbe Hunters*. 1926. New York: Harcourt, 1966.

Doyle, Arthur Conan. "The Doctors of Hoyland." *Round the Red Lamp*. 1894. London: Appleton, 1921. 295–315.

Eliot, George. *Middlemarch*. 1872. Ed. David Carroll. New York: Oxford UP, 1997.

Furst, Lilian R. *Between Doctors and Patients: The Changing Balance of Power*. Charlottesville: UP of Virginia, 1998.

Gaskell, Elizabeth. *Wives and Daughters*. 1866. New York: Penguin, 1969.

Jewett, Sarah Orne. *A Country Doctor*. 1884. New York: NAL, 1986.

Klass, Perri. *A Not Entirely Benign Procedure*. New York: Putnam, 1987.

Kleinman, Arthur. *The Illness Narratives: Suffering, Healing, and the Human Condition*. New York: Basic, 1988.

Klitzman, Robert. *Year-Long Night*. New York: Penguin, 1989.

Konner, Melvin. *Becoming a Doctor*. New York: Penguin, 1987.

Lewis, Sinclair. *Arrowsmith*. 1925. New York: Signet, 1961.

Morantz-Sanchez, Regina M. *Science and Sympathy: Women Physicians in America*. New York: Oxford UP, 1985.

Nuland, Sherwin B. *Doctors: The Biography of Medicine*. New York: Vintage, 1988.

Phelps, Elizabeth Stuart. *Dr. Zay*. 1882. New York: Feminist, 1987.

Reiser, Stanley Joel. *Medicine and the Reign of Technology*. Cambridge: Cambridge UP, 1978.

Rosenberg, Charles E. *The Care of Strangers*. New York: Basic, 1987.

Sacks, Oliver. *An Anthropologist on Mars*. New York: Knopf, 1995.

———. *Awakenings*. 1973. New York: Harper, 1990.

Trollope, Anthony. *Doctor Thorne*. 1858. New York: Penguin, 1991.

Verghese, Abraham. *My Own Country: A Doctor's Story*. 1994. New York: Viking, 1995.

Suzanne Poirier

The History and Literature of Women's Health

Any course is the product not only of its designers but also of the institution in which it is taught. The History and Literature of Women's Health, a semester-long elective, cross-listed in medical humanities and women's studies at the University of Illinois, Chicago, is a case in point. The medical humanities program sees one of its goals to be the creation of a space where students from across the health professions can explore, on an equal footing, the human dimensions of illness and health care. The women's studies program, whose audience has traditionally been undergraduate and graduate students in disciplines other than the health professions, encourages the study of women in relation to a world that is often hostile to or dismissive of women's achievements or potential. Both programs seek to give voice to those who may remain voiceless in situations of unequal power: patients, in the case of medical humanities; women, in the case of women's studies. In situations where women are patients, the goals of both programs seem to be conveniently matched. In terms of the constituencies of the two groups, though, students may perceive themselves to be at odds. Feminist research and theory has produced vocal—and effective—critiques of medicine; health professions students have, in choosing their careers, aligned themselves to some degree with this system. Can students in the health professions learn to question the assumptions and practices of medicine in ways that will improve their responsiveness to female patients? Can students from other disciplines undertake a nuanced critique of medicine that acknowledges the complex mix of history and circumstance in which many health professionals unwittingly find themselves? These are the challenges that created and have sustained this course for over fifteen years.

Margaret (Peg) Strobel, then head of the women's studies program, and I designed and initially taught the History and Literature of Women's Health. Given our respective fields of history and literature, neither of us knew the science of medicine. We chose to use history and literature as vehicles for exploring the ways that the medical sciences have regarded and treated women, that is, discipline was a means to a topical end. Our approach was guided by three principles. First, we both believe strongly that ideas about women and men are constructed and that social mores and cultural beliefs often guide or obfuscate scientific knowledge. Thus we approached women's health by examining the historical, social, economic, political, and cultural contexts in which women and medicine have interacted. Second, because we were cautious to claim any viewpoint as pertaining to all women, we realized that it was equally dangerous to claim monolithic positions for all medical practitioners or researchers. This tenet led us to present the diversity of situations and views of both women *and* medicine. Third, one early and abiding goal of women's studies has been to discover and reclaim women's accomplishments. We therefore sought to present not only social history but also the achievements of particular women in the area of women's health and to consider always the meaning of women's health and its history in the daily lives of women.

A practical issue also contributed to the design of the course. As a survey (albeit of a specialized area), the course was designated a mid-level undergraduate course. Thus we sought to teach concepts and ways of thinking about women and health rather than in-depth information about the evolution of specific medical knowledge or therapies. Students learn the historical material in informal lectures, interrupted often by questions and short discussions, and read a work of fiction or autobiography to accompany each topic. Discussion is essential to the course, and it is important that no student feel threatened or silenced because of unfamiliarity with some of the subject matter. For example, those who come to the course after taking other women's studies courses often know little or nothing about physiology, anatomy, or clinical practice. In turn, those in the health sciences are frequently unfamiliar with, and often skeptical about, feminism. Such diversity in a "safe" classroom allows students to learn from one another. Students are challenged to examine their own beliefs and ideas as well as those of their classmates and of the authors whose works they read.

Five themes have emerged from the content of the course.

Medicine and science have always been inexact. Whether the humoral theory of medicine, one of the various theories of evolution, or germ theory predominates, scientific "advance" (and the treatments it has produced) has always been imperfect. By recognizing the limits of these theories' attempts to define women or describe women's health and illness, students come to understand as well the fallibility and limitations of physicians trained in (and trusting to) the science of their times. Recognizing the medical errors made in prescribing treatment for the narrator of Charlotte Perkins Gilman's "The Yellow Wallpaper" is relatively easy. Less easy is identifying the social assumptions about the "good life" of intelligent, middle-class British women that lead to the suicide of Susan Rawlings in Doris Lessing's "To Room Nineteen." Difficult too is sorting out the late-adolescent Susanna Kaysen's scorn of adults—who see her only as a sweet but dizzy-headed girl—and her real fear of harming herself, in the autobiographical *Girl, Interrupted*.

Medical science both shapes and reflects the social biases of its day. Theories of evolution and eugenics and the medical practices that grew out of them are probably the most obvious examples of how racial and gender biases were often reinforced by science. Caught in self-fulfilling prophecies of scientific determinism, women have often found that speaking out against their doctors is the same as speaking out against their society and vice versa. Charlotte Perkins Gilman's utopian novel *Herland,* about a world of only (Aryan) women where violence is unheard of and each child is cherished, is filled with the ideals of feminist and health reforms of her day—but also with the social engineering of eugenics and an essentialist view of women as mothers. Margaret Atwood's *The Handmaid's Tale,* sometimes taught at the end of the course, offers a dramatic counterpoint to Gilman's novel. Atwood's dystopian novel also places motherhood at the center of a society's values, this time in an authoritarian, patriarchal, militaristic world in which female fertility is used to enhance male power.

Social and scientific change is not effected by any one person or event. Nearly all medical-social change has a history of individual and collective politics; scientific trial, error, and (reluctant) redirection; advocacy and battle on a number of legislative fronts; and ethical debate about the nature and consequences of scientific "progress." The lecture on the history of birth control, for example, demonstrates this complex dynamism by concluding with brief biographies of three women who advanced development and legitimation of birth control in the United States in important ways: Emma Goldman, a midwife and anarchist who was one of the first people to bring the issue of limiting family size to public consciousness; Margaret Sanger, a trained nurse who made the legalization of birth control her life's goal, suceeding eventually by conceding control of distribution and education to physicians; and Rachel Yarros, a physician who rallied her male colleagues to support the creation of numerous birth-control clinics in Chicago. The readings that accompany this unit—a local history of Jane, an underground abortion collective of Chicago students and housewives that operated from 1969 to 1973 ("Jane"),[1] and a paper by Toba Cohen, a former student of this class, about her work raising support in Illinois for a legislative bill to legalize abortion—also demonstrate the diversity of goals, personalities, and methods necessary to make change happen. (Both Cohen and Ruth Surgal, a former member of Jane, attend class the evening we discuss these readings, and they talk about their work.)

Women's health has no one, monolithic meaning agreed on by all women, not even by all feminists. The first women's movement in the United States brought together diverse women with interests in such issues as abolition, suffrage, property rights, education, and health reform. There was no agreement then on a unified platform of women's rights. Race and class were always at issue; most women came from white middle and upper classes. History teaches students not only that there is room for a variety of opinions about women's health today but also that proponents of women's health must themselves be sensitive to the assumptions and limitations of their views. In Kate Chopin's *The Awakening*, Edna Pontellier, finding no hope for a respectable, fulfilling life outside marriage in her Creole society, swims out to sea without a backward look. Students' responses to her act run the gamut: some insist that she eventually turns around and arrives safely back on land with new resolve to make a place for herself; others applaud her clearheaded defiance of an oppressive society; still others condemn her actions and reasoning as cowardly and nearsighted. Similarly, students are never unanimous in their conclusions about the events in Alice Walker's short story "Advancing Luna — and Ida B. Wells," in which a white woman chooses to remain silent about her rape by an African American civil-rights leader. While enthusiastically examining the extent to which ideals of female beauty and femininity drive Ruth in Fay Weldon's *Life and Loves of a She-Devil*, many students nevertheless have difficulty examining with equal criticism the ways these standards influence their responses to their own bodies. The sources of students' different reactions to these stories are as important as the different interpretations themselves.

In general, history shows women striving for ever-greater knowledge and choice in terms of their bodies, health, and health care. Women have unceasingly sought information about and control over their bodies, from the physiological societies in nineteenth-century New England, where women of leisure met regularly to read and study their husbands' or brothers' medical books, to women's various efforts to gain knowledge about and access to contraception and abortion, to Audre Lorde's refusal to wear a prosthesis after her mastectomy and her eloquent plea to health professionals to consider how a black lesbian feminist might think about breast cancer (*Cancer Journals*). The search for information that serves women's individual or collective needs extends to a search into the past to discover long-forgotten ways of thinking about women: Anne Cameron's "Old Magic" and "Copper Woman" revive a creation myth that finds strength and pride in the outpourings of women's bodies.

Both the historical and the literary content of the course explores the diversity of women's experiences. In addition to the lectures, which include information about women of color, lesbians, and women from all socioeconomic classes, special units consider issues of health for these women. Oral histories of the African American midwife Onnie Lee Logan and the Hispanic Native American midwife Jesusita Aragón recount the special skills of these women, their special sense of calling to their work, and the special needs of the patients they serve (Logan; Buss). Toni Cade Bambara's *The Salt Eaters* and Ana Castillo's *So Far from God* not only present traditional methods of healing in, respectively, African American and Mexican American (and Native American) cultures but also explore the complex relations among gender, health, culture, and oppression faced by women of color in the United States. June Arnold's *Sister Gin* closes with a discussion of race and violence, but its central characters are a lesbian couple who wrestle with menopause, aging, alcohol use, and a faltering relationship. In all the literature, but particularly in these novels, women's individual health and lives cannot be seen as separate from the family, friends, and formal and informal institutions that surround them.

The actual content of the course varies from year to year but includes most of the topics presented here. The course always begins with two overviews. The first, which introduces the course, invites students to name topics they consider relevant to women's health. The obvious ones are mentioned quickly and the discussion expands to such issues as violence against women, disease prevention, poverty, alternative treatment, and inclusion of women in medical research. The discussion highlights not only the breadth of women's health concerns but also many points of debate that appear in contemporary issues—and have appeared as well in past debates about women's health. The second (almost embarrassingly ambitious) overview is of women's history in the United States. We look in particular at the often paradoxical history of women in various reform movements and conclude with a visit to the Hull House Museum, the site of the United States's first settlement community. A tour of the Hull mansion and a slide presentation about the women of Hull House by Mary Ann Johnson, the museum's director, bring the reforms of the nineteenth and early twentieth centuries alive. By the end of the first three weeks of class, students are aware that women's health is of long-standing concern to women; that the obstacles and politics of the women's health movement are inseparable from the lives of women themselves; and that women have played important roles in seeking to improve the health of women, their families, and their communities, often in cautious but supportive conjunction with men and medicine.

The History and Literature of Women's Health was first taught in 1981. After the first few years, Peg Strobel's other responsibilities necessitated her resignation from the course, but I have found that the goals and structure we established still serve the course well. Time, however, does not stand still. When we designed the course, new historicism informed much of our approach. Today, work in critical theory, particularly in cultural studies, has brought new, even more nuanced interpretations to women's health. Because of the course level and format, I have chosen not to introduce the new theory qua theory, but its tenets and methods inform my lectures and the discussion of the literature; we speak today, for example, of women as the objects of others' gazes and women's bodies as carrying the effects of their social status. The students who enroll in the course have changed as well. Although the course continues to draw students about equally from professional and undergraduate programs, usually less than half the enrollment is Anglo-American. The continued emphasis on United States history, even though I encourage students to discuss their own ethnic traditions and beliefs, often seems narrow. Finally, when I first came to the university, the humanities program was a freestanding unit that served all the health professions colleges; today, the medical humanities program is housed in the Department of Medical Education in the College of Medicine, and my charge is primarily to teach medical students. The History and Literature of Women's Health, with its semester-long format, does not accommodate medical students' schedules.

However, women's health has recently received attention in the College of Medicine and has begun to be incorporated into the curriculum. Literary works about women's health now appear in a number of courses taught by me and by others. Thus several of the issues and debates in this course occur in other formats. Also, Peg and I have recently begun to explore two possibilities for renewing collaboration with the women's studies program: first, to recast this elective as an upper-division and graduate course that allows the instructor to deal more directly with the variety of theoretical approaches to women's health that exist today and, second, to discuss the creation of a new course, International Issues in Women's Health, which will address more political and cultural issues and expand our literary options to the wealth of world literature by women. In addition, the women's studies program has begun to build a collaborative master's degree in women's health with nursing, public health, and medical humanities. When the History and Literature of Women's Health was first designed, history and literature were the means to the end of teaching about a broad way to envision the health of women (and eventually of all people). The proliferation of venues in which such teaching is being done at the University of Illinois, Chicago, is a healthy sign. As the settings in which we teach about women's health continue to change, so will the nature of the courses and their content. Both the content and the contexts of these courses will continue to inform each other.

Course Readings

Overview of Women's Health
Origins and goals of the women's health movement that began in the 1970s.
Lorde, *The Cancer Journals*
Schwartz, "So You're Going to Have a New Body!"

Overview of Women's History
Origins of the first women's movement in the United States, nineteenth-century reform movements and women's roles in them; the entrance of women into medicine, nursing, and pharmacy; the work of the women of Hull House (with a tour of Hull House).
Gilman, *Herland*

Theories of Women's Sexuality
Shifting attitudes about what constitutes healthy sexual expression in men and women, social and legal attitudes toward homosexuality, considerations in interpreting early professional and personal writing about sexuality.
Chopin, *The Awakening*
Wharton, *Summer*

Women's Mental Health
Connection of women's emotional stability and instability with their reproductive systems, S. Weir Mitchell's treatment of nervousness with rest, advent of Freud and various Freudian theories.
Gilman, "The Yellow Wallpaper"
Kaysen, *Girl, Interrupted*
Lessing, "To Room Nineteen"
Steinem, "Ruth's Song (Because She Could Not Sing It)"

Birth Control and Abortion
History of birth control through development of the Pill, with particular attention to the groups and women who contributed to the various birth control movements; contraception and abortion legislation.
Cohen, "The Battle to Legalize Abortion in Illinois"
"Jane"
Walker, "The Abortion"

Childbirth
Midwifery and the rise of obstetrics, home birth and hospital delivery, interventive and natural childbirth.
Buss, *La Partera*
Logan, *Motherwit*

Theories and Myths of the Menstrual Cycle
Recent theories about the role of women in ancient religions, rise of theories about the onset and cessation of menses as times particularly dangerous to women's health, the effects on postmenopausal women of equating women with reproduction.
Arnold, *Sister Gin*
Cameron, "Old Magic," "Copper Woman"
Macdonald, *Look Me in the Eye*

Minority Issues in Women's Health
Health of African slave women, marginalization and its historical hazards to health, poverty and health, cultural attitudes toward health, cultural differences between white women and women of color regarding health.
Bambara, *The Salt Eaters*
Castillo, *So Far from God*
Kingston, *The Woman Warrior*
Lorde, *The Cancer Journals*
Morrison, *The Bluest Eye*

Violence against Women
Relation of rape to property laws and practices of war, evolution of definitions of family abuse and neglect as reported by social service agencies.
Walker, "Advancing Luna—and Ida B. Wells"

Beauty and Body Image
Changing standards of feminine beauty and the health consequences of these standards, race and beauty in a white-dominated society.
Grealy, *Autobiography of a Face*
Weldon, *The Life and Loves of a She-Devil*

Lesbian Health and Literature
The invisibility of female homosexuality and its health consequences, the growing visibility of lesbian literature.
Arnold, *Sister Gin*
Macdonald, *Look Me in the Eye*

Imagining the Future of Women's Health
Review of the themes of the course.
Atwood, *The Handmaid's Tale*

Notes

I would like to thank Peg Strobel for reading this paper during its preparation but most especially for her collaboration in the creating and early teaching of this course.

1. This reading, which comes from an underground newspaper that was published for a short period in Chicago, remains as disturbing and controversial today as when it was written. A book-length history of Jane was recently published (Kaplan).

Works Cited

Arnold, June. *Sister Gin*. New York: Feminist, 1989.

Atwood, Margaret. *The Handmaid's Tale*. New York: Fawcett, 1986.

Bambara, Toni Cade. *The Salt Eaters*. New York: Vintage-Random, 1981.

Buss, Fran Leeper. *La Partera: Story of a Midwife*. Ann Arbor: U of Michigan P, 1980.

Cameron, Anne. "Copper Woman." Cameron, *Daughters* 25–29.

———. *Daughters of Copper Woman*. Vancouver: Press Gang, 1981.

———. "Old Magic." Cameron, *Daughters* 15–24.

Castillo, Ana. *So Far from God*. New York: Plume-Penguin, 1994.

Chopin, Kate. *The Awakening*. 1899. New York: Bard-Avon, 1972.

Cohen, Toba. "The Battle to Legalize Abortion in Illinois: Recollections from a Twenty-five Year Perspective and an Update from the Trenches." Unpublished essay, 1994.

Gilman, Charlotte Perkins. *Herland*. 1915. New York: Pantheon, 1979.

———. *The Yellow Wallpaper*. 1892. Old Westbury: Feminist, 1973.

Grealy, Lucy. *Autobiography of a Face*. New York: Harper, 1994.

"Jane." *Voices* n.d. 1973: n. pag.

Kaplan, Laura. *The Story of Jane, the Legendary Feminist Abortion Service*. New York: Pantheon, 1995.

Kaysen, Susanna. *Girl, Interrupted*. New York: Vintage-Random, 1993.

Kingston, Maxine Hong. *The Woman Warrior*. New York: Vintage-Random, 1977.

Lessing, Doris. "To Room Nineteen." *"A Man and Two Women" and Other Stories*. New York: Simon, 1958. 278–316.

Logan, Onnie Lee. *Motherwit: An Alabama Midwife's Story*. Told to Katherine Clark. New York: Plume-Penguin, 1991.

Lorde, Audre. *The Cancer Journals*. Argyle: Spinsters, 1980.

Macdonald, Barbara, with Cynthia Rich. *Look Me in the Eye: Old Women, Aging, and Ageism*. San Francisco: Spinsters, n.d.

Morrison, Toni. *The Bluest Eye*. New York: Pocket-Simon, 1972.

Schwartz, Lynne Sharon. "So You're Going to Have a New Body!" *The Melting Pot" (and Other Subversive Stories)*. New York: Harper, 1987. 42–58.

Steinem, Gloria. "Ruth's Song (Because She Could Not Sing It)." *Outrageous Acts and Everyday Rebellions*. New York: Holt, Rinehart, 1983. 129–46.

Walker, Alice. "The Abortion." Walker, *You Can't* 64–76.

———. "Advancing Luna—and Ida B. Wells." Walker, *You Can't* 85–104.

———. *You Can't Keep a Good Woman Down: Short Stories*. 1971. New York: Harvest-Harcourt, 1981.

Weldon, Fay. *The Life and Loves of a She-Devil*. New York: Pantheon, 1983.

Wharton, Edith. *Summer*. 1918. New York: Harper, 1979.

Kendrick W. Prewitt

Teaching the Body in Texts: Literature, Culture, and Religion

Toward the end of John Donne's lyrical seduction piece "The Ecstacy," the suitor reminds his mistress that while "Love's mysteries in souls do grow," yet "the body is his book" (71–72). Donne's argument that the body encodes "love's mysteries" draws on a long tradition of reading messages scripted in the body and of encoding and decoding these embodied messages. I teach a course for fourth-year medical students in which we examine these messages, codes, and other aspects of the body as represented in selected texts from the "body" of Western literature.[1] We find that the human form is more than just the sum of its physical parts; it has a wealth of cultural, religious, and political baggage attached to it. In literature, the representation of the body has many possibilities; it might be a vehicle for perception, a register of social or political values, an instrument of sexuality, a part of a larger body politic, or a part of the collective ancestral body. Is the body the soul incarnate? the soul entombed? the animated flesh? The course brings to light through the readings two issues about the human body that are especially relevant in medical school, when students are first being exposed to cadavers and to a highly specialized understanding of the body. First, the reading list, which includes works by "difficult" writers from other places and time periods, such as François Rabelais and Donne, calls on us to historicize our conceptions of the body and to investigate how the traditional Western mind-body dualism shapes other dualisms as well, such as the intellectual-physical, male-female, and classical-grotesque. Second, these works at the same time illustrate how the body has been used as a register of cultural, political, and religious agendas.

The course invites students to reconsider many old assumptions about the body. Does the body itself remain the same through differences of time and place?[2] Accordingly, the course also challenges students to think broadly and to incorporate a wide variety of critical perspectives—historicist, psychoanalytic, feminist, Marxist, theological, biological—in order to place their growing anatomical knowledge in perspective. Today's medical students, moreover, need a frame of reference for tackling issues such as when life begins, the right to die, transplant and reproductive technologies, and gene therapy. How we distinguish, or refuse to distinguish, the mind and body—and how we define and conceive of the body and its relation to personhood—have much to do with decisions about these issues.

We start with the sixteenth-century anatomical woodcuts of Andreas Vesalius and his contemporaries, such as Juan de Valverde de Hamusco and Charles Estienne (see Traub 57–78; Sawday following 38, following 84; Harcourt 30–34, 46–48, 50–51). They provoke students accustomed to twentieth-century anatomical texts to think about poses and settings in the woodcuts and to consider what these aspects might suggest about culture, the body, and the practice of anatomy. For instance, in contrast to the tightly framed photographs and illustrations in modern anatomical texts, the "muscle men" in Vesalius's 1543 *De humani corporis fabrica* ("Of the Fabric of the Human Body") are depicted in a full, aesthetically pleasing context: towering over an Italian landscape, contemplating a skull, or striking poses that would be physically difficult to maintain (Saunders 95, 87, 99, 101). The classical forms and decaying ruins depicted in the woodcuts claim a certain dignity for the human body and for the practice of anatomy. Yet, as Valerie Traub argues, the sense of order and proportion that they lend is also intended to mitigate the "uncomfortable suspicion that the internal structure and workings of the body do not always express a beautiful, or what's worse, fully knowable design" (52). In an examination of other anatomical woodcuts from the period, Traub has identified significant differences in the representations of Estienne's female and male subjects. In one example of the gendered codes implicit in anatomical illustration, a female reclines in a fully furnished boudoir, hand over head, with her belly skin neatly pealed away to reveal the abdominal region. This sensual pose in a domestic setting, Traub argues, contrasts with the public poses struck by male subjects, who often hold scrolls or point to an explanatory text (81). These illustrations, in short, are not simply scientific reproductions of bodies but are cultural documents as well.

What explains these sixteenth-century conventions of representing the body, and why does medicine today not continue this tradition of representation? In addition to the pragmatic considerations of presenting the three-dimensional body on the two-dimensional page, anatomists are forced to take into account cultural and religious proscriptions. Glenn Harcourt argues that the labored artwork of the sixteenth-century anatomists is part of a larger strategy, perhaps an effort to assuage any anxiety about the enterprise of procuring and dissecting corpses or to obscure the unpleasant realities behind the practice of anatomy (37). Examining these anatomical illustrations provides an occasion for students to practice skills of interpretation and to come to terms with early anatomical texts in which the presentation of the body is conspicuously charged with cultural values. Students soon realize that depictions of the body in today's anatomy textbooks—illustrations or photographs with body parts radically abstracted and tightly framed—are also culturally determined and may well affect the way students understand the body.

Part of the strategy of Vesalius and others in presenting such compliant, well-built human specimens, gazing upward in contemplation, was to overshadow or atone for the morally questionable aspects of anatomy—the ripping up of the human body, the quasi-legal acquisition of corpses, and so forth. Such artistic control in the depiction of tidily individualized bodies requires the containment of a potentially messy setting and implies the subjugation of body to mind (Traub 51–53). The dualism of body and mind (or soul) is deeply ingrained in the Western philosophical tradition by the writings of Plato, which were appropriated into Christian thought through the Neoplatonism of the early church fathers and which typically privilege the mind or soul over the body or flesh. But this hierarchy of mind over body encounters a stiff challenge in the writings of the sixteenth-century Frenchman François Rabelais and more explicitly in the work of Rabelais's twentieth-century commentator Mikhail Bakhtin. Bakhtin's contribution to this course takes us deeper into questions of representation. In *Rabelais and His World*, he articulates two modes of bodily representation, the "classical" and the "grotesque." The classical mode celebrates the head as the seat of reason; it transcends the "merely bodily," sees the body as self-contained and individualized, and has analogues in authoritarian hierarchical society. The grotesque mode levels or even subverts the traditional (classical) mind-body hierarchy. It emphasizes those parts of the body that are open to the outside world—the open mouth, the sexual organs, and so forth—and celebrates dung as the fertilizer of material life. The grotesque body is on the whole unfinished; it outgrows itself and is not clearly separated from the world (Bakhtin 19–29). Students are asked to consider this distinction between the classical and the grotesque as we take up Rabelais, and Rabelais's presentation of the grotesque body becomes a point of reference and contrast for later readings.

Rabelais's *Gargantua and Pantagruel* presents lofty ideas about freedom and equality in the context of coarse, exuberant tales that celebrate the grotesque body. Rabelais's satire is directed at institutions and circumstances that students may not be familiar with, notably the late medieval church, monastic life, and humanist education. Indeed, *Gargantua and Pantagruel* can be heavy going for nonspecialist readers, and it may be prudent either to excerpt or to focus heavily on certain episodes, such as the birth and education of Gargantua and Pantagruel in books 1 and 2 and Panurge's adventures and dialogues in book 3. The account of Gargantua's origins provides a good dose of the Rabelaisian bawdy celebration of defecation, copulation, pregnancy, and birth. After eleven months of pregnancy, Gargantua's mother eats "sixteen quarters, two bushels, and three pecks" of tripe, which leads to a "disturbance" in her lower parts, causing her fundament to fall out (48). The ever resourceful Gargantua then makes his way out of the womb through his mother's ear (52–53). Rabelais is no less lyrical in describing how the infant drinks liquor, in praising the immensity of Gargantua's codpiece (eighty-one inches long), and in detailing Gargantua's precocious invention of the arse-wipe (53–54, 55, 66–69). These episodes epitomize Rabelais's combination of comic exaggeration and serious intent and have prompted students to discuss his purposes in celebrating the grotesque body.

In book 3, Rabelais joyously acknowledges the collective ancestral body. Panurge's discussion of how to build city walls (not with the bones of soldiers but with brick and mortar made of the connected genitalia of Parisian men and women) is offered not with moral condemnation but in praise of human fecundity. His speech honoring lenders and debtors conceives of the body as a model for how society should operate: all the organs lend to and borrow from one another, just as members of society ought to respond to one another's needs; it is divine to lend and heroic to owe. Finally, Panurge argues that since the codpiece protects the precious seed that is vital to the preservation of the species, it is the noblest piece in a warrior's armor and even more crucial than the helmet.

To read Rabelais is to see obscured the boundaries that separate the human, animal, and earthly realms. As Bakhtin argues, "In grotesque realism and in Rabelais's work the image of excrement, for instance, did not have the trivial, narrowly physiological connotation of today. Excrement was conceived as an essential element in the life of the body and of the earth in the struggle against death. It was part of man's vivid awareness of his materiality, of his bodily nature, closely related to the life of the earth." (224). Michael Holquist argues that Bakhtin's passionate engagement with the festive grotesque body in Rabelais reflects Bakhtin's own political situation in Russia in the 1930s. Bakhtin (1895–1975), who endured the Russian censorship of certain types of laughter, irony, and satire in the years after the revolutions of 1917, saw distinct similarities between the social and political revolutions that marked his and Rabelais's eras and saw in Rabelais a model for the subversion of official culture by means of folk culture (xiii–xxiii). Like Rabelais, Bakhtin sees the body as a locus for class conflict; he celebrates the Rabelaisian view of the connection of bodily representation and social order and highlights the implications of the grotesque as opposed to the classical body.

Medical students are at first shocked by Rabelaisian bawdy grotesquerie but then begin to see in Rabelais's celebration of the body the political and humanist ideas of liberation. A touchstone for the rest of the course, Rabelais's grotesque body provides a striking contrast with the classical body depicted in the next text, John Donne's *Devotions*. Writing the *Devotions* while in bed with a severe fever, Donne takes his sickly body not as a locus for class conflict or as a vehicle for celebrating human potential but as a symbol of the ills of the world. In "Meditation 4," Donne writes as an anatomist, or self-vivisectionist, to present his body as a microcosm of the world, likening his veins to rivers, his muscles to hills, and then his thoughts to creatures (*Devotions* 337–38). But while he is absorbed in his body, it is his body in classical isolation, far removed from any Rabelaisian sense of community. The body is significant only insofar as it fits into the cosmic scheme. Donne's meditations take his mind far from the immediate circumstances of his body and his sickbed to larger issues of the perils of solitude and the condition of humanity, as epitomized in one of his best-known writings, "Meditation 17" (*Devotions* 344–45). But where Rabelais's hopeful and recuperative image is of the bodily organs lending to and borrowing from one another, Donne's image is of isolated bodies on disparate continents striving for some form of spiritual communion. This spiraling away from the body contrasts markedly with Rabelais's grotesque celebration, which revels without apology in the stinking beauty of excrement. Where Rabelais formulates communal society as bodily,

Donne intellectualizes the body, bemoans isolation, and longs for community (see Scarry). Such an assessment suffices for this aspect of Donne's oeuvre, though in his poems and sermons Donne demonstrates a wide variety of postures toward the body; as John Carey argues, the body for Donne is both "a love-nest and a laboratory" (145).

As this discussion makes clear, a significant focus of the course is the way in which literary texts use the human body as a vehicle for social, political, and religious agendas. Recent studies of eighteenth-century thought in England have shown that various conditions both material (e.g., the crowdedness of London) and philosophical (e.g., Hobbes's insistently materialistic view of the soul and body versus Descartes's privileging of the mind with *cogito ergo sum*) conspired to create a good deal of turbulence in the ways in which the body was conceived (Flynn 1–7). Responding to these conditions, Jonathan Swift and his contemporaries either coped with, relished, or attempted to escape the reality of the body in various ways. The human body serves as a prism for Swift's social and cultural ideals throughout *Gulliver's Travels*—excerpts of which are assigned. Swift uses optical relativism in books 1 and 2, in which Gulliver visits the lands of dwarfs and giants, not only to unsettle eighteenth-century English attitudes about politics and religion but also to satirize what he saw as uncritical Enlightenment optimism about human nature. During a visit to the land of the giant Brobdingnagians (book 2), Gulliver is disgusted by his close-up view of the pockmarked faces and breasts of the ladies. In book 4, the visit to Houyhnhnm land, Gulliver is revolted by the Yahoos (irrational, human-shaped animals) and finds preferable the company of the horses, the perfectly rational Houyhnhnms. In other words, Swift attempts to restrict contemporary optimism about human nature by juxtaposing Enlightenment ideals with unsavory representations of the human body.

One of the most compact and striking instances of Swift's use of the body to make a sociological point is in his "excremental poetry," in which young men are stunned at the gross bodily realities revealed in the dressing room. In "The Lady's Dressing Room," they discover combs "Filled with dirt so closely fixed, / No brush could force a way betwixt" (21–22) and other unsavory items such as oily facial rags (25) and "ointments good for scabby chops" (36). One inventory leads to the unappetizing conclusion that "Celia, Celia, Celia shits!" (118). While these poems might well be of a piece with Swift's manifest agenda of leveling all forms of human pride, including vanity of dress and appearance, it is hardly a revelation to point out that Swift's vehicle for his corrective view of humankind is woman. And it is not difficult to detect in Swift's efforts to demystify the female body an uneasiness with female sexuality. While Rabelais revels in the farting and smelling, Swift distances himself from such bodily realities by inserting a stunned swain into his poems to feel and express the shock.[3]

Viewing the poetry of the body in historical context reminds us that the lines between disgust, revulsion, pride, vanity, and other attitudes toward the body are patrolled by philosophical and political controversy, as well as by the politics of gender and sexuality. The free-flowing, body-obsessed poetry of Walt Whitman has clear political and sexual overtones germane to the United States just before the Civil War. In "I Sing the Body Electric," Whitman sketches out in brief compass much of the thinking that informs his work as a whole. In one section, as Betsy Erkkila argues, the body serves as a vehicle for his redemptive description of the "dullfaced immigrants" (86) and for his criticism of the decade's prevailing anti-immigration sentiment, embodied in the Know-Nothing Party (*Whitman the Political Poet* 125). Whitman also enobles the "common farmer" by praising his physical beauty and vigor (33). In other sections, he describes the bodies of two slaves—a man and a woman—at auction, expanding his vision of the body to address issues of morality and public policy, including antiprostitution and abolitionism.

In all these examples, Whitman's vision of the body politic is self-consciously American and democratic. But significantly, his enthusiasm is for clean, healthy bodies, not filthy or diseased ones. Even the "lung-sponges, the stomach-sac, the bowels sweet and clean" are sanitized (148). One might expect his formative experience as a nurse in the Civil War to provoke graphic descriptions of wounded soldiers. In "The Wound-Dresser," though, while he mentions the "gnawing and putrid gangrene," his focus is primarily on the valor and heroism represented in the body of the soldier (54). Whitman's celebration of the body, then, is of a different order from Rabelais's—where Rabelais's is bawdy and full of an earthy humor, Whitman's tends toward the erotic and declamatory. Recent commentators have noted that Whitman's poetry reflects Enlightenment acceptance of the social and physical orders yet stands against the Puritan heritage that tended to deny the reality of the body (see Erkkila, *Walt Whitman* 32; Killingsworth 11). As Harold Aspiz has observed, Whitman used the body in a way that was unique among his contemporaries. Hawthorne used the head, heart, and spleen as metaphors in the realm of morality, not simple physiology. Thoreau, while certainly aware of the body and treating it in the course of his prose writings on nature, seems to have found little poetic inspiration in it; Melville's references to the body are heavily shrouded in parable, and Oliver Wendell Holmes's treatment of the body, in "The Living Temple," is "generally prayerful" (67–68). But Whitman takes satisfaction in recuperating and presenting the body as a vehicle for his democratic social and political beliefs.

The course has, by now, moved on to works and authors with which students are familiar. But as they discover, twentieth-century representations of the body are no less complex and conflict ridden than their precursors. Flannery O'Connor's short fiction demands that students reckon with her Catholic interest in the reality of the flesh as well as the spirit. The Catholic doctrine of transubstantiation posits the actual presence of the body and blood of Christ—not the mere representation of it—in the bread and wine of the eucharistic sacrament. We can especially see these religious dimensions of the body in O'Connor's short stories "Temple of the Holy Ghost," "Good Country People," and "Parker's Back." The first story narrates a twelve-year-old girl's grudging acceptance of the flesh and her effort to overcome her pride. The girl mocks the adolescent pretensions of her "positively ugly" older female cousins, who parrot back the lessons of their Catholic upbringing and their parochial school instructions on how to repel the advances of overly aggressive male suitors: "Stop, sir, I am a Temple of the Holy Ghost" (238). The girl is intrigued both by the phrase and by the cousins' account of seeing a hermaphrodite at a carnival freak show. The hermaphrodite, according to the cousins, asserted that God had simply made him that way, but when the young girl remembers the account, she imagines him saying that he was "a temple of the Holy Ghost" (246). Throughout the story we are presented with unsparing images of the flesh—from the protruding stomach of Mr. Cheatham to the round, sweaty chest of Alonzo Myers and the three folds of fat in his neck. The concluding scene, in which the young girl experiences grace when she is hugged by a corpulent nun, reinforces O'Connor's notion that all religious mystery must finally be grounded in matter and flesh (247–48).

We close the semester with a look at the tradition of poetic dialogues between the body and soul that seek, if wistfully, to revise the mind-body hierarchy.[4] We include Andrew Marvell's seventeenth-century "A Dialogue between the Soul and Body" and a selection of dialogues written by three twentieth-century poets. Richard Wilbur's insistent call to return to the material grounding of affections, in "Love Calls Us to the Things of This World" and "A World without Objects Is a Sensible Emptiness," gives poetic expression to dignifying the dirt under one's fingernails. W. H. Auden's "No, Plato, No" and Randall Jarrell's "A Dialogue between Soul and Body" both revisit the old themes of body and soul in efforts to reclaim the material realm for the spiritual.

The readings and considerations outlined here constitute one framework for a body-in-literature course, a framework that asks students to reappraise the mind-body dualism and that introduces several of the body's possible cultural, political, and religious meanings. But such a course might explore many other themes and draw on a variety of available texts. Issues of subjectivity, sexual politics, race, reproductive technologies, and cyborgs as well as the bodily stereotypes of social class could easily be treated. Possible twentieth-century texts would include Franz Kafka's *Metamorphosis* and "In the Penal Colony," Katherine Dunn's 1989 novel *Geek Love*, and even the strange underground cartoons of Robert Crumb. Holly-

wood, too, has provided fascinating explorations into the nature of
the body and human identity, including Ridley Scott's *Blade Run-
ner* and James Cameron's *Terminator* movies as well as numerous
films about gender politics and the body, such as Stephen Frears's
Dangerous Liaisons.

In this course students encounter bodies that are conceived of
in unfamiliar ways—as giants, dwarfs, and freaks—and that are represented from different angles—by first-person or third-person
voices in the mode of satire, comedy, irony, paean, or complaint.
The bodies may be viewed from a distance or magnified and scrutinized closely. In part these bodies make for striking images, fictions,
and poetry, but the preponderance of such freaks on the syllabus invites further investigation. Flannery O'Connor, speaking in 1960,
explained the attraction of the abnormal in cultural and theological
terms: If southern writers tend to write about freaks, it is because
they are "still able to recognize [them]. To be able to recognize a
freak, you have to have some conception of the whole man, and in
the South the general conception of man is still, in the main, theological" ("Some Aspects" 44). Further, she states, "I hate to think
that in twenty years Southern writers too may be writing about men
in gray-flannel suits and may have lost their ability to see that these
gentlemen are even greater freaks than what we are writing about
now" ("Some Aspects" 50). O'Connor, in her usual frank manner,
neatly deconstructs the notion of what constitutes a freak: abnormality may have little to do with physical appearance. Likewise, considerations of the body carry implications far beyond those for joints
and sinews. O'Connor's interest in the abnormal resonates with
medical students since much of their education focuses on the abnormal in order to teach about normal health and the relation between the two. Cutting up the body into little pieces in anatomy
class is, after all, in some sense an act of skewing the body.[5] Reading
through O'Connor's short stories and essays, accordingly, affords a
different purchase on the normal.

Students, with a little prodding, recognize that the unfamiliar
works and distant representations of the body met with in this class
bear on issues that are central to medical practice. The readings give

a broadened frame of reference to all sorts of current speculations about mind and body: Is mental illness an affliction of the mind or of the body? Should we treat mental illness with chemistry or with counseling? And how do issues about the body—and its baggage—come into play in medical practice?

In sum, this course reinforces the sense that our ideas about bodies (and even, perhaps, our bodies themselves) have changed and will change and that these ideas are not determined by any particular science. Indeed, scientific representations (like literary representations) are dependent on circumstances of time and place. In the first and second years of medical school, students are introduced to fundamentally new and highly specialized views of the body. These views have significant pragmatic uses as well as enormous symbolic consequences in our culture. Students can see that the symbolic power of the body is not to be taken lightly; that it resonates in social issues, politics, and religion; and (one hopes) that a complex understanding of the body will equip them well alongside the various tools that make up the practice of medicine.

Course Readings

Week 1 The Body Anatomized
        Anatomical illustrations from Vesalius, Hamusco, Estienne

Week 2 The Body Gloriously Grotesque
        Rabelais, *Gargantua and Pantagruel,* book 1, chapters 3–8,
            12–13; book 2, chapters 1–4, 15–16, 27–28; book 3,
            chapters 3–9
        Bakhtin, *Rabelais and His World,* 18–31, 224–27
        Auden, "The Geography of the House," "New Year Greeting"

Week 3 The Classical Body as a Microcosm
        Donne, "The Ecstacy"; meditations 1, 2, 4–6, 8, 14, 16, 17
            from *Devotions*

Week 4 Swift: The Body Denigrated
        Gulliver's Travels, book 1, chapter 1; book 2, chapters 4–6
        "The Lady's Dressing Room," "Cassinus and Peter," "Strephon
            and Chloe"

Week 5 The Body Sanctified: Flannery O'Connor
        "Temple of the Holy Ghost," "Parker's Back"

Week 6 More O'Connor: The Body Sanctified and the Grotesque
"Good Country People"
"Some Aspects of the Grotesque in Southern Fiction"

Week 7 The Body Celebrated and Scrutinized: Whitman and Dickinson
Whitman, "I Sing the Body Electric"
Dickinson, "The Body grows without—," "With Pinions of
Disdain," "The Spirit lasts—but in what mode—," "One need
not be a Chamber—to be Haunted—"

Week 8 Wrap-up: Five Poetic Treatments of Body and Soul, and
One Long Essay
Wilbur, "Love Calls Us to the Things of This World,"
"A World without Objects Is a Sensible Emptiness"
Jarrell, "A Dialogue between Soul and Body"
Marvell, "A Dialogue between the Soul and Body"
Auden, "No, Plato, No"
Porter, "The History of the Body"

Notes

1. I wish to thank the Department of Social Medicine at the University of North Carolina, Chapel Hill, for its generous support in funding the Senior Fellowship in Literature and Medicine, under the auspices of which this course was first taught.
2. For a helpful survey and extensive bibliography of works reflecting the recent upsurge of interest in cultural studies of the body, see Porter. See also Francis; Lefkowitz.
3. In a 1997 book, William Miller speculates about the role of gender differences in accommodating the loathsome and disgusting and about the double standards in various cultures regarding the production of disgusting matter or behavior.
4. For an excellent overview of the seventeenth-century tradition of the body-soul dialogues, see Osmond.
5. One anatomy student, while carrying an amputated leg over her shoulder from dissection table to sink, unnervingly realized that the only persons who would do such a thing are anatomy students and ax murderers.

Works Cited

Aspiz, Harold. *Walt Whitman and the Body Beautiful*. Urbana: U of Illinois P, 1980.

Auden, W. H. *Collected Poems*. Ed. Edward Mendelson. New York: Vintage, 1991.

———. "The Geography of the House." Auden, *Collected Poems* 698–700.

————. "New Year Greeting." Auden, *Collected Poems* 837–39.

————. "No, Plato, No." Auden, *Collected Poems* 888.

Bakhtin, Mikhail. *Rabelais and His World.* 1965. Trans. Hélène Iswolsky. Bloomington: U of Indiana P, 1984.

Carey, John. *John Donne: Life, Mind, and Art.* New ed. London: Faber, 1990.

Dickinson, Emily. "The Body grows without—." Dickinson, *Complete Poems* 282.

————. *The Complete Poems of Emily Dickinson.* Ed. Thomas H. Johnson. Boston: Little, 1960.

————. "One need not be a Chamber—to be Haunted—." Dickinson, *Complete Poems* 333.

————. "The Spirit lasts—but in what mode—." Dickinson, *Complete Poems* 654.

————. "With Pinions of Disdain." Dickinson, *Complete Poems* 609–10.

Donne, John. *Devotions upon Emergent Occasions.* Donne, *John Donne* 333–50.

————. "The Ecstacy." Donne, *John Donne* 121–23.

————. *John Donne.* Ed. John Carey. Oxford: Oxford UP, 1990.

Erkkila, Betsy. *Walt Whitman among the French.* Princeton: Princeton UP, 1980.

————. *Whitman the Political Poet.* Oxford: Oxford UP, 1989.

Flynn, Carol Houlihan. *The Body in Swift and Defoe.* Cambridge: Cambridge UP, 1990.

Francis, Anne Cranny. *The Body in the Text.* Victoria: Melbourne UP, 1995.

Harcourt, Glenn. "Andreas Vesalius and the Anatomy of Antique Sculpture." *Representations* 17 (1987): 28–61.

Holquist, Michael. Prologue. Bakhtin xiii–xxiii.

Jarrell, Randall. "A Dialogue between Soul and Body." *The Complete Poems.* New York: Farrar, 1969. 427–28.

Killingsworth, H. Jimmie. *Whitman's Poetry of the Body.* Chapel Hill: U of North Carolina P, 1989.

Lefkowitz, Lori Hope, ed. *Textual Bodies: Changing Boundaries of Literary Representation.* Albany: State U of New York P, 1997.

Marvell, Andrew. "A Dialogue between the Soul and Body." *The Complete Poems.* Ed. Elizabeth Story Donno. Harmondsworth: Penguin, 1972. 103–04.

Miller, William Ian. *The Anatomy of Disgust.* Cambridge: Harvard UP, 1997.

O'Connor, Flannery. *The Complete Stories.* New York: Farrar, 1971.

————. "Good Country People." O'Connor, *Complete Stories* 271–91.

————. "Parker's Back." O'Connor, *Complete Stories* 510–30.

————. "Some Aspects of the Grotesque in Southern Fiction." *Mystery and Manners.* Ed. Sally Fitzgerald and Robert Fitzgerald. New York: Farrar, 1961. 36–50.

————. "Temple of the Holy Ghost." O'Connor, *Complete Stories* 236–48.

Osmond, Rosalie. "Body and Soul Dialogues in the Seventeenth Century." *English Literary Renaissance* 4. (1973): 364–403.

Porter, Roy. "The History of the Body." *New Perspectives on Historical Writing*. Ed. Peter Burke. University Park: Pennsylvania State UP, 1992. 206–32.

Rabelais, François. *Gargantua and Pantagruel*. Trans. Burton Raffel. New York: Norton, 1990.

Saunders, J.V. de C. M., and Charles D. O'Malley. *The Illustrations from the Works of Andreas Vesalius of Brussels*. New York: World, 1950.

Sawday, Jonathan. *The Body Emblazoned: Dissection and the Human Body in Renaissance Culture*. London: Routledge, 1995.

Scarry, Elaine. "Donne: 'But Yet the Body Is His Booke.'" *Literature and the Body: Essays on Populations and Persons*. Ed. Scarry. Baltimore: Johns Hopkins UP, 1988. 70–105.

Swift, Jonathan. "Cassinus and Peter." Swift, *Jonathan Swift* 463–66.

————. *Gulliver's Travels*. Ed. Paul Turner. London: Oxford UP, 1971.

————. *Jonathan Swift: The Complete Poems*. Ed. Pat Rogers. Harmondsworth: Penguin, 1983.

————. "The Lady's Dressing Room." Swift, *Jonathan Swift* 448–52.

————. "Strephon and Chloe." Swift, *Jonathan Swift* 455–63.

Traub, Valerie. "Gendering Mortality in Early Modern Anatomy." *Feminist Readings of Early Modern Culture*. Ed. Traub, M. Lindsay Kaplan, and Dympna Callaghan. Cambridge: Cambridge UP, 1996. 44–92.

Whitman, Walt. *The Complete Poems*. Ed. Francis Murray. Harmondsworth: Penguin, 1975.

————. "I Sing the Body Electric." Whitman, *Complete Poems* 127–36.

————. "The Wound-Dresser." Whitman, *Complete Poems* 333–36.

Wilbur, Richard. "Love Calls Us to the Things of This World." Wilbur, *New Collected Poems* 233–34.

————. *New Collected Poems*. New York: Harcourt, 1988.

————. "A World without Objects Is a Sensible Emptiness." Wilbur, *New Collected Poems* 283–84.

Martin Donohoe

Exploring the Human Condition: Literature and Public Health Issues

Despite the amazing technological advances of American medicine, the United States has indicators of community health, morbidity, and mortality similar to or worse than those of countries that spend far less per capita on health care. Many Americans feel that medical education fails to address adequately the socioeconomic, cultural, occupational, environmental, and psychological contributions to individual illness and to community health problems. In response, reformers in medical education are calling for increased emphasis on topics traditionally associated more with the field of public health than with scientific or clinical medicine. Furthermore, the Association of American Medical Colleges, the American Board of Internal Medicine, and other groups have recommended that curricula be population-based and adjusted toward societal needs and that physicians be encouraged to act as agents of social change.

As a physician concerned about these issues, I have designed a course that combines literature (short stories, essays, and novellas) with articles from contemporary medical periodicals to promote discussion about the social, economic, and cultural determinants of illness. Literature, medicine, and public health share a fundamental concern with the human condition. Through literature, a reader can vicariously experience new situations, explore diverse philosophies, and develop empathy with and respect for others whose place in society may be very different from the reader's own. Reading about the experiences of those who suffer the consequences of poverty, racism, stigmatization, and impaired access to health care can help medical students identify more closely than before with their patients, whose complex lives they glimpse only during periodic clinic visits.

The course is an elective, small-group seminar for medical students that meets weekly over ten to twenty weeks. For each two-hour session students read prose selections along with research and review articles. The stories vividly describe such experiences as being homeless, being a victim of domestic violence, or finding oneself a stigmatized patient with a disfiguring or contagious illness. Other topics include alcoholism and substance abuse, aging and long-term care, torture, and mental illness. Occasionally participants read actual case histories. The journal articles augment the literary texts by providing background on the issues raised in the stories and by suggesting areas for discussion, debate, research, intervention, and physician activism. The course exposes students to the instructive and evocative powers of literature; introduces basic principles of social medicine and community health; facilitates discussion among students regarding the social determinants of illness, the health of populations, and the public health responsibilities of physicians; increases empathy, understanding, and appreciation of alternative viewpoints; and encourages students to undertake further study and research in public health and to work publicly toward solutions to sociomedical problems.

Each week the seminar focuses on a different topic. For the session on stigmatization, we read John Updike's "From the Journal of a Leper," in which the afflicted narrator describes the changes in his relationship with his girlfriend, the quality of his art, and the reactions of society during the course of his outwardly successful ultraviolet-light treatment for disfiguring psoriasis. Students examine why Updike's psoriasis victim seeks empathy and wants society to see beyond his disfigured exterior yet, as he recovers, becomes hyper-critical of his girlfriend's imperfections. They comment on how Updike's victim invests the ultraviolet-light therapy chamber with mysterious, nearly supernatural powers and how this mirrors society's desire for high-tech interventions, which may not always be as beneficial or cost-effective as less glamorous, preventive measures.

Updike's fictional account is complemented by Iona H. Ginsburg and Bruce Link's study examining the psychological consequences of rejection and stigma in psoriasis patients. This study serves as a springboard for the examination of stigmatization of AIDS patients. Students read an article documenting physicians' attitudes toward caring for patients with AIDS (Gerbert et al.). They are troubled by the results of a survey of health professionals asking if they would eat cookies prepared by an AIDS patient or a leukemia patient—and if not, why not (Wormser and Joline)—and by Mark Ragg's report on the Australian government's controversial plan to compensate only those AIDS patients who acquire the disease through blood transfusion.

Some students candidly share their fears of being stuck with a needle in the process of caring for patients with AIDS and hepatitis, though they also acknowledge that occupational infectious disease risks among physicians were much higher in the past (e.g., bubonic plague, secondary syphilis before the discovery of penicillin) than they are now. Students realize that if physicians cannot overcome irrational fears about HIV transmission, then medical professionals will not be able to persuade the public at large to overcome its superstitions.

We also discuss the degree of patient responsibility physicians associate with different afflictions, from alcoholism and obesity (where genetic disorders or character flaws can be judged as intemperance or gluttony) to childhood leukemia (which afflicts "blameless innocents"), and we consider how holding patients responsible for their diseases can compromise one's compassion for their suffering. I ask students to construct a scale of blame for various diseases: they debate where to place not only alcoholism and obesity but also lung cancer and multifactorial conditions such as coronary artery disease and adult-onset diabetes mellitus.

In the session on homelessness, Doris Lessing's "An Old Woman and Her Cat" provides a moving fictional entrée into the world of society's dispossessed. This short story details the daily struggles of two unwanted creatures, an aged gypsy and her adopted alley cat, trying to cope with life on the streets of London. When the woman becomes ill with pneumonia, she takes refuge in a dilapidated, condemned house. She feeds on pigeons caught by her cat, which she roasts on rotting floorboards, until she succumbs to a lonely death. Students discuss the reasons behind the woman's stubbornness and unwillingness to accept solutions proferred by social service agencies —as when, for instance, she refuses housing in a building where pets are not allowed. The disordered thinking associated with mild dementia does not seem to account entirely for her seemingly irrational and self-destructive behavior.

While some students initially express incredulity that the woman would rather starve to death in a hovel than accept charity, most come to appreciate her pride in not accepting handouts, her desire for independence, and her loyalty to the pet who is her only solace in a world where human beings ignore or even scorn her. An epidemiological study of the lifetime prevalence of homelessness alerts students to the dimensions of the problem (Link et al.), and a clinical review describes the health problems commonly experienced by homeless individuals (Usatine et al.). Through discussing the story and the articles, students gain an understanding of the survival skills necessitated by a life on the streets and come to appreciate why the homeless have low rates of preventive care and medication compliance and are more likely than others to visit emergency rooms for their primary care.

In the session on family issues, we read Grace Paley's "An Interest in Life," a single mother's somewhat tongue-in-cheek story of searching for companionship, trying to raise her children, and navigating through the vagaries of the welfare system after her husband leaves her. Students identify with the difficulties the mother faces and confront some of society's (and their own) stereotypes about "welfare mothers." Many struggle with whether or not to sympathize with the woman, who, despite being taken advantage of by her ex-husband and a friend, continues to turn to them for emotional support and sexual solace. Articles cover the economics of welfare, profile the American family, and discuss child care and parental leave (see, e.g., Zylke).

For the session on race and health care, we read "The Sky Is Gray," Ernest J. Gaines's story of a poor, single, African American farm mother trying to obtain dental care for her ill child. Students share in their struggle to overcome both overt and subtle racism. An essay by Todd L. Savitt on pre–Civil War medical care for slaves provides background on the origins of the two-tiered medical system portrayed in the story, and an overview of current black-white disparities in health care by the American Medical Association's Council on Ethical and Judicial Affairs illustrates that much progress still needs to be made in improving health care for minorities. We also discuss the de facto segregation of health care that continues to exist because of socioeconomic differences in access to care and diminishing funding for inner-city public hospitals, despite the fact that suburban facilities have an excess of MRI scanners and other high-tech equipment. Students wonder about their own roles in both perpetuating and responding to the two-tiered system of medical care in the United States.

After a brief introduction to different systems of health-care delivery, from single-payer to fee-for-service to capitation and managed care, I encourage students to voice their concerns about the future of medicine. They almost never worry about their future incomes, but, rather, they speak passionately about the primacy of the doctor-patient relationship. Many worry that increasing demands to see more patients in less time will prevent them from getting to know their patients intimately and from addressing socioeconomic and psychological contributors to illness. They worry that the corporatization of medicine will erode the bond of trust between physician and patient that is so critical to healing.

Another meeting covers domestic violence, including child and spousal abuse and the physician's response to victims. In William Carlos Williams's "The Insane," a young pediatrician shares with his physician-father his concern that emotional neglect and exposure to violence will have long-term effects on a child's mental health. In Michael LaCombe's "Playing God," a rural doctor covers up a woman's shooting of her alcoholic, physically abusive husband. Students interpret these short stories from the points of view of the abusers, the victims, and the physicians. While it is hard to garner sympathy for the abusers, students recognize that histories of child abuse, alcoholism, and financial stress and the acceptance in many cultures of male dominance within marriage provide fertile ground for the development of an abusive personality. And, while students grieve for the woman in LaCombe's story, they show frustration at her unwillingness or inability to follow the physician's repeated advice to extricate herself from the abusive relationship. Our accompanying discussion focuses on a review of mandatory reporting laws (Hyman, Schillinger, and Lo). Should physicians be required to report suspected cases of violence against women, the hope being, as it was in requiring reporting of child abuse, that formal recognition of the offense in time diminishes its occurrence? Or does mandated reporting, particularly when unaccompanied by measures to protect women from retributive violence and to assist them in exploring housing and economic opportunities, place them in acute danger and augment their sense of powerlessness? Interestingly, female students have been more likely than male students to conclude that La-Combe's physician did the right thing in covering up the shooting; male students have often been troubled by the doctor's extrajudicial handling of what many of them consider to be murder.

Articles describing the relevance of domestic violence for health care professionals and the deleterious effects that witnessing violence has on child development facilitate discussion of possible solutions to the growing epidemic of violence in our country (Council on Scientific Affairs; Groves et al.). Proposed solutions include strengthening gun control legislation, reducing the amount of violence in the media, legislating stricter sentencing and attempting rehabilitation of violent offenders, and emphasizing violence prevention through educational programs and peaceful mediation of disputes.

Another course meeting covers poverty and access to care.

Readings include "How the Poor Die," George Orwell's timeless essay describing the abysmal conditions in certain public hospitals; selections from Anton Chekhov's writings on his journey to Sakhalin, where he witnessed the detrimental health effects of extreme poverty ("Letter to A. F. Koni"; "Letter to A. S. Suvorin"); and "Phlebitis: At the Public Hospital," a chapter from the homeless author Lars Eighner's best-seller *Travels with Lizbeth*, in which Eighner provides a scathing, sarcastic account of being treated with derision and suspicion during his hospitalization for a swollen leg. The articles that complement these writings examine socioeconomic inequalities in health (Adler et al.), the costs of caring for the poor (Epstein, Stern, and Weissman) and the health consequences of economic recessions (Jones). Students become attuned to the barriers to care faced by the poor and learn a little about how medical care for the indigent is financed.

Students are frustrated when they realize that while medical technology has developed remarkably, medicine's approach to the detrimental health effects of poverty has in some ways changed little over time. Many of the topics we cover could lead to a sense of nihilism or inculcate pessimism among the students. However, most students appreciate being made aware of these issues and express a desire to explore them further through the vicarious approach of reading stories, through sharing their thoughts and experiences with fellow students in a supportive environment, and through community involvement. Throughout the course, we discuss our roles and responsibilities as physicians. These include improving our profession's attention to the socioeconomic determinants of disease, conducting research on underserved populations and disseminating our findings to colleagues and policy makers, volunteering in our communities, improving our understanding of the different cultures we serve (perhaps by learning a new language), and participating in organizations that fight violence and international human rights abuses.

It is not clear to what extent students' enthusiasm might wane over time. Offering similar courses to premedical and medical students and to physicians at other stages of training may help counteract the loss of compassion and the jadedness that can afflict them. I have developed an expanded version of this course for fourth-year medical students, and I am incorporating poems and brief stories into ward rounds and offering reading seminars for internal medicine residents. I will be interested to learn how these students respond to this teaching method.

The course I have described differs from and goes beyond other literature and medicine courses in several ways. Though the centrality of a close doctor-patient relationship to good medical care (often the focus of other courses) is acknowledged, equal emphasis is placed on sociocultural determinants of illness. Our patients' lives are stories; hence the usefulness of approaching a sympathetic understanding of their sufferings and dilemmas through fiction. However, the signs and symptoms of our patients' illnesses lose meaning when removed from their social contexts; hence the value of exploring patients' sociocultural milieus. The course's melding of fiction and journal studies parallels medicine's nature as both art and science. The stories are vehicles for vicarious experience that prepare students for the informative background material and foster their receptiveness to the suggestions for positive change advanced in the articles. Students are encouraged to develop the reading habits required for continuous, lifelong learning.

In conclusion, facilitating students' understanding of public health topics through stories coupled with journal articles is feasible, enjoyable, meets the professed goals of modern medical education, and should be undertaken more frequently than at present as a method of instruction. Including such a course in the curriculum requires verbal and financial support from deans and department heads, knowledgeable and enthusiastic faculty members, and adequate curricular time (ideally in both the preclinical and clinical years, as students' perspectives develop through increasing exposure to patients). I am convinced that such a course can contribute to the development of empathic, broad-minded clinicians and policy makers who are sensitive to the social, economic, and cultural determinants of illness. By learning to focus not just on problems affecting individuals but also on the broader determinants of health that can be changed only through widespread social action, students can grow into strong advocates for the public's health.

Course Readings

Week 1   Stigmatization
        Updike, "From the Journal of a Leper"
        Ginsburg and Link, "Psychosocial Consequences of Rejection and Stigma Feelings in Psoriasis Patients"
        Gerbert et al., "Physicians and AIDS: Sexual Risk Assessment of Patients and Willingness to Treat HIV-Infected Patients"
        Wormser and Joline, "Would You Eat Cookies Prepared by an AIDS Patient?"
        Ragg, "Australia: Compensation for Medically Acquired AIDS"

Week 2   Homelessness
        Lessing, "An Old Woman and Her Cat"
        Link et al., "Lifetime and Five-Year Prevalence of Homelessness in the United States"
        Usatine, et al., "Health Care for the Homeless: A Family Medicine Perspective"

Week 3   Family Issues
        Paley, "An Interest in Life"
        Sancton, "How to Get America off the Dole"
        Zylke, "Care for Working Parents' Children Grows as a Challenge for Nation"
        Grisso, et al., "Parental Leave Policies for Faculty in U.S. Medical Schools"

Week 4   Race and Health Care
        Gaines, "The Sky Is Gray"
        Savitt, "Black Health on the Plantation: Masters, Slaves, and Physicians"
        Council on Ethical and Judicial Affairs, American Medical Association, "Black-White Disparities in Health Care"

Week 5   Family Violence
        Williams, "The Insane"
        LaCombe, "Playing God"
        Hyman, Schillinger, and Lo, "Laws Mandating Reporting of Domestic Violence"
        Council on Scientific Affairs, American Medical Association. "Violence against Women: Relevance for Medical Practitioners"
        Groves et al., "Silent Victims: Children Who Witness Violence"

Week 6   Poverty and Access to Care
        Orwell, "How the Poor Die"
        Chekhov, "Letter to A. F. Koni," "Letter to A. S. Suvorin"
        Eighner, "Phlebitis: At the Public Hospital"

Adler et al., "Socioeconomic Inequalities in Health: No Easy Solution"

Epstein, Stern, and Weissman, "Do the Poor Cost More? A Multi-hospital Study of Patients' Socioeconomic Status and Use of Hospital Resources"

Jones, "The Health Consequences of Economic Recessions"

Week 7 Alcoholism and Substance Abuse
Taylor, "The Captain's Son"
Hughes, "Junior Addict"
Moore et al., "Prevalence, Detection, and Treatment of Alcoholism in Hospitalized Patients"
McNagny and Parker, "High Prevalence of Recent Cocaine Use and the Unreliability of Patient Self-Report in an Inner-City Walk-in Clinic"

Week 8 Occupational Health
Williams, "The Paid Nurse"
Powell, "Minamata Disease: A Story of Mercury's Malevolence"
Hendee, "Disposal of Low-Level Radioactive Waste"

Week 9 Aging and Long-Term Care
Canin, "We Are Nighttime Travelers"
Blumenthal, "Who Will Live in Our Houses When We Die?"
Lee, "Cider with Rosie"
Kemper and Murtaugh, "Lifetime Use of Nursing Home Care"

Week 10 War and Human Suffering
Trumbo, *Johnny Got His Gun*
Owen, selections from *War Poems and Others*

Note

I gratefully acknowledge the editorial guidance of Anne Hunsaker Hawkins and the support of the Robert Wood Johnson Clinical Scholars Program, the Palo Alto Veterans Administration Medical Center, and Oregon Health Sciences University, and I thank David B. Wheeler and Susan Schrag for their excellent technical assistance in the preparation of this manuscript.

Works Cited

Adler, Nancy E., et al. "Socioeconomic Inequalities in Health: No Easy Solution." *Journal of the American Medical Association* 269 (1993): 3140–45.

American Board of Internal Medicine. Subcommittee on Evaluation of Humanistic Qualities in the Internist. "Evaluation of Humanistic Qualities in the Internist." *Annals of Internal Medicine* 99 (1983): 720–24.

Association of American Medical Colleges. *Integrating Human Values*

Teaching Programs into Medical Students' Clinical Education. Washington: Assn. of Amer. Medical Colls. 1986.

Blumenthal, Michael. "Who Will Live in Our Houses When We Die?" *Days We Would Rather Know: Poems.* New York: Viking, 1984. 116.

Canin, Ethan. "We Are Nighttime Travelers." *The Emperor of the Air.* Boston: Houghton, 1988. 79–96.

Chekhov, Anton. "Letter to A. F. Koni." 26 Jan. 1891. Cousins 293–95.

———. "Letter to A. S. Suvorin." 9 Mar. 1890. Cousins 279–81.

Council on Ethical and Judicial Affairs. American Medical Association. "Black-White Disparities in Health Care." *Journal of the American Medical Association* 263 (1990): 2344-46.

Council on Scientific Affairs. American Medical Association. "Violence against Women: Relevance for Medical Practitioners." *Journal of the American Medical Association* 267 (1992): 3184–89.

Cousins, Norman, ed. *The Physician in Literature.* Philadelphia: Saunders, 1982.

Eighner, Lars. "Phlebitis: At the Public Hospital." *Travels with Lizbeth.* New York: St. Martin's, 1993. 141–59.

Epstein, Arnold M., Robert S. Stern, and Joel S. Weissman. "Do the Poor Cost More? A Multi-hospital Study of Patients' Socioeconomic Status and Use of Hospital Resources." *New England Journal of Medicine* 322 (1990): 1122–28.

Gaines, Ernest J. "The Sky Is Gray." Secundy 38–64.

Gerbert, Barbara, et al. "Physicians and AIDS: Sexual Risk Assessment of Patients and Willingness to Treat HIV-Infected Patients." *Journal of General Internal Medicine* 7 (1992): 657–64.

Ginsburg Iona H., and Bruce G. Link. "Psychosocial Consequences of Rejection and Stigma Feelings in Psoriasis Patients." *International Journal of Dermatology* 32 (1993): 587–91.

Grisso, Jeane Ann, et al. "Parental Leave Policies for Faculty in U.S. Medical Schools." *Annals of Internal Medicine* 114 (1991): 43–45.

Groves, Betsy McAlister, et al. "Silent Victims: Children Who Witness Violence." *Journal of the American Medical Association* 269 (1993): 262–64.

Hendee, W. R. "Disposal of Low-Level Radioactive Waste: Problems and Implications for Physicians." *Journal of the American Medical Association* 269 (1993): 2403–06.

Hughes, Langston. "Junior Addict." Secundy 185–86.

Hyman, Axiella, Dean Schillinger, and Bernard Lo. "Laws Mandating Reporting of Domestic Violence." *Journal of the American Medical Association* 273 (1995): 1781–87.

Jones, L. "The Health Consequences of Economic Recessions." *Journal of Health and Social Policy* 3.2 (1991): 1–14.

Kemper, P., and C. M. Murtaugh. "Lifetime Use of Nursing Home Care." *New England Journal of Medicine* 324 (1991): 1352–58.

LaCombe, Michael. "Playing God." *On Being a Doctor.* Ed. Lacombe. Philadelphia: Amer. Coll. of Physicians, 1994. 83–87.

Lee, Laurie. "Cider with Rosie." Excerpt. *The Oxford Book of Death.* Ed. D. J. Enright. Oxford: Oxford UP, 1983. 249–50.

Lessing, Doris. "An Old Woman and Her Cat." *The Doris Lessing Reader.* New York: Knopf, 1988. 98–105.

Link, Bruce G., et al. "Lifetime and Five-Year Prevalence of Homelessness in the United States." *American Journal of Public Health* 84 (1994): 1907–12.

McNagny, Sally E., and R. M. Parker. "High Prevalence of Recent Cocaine Use and the Unreliability of Patient Self-Report in an Inner-City Walk-in Clinic." *Journal of the American Medical Association* 267 (1992): 1106–08.

Moore, R. D., et al. "Prevalence, Detection, and Treatment of Alcoholism in Hospitalized Patients." *Journal of the American Medical Association* 261 (1989): 403–07.

Orwell, George. "How the Poor Die." *The Collected Essays, Journalism, and Letters of George Orwell, 1945–1950.* Ed. S. Orwell and I. Angus. New York: Harcourt, 1950. 223–33.

Owen, Wilfred. *War Poems and Others.* Ed. Dominic Hibberd. Sydney: Random, 1989.

Paley, Grace. "An Interest in Life." *We Are the Stories We Tell: The Best Short Stories by North American Women since 1945.* Ed. Wendy Martin. New York: Pantheon, 1990. 61–76.

Powell, P. P. "Minamata Disease: A Story of Mercury's Malevolence." *Southern Medical Journal* 84 (1991): 1352–58.

Ragg, Mark. "Australia: Compensation for Medically Acquired AIDS." *Lancet* 339 (1992): 419.

Sancton, Thomas. "How to Get America off the Dole." *Time* 25 May 1992: 44–47.

Savitt, Todd L. "Black Health on the Plantation: Masters, Slaves, and Physicians." *Sickness and Health in America: Readings in the History of Medicine and Public Health.* Ed. Judith Walzer Leavitt and Ronald L. Numbers. Madison: U of Wisconsin P, 1985. 313–30.

Secundy, Marian Gray, ed. *Trials, Tribulations, and Celebrations: African-American Perspectives on Health, Illness, Aging, and Loss.* Yarmouth: Intercultural, 1992.

Taylor, Peter. "The Captain's Son." *The Invisible Enemy: Alcoholism and the Modern Short Story.* Ed. Miriam Dow and Jennifer Regan. Saint Paul: Graywolf, 1989. 24–51.

Trumbo, Dalton. *Johnny Got His Gun.* New York: Bantam, 1939.

Updike, John. "From the Journal of a Leper." *American Journal of Dermatopathology* 4 (1982): 137–42.

Usatine, R. P., et al. "Health Care for the Homeless: A Family Medicine Perspective." *American Family Physician* 49 (1994): 139–46.

Williams, William Carlos. *The Doctor Stories.* Comp. Robert Coles. New York: New Directions, 1984.

———. "The Insane." Williams, *Doctor Stories* 104–07.

————. "The Paid Nurse." Williams, *Doctor Stories* 92–98.

Wormser, G. P., and C. Joline. "Would You Eat Cookies Prepared by an AIDS Patient?" *Postgraduate Medicine* 86 (1989): 174+.

Zylke, Jody W. "Care for Working Parents' Children Grows as a Challenge for Nation." *Journal of the American Medical Association* 266 (1991): 3255–57.

Iliana Alexandra Semmler

Ethics, Language, and Narrative

My class in literature and medicine serves as an undergraduate elective in the English department; it also draws a significant number of premed students (who are often asked to include several English courses in their curriculum) and a sprinkling of majors from other departments. This course is useful both for English majors interested in cultural studies and for premed students who want to enlarge and sharpen their understanding of the culture of medicine before embarking on their medical studies. At the outset, we look carefully at three short texts that play a large part in structuring the course: the Hippocratic oath, Dannie Abse's poem "Song for Pythagoras," and some material from Kathryn Montgomery Hunter's *Doctors' Stories: The Narrative Structure of Medical Knowledge*. These texts provide a framework for considering ethics, language, and narrative in the course readings.

The Hippocratic oath is the first text considered because of its force throughout the ages as a statement of ethical practice and commitment. We raise the question of what it means to "look upon him who shall have taught me this Art even as one of my parents," exploring a physician's responsibilities within the medical community to respect the history and practitioners of medicine and to pass on knowledge to those entering the field. We look at the ethical principles involved in beneficence and nonmaleficence (particularly as these concepts impinge on the refusal to give "deadly drug[s]" or help a woman to "procure abortion") in both historical and contemporary contexts. We explore the pledge to refrain "from all wrongdoing or corruption." What did it mean to the Greeks? Does it mean something different to us in the twentieth century? Is it this part of the oath that is invoked in the contemporary standard of maintaining boundaries between physician and patient? Is the principle of patient confidentiality a logical outgrowth of what appears in the oath as an injunction not to gossip about one's patients— "Whatsoever things I see or hear concerning the life of men [. . .] which ought not to be noised abroad, I will keep silence thereon [. . .] ("Medicine" 199)? Which issues not in the oath do we, today, believe to belong in the realm of medical ethics?

A consideration of "Song for Pythagoras" moves the discussion into the personal world of the physician:

White coat and purple coat
A sleeve from both he sews.
That white is always stained with blood,
that purple by the rose.

And phantom rose and blood most real
compose a hybrid style;
white coat and purple coat
few men can reconcile.

White coat and purple coat
can each be worn in turn
but in the white a man will freeze
and in the purple burn.

What distinction does Abse mean to show between white and purple? Students first observe that a white coat suggests a scientist or a doctor and recognize the importance to scientific medicine of an objective, rather than a subjective (and emotional), stance. But what does purple stand for, and which of its several connotations is applicable to the idea Abse puts forward in the poem? Discussion leads the students to pass over the connections to royalty and foreground the priestly and the passional aspects the color suggests. Although students recognize that the logical and the emotional are two poles that most of us try to "reconcile," they also come to see that priestly and passional qualities have special relevance to the life and work of a physician: healers serve a priestly, sometimes even shamanic, function in most cultures, including (perhaps subliminally) ours, and physicians often find themselves in situations involving intense emotion.

Other oppositions in the poem include "blood" (the reality of physical suffering) and "rose" (with its connotations of love and romance) and "freezing" and "burning." Further questions present themselves: What does Abse do with these images? What seems to be his message? It can be a struggle to engage students in focusing on the final pair of contrasts: if the coats are worn "in turn," the wearer will alternately freeze and burn; but wearing them together, in the "hybrid style," is something that few are capable of. The last question I raise is, What has Pythagoras to do with all of this? The answer would seem to lie in mathematics, which few connect with poetry. The Pythagorean theorem, $a^2 + b^2 = c^2$, suggests in this context that when a higher (squared) order of the white coat a is added to a higher order of the purple coat b, the result will be a higher order of that desirable quality c, the hybrid style.

In the third foundation text, *Doctors' Stories*, Hunter identifies three separate but interrelated narratives that come into play when a person consults a physician: the patient's story (his or her view of the onset of the condition that prompts seeking medical help and its potential relation to other life events); the physician's story, which sifts the medically relevant details from the patient's story and which, often with the help of tests and instruments, results in a diagnosis; and the retelling of the original story, altered and interpreted in the light of medical knowledge, to the patient in terms that he or she can readily understand. "The patient's account of illness and the

medical version of that account are fundamentally, irreducibly different narratives," Hunter explains (123), but it is in the "physician's
return of the story to the patient [that] the incommensurability of
the [first] two stories is most evident," and it is here that "any number of small—but to the patient earth-shattering—miscommunica-
tions" may enter (141). Unless carefully told, Hunter warns, "the
transformed and medicalized narrative may be alien to the patient:
strange, depersonalized, unlived and unlivable, incomprehensible or
terrifyingly clear" (13).

These ideas demonstrate the principles involved in narrative
bioethics, which maintains that ethics derives from stories, not from
fixed principles. Narrative ethics takes cognizance of the stories of all
the participants in a decision-making process. Although Hunter's
work is intended to describe real-life physician-patient encounters,
her paradigm serves equally well in analyzing and deconstructing
both fictional and nonfictional works in the field of literature and
medicine. It is important to remember here that language not only
communicates ideas but also expresses power. Examining the language in which a story is told and understanding whose story is the
controlling one are ways of illuminating both the work of literature
and the bioethical issues involved therein.

Students sometimes need help in grasping the meaning of *story*
as it is used in this course. They do not always realize that the same
events may have very different meanings in narratives constructed by
different people and that an undeterminable number of stories may
be formed around the same set of occurrences. Students are also
often not aware of the influence of language on the development of
individual narratives (the tone and tropes of dialogue, the degree of
intelligibility, and the kind of power positioning a formed story may
convey). To heighten understanding of these issues, I ask students
to write a short story about a medical encounter that they have had.
The story must contain dialogue that they feel accurately reflects the
nature of the encounter and must have a traditional beginning, middle, and end. Along with their stories, students submit papers that
show how well the verbal interchange facilitates communication of
information and determines the relative comfort and power posi-

tions of the participants. Students thus demonstrate through their own work the kinds of issues described by Hunter.

We discuss the core texts carefully and at some length because students need to understand their implications for the other readings in the course. As we approach the later readings, I point out that literature seldom fits into neat analytic frames and that students can expect the lessons of the three foundation texts to illuminate to various degrees and in changing configurations the literary works we consider. I begin this phase of the course with a group of readings by physician-authors, to examine possible interrelations between the work of doctoring and the work of writing. Next we consider how language operates in medical discourse. Then follows a selection of "plague" literature, including works about HIV and AIDS. The course finishes with some fictional pathographies (usually the most complex works), novels that focus on the progress of an illness and the resolution of that illness in death, recovery, or some state of equilibrium.[1]

A number of works, some by physician-authors, raise important ethical issues.[2] William Carlos Williams's story "Old Doc Rivers" treats the issue of the physician impaired by alcohol and drugs. It is particularly effective when read in connection with the Hippocratic oath because of the relationship between the young doctor who narrates the story and Doc Rivers, whose addiction poses a threat to the community.

In introducing discussion, I first ask, Why is the narrator telling this story? This question draws attention to the young doctor, whom most students, dismayed at Rivers's behavior, barely notice. They all agree that Doc Rivers should not be practicing medicine but have difficulty explaining the narrator's interest in him. That the narrator might be showing respect for an older doctor, one who acts as parent or teacher to him, is difficult to tease out.

The narrator, tacitly fulfilling his pledge to "look upon him who shall have taught me this Art even as one of my parents," examines Rivers's career in as impartial, even favorable, a light as is possible. We follow the young doctor as he examines hospital records and recalls ancedotes that show Rivers to have been exceptionally talented in both diagnosis and treatment. "[H]e had a record of thirty years behind him, finally, for getting there (provided you could find him) anywhere, anytime, for anybody [. . .] and for doing something, mostly the right thing [. . . ,] once he was there" (15). The narrator gives himself the difficult task of mediating between the respect demanded by the oath and its provision that the physician's first duty is to do no harm, a vow whose abrogation a doctor on drugs risks at every turn.

Once students have acknowledged the conflicting claims of the oath, I ask them to reflect on the reasons for Rivers's aberrant behavior and to respond to the narrator's mention of a sensitivity "that made [Rivers . . .] the victim of the very things he best served" (25). As a final point, I ask them to see Doc Rivers in terms of the Abse poem: we close on a consideration of the imbalance between the white and purple coats in this story, and the consequences of failing to achieve a "hybrid style."[3]

David Feldshuh's *Miss Evers' Boys,* a play about the Tuskegee syphilis study, raises a number of ethical issues, especially concerning the abuses that accompanied the government sponsorship of this "scientific" medical study carried out on poor black men in the rural South. Students often have not heard of the Tuskegee study, so I give them background information on the study itself and on its exposure in the press in 1972.[4] Students' first reaction is shock and disbelief that the United States government could have carried out an experiment with so little regard for subjects' well-being and rights. Feldshuh's play individualizes some of the participants, giving us Dr. Douglas, a white physician working under government auspices; Dr. Brodus, an African American doctor who is the administrative head of Memorial Hospital in Tuskegee; and Eunice Evers, an African American nurse who has close and caring relationships with four participants in the study, who represent a range of ages, beliefs, and sophistication.

Instead of focusing on the unethical nature of the study, which no student in my class has ever questioned, I ask the students to look again at Hunter and to identify the different stories at work in the drama. Dr. Douglas (the only fully unsympathetic character in the play) is seen as overcommitted to his research project: even after penicillin is available, he refuses to allow the men in his subject group to be treated because the study will be invalidated if not "taken to end point" (i.e., autopsy, 88). He wants to prove that the effects of untreated syphilis in African American males are different from those in white males. Dr. Brodus sees Dr. Douglas as trying to be both physician and scientist, "an uneasy combination," but at the same time Dr. Brodus is willing to stick with the study both for the renown it will bring Tuskegee and because he believes it will show there is no racial difference in the effects of syphilis (42). Nurse Evers is devoted to her "boys" and believes that they will be in a better position to benefit from advances in treatment if they remain in the study. Each of the four syphilitic men has a different story: Ben, older than the rest, is the most ready to submit to the study's rules; Hodman believes in magic cures and eventually drinks a poisonous concoction; Caleb is skeptical and leaves the study to get penicillin once it becomes available; and Willie, the youngest, who has great talent and zest for dancing, remains with the study and suffers the crippling effects of syphilis.

An important element in this play is the ethical dimension of language used in a medical context. When Dr. Douglas attempts to explain the course of syphilis to the men in technical medical terms, Miss Evers steps in and translates his explanation into terms they understand: "By frolickin' with the wrong women you can get a sore down below on your private parts and through that sore a bug can crawl inside you [. . . and] can go to sleep for twenty or thirty years. But when it wakes up, you can't walk, you can't breathe, you can't think. That's bad blood" (31). Generally, the students feel this translation performs a valuable service for the men. Then I ask them to look at a later scene, in which Dr. Douglas decides that the men should be submitted to painful spinal taps to provide evidence for his study. Describing the procedure to the men, he calls the spinal taps "backshots" (44). I ask about the difference between these two renderings of medical terms into colloquial language. Discussion leads to the conclusion that the first example serves the goal of clarification, the latter that of obfuscation, and that Dr. Douglas takes advantage of a difference in background and culture to gain his own ends.[5]

We next move to plague literature, which has a long history. I refer to the biblical plagues and particularly to *Oedipus Tyrannos*, which most students have read, to uncover the common view of plagues as a kind of deserved punishment—an attitude that often accompanies their occurrence. Uncovering this view leads to a consideration of the next assigned work, Albert Camus's *The Plague*, which mediates between the superstitious and the scientific, examining the psychology of government and of individuals facing an illness whose cause and method of spread are initially unknown and whose result is almost inevitably death.

Tony Kushner's two-part play *Angels in America* can be viewed in terms of the many different stories surrounding AIDS in the gay community and, by extension, in society at large.[6] When, in *Millennium Approaches* Prior Walter tells his lover, Louis Ironson, that he has AIDS, both men know that Prior will require a great deal of long-term care. In Prior's narrative, that care will come from Louis, but Louis's story does not accommodate that role.[7] Students need to recognize that Louis is tormented by his narrative; indeed, his eventual ability to change that narrative—to return to Prior—is one of the important character developments in the play. In another scene, the stories of Roy Cohn (a character from recent history) and his physician are very much at odds. Cohn rejects his physician's story, both the diagnosis of AIDS and the accompanying inference about his sexual orientation. Cohn takes control of the story by threatening his doctor: "Say: 'Roy Cohn, you are a homosexual.' And I will proceed, systematically, to destroy your reputation and your practice and your career in New York State." Characterizing himself as "a heterosexual man [. . .] who fucks around with guys," Cohn supplies his own diagnosis: "AIDS is what homosexuals have. I have liver cancer" *(Millennium Approaches* 44, 46*)*. I ask the students who controls the story at this point. They are surprised and amused by the reversal of the expected power structure in the physician-patient interchange and quickly see that the physician's power is eroded when his patient muzzles his use of language.[8]

Pathographies written by accomplished authors, such as Paul Monette's *Borrowed Time* and William Styron's *Darkness Visible,* are powerful pieces of literature that, by presenting the story of the patient as the patient understands it, have the important function of "return[ing] the voice of the patient to the world of medicine" (Hawkins 12). Fictional pathography has the same power. One of the best fictional pathographies is John Updike's *Rabbit at Rest,* in which Harry "Rabbit" Angstrom, disabled by his lack of will power, fails to follow the dietary advice of his physician and family and suffers two heart attacks—the second fatal. I ask students to chart the progress of his symptoms and to examine the way he connects his present plight to his own past and to current events (the crash of Pan Am flight 103 over Lockerbie, Scotland, is a particularly important image in the novel). They come to understand that part of a patient's story relies on context and that it is primarily the context that individualizes the story.

Rabbit at Rest is a gold mine for the study of language and trope: Harry experiences his angina as "a bad child inside his chest [who] keeps playing with matches" and feels "his body sag[ging] around his heart like a tent around a pole" (80, 94). It can be helpful at this point if students share metaphors that they themselves use in describing illnesses such as a bad cold or a headache. The language of the various physicians Rabbit encounters is illuminating, as it ranges from technical jargon—"We'd bypass both the RCA and the CFX, and the LAD depending on the restenosis," one doctor tells him—to a graphic description of the difference between angioplasty and coronary bypass surgery: "It's the difference between scrubbing out your toilet bowl with a long brush and actually replacing the pipes" (235, 236). I ask students to reflect on this juxtaposition of arcane terms, incomprehensible to the patient, with down-to-earth but less than attractive descriptions of the functioning of the human body. Clearly, neither is a constructive means of communicating information from physician to patient. Moreover, students realize, poor communication compromises truly informed consent for medical procedures.

The assignments connected with the course reflect the same

emphasis on ethics, language, and narrative foregrounded above. In addition to the early paper on a medical encounter, students sign up for a major project that is in part a group presentation to the class and in part an individual paper based on the presentation. In one such project, students prepare a courtroom drama in which Williams's Doc Rivers is tried for malpractice. A paper stemming from this project would give a fully developed rationale for its author's argument or testimony in the presentation. In another project, a group gives a presentation on some ethical issues explored in hospital dramas on television. The resulting papers would explore particular issues or provide an extended analysis of a particular television series. Another option allows students to present a scene or scenes from one of the dramas we read during the semester. In this case, individual papers would entail some library research, either on the work of the dramatist or on the issues explored in the play, and concentrate on the student's role in the performance. For a final assignment I find I must choose between breadth and depth, recognizing that each has its merits. If it is breadth I am looking for, I give an examination that allows students to draw together and put into perspective the semester's course content as a whole. If depth is the aim, I assign a substantial final paper on topics the students have chosen for themselves and for which they have submitted an abstract earlier in the semester.

Course Readings

Week 1   In-depth discussion of the Hippocratic oath, Abse's "Song for Pythagoras," and Hunter's paradigm of the three narratives

Week 2   Williams, *The Doctor Stories* (except "Old Doc Rivers")

Week 3   Williams, "Old Doc Rivers"
Selzer, selections from *Imagine a Woman*

Week 4   Selzer, "A Mask on the Face of Death"
Selzer, chapter 13 from *Down from Troy* (on physician-assisted suicide)
Short story about a personal medical encounter due

Week 5   Rabe, *A Question of Mercy*
Camus, *The Plague*
Presentation 1: Doc Rivers's trial (paper due one week later)

Week 6   Monette, *Borrowed Time*, chapters 1–10
            Presentation 2: McNally's "Andre's Mother" and AIDS and the
            family (paper due one week later)

Week 7   Monette, *Borrowed Time*, chapters 11–12
            Midterm test

Week 8   Feldshuh, *Miss Evers' Boys*
            Hemingway, "Indian Camp"

Week 9   Selzer, "Tube Feeding"
            Kushner, *Angels in America: Millennium Approaches*
            Presentation 3: The Tuskegee experiment and informed consent
            (paper due one week later)

Week 10 Kushner, *Angels in America: Perestroika*
            Presentation 4: *Angels in America*: What does it mean? (paper
            due one week later)

Week 11 DeLillo, *White Noise*
            Presentation 5: Ethical issues in TV medical dramas (paper due
            one week later)
            Abstract for final paper topics due (when final paper is substi-
            tuted for final exam)

Week 12 Updike, *Rabbit at Rest*, parts 1 and 2
            Presentation 6: Physician-patient relationships (paper due one
            week later)

Week 13 Updike, *Rabbit at Rest*, part 3

Week 14 Final exam (or final paper due)

Notes

1. Anne Hunsaker Hawkins defines pathography as "a form of autobiography or biography that describes personal experience of illness, treatment, and sometimes death" (1). The pathographies she considers are
not fictional, but the term applies equally well to fictional narratives.

2. Williams's stories "The Use of Force" and "A Face of Stone" are narrated by physicians who might be called "impaired" by their own emotions. The ethical issues involved in maintaining boundaries between
physician and patient can be seen in "The Use of Force," in Selzer's
"The Consultation," in Dr. Hullah's prying investigation into the
rooms of patients' homes during house calls in Davies's *The Cunning
Man*, and in Stone's "He Makes a House Call" and "The Long House
Call" (in both of which maintaining boundaries becomes a nonissue).
A physician's decision to terminate surgery and allow death to occur is
taken up in Selzer's "Sarcophagus" and the question of physician-
assisted suicide is explored in chapter 13 of Selzer's autobiographical
Down from Troy and in *A Question of Mercy*, Rabe's recent play based

on that chapter. Camus's *The Plague* presents an image of a healer whose ethical imperatives are not problematized as dilemmas; he self-lessly subjugates his personal life to the medical emergency at hand.

3. The issue of the impaired physician in a contemporary context is discussed in Keating and Ackerman.

4. See Caplan; Edgar; Jones, "Tuskegee"; and King—all in a section entitled "Twenty Years After: The Legacy of the Tuskegee Syphilis Study" in the *Hastings Center Report*. Jones's *Bad Blood: The Tuskegee Syphilis Experiment* is a longer work on the subject.

5. Feldshuh's play demonstrates how Western medicine forces itself on the African American culture of the rural South. Other works that prove helpful in discussing the incursion of Western medicine on other cultures are Hemingway's "Indian Camp" and Walker's "Strong Horse Tea." See also Payer's *Medicine* and *Culture* and Eisenstein's *Encounters with Qi*. Sontag's *Illness and Metaphor* and *AIDS and Its Metaphors* can sensitize students to words and images that literature and culture employ for different illnesses.

6. Students are quick to note that AIDS is not simply a disease of gay men; indeed, that it is currently spreading most rapidly among women and racial minorities. Literary output, however, does not follow the epidemiological spread pattern, and it is a fact that most—and the best—AIDS literature still has as its context the gay male community. It is also true that *Angels in America* is about a great deal more than the impact of AIDS on homosexuals: it is more significantly about the limits of caregiving; the destructive effects of existence in any kind of "closet"; and, finally, the triumph of love, hope, and courage in the face of an uncertain and unknowable future.

7. Before I introduce this play, I ask students to read and discuss Selzer's "Tube Feeding." This piece shows a loving husband who can no longer bear to continue tube feeding his terminally ill wife after a mishap with the process. She agrees that "it is enough" (165), so their individual stories come to the same end. "Tube Feeding" enables students to see that the details of physical care may be more than a person can rise to.

8. In Gilchrist's *The Anna Papers,* Anna Hand, ill from breast cancer, controls her story by refusing to see a physician until near the end of her life, refusing to take his advice, and committing suicide. In DeLillo's *White Noise*, the controlling story is that of the computer, whose role overrides the physician's and finds voice through a technician.

Works Cited

Abse, Dannie. "Song for Pythagoras." *White Coat, Purple Coat: Collected Poems, 1948–1988*. New York: Persea, 1991. 273–74.

Camus, Albert. *The Plague*. Trans. Stuart Gilbert. Vintage Intl. ed. New York: Vintage, 1991.

Caplan, Arthur L. "When Evil Intrudes." *Hastings Center Report* 22.6 (1992): 29–32.

Davies, Robertson. *The Cunning Man.* New York: Penguin, 1996.

DeLillo, Don. *White Noise.* New York: Penguin, 1986.

Edgar, Harold. "Outside the Community." *Hastings Center Report* 22.6 (1992): 32–35.

Eisenstein, David, with Thomas Lee Wright. *Encounters with Qi: Exploring Chinese Medicine.* New York: Penguin, 1987.

Feldshuh, David. *Miss Evers' Boys.* New York: Dramatists, 1995.

Gilchrist, Ellen. *The Anna Papers.* New York: Little, 1989.

Hawkins, Anne Hunsaker. *Reconstructing Illness: Studies in Pathography.* West Lafayette: Purdue UP, 1993.

Hemingway, Ernest. "Indian Camp." *The Nick Adams Stories.* New York: Bantam, 1973. 6–10.

Hunter, Kathryn Montgomery. *Doctors' Stories: The Narrative Structure of Medical Knowledge.* Princeton: Princeton UP, 1991.

Jones, James H. *Bad Blood: The Tuskegee Syphilis Experiment.* New York: Free, 1993.

———. "The Tuskegee Legacy: AIDS and the Black Community." *Hastings Center Report* 22. 6 (1992): 38–40.

Keating, Herbert J., and Terrence F. Ackerman, commentators. "Case Studies: When the Doctor's on Drugs." *Hastings Center Report* 21.5 (1991): 29–31.

King, Patricia A. "The Dangers of Difference." *Hastings Center Report* 22. 6 (1992): 35–38.

Kushner, Tony. *Angels in America: Millennium Approaches.* New York: Theatre, 1993.

———. *Angels in America: Perestroika.* New York: Theatre, 1994.

McNally, Terrence. "Andre's Mother." *The Way We Live Now: American Plays and the AIDS Crisis.* Ed. M. Elizabeth Osborn. New York: Theatre, 1990. 189–93.

"Medicine." *The Encyclopedia Britannica.* 14th ed. 1962.

Monette, Paul. *Borrowed Time: An AIDS Memoir.* New York: Avon, 1990.

Payer, Lynn. *Medicine and Culture: Varieties of Treatment in the United States, England, West Germany, and France.* New York: Penguin, 1989.

Rabe, David. *A Question of Mercy: Based on the Essay by Richard Selzer.* New York: Grove, 1998.

Selzer, Richard. "The Consultation." *Rituals of Surgery.* New York: Morrow, 1987. 18–23.

———. *Down from Troy: A Doctor Comes of Age.* New York: Morrow, 1992.

———. *Imagine a Woman.* East Lansing: Michigan State UP, 1990.

———. "A Mask on the Face of Death." *The Best American Essays 1988.* Ed. Annie Dillard. New York: Ticknor, 1988. 207–19.

———. "Sarcophagus." *Confessions of a Knife.* New York: Morrow, 1987. 50–60.

———. "Tube Feeding." *Confessions of a Knife.* New York: Morrow, 1987. 159–66.

Sontag, Susan. Illness as Metaphor *and* AIDS and Its Metaphors. New York: Anchor-Doubleday, 1990.

Stone, John. "He Makes a House Call." *In All This Rain.* Baton Rouge: Louisiana State UP, 1980. 29–37.

———. "The Long House Call." *In the Country of Hearts: Journeys in the Art of Medicine.* New York: Dell, 1992. 4–5.

Styron, William. *Darkness Visible: A Memoir of Madness.* New York: Vintage, 1992.

Updike, John. *Rabbit at Rest.* New York: Ballantine, 1991.

Walker, Alice. "Strong Horse Tea." *Trials, Tribulations, and Celebrations: African-American Perspectives on Health, Illness, Aging, and Loss.* Ed. Marian Gray Secundy. With the literary collaboration of Lois La Civita Nixon. Yarmouth: Intercultural, 1992. 76–82.

Williams, William Carlos. *The Doctor Stories.* Comp. Robert Coles. New York: New Directions, 1984.

———. "A Face of Stone." Williams, *Doctor* 78–87.

———. "Old Doc Rivers." Williams, *Doctor* 13–41.

———. "The Use of Force." Williams, *Doctor* 56–60.

Janice L. Willms

Madness and Suicide as Themes in Western Literature

Madness and suicide, whether presented as relatively peripheral themes or as central ones, appear with considerable frequency in Western literature. The two may be linked, or they may occur in the same work without relation to each other. It is not difficult for the reader familiar with a broad spectrum of fiction and drama to identify works that draw on these themes as sources of conflict and tension. These are topics of universal significance to the human condition and thus serve both medical and humanities curricula.

A multidisciplinary approach to madness and suicide in literature is essential to the effective use of these topics in the medical humanities curriculum. The cultural attitudes that underlie a literary work inform how we interpret it, and the presentation of madness or suicide in a work of fiction or drama is a cultural artifact of the author's society. For example, one might ask why Tom O'Bedlam is free to roam about the English countryside in *King Lear*. In the late sixteenth century, British society had not yet decreed that all persons who behaved strangely needed to be tranquilized or straitjacketed.

119

Harmless lunatics could in fact be on their own as long as they could sustain themselves. Tom's madness is both a metaphor for a kingdom that is going mad and an illustration of the contemporaneous attitude toward the benign "crazy" man.

In the spirit of interdisciplinary analysis, I present here a brief overview of the evolving social and medical responses to madness and suicide and discuss how these attitudes are reflected in selected literary works from the Renaissance forward. What emerges is a demonstration of how the themes of madness and suicide (in all their human, medical, and social dimensions) can be used in the classroom to teach literary analysis, foster an appreciation of cultural history, and encourage the assessment of society's role in evaluating and caring for those who are mad or suicidal.

Although the culture of medieval Christianity borrowed from Greek and Arabic medicine the idea that madness could be a result of moral trauma or organic disease, it emphasized another interpretation—that madness is a mark of divine providence. According to Roy Porter, in the medieval and Renaissance eras one could comprehend madness as a moral, a medical, or a religious issue; as good or bad; as divine or diabolical (13). The lunatic, since he or she was often viewed as divinely directed, was allowed to mingle with the populace at large. This practice was to change dramatically during the seventeenth-century Age of Reason, with its celebration of the rational and its need to establish sovereignty over its adversary, irrationality. With the Enlightenment, madness became a "disorder," a disease state whose victims needed to be captured and sequestered. Insanity gradually lost its moral and religious implications and became a social outrage to be hidden from view. The late nineteenth century saw the limits of acceptable behavior constricted and fear of the irregular, the irrational, grow. Increasing numbers of people were institutionalized for disordered thinking that resulted in disordered behavior. This trend, Judith S. Neaman suggests, began to shift in the last decades of the twentieth century as the modern world's enhanced variety of choices—religious, social, economic, and philosophical—once again extended the boundaries of the normal. She argues that "the result has been increased flexibility and increased confusion, manifest in an unwillingness and even an inability to say what is rational or irrational, sane or insane" (146).

Attitudes toward suicide vary dramatically across cultures. There were periods and societies in which suicide was perceived as a heroic act. In other times and places suicide was a mortal sin and a felonious crime. Eventually attitudes evolved to the highly secular "die if you wish, and let die" ideology familiar today. In the early Middle Ages, evangelists preached that suicide—self-murder—was incited by the devil and punishable as a crime against God and state. Suicide became tolerated only when it was perceived as a disease— this perception resulting from a complex transition in culture, politics, and science that was incomplete until well into the nineteenth century. The suicidal person, designated non compos mentis, was no longer culpable but rather needed to be protected from self-harm. However, there remained a vestige of shame, in some instances based on the inability of family members and friends to fully accept a diagnosis of mental disturbance and in others associated with religiously grounded uncertainty about the ultimate fate of the self-killer.

The following considerations are important in choosing texts and developing a syllabus for a course focusing on the literature of madness or suicide. The instructor should begin by examining the target audience. Are the students coming from humanities disciplines to explore medical issues as they appear in literature? Are the students future health professionals wishing to gain a broad, humanities-based perspective on problems they encounter in the clinic? Or, in the ideal situation, are the students a mixture of the above? The humanities student may require some preliminary work in the language of medical discourse, whereas the student of medical science may require instruction in how to approach a literary text. The history of societal responses to insanity and suicide will likely be new to both groups.

Given the projected makeup of the student population, what are the instructor's objectives? Is the principal goal to enable medical students, through the insights of literature, to approach an understanding of what madness or suicide means to the patient and his or

her loved ones? Or is it to give the student of history a narrative vision of cultural attitudes toward suicide and madness? Perhaps the
students are asking just how the literature they study relates to the
real world of medicine. It is important to define a set of objectives
that are narrow enough to be achieved in the time available yet
broad enough to accommodate the interests of the target audience.

Readings may be clustered to illustrate a specific societal issue,
to demonstrate gender-specific cultural or medical pressures, or to
show the differences between genres, novels and plays for example,
in dealing with the themes of madness and suicide. Conversely, texts
may be organized chronologically to illustrate (or question) the evolution of attitudes. Texts could also be chosen for their ability to explore a literary device such as symbol or metaphor or to examine
how the reader's interpretation of a text may be affected if the narrator's mental status is in question.

Having selected the course texts, the instructor identifies preliminary readings or extratextual background. Carefully crafted
questions presented before reading and during discussion help
guide the student toward the richest experience with both the primary and the secondary texts.

Following are some possible ways to design a course. One approach is to use a text to demonstrate a particular set of clinical or
literary insights into madness or suicide. For example, in Shakespeare's *King Lear* the symptoms and signs of madness in the elderly
are as clearly discernible in the characters of Lear (dementia with superimposed delirium) and Gloucester (depression presenting as
pseudodementia) as they would be on a late-twentieth-century psychiatric ward. There is considerable evidence that Lear has already
begun to slip when he divides his kingdom, a most unkinglike thing
to do. Long before the central act 3, even the fool recognizes that
the king is no longer thinking clearly. The storm-driven delirium on
the heath substantiates Lear's craziness, and one might argue that
even though the delirium passes, Lear never regains normal mental
function. Gloucester exercises poor judgment, which results in the
loss of his son, his eyesight, and his home and property—leading
him to profound depression and suicidal ideation. When he is re-

united with his son, all signs of despair or disordered thinking dissolve as his situational depression lifts. The value of this approach to the play, which can be combined with more traditional literary interpretations, is that it encourages careful reading for textual clues to the evolving mental status of the characters and to the artistic relation of these changes to the larger issues of the drama. *Lear* also demonstrates the power of madness as a metaphor for chaos. As students carefully dissect events from the poetry of the play, the congruity of the storm on the heath, the figurative storms in the minds of the old men, and the tempest dismembering the body politic elicit reactions of comprehension and admiration from even the least committed reader of drama.

Preliminary reading for the instructor (and possibly for students as well) on the subject of madness in the sixteenth century could include selections from Porter's *A Social History of Madness: Stories of the Insane* and passages describing the signs and symptoms of depression from Robert Burton's *The Anatomy of Melancholy*. A brief lecture on depressive and delusional language helps students analyze the words of Lear and Gloucester for signs of decreasing rationality and understand their words in relation to accelerating disorder in their environment.

Anton Chekhov uses the psychiatric hospital in "Ward Number Six" as a powerful political metaphor. How does madness work in this metaphor? The dissolution of the prerevolutionary Russian government can be likened to the madness within the ward or to the madness of the world without. The evolution of the physician into the role of insane patient presents an interesting opportunity to study the unresolved question of the blurred boundary between sanity and insanity, a question that haunts literary interpretation as well as society's collective social consciousness. In preparation for this text, students benefit from a survey of the political state of Russia in the last twenty-five years of the nineteenth century. Russia's mental health care system can be viewed as a microcosm of the political situation of the period. A discussion of Michel Foucault's *Madness and Civilization* and a lecture summarizing the institutional management of insanity in the Age of Reason help illuminate the text, particularly if insanity is interpreted as metaphoric. Students might be asked to consider the following questions as they read Chekhov: Are any of the men on the ward crazy? If so, which ones and by the authority of whose definition of madness?

A second approach to organizing texts is to cluster selected readings around a particular set of themes and perspectives. Gustave Flaubert's *Madame Bovary*, Kate Chopin's *The Awakening*, Federico García Lorca's *The House of Bernarda Alba*, and Sylvia Plath's *The Bell Jar* all deal with a woman's decision to take her own life. Each work reflects a unique perspective on self-destruction. Emma Bovary is a self-centered, self-deluded dreamer with insufficient insight into her own motivations to survive the ultimate destruction of her fantasies. She escapes in a dramatic and protracted dying scene which amplifies not only her character but also the consequences of her act for her family and community. Chopin's Edna, a nineteenth-century, upper-middle-class American wife, seeks excitement and meaning in her dreary life. She tells us exactly why she chooses death over what she has. We must evaluate her in the context of what it meant socially for the wife of a wealthy Creole to give up everything, including her children, and walk into the sea. In García Lorca's play repressed sexuality and the heavy hand of Spanish Catholicism push young Adela, daughter of Bernarda Alba, to hang herself. This dark play, filled with images of death, serves as an especially useful tool for teaching the dramatic power of symbolism. Plath's central character, Esther, is an American woman of the 1950s who is single, discontent, confused, and depressed. Her story takes us into the morass of modern psychiatric theory and depression management.

Although all these texts are modern, the differences among them in terms of the religion and social class of the characters exemplify the personal and social significance of each of the suicides. Selected readings from Alfred Alvarez's *The Savage God* and Barbara Gates's *Victorian Suicide* provide background for this differentiation. Students can benefit from considering both the common theme of women in despair and the distinctions among the suicides. Are any of these suicides justifiable? On what grounds? Are any of the women psychiatrically ill as defined in their time and place or in ours? How does each suicide serve the purpose of the plot or of characterization? Does narrative point of view affect the reader's response to the self-destructive acts?

In another cluster of texts, Herman Melville's classic short story "Bartleby, the Scrivener" and J. D. Salinger's "A Perfect Day for Bananafish" encourage the reader to question a man's death. The works, both American, were written more than a century apart, but in both periods self-destruction was considered an act of desperation generated within a disordered mind. The tension in each story is created by filtering the central character's worldview through the interpretation of a third-person narrator. It may be helpful for students to review the ethical and the legal implications of the characters' unfolding medical histories. Is Bartleby's death a suicide? Is the narrator or the society responsible for Bartleby's death? In Salinger's story, does the medical establishment fail Seymour Glass? Are the narrators' interpretations consistent with the reader's observations? Do these interpretations reflect contemporaneous attitudes toward self-willed death or do they speak only to the narrator's (or the author's) personal concerns with the psychology of suicide? Is either death the result of mental disorder, or can we view each as a rational act, given the time, the place, and the circumstances?

Why use literary texts rather than clinical case studies to shed light on real life psychiatric disorders and the personal events that shape the decision to take one's life? My training and experience as a physician have convinced me that the complex characters and circumstances found in literature offer a comprehensive model with which to study aspects of human behavior that emerge in the clinic. In contrast, medical narratives are more narrow and personally guarded. Testing our humanity in the relative safety of fiction, we may cry out at the moral blindness of Gloucester as he denounces his son. But around our real patient or friend we may be unable to openly examine motives and feelings—either our own or those of others. Literature frees us to explore unlimited possibilities and draw interpretive conclusions without fear of harming ourselves or others.

Course Readings

This design is for a fifteen week, three-credit course at the upper-division undergraduate level. Target students include both science majors preparing for health professions and humanities majors.

The objectives of the course are to examine madness and suicide as themes in literature and as devices that can create, develop, or resolve conflict; to understand madness and suicide as cultural artifacts of the time and place in which each work was written; to analyze the roles of gender, race, and economic status in framing society's perceptions of madness and suicide; and to explore, through the study of fictional characters, the feelings and behaviors of the actors involved in a story of madness or suicide. With adaptations in emphasis, the same core readings and design are useful for medical students as well. The course begins with a lecture on the cultural history of madness and suicide in the West from the Renaissance to the present. The following are the subjects for weekly readings; in addition selected readings from pertinent secondary sources (listed in Works Cited) may be assigned.

Shakespeare, *King Lear*
Flaubert, *Madame Bovary*
Melville, "Bartleby, the Scrivener"
García Lorca, *The House of Bernarda Alba*
Chekhov, "Ward Number Six"
Chopin, *The Awakening*
Wharton, *Ethan Frome*
Faulkner, *As I Lay Dying*
Miller, *Death of a Salesman*
McCullers, *The Heart Is a Lonely Hunter*
Plath, *The Bell Jar*
Norman, *'Night, Mother*
Salinger, "A Perfect Day for Bananafish"
Review: discussion of Alvarez's *The Savage God* and Porter's *A Social History of Madness*

Works Cited

Alvarez, Alfred. *The Savage God: A Study of Suicide*. New York: Random, 1972.

Burton, Robert. *The Anatomy of Melancholy*. 1621. New York: Tudor, 1927.

Chekhov, Anton. "Ward Number Six." *"Ward Number Six" and Other Stories*. Trans. Ronald Hingley. New York: Oxford UP, 1974.

Chopin, Kate. *The Awakening*. Ed. Margaret Culley. New York: Norton, 1976.

Faulkner, William. *As I Lay Dying.* New York: Vintage, 1987.

Flaubert, Gustave. *Madame Bovary.* Trans. Francis Steegmuller. New York: Random, 1957.

Foucault, Michel. *Madness and Civilization: A History of Insanity in the Age of Reason.* 1965. New York: Vintage-Random, 1988.

García Lorca, Federico. *The House of Bernarda Alba. Three Tragedies.* New York: New Directions, 1955. 157–211

Gates, Barbara. *Victorian Suicide: Mad Crimes and Sad Histories.* Princeton: Princeton UP, 1988.

McCullers, Carson. *The Heart Is a Lonely Hunter.* New York: Bantam: 1953.

Melville, Herman. "Bartleby the Scrivener." *The Norton Anthology of American Literature.* 4th ed. Vol. 1. New York: Norton, 1994. 2234–58.

Miller, Arthur. *Death of a Salesman.* New York: Penguin, 1976.

Neaman, Judith S. *Suggestion of the Devil: The Origins of Madness.* Garden City: Anchor-Doubleday, 1975.

Norman, Marsha. *'Night, Mother.* New York: Hill, 1983.

Plath, Sylvia. *The Bell Jar.* New York: Harper, 1971.

Porter, Roy. *A Social History of Madness: Stories of the Insane.* London: Weidenfeld, 1987.

Salinger, J. D. "A Perfect Day for Bananafish." *Nine Stories.* Boston: Little, 1953. 7–18.

Shakespeare, William. *King Lear.* Ed. Kenneth Muir. New York: Random, 1964.

Wharton, Edith. *Ethan Frome.* New York: Macmillan, 1986.

Jan Marta

Mind and Body, Psyche and Soma: Metaphors from Greek Myth through Literature to the Clinic

The mythical figure of Psyche, beloved of Cupid or Eros, resonates in Western prose, poetry, and drama—from Apuleius's second-century Latin story through works by Marino, Milton, and Molière, as well as Cervantes and La Fontaine in the seventeenth century to Keats's nineteenth-century "Ode to Psyche." Psyche has found her way into the twentieth-century works of C. S. Lewis, Zora Neale Hurston, and Doris Lessing, among others. Contemporary criticism focuses on Psyche's story as a quest myth, a tale of female development, and an exemplar of feminine heroism and integrates her figure into various psychoanalytic approaches including Jungian archetypes and Derridean semiotics.

In the approach to teaching literature and medicine outlined here, the figure of Psyche is the leitmotiv for an interdisciplinary study of Western conceptualizations of the mind-body relation as represented in literary, philosophical, medical, psychiatric, and psychoanalytic writings.[1] The course, Mind and Body, Psyche and Soma: Metaphors from Greek Myth through Literature to the

Clinic, employs an innovative theme-specific mode of interdisciplinary study, a mode that uses the transformative potential of metaphor (and of literary representations as living macrometaphors) to show the philosophical and clinical value in articulating the links between literature and medicine. Poststructuralist literary theory — emphasizing textual analysis, linguistic approaches, and an understanding of the text as part of a broader sociocultural communication process — provides the overall framework for the study of mind, body, and metaphor; their interrelations; and their impact on lay and professional views and on manifestations of illness and disease. Within this framework the course relies on Paul Ricoeur's "living metaphor" as a specific theoretical and methodological anchor for the textual readings. Aimed at senior students in the arts and sciences and in medicine, this one-term seminar (of three hours per week) highlights the role of literature as re-presentation, that is, as both reflector and creator of sociocultural and medical paradigms.

Throughout the course, relevant philosophical texts help foster a nuanced understanding of Western ideas of mind, body, and soul. The representation within a literary text of a specific malaise such as grief or of an explanatory model of illness such as psychological trauma or of a clinical syndrome such as depression fuels the examination of current lay and professional manifestations of mind-body disturbances, called psychosomatic illnesses. Class discussions emphasize that clinical syndromes are themselves mental and physical metaphoric expressions of mind-body relations. The construction of meaning, the constructedness of scientific knowledge, and the relation of sociocultural ideas and practices to metaphor are addressed. A major focal point is the role of living metaphors and of literary texts as living macrometaphors in the development of a transdisciplinary, holistic concept of mind and body.

The course begins with an introduction to metaphor, then elaborates on Ricoeur's living metaphor, George Lakoff and Mark Johnson's "metaphors we live by," and the integration of the two concepts. Given the multidisciplinary composition of the class, it is especially important to start with basic definitions. These could include the etymological derivation of the word *metaphor*; the standard rhetorical definitions of metaphor as a figure of speech distinct from related ones like simile, metonymy, and synecdoche; and Aristotle's writings on the topic. Examples from well-known literary works (such as those often taught in high school) make particularly helpful illustrations, especially when they invoke mind and body. The concepts of naming, substitution, and tenor and vehicle should be highlighted. The decorative function of metaphor and its role in creating meaning should be discussed as should the idea of the dead metaphor or cliché — a metaphor that is so common as to go almost unrecognized, rather than startling through new comparison.

Ricoeur's concept of living metaphor is one of tensions, not substitutions. In a living metaphor, tensions occur between tenor and vehicle, similarity and difference, existence and nonexistence, truth and nontruth. Tensions turn on the literal "is not" and the figurative "is" of the implied copula "to be" and its extension "to be like." A living metaphor creates new meaning and a new referent in the world while holding in tension the already existing meanings and referents of the tenor and vehicle that participate in its creation. It is alive in that it is never merely decorative but always transformative. A living metaphor transforms meaning, our construct of reality, our worldview, and our notion of truth. It is analogous to a scientific model in that it serves the heuristic function of taking us beyond the known while representing it. Ricoeur's definition of living metaphor, which allows one to trace patterns from the past in current and future formulations, is thus particularly well suited to the enterprise of examining the evolution of ideas over centuries.

Lakoff and Johnson's notion of metaphors we live by is especially apt; it reveals the metaphoric structure of everyday words. The authors demonstrate how to revive the long-dead metaphors or clichés that transmit accepted ideas. They argue that the abstract or figurative is based on the mental (cognitive) transformation of perceptions grounded in the concrete, literal, and spatial relations of the body in the world. Their exposition of this process and their many examples amply illustrate how yesterday's living metaphor becomes a metaphor we live by, a set of seemingly unobtrusive norms that frame our conceptualizations of ourselves in our physical and social (received linguistic) worlds.[2]

This background on metaphor sets the frame for the next phase in the course — the analysis of key pairings of mind and body, body and soul, and psyche and soma in Apuleius's "Cupid and Psyche" and in further reinterpretations of the myth by Milton and by Keats. "Cupid and Psyche" is the longest, most elaborate tale in Apuleius's classic novel *The Golden Ass.* It tells the story of the youngest of three daughters, Psyche, whose great beauty invites adoration equal to that enjoyed by Venus. Initially, Psyche is an empty vessel, a maiden loved from afar, and a mortal. Her status as a human Venus puts her in an untenable position. The tensions between embodiment and soul, physical beauty and human spirit, mortality and immortality are irreconcilable in the world of the text. Unmarriageable and barren, Psyche is ordered by the jealous Venus to be put to the living death of marriage to a human beast. Cupid rescues, marries, and impregnates Psyche. However, her transgression of his injunction never to look at his face sends them separately wandering and suffering through travails of body and soul. As Psyche struggles against despair and suicide, Cupid battles a fatal wound and imprisonment.

Ultimately, Psyche's existence depends on the relational function of the copula "to be." For her "to be" she must "be like" Cupid, and vice versa, without either of them ceasing to exist. This relationship is marked by each one's submission to a higher authority (Psyche's to Venus, Cupid's to Jupiter) in order "to be" together. The metaphoric transformation is completed when Jupiter naturalizes their union by making Psyche immortal and sanctions their marriage through social law. The confluence of spiritual love and physical desire, of body and soul, engenders a new reality, Pleasure, the child born to Psyche and Cupid at the close of the story. Psyche, as a metaphor of love and desire, spirituality and physicality, mortality and immortality, becomes a metaphor of mind-body integration, preservation, and creation. She who begins as a decorative but empty embodiment of soul is transformed by her union with desire.

Psyche is the tenor and Venus, then Cupid, the vehicles of living metaphors that generate new meanings and new references in the world of the text and, by analogy and extension, that of the reader.

As Psyche's story becomes inextricably entwined with Cupid's, the relation between mind-soul-spirit and body is neither clearly dualistic nor clearly monistic, neither Cartesian nor materialistic. D. W. Hamlyn's chapter on minds provides an overview of philosophical concepts of the mental and physical that helps elucidate these paradigms and furthers discussion of the possible metaphoric combinations in Apuleius's text. Psyche's sufferings can also lead to discussion of current conceptualizations of the biological, psychological, and social factors contributing to the onset, manifestation, and treatment of clinical depression and one of its symptoms, suicidal impulses. A feminist critique of the genderization of minds and bodies, of spirit and passion, and of forms of illness and suffering enlivens and adds nuance to these philosophical and clinical topics of discussion (see Ehrenreich and English; Gilligan).

In *Comus* and *Areopagitica,* Milton reinterprets the Psyche myth as an illustration of the importance and necessity of enduring physical trials to achieve spiritual triumph over "sensual folly [. . .] and intemperance" (*Comus* 106). He invokes the Psyche myth specifically to emphasize the "incessant labour of the fallen to cull good from evil" (*Comus* 106). In Milton, the human Psyche is initially a fallen soul analogous to Eve. Her redemption and immortality come only through the suffering and rejection of the flesh, not through "a fugitive and cloistered virtue" (*Areopagitica* 166). Psyche apotheosized is chaste—a virgin bride joined for eternity with Cupid, a virgin mother who gives birth to Youth and Joy (*Comus* 107). Gone are the erotic jealousies and sensual "Pleasure" of Apuleius's story.

Milton's elaboration of the Christian dichotomy of body and soul precedes and in its duality foreshadows the Enlightenment ideal of the secular mind-body split that has predominated in Western thought ever since. Hamlyn's chapters on mind and on personal identity provide the philosophical correlates for these developments and for the development of the related Western notions of personhood and identity—notions consolidated in the late eighteenth century, which have become key preoccupations of modern thought (161–86; 187–218). *The Languages of Psyche: Mind and Body in Enlightenment Thought* contains various papers addressing the history of mind-body relations from the seventeenth through the eighteenth centuries, as expressed not only in philosophy but also in literature and in medicine (Rousseau).

"Ode to Psyche," Keats's nineteenth-century poetic transformation of Apuleius's prose "Cupid and Psyche," marks the literary advancement of the themes of mind, body, and personhood toward modern conceptualizations. The poem begins after the deification of Psyche, then returns to the themes of her birth and youth. At the same time, "Ode to Psyche" recounts the birth of the poet, who is transformed from one who wrings "tuneless numbers" to one who sings praises of the goddess (line 1). In the final stanza, Psyche and the poet are reborn together. Enraptured, the poet becomes Psyche's priest and creates a temple for her within his "mind" (51). The goddess who first was "espied" in a bower now lives in a "rosy sanctuary" within the poet's "working brain" (12, 59, 60). Yet the open casement that would let Eros in could let the "wingèd Psyche" out (6). Ultimately, the poet's ecstasy is modulated by the "pleasant pain" of the tenuousness of his internalization of the goddess (52).

Keats's portrayal of Psyche as the "other within" (Marta, "Internalizing Psyche") holds forth a new tension between body and soul that transforms the cold Enlightenment philosophies of Cartesian mind-body dualism and Lockean consciousness through the "warm Love" of eroticism, emotion, "Fancy," and imagination ("Ode to Psyche" 67, 62). In "Ode to Psyche," Keats draws seventeenth- and eighteenth-century thought into nineteenth-century Romanticism and pushes it toward the modernist and postmodernist subjectivity and alterity of the twentieth century. At the same time, the movement in the poem mirrors the development in Western medicine, psychiatry, and psychoanalysis of the concept of an "intrapsychic" unconscious.[3]

"Ode to Psyche" marks a transition in the course from early to contemporary literary works and intellectual constructs. At this point a number of nonliterary texts help elucidate the ideas that shape the movement in modern Western thought from "mind and body" to "psychosomatic." In brief, Mark Johnson provides a philosophical overview and critique of nineteenth-century objectivist theories of meaning and rationality and argues for the inclusion of embodied human imagination as a twentieth-century way of bridging the Cartesian mind-body split (xix–xxxvi).[4] Chase Patterson Kimball traces the development in the twentieth century of psychosomatic medicine, a branch of medicine that explicitly regards all illness as dependent on "a multiplicity of factors involving the somatic and psychological processes of the individual in relationship to the environment" (307). The psychiatrist and philosopher Aviel Goodman synthesizes this biopsychosocial model with Spinoza's mental-physical identity theory to propose an "organic unity theory." This theory is a clinically relevant concept of mind and body as two linguistically distinct conceptualizations of the same phenomenon—in Ricoeurian terms, the (interchangeable) tenor and vehicle of a single living metaphor (or scientific model)—currently represented by the words "biopsychosocial" or "psychosomatic."[5]

Two twentieth-century novels, Marie Cardinal's *The Words to Say It* and D. M. Thomas's *The White Hotel,* offer literary representations of psychosomatic illnesses and their treatments rather than overt interpretations of the Psyche myth. Each novel reflects the mind-body paradigms dominant at the time of its writing. Each challenges specific Western ideas about the mind-body relations and proposes alternative configurations.

In *The Words to Say It,* a novelization of Cardinal's own seven-year Freudian psychoanalysis, the author admirably portrays the formation of her psychosomatic symptoms, her love-hate relationship with those symptoms, and the reasons medical and biological psychiatric interpretations and treatments failed to give meaning to, or relief from, her mental and physical anguish. The stories of her early relationships (particularly with her mother), her life in French Algeria from the 1930s to the 1950s, and her adult relationships as wife and mother are told through the associative processes of psychoanalysis. Not only free association but also the analytic phenomena of resistance, transference, and acting out are beautifully and accurately rendered as she is shown growing into a healthy, fulfilled woman and writer. Cardinal clearly implies that the relation between the actual process of psychoanalysis and the attempt to represent it resembles that between reality and fiction. She sustains an apt and lyrical metaphor for her relation to the protagonist who is her former self (or selves): that of two sisters who are alike but not identical (see Marta, "Annotation," "Lighting").[6]

Thomas's *The White Hotel* at once represents and challenges Freudian psychoanalysis. The life story of the opera singer Lisa Erdmann, the novel includes her analysis by, and written correspondence with, a fictionalized Freud. The Freud character analyzes the physical symptoms for which Lisa seeks treatment (pelvic and breast pain) and diagnoses her with hysteria arising from childhood trauma and from latent homosexuality. In his formulation the body is understood as the repository of repressed psychological symptoms, and the treatment focuses on their mental undoing. Later events in Lisa's life reveal that her physical symptoms are premonitions of future injuries. Ultimately psyche and soma are revealed to be two conjoined and misunderstood aspects of a prophetic capacity that Lisa had attributed to her maternal cultural heritage, "a strain of the Romany" (197), and that the Freud character initially had dismissed, then eventually and simultaneously acknowledged and discredited (see Marta, "Lighting" 155).

Freud's case history of Dora (on hysteria) makes a good foil for Cardinal's fictionalized autobiography and Thomas's novel. Later psychoanalytic theorizations of the mind-body relation—particularly the mirror's role in the process of creating and becoming aware of one's mental and physical self, in the work of Jacques Lacan and of D. W. Winnicott—challenge Freudian theory from within psychoanalysis (Lacan 1–7; Winnicott 130–38). Such theorizations also foreground the narcissism of our cultural preoccupations with our bodies *as* our selves. These preoccupations and their impact on psyche and soma can be demonstrated graphically by study and discussion of anorexia nervosa—one of our culture's most prevalent psychosomatic disorders.[7]

Study and discussion of a disorder like anorexia nervosa help show how the metaphor "psychosomatic" subtends the illnesses our culture lives and dies by. As a union of mind and body that holds in tension the two constituent elements and their respective paradigms, "psychosomatic" neither subsumes one in the other nor recognizes the truth claim of one over the other. The metaphor goes beyond the combined knowledge of our letters and sciences. This knowledge is continually evolving, keeping the metaphor alive to further transformation. The course described here aims to contribute to that transformation by showing students the paradigms that historically underpin the existing metaphor and by encouraging them to critique and reconstruct those paradigms.

In class discussions students drew on knowledge gained not only through formal study of a broad range of disciplines from art history to zoology but also through their extracurricular activities, whether in the creative arts (painting, writing) or in corporal expression (sports, nonverbal therapies). The life experiences of motherhood, part-time work as a hospital ward clerk, and middle age became the wellsprings of impassioned debates about the role of development in mind-body understanding, the social structures of health care, and the biological and cultural assumptions that define the "middle." During one seminar, we listened entranced as a former dancer described her mental, physical, and spiritual transformations, beginning with the effort of rehearsal and culminating in the rapture of performance.

Mind and Body, Psyche and Soma has the capacity to remind premedical and medical students of their pluripotent earlier and current selves, to draw on past and current academic and extracurricular interests, and to give validation to a sociohistorically contextualized approach to the minds and bodies with which the students will be professionally entrusted. The course affirms the importance and validity of the biological sciences that are these students' main fare, while placing those sciences within a broader sociocultural context that encompasses both physician and patient. In other words, this course provides the tools for critical thinking about the metaphoric underpinnings of the medical model and of the biopsychosocial and psychosomatic constructs that inform students' current and future practice. The course reminds students of the shared space of human knowledge and experience beyond the artifice and heuristic of disciplinary boundaries. For future doctors, this reminder can serve as an inoculation against the physicians-versus-patients attitude that can be such an endemic and virulent part of their apprenticeship.

Course Readings

Ricoeur, *The Rule of Metaphor*
Lakoff and Johnson, *Metaphors We Live By*

Apuleius, "Cupid and Psyche"
Milton, *Comus, Areopagitica*
Keats, "Ode to Psyche"
Hamlyn, "Minds" and "Persons and Personal Identity"
Rousseau, *The Languages of Psyche*

Johnson, *The Body in the Mind*
Kimball, "Conceptual Developments in Psychosomatic Medicine, 1939–1968"
Goodman, "Organic Unity Theory"

Cardinal, *The Words to Say It*
Thomas, *The White Hotel*

Freud, "Dora"
Lacan, Ecrits: *A Selection*
Winnicott, *Playing and Reality*

Notes

1. The terms *disciplinary, cross-disciplinary, multidisciplinary, interdisciplinary,* and *transdisciplinary* have gained currency and cachet in teaching and research despite their often imprecise and contradictory use. Here they are understood in the following manner, adapted from Rosenfeld. *Cross-disciplinary* is a generic term for research, whether individual or collaborative, that goes beyond disciplinary boundaries. *Multidisciplinary* refers to work done sequentially or concomitantly from different disciplinary bases on a specific topic; *interdisciplinary,* to the integration in a rigorously scholarly manner of different disciplinary

approaches to a specific topic; and *transdisciplinary*, to the development or application of a theoretical or conceptual model that goes beyond the disciplinary, multidisciplinary, or interdisciplinary boundaries of the topic and approaches involved.

2. Among the most relevant metaphors discussed by Lakoff and Johnson are those pertaining to the paradigm "health and life are up; sickness and death are down"—"He's at the *peak* of his health. [. . .] He *fell* ill. [. . .] He *dropped* dead" (15). Also relevant are metaphors pertaining to the related paradigm "rational is up; emotional is down"—"The *rational* plane [. . .]. He couldn't *rise above* his *emotions*" (17). Both paradigms derive from the overarching "good is up; bad is down" (16).

3. This reading reflects material elaborated in my "Internalizing Psyche," for which Abrams (57–69) was particularly useful, as were selected letters of Keats written between 21–27 December 1817 and 30 April 1819 (Perkins 1209–26).

4. Building on ideas introduced in *Metaphors We Live By* (Lakoff and Johnson), Johnson argues in *The Body in the Mind* that human beings, as rational animals, are both rational and embodied. As such, the meanings humans make are directly influenced by patterns of bodily movement and of existence in space and time that function as "image schemata"—as gestalts for ordering experience. Imagination is the capacity to use image schemata to order human experience from the bodily through the rational to the abstract.

5. Aviel Goodman elaborates on the clinical relevance and impact of his theory with specific reference to the following topics: a general approach to patients as "whole organic unities" that requires the physician to be "fluent in both physical and mental languages and to appreciate and have the ability to evaluate both objective and subjective data" (562); diagnostic systems that recognize both objective (physical) and subjective (mental) data; and the recognition that all treatments, whether primarily physical (pharmacological) or mental (psychotherapeutic), affect both body and mind—a recognition that should lead to greater openness by the psychiatric profession and by individual clinicians to both modalities (561–62).

6. Wallace's history, "Freud and the Mind-Body Problem," and McDougall's more contemporary Freudian approach to psychosomatic illness are informative reading for a fuller appreciation of the sociocultural context of this novel and the next.

7. Anorexia nervosa affects women eight to ten times as often as men and has a fifteen percent mortality rate. Work on this topic abounds in women's and culture studies. Helpful mainstream psychiatric texts include the American Psychiatric Association's *Diagnostic and Statistical Manual of Mental Disorders*, Kaplan and Sadock's textbook of psychiatry, and, more particularly, works by Minuchin and by Bruch ("Anorexia"; "Four Decades").

Works Cited

Abrams, M. H. *The Mirror and the Lamp: Romantic Theory and the Critical Tradition*. New York: Oxford UP, 1953.

American Psychiatric Association. *Diagnostic and Statistical Manual of Mental Disorders*. 4th ed. Washington: Amer. Psychiatric Assn., 1994.

Apuleius. "Cupid and Psyche." *The Transformations of Lucius, Otherwise Known as* The Golden Ass. Trans. Robert Graves. New York: Noonday-Farrar, 1998. 96–143.

Bruch, Hilde. "Anorexia Nervosa: Therapy and Theory." *American Journal of Psychiatry* 139 (1982): 1531–38.

———. "Four Decades of Eating Disorders." *Handbook of Psychotherapy for Anorexia Nervosa and Bulimia*. Ed. David M. Garner and Paul E. Garfinkel. New York: Guilford, 1985. 7–18.

Cardinal, Marie. *The Words to Say It*. Trans. Pat Goodheart. Cambridge: VanVactor, 1983.

Ehrenreich, Barbara, and Deirdre English. *For Her Own Good: 150 Years of the Experts' Advice to Women*. Garden City: Anchor-Doubleday, 1979.

Freud, Sigmund. "Dora." 1905. Trans. Alix Strachey and James Strachey. *Case Histories 1: "Dora" and "Little Hans."* Ed. Angela Richards. New York: Penguin, 1977. 29–164. Vol. 8 of *The Pelican Freud Library*.

Gilligan, Carol. *In a Different Voice: Psychological Theory and Women's Development*. Cambridge: Harvard UP, 1982.

Goodman, Aviel. "Organic Unity Theory: The Mind-Body Problem Revisited." *American Journal of Psychiatry* 148 (1991): 553–63.

Hamlyn, D. W. *Metaphysics*. New York: Cambridge UP, 1984.

———. "Minds." Hamlyn, *Metaphysics* 161–86.

———. "Persons and Personal Identity." Hamlyn, *Metaphysics* 187–218.

Johnson, Mark. *The Body in the Mind: The Bodily Basis of Meaning, Imagination, and Reason*. Chicago: U of Chicago P, 1987.

Kaplan, Harold I., and Benjamin J. Sadock, eds. *Comprehensive Textbook of Psychiatry*. 6th ed. 2 vols. Baltimore: Williams, 1995.

Keats, John. "Ode to Psyche." Perkins 1183–84.

Kimball, Chase Patterson. "Conceptual Developments in Psychosomatic Medicine, 1939–1969." *Annals of Internal Medicine* 73 (1970): 307–16.

Lacan, Jacques. Ecrits: *A Selection*. Trans. Alan Sheridan. New York: Norton, 1977.

Lakoff, George, and Mark Johnson. *Metaphors We Live By*. Chicago: U of Chicago P, 1980.

Marta, Jan. "Annotation of Marie Cardinal's *The Words to Say It*." *On-Line Database of Literature, Arts, and Medicine*. Ed. Felice Aull et al. New York: New York UP, 1996. 51–52.

———. "Internalizing Psyche: Keats' Ode to the Other Within." Unpublished essay, 1997.

———. "Lighting the Way: The Temporal Dimension of Narrative in Psychotherapy." *Literature and Medicine* 13 (1994): 143–57.

McDougall, Joyce. *Theaters of the Body: A Psychoanalytic Approach to Psycho-somatic Illness.* New York: Norton, 1989.

Milton, John. *Areopagitica.* 1644. *The Portable Milton.* Ed. Douglas Bush. New York: Viking, 1949. 151–205.

———. *Comus.* 1634. *The Portable Milton.* Ed. Douglas Bush. New York: Viking, 1949. 76–107.

Minuchin, Salvador. "Perspectives on Anorexia Nervosa." *Psychosomatic Families: Anorexia Nervosa in Context.* Ed. Minuchin, Bernice L. Rosman, and Lester Baker. Cambridge: Harvard UP, 1978. 1–22.

Perkins, David, ed. *English Romantic Writers.* New York: Harcourt, 1967.

Ricoeur, Paul. *The Rule of Metaphor: Multi-disciplinary Studies of the Creation of Meanings in Language.* Trans. Robert Czerny with Kathleen McLaughlin and John Costello. Toronto: U of Toronto P, 1977.

Rosenfeld, Patricia L. "The Potential of Transdisciplinary Research for Sustaining and Extending Linkages between the Health and Social Sciences." *Social Sciences and Medicine* 35 (1992): 1343–57.

Rousseau, G. S., ed. *The Languages of Psyche: Mind and Body in Enlighten-ment Thought.* Clark Library Lectures 1985–1986. Berkeley: U of California P, 1990.

Thomas, D. M. *The White Hotel.* London: Penguin, 1981.

Wallace, Edwin R., IV. "Freud and the Mind-Body Problem." *Freud and the History of Psychoanalysis.* Ed. Toby Gelfand and John Kerr. Hillsdale: Analytic, 1992. 231–69.

Winnicott, D. W. *Playing and Reality.* London: Penguin, 1988.

Lois S. Spatz and Kathleen Welch

Literature and Medicine as a Writing Course

Writing, Healing, and the Humanities was a sophomore writing course at the University of Missouri, Kansas City, that was offered, thanks to a Culpeper Foundation grant, to meet the needs of students interested in the health-care professions. Faculty members from the English department and the School of Medicine developed the syllabus and shared the teaching. Students were divided into seven sections, each made up of fifteen to twenty students. Sections were taught at the same time so that all students could meet together for special activities. "Being human" was chosen as the unifying theme of the course, and essay assignments were matched with four topics relating to this theme. For the personal essay, students focused on self and other; for a research paper, on a social crisis; for the persuasive essay, they wrote about making moral choices; and for their imaginative essay, creativity was the topic. Besides the formal essays, students were given briefer writing assignments, or prompts, on which they reflected in their logs. Students were also asked to do freewriting exercises in class. Albert Camus's *The Plague* was the central text of the course; that and several shorter texts provided topics for most of the short writing assignments.

The various assignments were intended to introduce health science students to exploratory writing as a means of acquiring and processing knowledge. Scientific discourse, in order to objectify knowledge, is "stripped of context" and is "absolute" (Bazerman 64). In most science classes the dominant modes of learning are memorization and objective tests. When students go on to medical school or graduate school in the sciences, they learn to write non-contextually — without reference to intangible aspects of patient or subject. Since we required students to reflect on the readings and connect them to personal experiences, beliefs, and views, students learned how to formulate, express, and defend their opinions; how to reexamine prior ideas; and how to explore subjectivity as a positive and complementary mode of perceiving and responding. Students appreciated the opportunity to analyze experiences and express unresolved feelings on paper, particularly in the log entries and in-class responses, two less structured modes of expression.

The Plague worked well as a means of defining the course themes and focusing student thinking. Its protagonist, Rieux, is a selfless doctor who faces a medical crisis similar to AIDS or Ebola. The novel features a variety of responses by different characters to the crisis. Moreover it depicts social activism coupled with reflection: as Rieux bonds with others in fighting the disease, he and his friends ponder the relative merits of objectivity and feeling and discuss personal priorities as well as philosophical and religious questions. With issues like these as bait, we hoped to lure our students to examine what it means to be human from a perspective different from that of the biophysical model provided by their science courses.

The Plague is an excellent instrument for teaching writing as well as critical thinking. At its most literal level it is an objective chronicle that traces the course of the plague in Oran. The anonymous narrator pledges to record "what happened [. . .] and how it affected the life of the whole populace," based on "what he saw himself, [. . .] general accounts of other eyewitnesses, their personal impressions, [. . .] and lastly, documents that [. . .] came into his hands" (6–7). The narrator's account illustrates the careful observation, clear and precise description, and rigorous analysis that we encourage in student writing. Father Panloux's public sermons and the private conversations they provoke exemplify principles of deliberation and persuasion. The narrator's eyewitnesses take readers beyond the general to the particular and the personal. For example, Tarrou's journal records what "[t]he normal historian [. . .] passes over" (3), and Tarrou has an intimate conversation with Rieux when swimming. The shared confidences and "unburden-[ings]" (81) of emotion often occur after the characters witness scenes of great suffering, such as the death struggle of the magistrate's young son, and these confessions help students tell their own stories. Moreover, the characters, in struggling to communicate, realize the necessity of finding the right word and speaking the whole truth accurately, while recognizing the failure of words to express the fullness of thought and feeling. Grand—the clerk, Latin student, aspiring author, and husband "who couldn't find his words" —embodies both the need for and the frustrations of communication (45).

As the collection of essays edited by Stephen Kellman indicates, *The Plague* proves an excellent vehicle for developing students' ability to see beneath the surface. Camus himself invites interpretation with the epigraph from *Robinson Crusoe*: "[I]t is as reasonable to represent one kind of imprisonment by another as it is to represent anything which really exists by that which does not." The alert reader recognizes the theme of imprisonment running throughout the entire story, from the flat description of the ugly commercial town turned in on itself, to the literal facts of the disease and quarantine, to the use of the word *plague* to symbolize imprisonment in the human condition. The novel has a social or political level as well, including analogies to the French Resistance in World War II. Unlike war or imprisonment, however, the plague offers no human enemy. While different characters may accept or reject divine causation, the narrator suggests a universe indifferent to humankind.

During the first week of class, our physician-instructors

introduced the goals of the course by connecting the arts of writing, healing, and the humanities. After a brief lecture on the practical aspects of good writing skills for physicians, students were asked to complete a freewriting exercise in class. They were shown a slide of an infant hooked up to tubes and life-support systems and asked to describe what they saw and then to reflect on their response to the image. The prospective physicians differed from the liberal arts majors in the details they focused on and the vocabulary they used. Everyone, of course, sympathized with the child and its parents, but the group did not agree about whether the baby was a victim or a patient, whether the medical establishment was torturing or healing, or even whether the baby was a male or a female. These discrepancies, which surfaced as the students discussed their writings about the slide, convinced them that what individuals bring to any observation affects what and who they see. Students learned firsthand that they, like the writers in *The Plague* (Rieux, Tarrou, and Grand), impose their own points of view on what they see. Following this exercise, the physician-instructors commented on the difficulty of maintaining the objective, "scientific" gaze fostered in medical training; the importance of being aware of one's own biases and assumptions; and the importance of empathy in the medical encounter. Reading good fiction, these medical instructors claim, develops and sustains empathy.

In unit 1, "Self and Other," students reflected on who we are, how we are perceived, and how we perceive those around us. Students began reading *The Plague*, becoming acquainted with the major characters in parts 1 and 2. Shorter texts were assigned as well. To suggest how new discoveries and technologies are changing old ideas about "being human," we assigned the introduction to *The Mind's I*, which concerns an astronaut who can return to earth only in a cloned form (Hofstadter). Our internist-instructor lectured on brain physiology; consciousness; and the elusive notions of self, soul, and spirit and then asked the students to freewrite about their definition of the word *I*. Students also read Eudora Welty's story "A Worn Path," in which an elderly black woman prevails over rugged terrain, wild animals, and insensitive people on a journey from the country to the city to get medicine for her grandchild. Students noted in their logs and class discussion the discrepancy between the woman's courage, cunning, and dignity and the labeling of her as poor, old, 'stupid, and greedy—"a charity case"—by those she encountered (361). We pointed out that Camus too, in part 1 of *The Plague*, introduced the major characters primarily by appearance or labels: for example, name, profession, disease. One must read further to appreciate the fullness of the humanity of these characters.

Students were asked in the initial prompt for their reading logs about *The Plague* to cite a descriptive passage that they found meaningful and to discuss the images, memories, or ideas it evoked. Several students chose the passage in which Dr. Rieux acknowledges *plague* as a word and a fact; they reflected on whether the author intended to emphasize Rieux's feelings of helplessness and despair or his heroism in "pull[ing] himself together" (41). Others selected the detailed description at the beginning of the book of the ugly commercial town facing away from the sea or the scene of the rats pouring out from the sewers onto the street. Class discussion of log entries led students to consider the major themes of the novel and the course: confronting feelings, triumphing over despair, examining priorities, and enduring imprisonment. Instructors were able to show students how descriptions create mood and meaning through diction, selection of detail, and the juxtaposition of the documentary and the poetical.

In the first formal essay, students were asked to relate the readings to their personal experiences, either by describing a situation in which they felt like a character in "A Worn Path" or *The Plague* or by connecting ideas presented in *The Mind's I* to an experience that could not be fully explained in scientific terms. As students worked alone and in groups to brainstorm, draft, review, and revise, they learned more about themselves, one another, and the course materials. Almost every minority student had had a bitter experience of alienation or rejection, but so had the student who flunked engineering school and the religious woman who refrained from premarital sex. Some wrote about the different masks they wear and the inner conflicts they often feel that make them aware of deeper parts of themselves. Before completing their final drafts, students watched videotaped excerpts from *Nostradamus* and *The Band Played On* in which characters, limited by their own interests and assumptions, deny their vulnerability to some common danger. Students wrote entries in their logs comparing these scenes with similar passages in *The Plague,* in which Oran's leaders deny the reality of the epidemic.

This exercise led directly to our second unit, "Communities in Crisis: Positioning Ourselves in Relation to Others." Camus himself related the plague to the man-made catastrophe that was World War II, but he also observed that "*The Plague* can apply to any resistance against tyranny" (*Essays* 40). As students progressed further into the novel, they were encouraged to relate the fictional events in Oran to problems that plague our society. They were assigned various texts that analyze crime as a disease, including Malcolm Gladwell's article "The Tipping Point" and Tillie Olsen's short story "I Stand Here Ironing." Like the quarantine officials in *The Plague,* the "experts" in Olsen's story are pitted against the sufferers. For a guest lecture, we organized a panel of AIDS patients, insurers, and health-care providers whose discussion suggested the complexity of balancing community resources, the needs of patients, and the lives of health professionals—topics that are also debated by the officials, doctors, and volunteers in *The Plague.*

For this unit, students were required to research a particular social crisis and write an essay, with documentation, in which they reported the response of individuals and groups to a common danger. We suggested topics directly related to those in *The Plague,* such as public health issues, examples of social crises from the history of medicine, and Algerian healing practices, but we did not limit students' choices. Several students researched issues in which they were personally involved. One student, whose church condemns homosexuality, constructed a detailed survey about the clergy's attitudes toward parishioners dying from AIDS. She administered the survey by telephone to thirty religious leaders in Kansas City, discovering that the majority sympathized with the sufferers but still considered them sinners condemned to eternal damnation. Using journal articles, scientific reports, and newspapers, she traced this attitude in recent religious history and popular culture. She also included her opinion of its cruelty, based on her personal experience as both the daughter of a fundamentalist minister and the friend of a homosexual. Some students found that the collapse of the Hyatt Regency walkway in Kansas City and the Oklahoma City bombing inspired the kind of solidarity and determination Camus describes in *The Plague*. One student examined a crisis that produced negative effects: the Rodney King beating trial. Using media reports, books and articles on the history of race relations, and telephone interviews with relatives who live in Los Angeles, he argued that the riots following the verdict left the city more racially divided than it was before. The reason, he concluded, was that a few chose to benefit from the chaos — as Cottard and other profiteers do in *The Plague*.

Unit 3 emphasized ideas about free will and moral choice. Having completed *The Plague*, students could examine the lives of the individual characters, analyzing the limits, opportunities, and decisions which led up to their life situations. This discussion seemed to us to exemplify Robert Coles's description of literature as "moral inquiry of the wide-ranging kind" (446). Because Camus's characters reveal themselves more fully as they move toward death, we know why they chose their careers, what they value most, where they feel they have failed, what their certainties and doubts are, and what they think awaits them in life and in death. Most important, we see characters respond to the plague and to their common struggle in idiosyncratic ways.

Through outside readings and writing assignments in their logs, students had the opportunity to relate fictional dilemmas and moral inquiries to their own lives. Richard Selzer's "Toenails," a story in which a physician cuts the toenails of indigent patients he meets in a local library, helped students examine career choices. Selections from *Man's Search for Meaning*, Victor Frankl's account of his attempts to keep himself and others alive in a Nazi concentration camp, provoked students to speculate on their own responses to the threat of imminent death. Michel Foucault's "The Eye of Power" led to considerations of how the panoptic structure of hospitals and prisons can promote either healing or terror. Selzer's "Tube Feeding" and "A Question of Mercy" prompted reflection on euthanasia and helped students deal with issues in *The Plague:* Cottard's attempted suicide, Tarrou's intense aversion to capital punishment, Father Paneloux's decision not to seek medical help, and Rieux's attempts to preserve life.

For the third formal essay, students were asked to argue a position about living a moral life, using as evidence *The Plague,* one other reading, and their own experience. We posed such questions as, Who is changed most by the experience of the plague? Who is most heroic and why? What does your reading and experience so far suggest about free will or the moral nature of human beings? Most students argued that Rieux is the hero of the novel. Several claimed that Rambert displays the most heroism because his choice to remain in Oran and fight the plague is so contrary to his initial desire to flee to his lover in Paris. Others maintained that Othon's turnabout from stern magistrate, husband, and father to empathetic servant encapsulates the reversal from abstraction to acknowledgment of feeling that is experienced by all the characters, especially the doctor.

The fourth unit concerned creativity, which we defined not only as producing works of art but also as solving old problems in new ways, or working with others to build on what came before. For the final assignment, students could either write a creative essay or complete a creative project. As an in-class exercise, we asked them to write about whether they saw themselves as makers or appreciators, artists or problem solvers and to demonstrate, if possible, a product or action they were particularly proud of. Our tense and grade-conscious students came alive as they exhibited extracurricular interests such as scat singing, rebuilding junk cars, and inventing ingenious contraptions.

While these in-class activities were occurring, students were working on their creative essays and projects. Some wrote papers that defamiliarized the familiar: one student wrote about the plague from an Algerian woman's perspective, another, about a soccer game from a benchwarmer's point of view. But most chose to complete a project, which they were required to comment on in an essay. One student videotaped a class engaged in a role-playing exercise in which medical colleagues must decide whether they are willing to work with a partner who has AIDS. Another student created a poster to educate young adults about STDs, using pictures from a microbiology textbook blown up to terrifying size. We felt that projects were appropriate to a writing course because in the process of completing them, students were replicating activities required in writing. Students selected a topic or theme, investigated the facts about it (if necessary), chose a form for conveying it to a targeted audience, wrote text and picked visuals appropriate to the form, and then organized the materials in such a way as to interest, inform, and persuade readers or viewers. As we were going through peer reviews and revision, we were able to compare steps and missteps in students' creative processes with Camus's accounts in his journal of the process of writing *The Plague (Essays)*.

In this course, writing functioned as a bridge connecting reading assignments to lecture materials, class discussions to personal experiences, and personal experiences to course materials. Moreover, discussing students' writings in class encouraged students to step back from themselves and to realize not only that they are passively shaped by their day-to-day learning but also that they can actively participate in expanding or countering one another's interpretations of reality. These activities are crucial to becoming empathetic human beings as well as good physicians.

Course Readings

Camus, *The Plague*
Hofstadter, Introduction, *The Mind's I*
Welty, "A Worn Path"
Gladwell, "The Tipping Point"
Olsen, "I Stand Here Ironing"
Selzer, "Toenails," "Tube Feeding," "A Question of Mercy"
Frankl, *Man's Search for Meaning*
Foucault, "The Eye of Power"

Works Cited

Bazerman, Charles. "From Cultural Criticism to Disciplinary Participation: Living with Powerful Words." *Writing, Teaching, and Learning in the*

Disciplines. Ed. Anne Herrington and Charles Moran. New York: MLA, 1992. 61–68.

Camus, Albert. *Lyrical and Critical Essays.* Trans. Ellen Conroy Kennedy. Ed. Philip Thody. New York: Knopf, 1968.

———. *The Plague.* Trans. Stuart Gilbert. Vintage Intl. ed. New York: Vintage, 1991.

Coles, Robert. "Occasional Notes: Medical Ethics and Living a Life." *New England Journal of Medicine* 301 (1979): 444–46.

Foucault, Michel. "The Eye of Power." *Power/Knowledge: Selected Interviews and Other Writings.* Ed. Colin Gordon. Trans. Leo Marshall. New York: Pantheon, 1980. 146–65.

Frankl, Victor. *Man's Search for Meaning: An Introduction to Logotherapy.* New York: Pocket, 1963.

Gladwell, Malcolm. "The Tipping Point." *New Yorker* 3 June 1996: 32–38.

Hofstadter, Douglas R. Introduction. *The Mind's I: Fantasies and Reflections on Self and Soul.* Ed. Hofstadter and Daniel Dennet. New York: Basic, 1981. 1–15.

Kellman, Steven G., ed. *Approaches to Teaching Camus's* The Plague. New York: MLA, 1985.

Olsen, Tillie. "I Stand Here Ironing." *"Tell Me a Riddle" and Other Stories.* New York: Bantam, 1956. 1–12.

Selzer, Richard. "A Question of Mercy." *New York Times Sunday Magazine* 2 Sept. 1991: 32–36.

———. "Toenails." *Letters to a Young Doctor.* New York: Simon, 1982. 64–66.

———. "Tube Feeding." *Confessions of a Knife.* New York: Simon, 1979. 159–66.

Welty, Eudora. "A Worn Path." *"A Curtain of Green" and Other Stories.* New York: Harcourt, 1941. 357–63.

Elizabeth M. Willingham

Light to the Mind: Literature in the Medical Spanish Course

Language is more to the mind than light to the eyes.
Annie Sullivan, teacher

By incorporating literary and scientific readings into the medical Spanish class for undergraduates with a premedical concentration at Baylor University, we have created an increasingly vigorous and rewarding cap course for specialized foreign language study. We have expanded the range of materials to include authentic, unedited texts and have moved away from the standard vocabulary lists and pedagogical dialogues that are the norm in specialized language classes in business, premedicine, communications, and so on. To meet reading and writing requirements and oral proficiency standards for courses at this level, we incorporate literary and scientific readings that relate to the interests of premedical students and whose quality meets the expectations of competitive foreign language departments. This mixture of literary and expository prose challenges students to improve language skills in a context in which they are continually exposed to elements of culture and in which they read, write, perform, and discuss the kinds of issues they will one day confront when they apply science to human life.[1]

Many students who take the course already appreciate the value

151

of understanding Hispanic culture and the Spanish language as these relate to medical practice. About half the students have concurrent or previous experience in medical settings as volunteers in local emergency rooms or as paid hospital and clinic staff, and they are motivated to make the most of the classroom experience. Because oral translation is used in hospital and clinic situations, students practice explaining medical conditions and instructions accurately and sensitively. Reading both literature and science presents students with more vocabulary and a greater range of expression than do other pedagogical materials. The understanding students gain of fictional characters can facilitate their relationships with patients and patients' families, helping the students to see other viewpoints sympathetically and to avoid cultural blunders. Intensive and extensive practice based on the readings produces increased confidence in translation and in real-world interactions with Spanish speakers.

To improve students' vocabulary, grammar skills, and cultural understanding, the literary texts must have medical content and cultural value and must also fit one of the units of study. These units currently include such topics as mental health and substance abuse; sexually transmitted diseases; family planning, pregnancy, and birth; and aging, death, and dying. In addition to literature, students read periodical articles, essays, pamphlets, and material found on relevant internet sites. Students write synopses of all readings in their notebooks to prepare for class discussion and essay writing. This exercise gives students immediate feedback about whether their command of vocabulary and syntax is adequate to explain material or defend a position. A student can remedy any perceived gap with additional reading and use of the dictionary. Groups of students also write and perform skits using the scientific content and clinical vocabulary. These skits may incorporate literature, but must include reflections on culture. In addition to these exercises, students take notes, write short-answer essays on quizzes and exams, and submit papers related to the readings. Careful reading and well-constructed synopses are engines on which subsequent work runs or stalls.

Students perform best when the material and ideas they work with are at the same level as those they encounter in other classes.

Unedited, unglossed literary readings give the students linguistic information and foster high-level proficiency. Reading literature, producing skits, and role-playing show students that understanding and responding to people sincerely is a part of successful medicine. The complex of language and culture recorded in literature gives students the raw material with which to create authentic relationships with Hispanic patients.

Choosing the readings to foster the visionary goals of the course —as well as its objectively measurable ones—is a challenge because many good texts are available. The current selection includes Miguel de Cervantes's *Don Quixote de la Mancha*; Carlos Fuentes's *La muerte de Artemio Cruz (The Death of Artemio Cruz)*; Laura Esquivel's *Como agua para chocolate (Like Water for Chocolate)* and *La ley del amor (The Law of Love)*, and Gabriel García Márquez's *Crónica de una muerte anunciada (Chronicle of a Death Foretold)*. We use a short story, also by García Márquez, "Un día de estos" ("One of These Days"), and poetry by Federico García Lorca and Amado Nervo. In some semesters, various texts are omitted because of time constraints. In each literary reading, students focus on reader response and point of view in addition to plot, character, and culture. Students must learn to strike a balance between close reading—in this case, picking up key information about character and motivation from setting, description, and dialogue—and resisting the urge to consult the dictionary until they have exhausted their existent language skills. Students use context clues and grammatical knowledge to read—and reread—for understanding until they can run through the text without translating.

We begin with García Márquez's short story "Un día de estos." Its subject, brevity, and limited complexity make it an excellent place to start. The students' first task is to determine as much as possible about the two characters—the dentist and the mayor—and to decide how we know this or why we think that about them. Students focus on details that reveal information about each character's attitude and values, using the language of the text to work toward understanding the characters and their culture from the inside. In the synopses students write, they respond to questions about character:

With whom or with what is the character in conflict? Has he or she suffered a loss? Does the character feel misunderstood? If so, in what way? What noun or verb is most descriptive of the character's desires and goals? What adjectives best describe the character? Every conclusion must be supported by the text and must answer another question: How do you know? Thus students explore various aspects of the text and begin organizing and expressing their ideas for discussion and essay writing even before the class meets.

"Un día de estos" tells of a brief encounter between an unlicensed dentist named Don Aurelio Escovar and a brutal and powerful village *alcalde* ("mayor"). The proverbial "one of these days" arrives when the mayor, suffering from an abscessed molar, seeks the dentist's help; for a few minutes the dentist assumes a position of power. When the mayor shows up early at the dentist's house-cum-office, the dentist's eleven-year-old son shouts the mayor's request through the walls. The dentist tells the boy to say that he is not in, and continues polishing another patient's gold tooth. Of course the mayor hears the exchange, and the boy reports the fact to his father. This time the dentist does not reply until he has finished his polishing, and his response is simply, "mejor" 'very well' or 'so much the better.'[2] The boy shouts back that the mayor will shoot the dentist unless the dentist pulls his tooth, and the dentist, casually interrupting his polishing to open the drawer where he keeps a revolver, responds, "Bueno. . . . Dile que venga a pegármelo" 'Good. . . . Tell him to come on and shoot me' (24). The dentist seems to toy with the prospect of his own death and with the mayor's capacity for violence, but he is deliberate and his risk is calculated: the mayor needs him, and the dentist has a revolver at hand.

The tension in the story arises from the two portrayals of machismo: one represented by the mayor, swaggering and ready with threats and—so we imagine—backed by hardware and bodyguards; the other represented by the dentist, whose professional routines and ordinary dignity give him a cool boldness and restrained compassion.[3] The dentist notices the "noches de desesperación" 'nights of desperation' in the eyes of the mayor and silently observes that the right cheek, "hinchada y dolorosa" 'swollen and painful,' has a five-days' beard while the other is clean-shaven. The dentist's methodical preparation for the extraction—which is to be done without anesthesia—fuels the tension: "Llevó a la mesa de trabajo la cacerola con los instrumentos hervidos y los sacó del agua con unas pinzas frías, todavía sin apresurarse" 'He carried the bowl with the boiled instruments to the work table and removed them from the water with some cold forceps, still without rushing himself.' Later, "El dentista abrió las piernas y apretó la muela con el gatillo caliente [. . .]" 'The dentist opened the hot pliers and grasped the molar [. . .].' The mayor has a death grip on the dental chair at this point—and the reader is probably with him. A small, climactic moment follows: "El dentista sólo movió la muñeca" 'There was only a slight movement of the dentist's wrist' (25). Bones crunch, tears flow, the mayor perspires profusely, and the molar that caused five nights of torture is out.

None of the chilling outcomes the reader might have predicted comes to pass. The dentist offers the mayor a clean rag to dry his tears and recommends rest and saltwater lavages. As the mayor leaves, the dentist asks whether to send the bill to the mayor or to the town. The trembling mayor, neglecting to button up his soldier's jacket, calls back through the grillwork, "Es la misma vaina" 'It's the same thing' (26). The story is ironic and painful and full of humanity. The mayor needs the dentist, and, though the dentist has a small run of jokes at the mayor's expense, the dentist understands the mayor's pain and offers him relief. The dentist is cavalier when threatened with death. His behavior, however, is based on a correct calculation of his worth to the "town" (i.e., the mayor): the mayor cannot harm the dentist as long as the mayor has teeth. In a final twist, the dentist will get payment from the "town" for mitigating the pain of someone who has caused its citizens much suffering in the past.

Readings from Laura Esquivel's *Como agua para chocolate* and *La ley del amor* focus on the lives of two women, Tita and Citali, respectively. In Esquivel's work nothing is routine except the unexpected: twists of fate are a staple and events are mystical and magical. Esquivel's protagonists struggle to form their own destinies by the force of a passionate will. Their stories provide readings on birth, death, depression, and insomnia—among other things. The present discussion, however, is limited to the birth scenes from each novel. *Como agua para chocolate* opens with the precipitous and magical birth of Tita on the kitchen table. Tita arrives in a torrent of tears provoked by Mamá Elena's cutting of onions. When the child's father dies two days later, Mamá Elena's milk dries up, and Tita must be nourished in the kitchen by mixtures that Nacha, the family cook, prepares for her. The ironies of Tita's birth come full circle in Tita's mystical delivery of her sister's baby and in Tita's subsequent nursing of the child when her sister cannot.

In *La ley del amor*, compelling events frame the novel's first chapter. This reading is an excellent choice to illustrate point of view because its three characters—Citali, Rodrigo, and Isabel—form a closed triangle, and none of the three has a shred of understanding of the other two.[4] Their passion, fear, honor, and desire for vengeance maintain the tension of the triangle. The narrative voice explains that the three characters are separated utterly by their points of view—there can be no "encuentro" 'meeting' of their desires, goals, or personalities (7) because they come from different experiences (8). Citali, an Aztec princess, delivers her son in the midst of the fall of Tenochtitlan, and the child is immediately smashed against the stones by Rodrigo Diaz, a Spanish *capitán*. For his valor in battle, Rodrigo is allowed to destroy the Aztec pyramid to the goddess of love so that he can establish himself and his progeny on the site. Citali is enslaved and repeatedly raped by Rodrigo, who is drawn to Citali by an irresistible force—the Aztec goddess of love whose pyramid he has violated. Citali takes her vengeance on Rodrigo and his Spanish race by aborting the children he impregnates her with, one after the other. Citali's final act is to kill Rodrigo's newborn son by Isabel, Rodrigo's Spanish wife. In this world, there is an ironic perception of violence: rape is matter-of-fact, abortion is a means of preserving honor, and death is a welcome sacrifice. Love and hate are inextricable forces in Esquivel's vividly imagined post-conquest world; Esquivel presents the reader with opposed experiences dramatically juxtaposed in the same narrow temporal and geo-graphical dimensions.

Students leave Esquivel's electric accounts of depression, passion, and vengeance to take up the same issues in the stately and ironic prose of Cervantes's *Don Quixote de la Mancha*. Because of the novel's length, we limit our reading largely to the first eight chapters. These include Don Quixote's preparations and first, failed, effort to become a knight errant; the episode of the master beating his servant; the burning of Don Quixote's books in an effort to cure him; and Don Quixote's second, successful, attempt at knight errantry.

Don Quixote's delusions are grandiose, and his whole life is governed by his obsession. His little family—a housekeeper, teen-aged niece, and young laborer—eat well but simply, and Don Quixote has begun selling off his lands, his only source of income, to buy books. This fact tells us not only about the price of books in seventeenth-century Spain but also about the extent of Don Quixote's disorder: we are only mildly surprised when he mistakes an inn for a castle and, later, windmills for giants. The arguments Don Quixote uses to persuade Sancho to join him are logical, even though they are built on delusions of grandeur. Don Quixote promises Sancho an island to govern and great wealth, as spoils of Quixote's knight errantry, and Sancho, one of Spain's overtaxed poor and a practical materialist by necessity, is sufficiently tempted by the promise of wealth to overlook the improbability of Don Quixote's story. Don Quixote's great dignity, ludicrous imaginings, and real injuries elicit laughter as well as respect and sympathy from the reader. In Don Quixote students see the deluded idealist with his mind on "what ifs," and in Sancho, the hungry common man looking for the next McDonald's. It is Don Quixote's inability to separate the fictions of his life from life's realities that causes him and those around him consternation and suffering—a good lesson for any of us likely to be misled by alluring fictions and obsessions in our professional lives.

For the topic of death and dying, the choices of literary readings are especially strong. We read several lyric poems by the Spanish poet Federico García Lorca, including "Canción de jinete" (Song of the Horseman) and "Malagueña," lingering over García Lorca's gypsy-guitar rhythms and vivid images of southern Spain. If time permits we read three of Amado Nervo's poems about the death of his young wife, "Me besaba mucho," "Impaciencia," and "Dilema." We also read the final chapter of *Don Quixote*, where the old dreamer, finding death unexpectedly at his bedside, regains his sanity, renounces his obsessions, offers advice to Sancho, and dies as Alonso Quijano the Good. Students then return to modern themes presented in modern formats: García Márquez's *Crónica de una muerte anunciada* and Fuentes's *La muerte de Artemio Cruz*, texts that set a dispassionate rendering of the clinical event of death against the desperate emotions experienced by the characters involved.

Crónica de una muerte anunciada is deeply involved with the culture of the coastal Colombian village of the 1960s in which the story is set. Its themes of honor, fate, religiosity, village secrets, and tangled relationships are all compressed into a retrospective, first-person account of the slaughter of Santiago Nasar by two brothers who had sworn to kill him for deflowering their sister. Nearly everyone in the village is aware of the impending murder, and the irony is that no one and nothing stops it. Fate, complacency, plans gone awry, judgment weakened by the fatigue of an extended wedding celebration—all may be to blame. But Nasar, who is young, rich, handsome, popular (and possibly innocent), dies despite all the reasons that he should have lived. The fictional voices flow as in a documentary in which camera and interviewer return to the scene of a crime: one aging face after another fills the screen, speaking to us of personal confusion and the search for an answer.

In contrast to *Crónica de una muerte anunciada*, the final reading, *La muerte de Artemio Cruz*, is unified by the presence of a single narrator. Its style is rigorously economical and occasionally fragmentary but at the same time dense and expansive: a stream of consciousness combining present sensory impressions with recollections of the past and reflecting the common belief that one's life passes before one's eyes in the moments before death. Fuentes makes his protagonist a symbol of Mexico and of a corrupted nation in search of itself.[5] Artemio Cruz seeks his true identity among the shadows and mirrors of his past. While medical caregivers see only the dying old man, the reader perceives what life has been for Artemio Cruz and what he has been in life: "the bastard child of a raped mulatto servant and her *patrón*"; the opportunistic soldier who kidnaps—then loves—the woman he desires; the traitorous comrade and, paradoxically, a hero of the revolution; the calculating suitor of Catalina, sister to the man he betrays and heiress to her father's fortune; and, finally, the voracious capitalist, exploiting Mexico's resources and people.[6] Returning to the present, Artemio registers the events occurring within and around his dying body and makes futile attempts to be understood; abandoning the effort, he drifts inward again and again to search through memory for self.

It is satisfying for students to unravel Artemio's life from the fragments presented and to find themselves sympathizing with such an unlovable character. The reader discovers what the decay of the mortal body obscures: the mind's effort to relive the passions and errors of a lifetime and to reconcile them, together with the present impressions of medical procedures, pain, odors, tastes, and sounds in the hospital room. Students leave *Artemio Cruz* having encountered death in its cultural, emotional, and clinical aspects.

Reading such works of literature creates lasting impressions of situations, histories, characters, and cultures that may be different from one's own. Even if students allow their Spanish to grow rusty, images from the readings are likely to endure. The specific aim of this course is to acquaint students with Spanish language and literature and with the cultures of Spanish-speaking peoples, but a further aim is to enable students to serve their patients with confidence and compassion in that "rag-and-bone-shop" (to borrow a phrase from Yeats) where pain, fear, and death must be confronted. I trust that as physicians my students will be able to mitigate these burdens for their patients, partly because they carry the light of Cervantes's language in their minds and his dignity and comedy in their hearts.

Course Readings

Week 1   Web resources; Herrera McElroy and Grabb, *Medical Dictionary*, review uses and parts of medical dictionary and practice pronunciation and vocabulary

Week 2   Herrera McElroy and Grabb, *Medical Dictionary*, practice pronunciation and vocabulary; Cervantes, *Don Quixote*

Week 3   Herrera McElroy and Grabb, *Medical Dictionary*, practice pronunciation and vocabulary; presentation 1; García Márquez, "Un día de estos," synopses, characters, setting, narratological questions

Week 4   Herrera McElroy and Grabb, *Medical Dictionary*, practice pronunciation and vocabulary; García Márquez, *Crónica de una muerte anunciada*, chapter 1, synopses, characters, setting, narratological questions

Week 5   Herrera McElroy and Grabb, *Medical Dictionary*, practice pronunciation and vocabulary; García Márquez, *Crónica de una muerte anunciada*, chapter 2

Week 6   Herrera McElroy and Grabb, *Medical Dictionary*, practice pronunciation and vocabulary; García Márquez, *Crónica de una muerte anunciada*, chapters 3 and 4

Week 7   Herrera McElroy and Grabb, *Medical Dictionary*, practice pronunciation and vocabulary; García Márquez, *Crónica de una muerte anunciada*, chapter 4

Week 8   Herrera McElroy and Grabb, *Medical Dictionary*, practice pronunciation and vocabulary; García Márquez, *Crónica de una muerte anunciada*, chapter 5

Week 9   Exam; Herrera McElroy and Grabb, *Medical Dictionary*, practice pronunciation and vocabulary; Fuentes, *La muerte de Artemio Cruz*

Week 10 Herrera McElroy and Grabb, *Medical Dictionary*, practice pronunciation and vocabulary; Fuentes, *La muerte de Artemio Cruz*; exam 2: readings, presentations; poetry

Week 11 Herrera McElroy and Grabb, *Medical Dictionary*, practice pronunciation and vocabulary; poetry; Esquivel, *Como agua para chocolate*, chapter "enero"

Week 12 Esquivel, *Como agua para chocolate*, chapters "febrero," "marzo," "abril"

Week 13 Esquivel, *Como agua para chocolate*, chapters "junio," "julio"

Week 14 Esquivel, *Como agua para chocolate*, chapter "agosto"

Week 15 Esquivel, *Como agua para chocolate*, chapters "septiembre," "octubre," "noviembre"

Week 16 Esquivel, *Como agua para chocolate,* chapter "diciembre"; final
exam: oral and written presentation; final interview

Notes

1. Betsy Keller addresses the question of how to read second-language literature in a language-learning class. She emphasizes the efficacy of using the student's knowledge and experience to explore the text and of assigning specific tasks that get the student involved with the literature. Keller cites a number of articles on this subject.
2. All translations are my own.
3. For a commentary on Spanish machismo, see Ramón Sender, especially where he refers to his protagonist as "the kind of Spaniard to whom dignity is a kind of a religion" (9). I take this description to fit an authentic — that is, earned or deserved — portrayal of machismo. The false sort of machismo is seen in characters who are drunks, tyrants, and wife beaters and is more often found in Latin American fiction, for example, in the character of Artemio Cruz, than in peninsular fiction. The fiction of Emilia Pardo Bazán is the exception.
4. The anthropologist René Girard's theory of triangular rivalries and his explanations of mediated desire and sacrifice as components of fiction have been applied to Spanish fiction (specifically to *Don Quixote*) by Girard and Andrist.
5. We make no attempt to teach literary criticism or theory in a second-language course at this level, but critics and theorists provide insights and approaches that are useful in teaching. See, for example, Georg Lukács on Balzac and Tolstoy (213–14). Lukács's awareness of time and place and of the novelist's role parallels that of Fuentes in *Artemio Cruz.* See also Julia Kristeva, whose theoretical framework, informed by Marxist and Hegelian dialectics, can shed light on the development of narrative and character in *Artemio Cruz.*
6. For other, similar characterizations of Artemio Cruz, see Gyurko (64); and Parmies and Berg (68). Tzvetan Todorov's remarks on narrative voice and point of view seem particularly applicable to Fuentes's novel.

Works Cited

Andrist, Debra D. *Deceit plus Desire Equals Violence: A Girardian Study of the Spanish "Comedia."* New York: Lang, 1989.

Cervantes Saavedra, Miguel de. *El ingenioso hidalgo don Quixote de la Mancha.* Madrid: Calleja, 1917.

Esquivel, Laura. *Como agua para chocolate.* New York: Doubleday, 1992.

———. *La ley del amor.* New York: Crown, 1996.

Fuentes, Carlos. *La muerte de Artemio Cruz.* México: Fondo de Cultura Económica, 1962.

García Lorca, Federico. "Canción de jinete." García Lorca, *Selected Verse* 140–42.

————. "Malagueña." García Lorca, *Selected Verse* 46–47.

————. *Selected Verse*. Ed. Christopher Maurer. New York: Farrar, 1994.

García Márquez, Gabriel. *Crónica de una muerte anunciada*. Bogóta: Oveja Negra, 1981.

————. "Un día de estos." *Los funerales de la Mamá Grande*. Buenos Aires: Sudamericana, 1974. 21–26.

Girard, René. *Deceit, Desire, and the Novel*. Trans. Yvonne Freccero. Baltimore: Johns Hopkins UP, 1978.

Gyurko, Lanin A. "*La muerte de Artemio Cruz* and *Citizen Kane:* A Comparative Analysis." *Carlos Fuentes*. Ed. Robert Brody and Charles Rossman. Austin: U of Texas P, 1982. 64–94.

Herrera McElroy, Onyria, and Lola L. Grabb. *Spanish-English English-Spanish Medical Dictionary / Diccionario Médico Español-Inglés Inglés-Español*. 2nd ed. Boston: Little, 1996.

Hoffman, Michael, and Patrick Murphy, eds. *Essentials of the Theory of Fiction*. Durham: Duke UP, 1995.

Keller, Betsy. "Rereading Flaubert: Toward a Dialogue between First- and Second-Language Literature Teaching Practices." *PMLA* 112 (1997): 56–68.

Kristeva, Julia. *Desire in Language: A Semiotic Approach to Literature and Art*. Ed. Leon S. Roudiez. Trans. Thomas Gora, Alice Jardine, and Roudiez. New York: Columbia UP, 1980.

Lukács, Georg. "Marxist Aesthetics and Literary Realism." Hoffman and Murphy 203–17.

Nervo, Amado. *La amada inmóvil*. México: Espasa-Calpe, 1968.

————. "Dilema." Nervo, *La amada* 115.

————. "Impaciencia." Nervo, *La amada* 115.

————. "Me besaba mucho." Nervo, *La amada* 71.

Parmies, Alberto N., and C. Dean Berg. *Carlos Fuentes y la dualidad integral mexicana*. Miami: Universal, 1969.

Sender, Ramón J. *Crónica del alba, I*. Barcelona: Destino, 1973.

Todorov, Tzvetan. "Reading as Construction." Hoffman and Murphy 403–18.

Carol Donley and Sheryl Buckley

The Tyranny of the Normal

In Greek legend, Procrustes placed all people who fell into his hands on an iron bed. If they were longer than the bed, he chopped off the overhanging parts; if they were shorter, he stretched them until they fit. The legend has become a metaphor for a tyrannical force-fitting of people to one standard. While the myth presents an absurd extreme, in everyday life we usually exert pressures to normalize those who are outside our culture's standards. We half believe fairy tales in which beasts become charming princes and ugly ducklings turn into swans. In fact we think the beasts and ugly ducklings *should* change. If we cannot somehow repair or transform abnormal people, we tend to cast them out because they disturb us deeply. We want our Rumplestiltskins to disappear, our Quasimodos to stay out of sight. Leviticus 21.23 orders that none of Aaron's descendants "who has a deformity shall draw near the veil or approach the altar [. . .] that he may not profane my sanctuaries." Some of our religious and cultural traditions tend to equate beauty with goodness and deformity with evil, appearing to justify rejection of those who aren't like us.

What's Normal? is a course we team-teach annually at Hiram College. It satisfies part of the general education requirements for interdisciplinary study, especially for students in the health-care humanities minor and in the medical humanities major. Several years' experience teaching the course led us to publish an anthology, *The Tyranny of the Normal*, which includes many of the readings on physical disabilities (and most of the readings referred to in this essay). Throughout the course we examine articles from health-care journals and bioethics texts as well as several works of drama, fiction, and poetry, all of which portray people whose physical and mental abnormalities make them disturbingly deviant from cultural norms.

Both of us have participated in a summer seminar on narrative bioethics that provided theoretical insights and practical pedagogical assistance, some of which we suggest in this essay. We are both in the classroom throughout the course, sharing lectures and jointly leading discussions as well as reacting to each other's ideas. Sheryl Buckley is a practicing physician who brings concrete clinical experience to our discussions. She teaches medical ethics in addition to this course. Carol Donley is a professor of English who also has a master's degree in bioethics. We have collaborated in teaching this course for several years.

The essay that serves as one theoretical base for the course and provides the title for the anthology is Leslie Fiedler's "The Tyranny of the Normal," originally published in a collection of essays addressing the question, Which babies shall live? Fiedler points out that our reaction to extremely abnormal people is to pity them and fear them and that we try to get rid of that fear by "normalizing" the others or by putting them out of sight. "What begins with a fear of difference eventuates in a tyranny of the Normal. [. . .] The grosser abnormalities [are] prevented, repaired, aborted or permitted to die at birth so that those of us allowed to survive by the official enforcers of the Norm will be free to become even more homogeneously, monotonously beautiful" (Donley and Buckley 9). We may know how technically to normalize others, but we have done little thinking about important ethical questions: Who decides what is normal? What should happen to those outside the norm? Who has the authority or right to make changes? Who has access to "miracle fixes" such as facial reconstructions and who does not? The class reads both clinical articles and literary works, and discusses how the tyranny of social norms affects not only the psyche of the abnormal person but also the attitudes and behaviors of the normal population toward those who are different.

Most norms are culturally specific: what is devalued in one culture might be honored in another. Anorexia, for instance, seems to be unknown in Third World countries that do not equate thinness with beauty. In many Third World countries, the image of a very thin woman conveys a negative message: people are malnourished because there is not enough food to go around. But in the United States, a land of plenty where food is abundant and women have choices, the cultural ideal can "afford" to be skinny. Other examples of culturally specific norms are ideas about the elderly, who may be honored and respected in one place and shunted aside in another, and beliefs about what parts of the body must be covered up.

Often the cultural pressures to normalize are psychologically reinforced through advertising and other media. In the United States, a cult of slimness and youth, announced on the covers of magazines and represented in movies and TV shows, drives people to desperate diets, exercise programs, cosmetics, and plastic surgery. Norms of female beauty lead women to seek breast implants and other enhancement surgeries. The medical profession seems to encourage this pressure to normalize: plastic surgeons cash in on their patients' anxiety about their appearance, pediatricians give growth hormones to children who are not as tall as their parents want them to be, and various other health-care professionals offer fixes for those who fall outside the norm. Fueled by stories and poems, class discussions on the ethical and social implications of these issues are very lively.

An important collection of articles that were originally published in the *Journal of Clinical Ethics* is included in *The Tyranny of the Normal*. These articles begin with Jonathan Sinclair Carey's essay "The Quasimodo Complex," in which Carey shows that deformed people read the extent of their abnormality not in mirrors but in the implicit and explicit reactions of other people. Like

Quasimodo, who finally understands how repulsive his body is when Esmeralda cannot look at him without expressing shock, severely deformed people learn that they will always be judged by how they look, even if those who look at them feel sympathy for the person inside. Perhaps one of the biggest hardships deformed people face is that normal people find them too ugly to accept and love. Why are we so repulsed and yet so curious about these others that we line up to look at them (in freak shows or, these days, in movies)? In "The Tyranny of the Normal" Fiedler writes that freaks, "who at first appear to represent what is most absolutely 'Other' (thus reassuring us who come to gape that we are 'Normal') are really a revelation of what in our deepest psyches we recognize as our Secret Self." We are somehow afraid of being too small or big or ugly or crazy or dumb and "in the depths of our unconscious (where the insecurities of childhood and adolescence never die) we are, forever, freaks to ourselves" (Donley and Buckley 7–8). We remember as children being confused and scared about our size, about our sexuality and sexual roles, about what distinguishes us from animals. Our children's stories are full of giants, tiny folk, people changing size, human beings transformed into beasts and vice versa, animals that talk like us — all kinds of ambiguous borders between normal and abnormal. Students enjoy recalling stories that particularly affected them and often make links between those archetypal children's stories and the feelings they confront as adults dealing with others.

The course makes use of clinical and ethical readings and fictional literature to generate discussion of several topics: abnormal physical appearance (including disfigurement, obesity and anorexia, and dwarfism), abnormal behavior (including madness and deviance), and abnormal mental ability (particularly the extremes of the mentally retarded and the extraordinarily gifted). We begin with Fiedler's and Carey's essays. Once we have grasped their theories, we read Bernard Pomerance's *The Elephant Man,* Nathaniel Hawthorne's "The Birthmark," a selection from Victor Hugo's *Hunchback of Notre Dame,* John Updike's "Journal of a Leper," and several poems about malformed children such as Marilyn Davis's "Song for My Son," and Miller Williams's "The Ones That Are Thrown Out."

We note that the "abnormal" characters in these works do not interpret how they look by gazing at themselves in mirrors (none of them resembles Narcissus); rather, as Carey would predict, they read the extent of their malformity in the reactions of other people, especially those who make an effort to be close to them. And we observe, following Fiedler's lead, that much of the caregivers' effort is focused on making the abnormal person more normal, though doing so is not always possible or even desirable. Fiedler worries about the loss of diversity and variety, and, indeed, this normalizing often seems to be done at great cost: Hawthorne's character loses her life; Updike's narrator, his artistic distinctiveness and much of his humanity.

On the topic of eating disorders, we read Mary Mahowald's "To Be or Not to Be a Woman: Anorexia Nervosa, Normative Gender Roles, and Feminism" and selections from Barbara McFarland and Tyeis Baker-Baumann's *Shame and Body Image* and Carol Tavris's *Mismeasure of Woman*. Several poems and stories describe the experience of eating disorders from the perspective of the persons suffering the problem, whether a teenager, as in Pamela Hadas's "Diary of an Anorexic" or Rennie Sparks's "Skanks," or an adult woman, as in Sharon Olds's "The Meal" and Monica Wood's "Disappearing." Men with eating disorders appear in Raymond Carver's story "Fat" and in Jack Coulehan's poem "The Six Hundred Pound Man." Students first respond to these works with surprise, then begin to develop a sympathetic understanding of the narrators' lack of control over their lives. Mahowald suggests that anorexics try to conform to a socially induced, unhealthy stereotype of thin as beautiful while rejecting the sexist connotations of being female. We discuss Mahowald's formulation and consider questions raised in class, such as why mature womanhood is so repulsive and terrifying to many anorexics. Then we look closely at the young teenagers in our readings, noting, for instance, that the girl narrating Hadas's "Diary of an Anorexic" claims, "I'm *king* of my body now" (emphasis added), and expresses disgust at the "tapioca" thighs of her mother (198).

The section on mental illness and dementia includes such clinical articles as Rebecca Dresser and Peter Whitehouse's "The Incompetent Patient on the Slippery Slope" and Thomas Szasz's "The Myth of Mental Illness." Szasz's controversial article claims that "when one speaks of mental illness, the norm from which deviation is measured is a *psychosocial and ethical* standard. Yet the remedy is sought in terms of *medical* measures" (Caplan et al. 112). For Szasz it is absurd to seek medical solutions to psychosocial and philosophical problems or to call someone mentally ill because that person does not conform to certain social or ethical norms. In another article, H. Tristram Engelhardt, Jr., points out that society often medicalizes behavior that does not fit the norms of that particular culture: for example, in the nineteenth century drapetomania was a disease that caused slaves to run away and masturbation a disease that caused blindness, loss of hearing, headaches, rickets, and numerous other maladies. The class examines this concept of socially constructed illness in several works, noting, for instance, how the doctor-husband in Charlotte Perkins Gilman's story "The Yellow Wallpaper" imposes a popular concept of female illness (neurasthenia) on his wife and then "treats" her for it with a "rest cure" that deprives her of all normal interactions. This story tends to make students angry but also makes them see that many of our current illnesses are value-laden explanatory models of deviations that have no more objective reality than did drapetomania.

Discussion of mental retardation begins with a focus on several cases that address sterilizing retarded (or supposedly retarded) children (Levine). Again students note how strongly social context affects both the definitions of the "abnormalities" and the appropriate ways to treat them. Eugenics is, after all, a way of normalizing a population and includes determining who should survive and reproduce. Discussion also focuses on the tremendous burden the mentally retarded place on their caregivers. Marriages may break up, as happens in Peter Nichols's play *Joe Egg*, in which the father is so burdened that he tries to kill his severely retarded child. In Steinbeck's *Of Mice and Men*, murder (or, to be euphemistic, euthanasia) resolves the caregiving problem. Questions raised in class concern what options caregivers have when the burden of caring for the mentally disabled is overwhelming. Usually, students feel a sense of injustice, believing that society does not take its fair share of responsibility and, instead, leaves the disabled and their caregivers to fend for themselves.

The interdisciplinary nature of the course is based on two main theoretical foundations: medical ethics and narrative. They have a complementary working relation in narrative ethics, which begins with the patient's story in context and then incorporates principles when they fit the particular story. Case-based reasoning, care ethics, narrative ethics, and some feminist ethics all take this inductive approach rather than restricting themselves to the traditional deductive, principle-based method familiar to bioethics.

For example, if we were to use a strictly principle-based approach to *The Elephant Man*, we would describe conflicts between the patient's autonomy and the physician's and hospital's commitment to beneficence and nonmaleficence. These abstract principles often appear in descriptions of doctor-patient relationships. In this case, Dr. Treves's paternalism, however well-meaning, denies the patient, Merrick, his autonomy. Principles of justice are compromised when Merrick is used as a means to raise money and gain fame (first by the freak-show manager and then by the hospital administration and the doctor).

Instead of considering only such conflicting principles, however, narrative ethics focuses on the concrete particulars of Merrick's story, including his perspective; on the differing voices of other tellers of his story; and on the different audiences to whom the story is told. It is instructive to listen to the various versions of the story. Dr. Treves, as he lectures to a medical audience, gives a detailed, objective description of Merrick's physical abnormalities, as if the case history adequately "captures" Merrick:

> The most striking feature about him was his enormous head. [. . .] From the brow there projected a huge bony mass like a loaf. [. . .] From the upper jaw there protruded another mass of bone. It protruded from the mouth like a

pink stump, turning the upper lip inside out, and making the mouth a wide slobbering aperture. (5)

This detached medical case description is ironically reversed by Merrick's powerful parodic description of Dr. Treves's "condition," given near the end of the play to an imaginary audience:

The most striking feature about him, note, is the terrifyingly normal head. [. . .] From the brow projected a normal vision of benevolent enlightenment, what we believe to be a kind of self-mesmerized state. The mouth, deformed by satisfaction at being at the hub of the best of existent worlds, was rendered therefore utterly incapable of self-critical speech, thus of the ability to change. (61)

These contrasting narratives comment on each other in such a way that the reader or theatergoer rehears the first account when the second is voiced. Differing values and ways of seeing are juxtaposed until the ironies become excruciating. The narrative structure of *The Elephant Man* continually balances one story against another; an interpretation always receives at least one countering interpretation and sometimes several. By listening to and evaluating these contradictory voices and by appreciating the ambiguities, the reader comes to a richer, thicker description of the case and the several people involved.

Often narratives are in the voice of the "abnormal" person, as in Updike's "Journal of a Leper," allowing the reader at least temporarily to experience the "other's" perspective. Sometimes the narrator is a parent or friend or caregiver who looks at the "other" from the outside but from a certain biased perspective. We study different narrators and their often contradictory versions of what is going on, noting what they include, emphasize, and leave out of their accounts and observing how different contexts (race, gender, socioeconomic condition, historical era) affect how they see and interpret events. For example, *The Elephant Man* dramatically presents multiple perspectives on the patient's condition as well as on what the condition means for the patient himself and for the different characters who visit him. Whether Merrick is in a freak show or in his hospital room, people come to see him because he is different. His visitors bring their own biases and assumptions to the encounter; they see reflected in the elephant man what they themselves project onto him. The clergy, the hospital administration, the nursing staff, and the society ladies all see different qualities in him, while the man himself is hardly recognized. Students learn that no one way of seeing—including Dr. Treves's "objective" case presentation—is the right one. Dr. Treves, though he gives his patient good medical care, refuses to see Merrick as a mature man and continues to treat him as a child.

Paying attention to narrative requires realizing that language is not transparent. Whether in a poem or a medical case history, language is not a clear glass revealing the truth about the real world. Language is culturally constructed and carries hidden assumptions and perspectives that we often overlook. For example, many terms that are used to describe people outside physiological norms are negative and stigmatizing—freaks, mutants, monsters, mistakes of nature. Clinical terminology, such as *terata*, seems euphemistic. And such terms as *abnormal, disabled, malformed*, and *deviant* begin with a negative prefix that puts the person being described in opposition with the normal, the able, the formed, and those on the right path. A person with an abnormal appearance or behavior is always measured against the norm and is always, by definition, outside the bell curve. That we have not found a neutral term, let alone a positive one, for such a person indicates the tyranny of the normal in our culture. But any label, even a diagnosis, tends to serve as a shortcut and reduces our thinking and awareness: we are likely to believe that once we have named something or someone, we understand it. Class discussions of the readings tend to be especially sensitive and alert to the language used and its effect on the characters.

Some pedagogical techniques that have proved useful in the course include reading parts of the plays in a "reader's theater" format, followed by class discussion of what it feels like to take the role of each character. Sometimes students swap characters after they have got into their roles, so that they can experience the wrench of shifting points of view and can ask themselves why they might feel more comfortable with one role than with another. In a writing exercise, students are asked to take a different narrative position from the one in the story. For example, if the story is narrated by a doctor, then students are asked to retell it from the perspective of the patient or a family member; if it is narrated by an adult, they may retell it from a child's perspective; if it is told by a man, they may give a woman's interpretation; if a character seems to be silenced in the text, students attempt to give that person a voice. If students think a different racial or religious perspective should be heard, they try to give it a voice and an audience in their papers. In another writing exercise, students are asked to continue the story, predicting what is likely to happen and envisioning how a character will feel and act at that time. One or more of the literary works often remind students of something in their own experience; we encourage comparison papers linking personal experience to issues raised in the literature. Often we ask students to share especially effective papers with the class.

Because the readings for this course are extensive and diverse, we ask students to keep a journal, in which they respond to the clinical and ethical articles as well as the literary readings. For drama and fiction, we ask them to consider whether any of the characters changes or realizes something, what the conflicts are and whether they come to some resolution, who is narrating the work, and what the narrative viewpoints are. For poetry, we ask students to note any striking metaphors and describe how they work in the poem. Students are encouraged to add other comments or reactions they have to the readings, including feelings of being insulted or challenged or heart warmed. The journals help students to participate in class discussions and to prepare for papers and take-home exams.

In conclusion, it is obvious that in our encounters with deformed or mentally abnormal people we ought to control reactions, both verbal and nonverbal, that might be hurtful. But even if we can accomplish that difficult task, we still need to meet these people as they are, where they are, and in their context. Literature can help us develop the ability to put ourselves imaginatively in another person's position. If we understand, even indirectly, what it is like to be an "other," we can develop a genuine sense of empathy for such persons.

Course Readings

Donley and Buckley, selections from *The Tyranny of the Normal*
Dresser and Whitehouse, "The Incompetent Patient on the Slippery Slope"
Gilman, "The Yellow Wallpaper"
Nichols, *Joe Egg*
Pomerance, *The Elephant Man*
Shaffer, *Equus*
Steinbeck, *Of Mice and Men*
Szasz, "The Myth of Mental Illness"

Works Cited

Caplan, Arthur L., et al., eds. *Concepts of Health and Disease.* New York: Addison, 1981.

Carey, Jonathan Sinclair. "The Quasimodo Complex: Deformity Reconsidered." *Journal of Clinical Ethics* 1 (1990): 212–21. Rpt. in Donley and Buckley 27–52.

Carver, Raymond. "Fat." Donley and Buckley 147–50.

Coulehan, Jack. "The Six Hundred Pound Man." Donley and Buckley 145–56.

Davis, Marilyn. "Song for My Son." Donley and Buckley 305.

Donley, Carol, and Sheryl Buckley, eds. *The Tyranny of the Normal: An Anthology.* Kent: Kent State UP, 1996.

Dresser, Rebecca, and Peter Whitehouse. "The Incompetent Patient on the Slippery Slope." *Hastings Center Report* 24.4 (1994): 6–12.

Engelhardt, H. Tristram, Jr. "The Disease of Masturbation: Values and the Concepts of Disease." Caplan et al. 85–88.

Fiedler, Leslie. *Freaks: Myths and Images of the Secret Self.* New York: Simon, 1978. Excerpt rpt. in Donley and Buckley 11–26.

———. "The Tyranny of the Normal." *Which Babies Shall Live?* Ed. Thomas Murray and Arthur Caplan. Continuing Issues in Biomedical Ethics Series. Clifton: Humana, 1985. 151–66. Rpt. in Donley and Buckley 3–10.

Gilman, Charlotte Perkins. "The Yellow Wallpaper." *"The Yellow Wallpaper" and Other Writings.* Ed. Lynne Sharon Schwartz. New York: Bantam, 1989. 1–20.

Hadas, Pamela. "Diary of an Anorexic." Donley and Buckley 192–94.

Hawthorne, Nathaniel. "The Birthmark." Donley and Buckley 334–48.

Hugo, Victor. *The Hunchback of Notre Dame.* London: Penguin, 1987. Excerpt rpt. in Donley and Buckley 349–51.

Levine, Carol, ed. *Cases in Bioethics.* New York: St. Martin's, 1985.

Leviticus. Bible. Rev. Standard ed.

Mahowald, Mary B. "To Be or Not to Be a Woman: Anorexia Nervosa, Normative Gender Roles, and Feminism." *Journal of Medicine and Philosophy* 17 (1992): 233–51. Rpt. in Donley and Buckley 121–38.

McFarland, Barbara, and Tyeis Baker-Baumann. *Shame and Body Image: Culture and the Compulsive Eater.* Deerfield Beach: Health Communications, 1992.

Nichols, Peter. *Joe Egg.* New York: Grove, 1967.

Olds, Sharon. "The Meal." Donley and Buckley 197–98.

Pomerance, Bernard. *The Elephant Man.* New York: Grove, 1979.

Shaffer, Peter. *Equus.* New York: Avon, 1974.

Sparks, Rennie. "Skanks." Donley and Buckley 154–62.

Steinbeck, John. *Of Mice and Men.* New York: Viking, 1937.

Szasz, Thomas. "The Myth of Mental Illness." Caplan et al. 110–14.

Tavris, Carol. *The Mismeasure of Woman.* New York: Simon, 1992.

Updike, John. "Journal of a Leper." Donley and Buckley 286–96.

Williams, Miller. "The Ones That Are Thrown Out." Donley and Buckley 306.

Wood, Monica. "Disappearing." Donley and Buckley 201–03.

Dieter J. Boxmann

Rhetoric and the Politics of Medical Persuasion

Literature about medicine confirms the central role of persuasion in shaping the character and practice of medicine.[1] Medical practice as we know it stems as much from the way public discourse (rhetoric) establishes and maintains medicine's authority, insight, and ability as it does from advancements in scientific knowledge and technique.[2] Literature is one of many forms of public discourse that not only reflects prevailing attitudes about medicine but also influences our internalization of those attitudes. In teaching literature and medicine from a rhetorical perspective, I explore how literature articulates the values and struggles of medical practice, of the professional medical community, and of specific patient populations.

As an avenue of social criticism, rhetoric remains curiously underacknowledged in the modern academy. In rhetoric's 2,500-year history as a discipline, it has repeatedly been reduced to concern with formal mechanisms of style and eloquence and has sometimes disappeared almost entirely from the academy. Rhetoric's periodic disappearance and reemergence may be directly linked to its dialectical opposition to the aims and claims of science. Rhetorical appeals are characterized by the primacy of appearances, the contingency of particular occasions, the emotions experienced by audiences and speakers, and the probability that what may prove truthful and effective in one set of circumstances may not be equally so under different conditions. Scientific inquiry is grounded in the primacy of reality over appearance, necessity over contingency, reason over emotion, and truth over probability. Science bases its understanding of the world on universal laws of causality, and while it admits that psyche and circumstance play a part in human affairs, it strives to control these variables in favor of a reasoned approach to problems that may be diagnosed, isolated, and solved.

In almost any medical text, one can discover some failure to achieve the rigor promised by science's positivist ethos. Even Hippocrates recognized as much when he wrote:

> Medicine cannot be learned quickly because it is impossible to create any established principle in it, the way that a person who learns writing according to one system that people teach understands everything. [. . .] Medicine [. . .] does not do the same thing at this moment and the next, and it does opposite things to the same person, and at that things that are self-contradictory. (81)

Modern medicine has achieved far greater consistency in its therapeutic and diagnostic algorithms, but Hippocrates's assessment of the complexity of applied medicine remains as accurate today as it was when Hippocrates wrote it. Medicine still has to take into account how health is related to situational and environmental variables. Typically medicine censors its own rhetoricity by trying to appear neutral, objective, focused on patient outcomes, and transparently good. Medical scientists and sometimes even literary critics perceive persuasion as having little to do with either the business of securing health or the literary enterprise of exploring universal themes and the forms in which they are expressed. But since both endeavors are grounded in conflict, struggle, and communicative interaction, they unavoidably involve rhetoric. In my course on literature and medicine, I contend that medicine and rhetoric ought to be complementary.

As Hans-Georg Gadamer points out in *The Enigma of Health*, there is a deep and ancient affinity between rhetoric and medicine. Both begin by approaching a problem without a precise conception of the object under investigation or of how to control the problem effectively. Health and the dynamics of persuasion are, in important senses, enigmas (31–44). Understanding illness and facilitating persuasion both require an understanding of context. A good doctor knows her or his patients and their history; a good rhetor understands the desires, needs, and interests of a particular audience. Ultimately, the goal of rhetoric and of medicine is to find the intervention (discursive or physiological) that in each case produces the best possible outcome without too many unwanted side effects.

The underlying affinity between rhetoric and medicine was obvious in the political culture of ancient Greece; today it goes largely unrecognized. Yet medical professionals practice rhetoric, competing for the right to represent public interest. Rhetoric does not have to be antithetical to medicine but instead may humanize and sophisticate the manner in which medicine achieves its goals. Rhetoric exposes ambiguity, uncertainty, conflict, and debate over ends and means; it asks medicine to be accountable to its own political and value preferences and to take responsibility for its institutional forms and weaknesses. In the debate over a health-care issue such as when and how to develop expensive imaging technology, rhetoric ought to serve as a corrective—a way for the profession to build perspective by understanding the grounds, acknowledged and unacknowledged, for competing interests. A rhetorical reading of literature permits students to explore the power of language as it is manifested in style, motive, medical ideologies, ambiguities, patterns of inclusion and exclusion, and strategies of persuasive appeal and influence. Such an approach, moreover, helps students understand language as symbolic action.

In my course students read literary texts with a view to ascertaining what medicine does well, what its strengths and limitations are, and how current medical practice meets and sometimes does not meet our biological, psychological, social, and spiritual needs. The novels used in my course are chosen for the key medical issues they represent. Four texts have provided especially rich material for discussion of the rhetorical dimensions of medical practice.

Mary Shelley's *Frankenstein* has proved a useful point of departure for reflection on how medicine struggles over the meaning and value assigned to the healthy and diseased states possible to human beings. The tale exhibits interesting and profound tensions between Romantic ideas of health and Enlightenment notions of progress that entail the conquest of nature. Shelley underscores the role of the passions, associating the well-being of characters with simple manners, grace, and the tranquility of domestic relations and stressing the dangers of overexertion, overemotionality, and transgressing the boundaries of nature. The story raises useful questions about the impact of external environments on internal states. Its treatment of disease and deformity in the depiction of Frankenstein's monster as a depraved, stigmatized, and morally suspect "other" echoes the culture's propensity to treat the "abnormal" as abject and suspect. I ask students to think about these attitudes toward health and to address the following directives:

1. On the basis of specific action, narration, and description, discuss the novel's overall attitude toward the human body, our "frame."
2. Think about the characteristics Victor Frankenstein attributes to the "monster" he has created and about possible motivations for and implications of his seeing it as depraved, alien, and totally other.
3. Think about how a mechanic or an inventor would make a monster. What conclusions can you draw about the novel's approach to scientific techniques of production? What metaphors dominate description of the technical details of making the monster?

My initial impulse in using *Frankenstein* was to explore a work that occupies an established place in our cultural mythology as a harbinger of the evils made possible by technology. The novel's metaphors of invention and technology evoke sustained cultural fears about grafting body parts, experimenting with the dead, and tinkering with natural biological processes.

Some of the most interesting political persuasion in literature about medicine expresses the limits, futility, and downsides of medical practice while at the same time accounting for American medicine's growing power and prestige throughout the nineteenth and twentieth centuries. Sinclair Lewis's *Arrowsmith* offers a bold satire of institutionalized medicine's infatuation with germ theory and medicine's only partially successful struggle to perfect the germ model. *Arrowsmith* addresses the limitations of various medical practices and the unexamined terms of medical research in the early twentieth century. It locates these practices in the context of the enormous financial, social, and political pressures on medicine to provide unprecedented cures. As the novel shows, much medical practice at that time (1925) was more packaging than it was science. Examining that packaging exposes new questions about what we take to be scientific, and opens up critical inquiry into the strengths and flaws of medical decision making and its institutional forms and constraints.

Not infrequently literature offers a complex assessment of the institutions in and through which medicine is practiced. Aleksandr Solzhenitsyn's *Cancer Ward* provides both an inside view of institutional medicine and a broad social critique and raises issues of professionalism, the social dimensions of illness, the effects of culture on perceptions of illness, and the way medical practitioners communicate with patients. To encourage my students to think about these issues as they read Solzhenitsyn, I offer the following critical directives and questions:

1. Analyze instances in the story of medical attitudes toward intervention. What arguments and language do medical personnel use to speak of surgeries and other procedures? What are some implications of their arguments and attitudes?
2. Discuss the tropes and metaphors Solzhenitsyn employs to explore the experience of cancer. What kinds of moral, emotional,

and symbolic language are associated with cancer? To what is cancer compared or related? Consider also the opposite question: How is cancer metaphoric (and how is the cancer ward allegoric) for the various social, political, and existential ills that are the subject of this novel?

3. Discuss positive and negative aspects of the communication between patients and caregivers. In analyzing this communication be sure to consider nonverbal factors, paralinguistics (intonation, rate, pitch, volume, etc.), facial and eye expressions, proxemics (the impact of human spacing and distance), chronemics (the impact of time and timing), touch, perceptions of personal appearance and body shape, artifacts (objects people use to decorate themselves and their environment), body movements and positionings, whether the setting influences the dialogue, and medical jargon.

As these questions and directives suggest, a rhetorical perspective considers symbolic communication as it is used both formally and informally. For example, discussing issues of power in *Cancer Ward*, one student writes:

> On Ward 13, the patients have no control over their lives. [. . .] The controlling group (i.e., doctors or apparatchiks) makes sure its subjects are kept unaware of the alternatives, be they the various medical treatments (no discussion even takes place on the nature of their illness) or various forms of government (all of which are flatly denounced as inferior to communism). A thinking patient is a challenge to a doctor's authority, just as an intellectual is a challenge to communist nomenclature. (Repovic)

Analysis of Ken Kesey's *One Flew over the Cuckoo's Nest* provides examples of critical opportunities opened up by a rhetorical approach. The novel critiques medical culture through the perspectives of characters who are participant-observers as well as through the implied metacommentary of the narrating consciousness. When I ask students to read this story of ongoing power struggles between patients and staff in a mental institution, I draw students' attention to the rhetorical questions of who has what kind of power and by what means power is obtained. I ask students to reflect on modes of perception, acknowledged and unacknowledged motives, and competing perspectives.

Kesey's depiction of nurses opens some interesting points of discussion about the situations of female health-care workers; somewhat disturbing is the novel's lack of acknowledgment of the dehumanizing conditions under which health-care workers are often expected to practice. In the novel, nurses are conscious and manipulative agents of control. Big Nurse has direct control over the "Combine" (a machinelike power that both mows down and vaporizes the initiative of the ward's patients), but there is no suggestion of the extent to which she herself is reaped and discarded by the oppressive, mechanistic force. While Kesey's observations about the psychiatric hospitals of the time are disturbing and compelling, his focus obscures some forms of institutional control. The power of Big Nurse, while believable in some respects, is in others distorted by the stereotype of female manipulation that is invoked but that remains partly unexamined.

The only kind of power invested in the characters is the power to resist or escape. Readers who respond to *Cuckoo's Nest* primarily in terms of its surface conflicts may miss the ambiguities, complexities, and contradictions in the motives of the ward's staff. Reading the story simply in terms of conflict between protagonists and antagonists may be comparable to blaming institutional abuses on corrupt and controlling individuals.

A rhetorical approach helps instructor and students foreground the way creation of meaning, dispute, negotiation, argument, and advocacy shape medical practice and medical values. In my teaching I have found Robert Hariman's *Political Style: The Artistry of Power* helpful. Hariman offers an explanation of how literature both enacts and challenges the political culture of particular professional realms like medicine. He argues that different sorts of texts, particularly literary ones, may be classified according to what he calls their political style. Each political style, he writes, "draws on universal elements of the human condition and symbolic repertoire, but organizes them into a limited, customary set of communicative designs. Each evokes a culture—a coherent set of symbols giving meaning to the manifest activities of common living [. . .]" (11). Hariman's perspective invites us to look at works of literature as rhetorics expressing a political and social worldview performed as the product of everyday activities, behaviors, and patterns of interaction.

Of course one must be cautious in pursuing a rhetorical analysis of literary texts. As Martha Nussbaum demonstrates in her compelling analysis of the role of the poetic imagination in justice and social practices (like medicine), the literary real may not always accurately reflect the political real; made-up circumstances may be poor representations of concrete practices and situations. Also confounding the equation between reality and fiction are the limited medical authority of fiction writers, their creation of intentionally unreliable characters and fictive plot elements, and the likelihood, even desirability, that the writers are biased. However, what is most at stake in the politics of literary persuasion is not the real per se but how the real is constituted, depicted, packaged, and developed and how literary representations reflect and influence broader social and political cultures in a dialectical and reciprocal fashion.

Oliver Sacks has argued that American culture pretends modern medicine is a rational science, "but we have only to tap [medicine's] glossy veneer to split it wide open and reveal to us its roots and foundations; its old dark heart of metaphysics, mysticism, magic, and myth" (48). Because literary texts employ rich detail in exploring the human condition, they enable students to examine the problems, conventions, and myths of Western medicine. Using rhetoric as a conceptual framework, the issues students raise about the conventions and priorities of medical problem solving can lead to a careful study of the intricacies of the relation between literary texts and lived experience.

Course Readings

Foucault, *The Birth of the Clinic*
Gadamer, *The Enigma of Health*
Gilman, *Picturing Health and Illness*
Hudson, *A Case of Need*

Kesey, *One Flew over the Cuckoo's Nest*
Lewis, *Arrowsmith*
Shelley, *Frankenstein*
Solzhenitsyn, *Cancer Ward*

Notes

1. I use the phrase "literature about medicine" to refer to texts with generally acknowledged literary merit that invoke themes related to medical concerns. I use the phrase "other writing about medical practice" to refer to a wide array of writing that in some way explores medical conventions, reasoning, and values. Such writing includes philosophy, medical theory, popular science fiction, illness narratives, sociological and anthropological studies of medicine, and writing by practitioners for other professionals.
2. I employ the term "discourse" in Michel Foucault's sense of language practices that systematically construct the realities they attempt to describe. Thus discourse and rhetoric perform largely the same function as forms of civic deliberation that contribute to the establishment of institutional power relations.

Works Cited

Foucault, Michel. *The Birth of the Clinic: An Archaeology of Medical Perception*. Trans. A. M. Sheridan Smith. New York: Vintage, 1975.

Gadamer, Hans-Georg. *The Enigma of Health*. Trans. Jason Geiger and Nicholas Walker. Stanford: Stanford UP, 1996.

Gilman, Sander. *Picturing Health and Illness*. Baltimore: Johns Hopkins UP, 1995.

Hariman, Robert. *Political Style: The Artistry of Power*. Chicago: U of Chicago P, 1995.

Hippocrates. *Volume VII*. Trans. Paul Potter. Loeb Classic Library. Cambridge: Harvard UP, 1995.

Hudson, Jeffrey [Michael Crichton]. *A Case of Need*. New York: Signet, 1968.

Kesey, Ken. *One Flew over the Cuckoo's Nest*. New York: Viking-Penguin, 1996.

Lewis, Sinclair. *Arrowsmith*. New York: New Amer. Lib., 1961.

Nussbaum, Martha. *Poetic Justice: The Literary Imagination and Public Life*. Boston: Beacon, 1995.

Repovic, Pavle. "Quiz Six: Cancer Ward." Unpublished essay, 1997.

Sacks, Oliver. *Awakenings*. New York: Harper, 1990.

Shelley, Mary. *Frankenstein*. Ed. Joanna M. Smith. Boston: Bedford, 1992.

Solzhenitsyn, Aleksandr. *Cancer Ward*. Trans. Nicholas Bethell and David Burg. New York: Noonday, 1974.

Part II

Texts, Authors, Genres

Marilyn Chandler McEntyre

Touchstones: A Brief Survey of Some Standard Works

Few of us who read *Little Women* will forget the death of angelic Beth March, who contracts to scarlet fever at age thirteen after caring for the sick infant of a poor immigrant family and wastes away— a saintly demise, typical of a whole generation of Victorian heroines whose perfection seemed to lie in death. Consider Dickens's Little Nell. Or Hugo's mother-prostitute Fantine. Or the wife of the mad scientist in Hawthorne's "The Birthmark," a woman who dies of her husband's misguided efforts to rid her of her one blemish. Or even James's Milly Theale, who turns her face to the wall and leaves her fortune behind, to the moral confusion of her survivors. Literary deaths reward close scrutiny by revealing a spectrum of attitudes toward health, illness, medicine, doctors, women and children, and religion and thus providing a window on cultural history in general and medical history in particular.

Medical themes may be traced across the landscape of literature. The image of the doctor emerges in a variety of guises: the priestly figure who brings more comfort than cure; the buffoon who provides patients with little but an incentive to get well just to get rid of him; the Faust figure who desires medical knowledge more than human good; the benevolent family physician who makes house calls in horse and cart; and finally, the godlike bearer of antibiotics, vaccines, and high-tech salvation. A history of attitudes toward medicine and medical authority may be investigated through doctor figures who are butts of satire; icons of popular romance; or, at their best, complex figures, neither heroes nor saints, whose consent to responsibility for the health of their fellow mortals sets them apart and gives them leading roles in human dramas.

The literature of plagues and epidemics serves similarly to organize an understanding of medical and social history. In Exodus, *The Iliad*, and *Oedipus Rex* the plague is a punishment; in the *Decameron* and, later, in Poe's "The Masque of the Red Death" it is a context and a pretext; in *Paradise Lost* and Manzoni's *The Betrothed* it serves as a means of understanding human history; in Lewis's *Arrowsmith* it is a backdrop for heroic science; in Camus's *The Plague* it is an analogue for political and moral corruption.

The essays in part 2 show how literature can illuminate these and other medical themes and issues. The following brief survey of some of the texts most widely used in literature and medicine courses may serve to introduce and contextualize the readings.

Short Stories

For obvious reasons, short stories are the best kind of text for articulating a variety of medical themes over the course of a semester. They allow instructors to introduce narratological questions and questions of point of view, literary strategy, characterization, and tone, while offering various situations for analysis and comparison. Novels may develop medical themes in more detail and depth, but short stories can throw a particular aspect of a medical issue into high relief and can sometimes focus discussion more effectively than a longer work. Organized thematically, short stories allow classes to consider the same problem from different historical or cultural points of view. They are also much more manageable than longer works for medical students whose study time is limited and for whom a literature and medicine course is usually an elective. Stories, it may also be said, are less threatening than poetry to the lab-bound, some of whom find literary analysis tantamount to arcane cultic practice.

One of the most widely used short stories, by now a chestnut in literature and medicine courses, is William Carlos Williams's "The Use of Force." The story appears in a collection called *Doctor Stories,* which many instructors use in its entirety as a course text. Based on Williams's experiences as a general practitioner in the 1930s, the stories are surprisingly blunt, sometimes throwing a harsh light on the discomforts and dilemmas of the clinical encounter. The doctor hardly comes off as a hero; in a number of stories he seems to have suffered from emotional burnout and moral erosion. Worn from the tedium of other people's pain, he often reflects on his failure to feel compassion even as he acts compassionately toward patients who seem ignorant, recalcitrant, and ungrateful. The tales are unrelenting in representing the difficulties, frustrations, and disappointments of medical life, but they are also (perhaps because of their darkness) powerful in their affirmation of medicine's hard-won rewards. Williams's stories deromanticize the doctor even as they honor his quotidian virtues.

Mention of "The Use of Force" almost amounts to a club handshake among medical humanists. The story's importance lies in the way it succinctly brings into focus a whole cluster of everyday dilemmas that characterize the medical encounter. The tension that arises between a doctor, a child who won't open her mouth for a throat exam, and the child's two parents opens up discussion of medical authority, bedside manners, assignment of medical responsibility, doctor-patient dialogue, children's rights, and fear as a factor in treatment. Because the story is essentially a confession by the doctor-narrator—who retrospectively recognizes his antagonism and emotional, even psychosexual attraction, to the child—it also lends itself to discussion of gender issues and of the delicate matters of propriety and symbolic violation in the medical encounter, particularly between a male doctor and a young female patient. Some instructors have asked students to rewrite the story, making the child a boy or the doctor a woman, and to consider how such changes affect meaning, logic, and plot.

A child also figures in Ernest Hemingway's "Indian Camp," a similarly brief tale about an emergency cesarean section performed by a white male doctor on an Indian woman. The story, in which no character is particularly sympathetic, facilitates discussion of cross-cultural medical encounters. While on a fishing trip, the doctor, his young son, and his brother are led into a squalid cabin where a woman is in labor. Her husband lies on an upper bunk, crippled with an axe wound. The doctor's inattention to the woman's emotional distress, to the husband, to anything but the technical problem of performing the operation under such conditions frequently provokes strong negative reactions, especially among women students. These reactions are further complicated by discussion of the husband's suicide: during the operation the man has quietly slit his throat, an act that suggests the shame he has experienced in his helplessness. The story's symbolic representation of imperialistic attitudes and transgressions invites consideration of how the politics of manifest destiny and white privilege still shape attitudes about crossing cultural boundaries. The story is refracted through the child's point of view, foregrounding the problematic way the doctor models manhood for his son and emphasizing how the doctor's professional behavior manifests narrowly patriarchal ideas of virility, heroism, and empowerment.

Rewriting the story from the woman's point of view, like altering point of view in "The Use of Force," is an effective way of getting at some of the cultural and gender issues, including the issue of shame. The story pairs nicely with Richard Selzer's "Imelda," about an American surgeon who makes a yearly trip to a country south of the border to perform operations and who is profoundly changed when he loses a patient (and his pride) in a freak accident on the operating table.

Among the stories that deal with doctors' costly misperceptions of patients' experiences is Charlotte Perkins Gilman's short tale of mental illness, "The Yellow Wallpaper." This story provides a chilling but empathetic representation of a woman's slow transition from sanity to insanity as a response to repression. One of the most useful ways of working with the story in class is to have students identify points in the narrative where slippage takes place, often indicated by changes in syntax, rhythm, verb choices, dimensions of the visual field, and so on. This process of identification brings up analogies between critical reading and diagnosis. Poe's "The Telltale Heart" and Dostoyevsky's *Notes from the Underground*, both narrated by male characters in the throes of delusion, are useful points of comparison. These stories and others with similarly problematic points of view allow readers to consider subtle differences of perception and behavior that distinguish what we define as mental illness from what we consider "normal."

"The Yellow Wallpaper" is a handy touchstone for considering the dramatic spread of psychosomatic disorders among women of Gilman's generation, women whose diagnoses ranged from hysteria to neurasthenia to spinal irritation to intellectual overexertion. Alice James's *Diary* and Kate Chopin's *The Awakening*, as well as Hawthorne's "The Birthmark," prove useful companion pieces in that they also introduce questions about gender bias in medical reasoning, about diagnostics, about sources and manifestations of depression and dementia, and about patients' tactics for responding to abuses of medical authority.

In Chekhov's "Ward Number Six," another story that dramatizes dementia, a doctor decides that in the light of inevitable death there's no point in caring for the sick. He retreats to his books but finds himself fascinated with the mentally ill patients in ward 6 of his hospital. He befriends a patient with whom he engages in lively debate. The doctor is fired for his peculiar behavior and later himself incarcerated in the ward, where he dies. This bleak tale of medical skepticism raises questions about institutional authority, utilitarian reasoning, and doctors' responsibilities. Paired with the now classic film *One Flew over the Cuckoo's Nest*, the story generates useful discussion of the history of diagnosis and treatment of mental illness. Both works boldly expose what might be called medicine's dark side.

In another dark story, Tolstoy's "The Death of Ivan Ilych," a dying man confronts his past and the choices he has made. Awaiting death, Ivan Ilych is attended by five physicians whose ability to help is limited and whose attitudes are alienating. The family grows tired of Ivan Ilych's suffering and starts to resent him; only a servant is able to care for him compassionately. This is one of several works that examine attitudes toward death and dying. Other works commonly used are Selzer's "Mercy," Chekhov's "Misery," and Hemingway's "A Clean, Well-Lighted Place."

An important subgenre that provides a bridge between short stories and case histories is the "clinical tale," a term coined by Oliver Sacks, whose *The Man Who Mistook His Wife for a Hat* is still one of the most popular (and controversial) collections of its kind. The stories, which document the unorthodox work of a neurologist with exceptional patients, call attention to questions that broaden and humanize medical inquiry. The controversy over Sacks's use of actual case histories is itself a worthy topic of discussion.

Novels

Though teaching full-length novels involves some sacrifice of thematic and stylistic variation, certain novels have become classics in the field and reward the time they take with the depth of discussion they generate. Two of the most widely taught are Thomas Mann's *The Magic Mountain* and Aleksandr Solzhenitsyn's *Cancer Ward*. The first is the story of Hans Castorp, who goes to a sanatorium in the Swiss mountains to visit a cousin and ends up staying, ostensibly to recuperate from his own case of previously undiagnosed tuberculosis. *Cancer Ward* takes place in an urban hospital in the Soviet Union. The main character is a young man recently discharged from prison and now in exile, undergoing radiation therapy. As in *Magic Mountain*, medical themes are treated both literally and metaphorically; the culture of the cancer ward provides a prototype of the state, and cancer, a metaphor for totalitarianism. Issues of medical authority, patients' rights, and informed consent are particularly foregrounded in this novel. Both books lend themselves to complex discussion of institutional culture, of the psychodynamics of healing and incentives to remain ill, of strategies of adaptation to chronic illness, of the respective responsibilities of patients and caregivers, and of social and political contexts of illness.

Arrowsmith, by Sinclair Lewis, is another widely used novel that treats a variety of medical themes. Few readers today would praise its literary excellence, but it is a useful period piece. Chronicling a young doctor's medical education, the novel addresses the problems of institutional life in both clinic and academy; the choice between practice and research; the pressures from patients, colleagues, and professors; and the ethical dilemmas that arise when the demands of research conflict with patients' needs. In a heavy-handed way, the book leads readers to consider the institutional, social, and ethical pressures on doctors and those who train them. As a mirror of social history, the novel also raises interesting issues about the institutionalization that medicine underwent from the beginning of the twentieth century through the two world wars and about professional constraints that not only safeguarded the integrity of medical practice and authenticated licensing but also frequently prohibited individual practitioners from making judgment calls that conflicted with institutional solidarity. Two interesting works for comparison are A. J. Cronin's *The Citadel*, a bildungsroman about a young Welsh doctor, and George Eliot's *Middlemarch*, in which Dr. Lydgate's discussions of medical reform in mid-nineteenth-century England provide a valuable opportunity to consider the generic difficulties medical reformers encounter. *Middlemarch* is, of course, too long to handle in most semester-long courses, but many instructors have used excerpts successfully, and the quality of Eliot's prose offers a leaven that the other two novels lack. The three novels together frame questions not only about medical history but also about cultural variations in practice, in training, and in attitudes toward health and illness. Discussion of differences between European and American medical practices may be facilitated by accompanying these novels with Lynn Payer's *Medicine and Culture*, an engaging survey and analysis of differences among French, German, English, and American medicine.

A more recent novel that has proved its pedagogical value in articulating doctors' dilemmas is Perri Klass's *Other Women's Children*. In the novel a pediatrician becomes deeply involved with a young AIDS patient. The story focuses on the doctor's emotional dividedness between the children she cares for in the hospital and her own child and husband, who often feel neglected. The novel provides an interesting point of comparison with classic nineteenth-century novels by Alcott, Dickens, and Stevenson, in which sick children are featured.

Plays

From *Oedipus* and *Antigone* to Larry Kramer's *The Normal Heart* and Tony Kushner's pair of plays about AIDS, *Angels in America*, the history of theater is rich with medical themes. *Macbeth* and *Hamlet* feature humoral theory and poisonings, Molière's *The Doctor in Spite of Himself* and *The Imaginary Invalid* satirize doctors and hypochondriacs, and Ibsen's *An Enemy of the People* is a bitter social critique of how commercial interests override a doctor's informed concern for public health.

A particularly powerful play to find its way into courses in literature and medicine is *Miss Evers' Boys*, by David Feldshuh. Based on James Jones's *Bad Blood: The Tuskegee Syphilis Experiment* and on oral testimony related to that experiment, the play portrays the relationship between an African American public-health nurse and four men participating in the study. The government is complicit in this unethical study in which men being treated for syphilis are not informed when actual treatment is discontinued and are then kept under observation to determine the course of the disease. In the interests of that goal they are even deprived of penicillin when it becomes available as an effective treatment for syphilis. The play examines in particular the issue of informed consent and the role of the government, the medical institutions involved, the doctors, and the nurse, whose compromise is the most complicated moral issue of the play.

A play that is similarly unsettling and equally helpful for generating discussion of difficult medical issues is *The Elephant Man,* by Bernard Pomerance. The play is based on the life of John Merrick, a nineteenth-century Englishman suffering from severe deformity who, when abandoned by the traveling freak show that exhibited him, enters Whitechapel Hospital under the care of Dr. Frederick Treves. There Merrick is kept, educated, and introduced into London society, where he is received, but, as he realizes, never as an ordinary person. He dies in his sleep, attempting to sleep lying down like "normal" people. Discussion of the play may take a variety of directions, the most obvious being treatment and adaptations of the severely deformed and social and institutional responses to untreatable deformities. Shakespeare's Caliban and Hugo's Quasimodo make interesting points of comparison for reflection on characterization of the outcast "other." The movie *Mask,* about a young boy with a bone disease that makes his face progressively more deformed (also based on an actual case), offers a close parallel.

Poems

Poetry can be an extremely satisfying section of a literature and medicine course, for the paradoxical reason that poetry is often the most alien genre for premedical and medical students and requires skills and analytical processes that run counter to the kind of thinking demanded in the students' other courses. A fair number of contemporary poems, some mentioned in the following essays, have become standard offerings (see the anthologies of primary sources in part 4 of this book for titles of several widely used collections). Contemporary poetry has the advantage of familiarity of reference, but older poetry serves an important function partly by defamiliarizing issues of sickness, pain, treatment, death, caregiving, and mourning. John Keats's "Ode on Melancholy" stands high among such historical touchstones. Keats, who received medical training and who died at age twenty-nine of tuberculosis, argues against suicide as a response to depression, or melancholy, by focusing and feasting on beauty. Melancholy, he reasons, sharpens the experience of aesthetic pleasure by throwing the experience into high relief. The poem reminds us of the fleetingness of life and the importance of consenting to joy on the only terms available.

Whitman's "The Wound Dresser" speaks with the voice of a caregiver who witnesses suffering he can't relieve. The speaker recalls the faces of the young men dying in the battlefield hospitals, referring to the men as "my wounded" (26). As he dresses their wounds he reflects on what binds him to them in such a powerful way that he "could not refuse this moment to die for [them], if that would save [them]" (38). The poem's passionate representation and affirmation of deep emotional empathy with those who are suffering raise sharp questions about the ideal of clinical detachment and about the attitudes of healers toward their patients.

W. H. Auden's "Musée des Beaux Arts" offers another reflection on human suffering, providing a point of departure for considering the social contexts of illness and pain, the idea of suffering as personal fate, and in what sense suffering is about the life of the community. The poem raises some useful questions about the obligations of the healthy to those who suffer.

Denise Levertov's "Death Psalm: O Lord of Mysteries," structured both like a biblical psalm and like a litany, details a woman's process of preparing for death. The sad gracefulness of the process is undermined by the fact that the woman, called only "she," does not die when her time seems to have come. The jarring second half of the poem describes the lingering on of someone ready in every respect to die—a reality of modern technologically assisted death. The mystery of death ironically becomes the mystery of why the woman does not die, and the prayer turns from acceptance to bafflement, reminiscent of Job, of the psalmist's laments, and of more recent existentialist outcries about the absurdity of existence.

Nonfiction

Nonfiction prose—medical treatises, case histories, journalistic accounts of plagues and epidemics, sermons on sickness and sin—

raises interesting questions about the literary treatment of fact, that is, what makes writing literary. Several examples of widely used literary nonfiction may serve here to define the place of such works in a literature and medicine course. John Donne's *Devotions*, meditations written in time of illness, ponders the meaning and experience of sickness in the light of faith, the role and responsibility of the physician, the work of medicine, and the purpose of sickness for the health of the soul. Chronicling Donne's typhus from symptoms to diagnosis to crisis and confrontation with death to cure, the devotions conclude with the physicians' warnings about relapse. All these stages give rise to reflections not only on medicine itself but also on analogies between medicine and religion, sickness and sin. Virginia Woolf, like Donne, reflects on the experience of being ill and on the new perspectives it offers. In "On Being Ill" she claims that illness turns one toward poetry, whose language can approximate most closely the extremities of human experience.

Audre Lorde's *Cancer Journals* offers a stark contrast to Woolf's highly literary musings. Composed primarily of journal entries written during the author's treatment for breast cancer, the book also includes interpolations of later prose and poetry that complicate what would otherwise be a conventional chronicle of illness. Lorde writes as a black lesbian feminist, each of those aspects of identity serving to define a particular medical and social situation. The book emphasizes the role of community among woman and sharply criticizes the pressures on women to make choices aimed at pleasing men and minimizing social discomfort after mastectomy. *Cancer Journals* is one book among many that raise questions about "normality": Who defines it, and what price is paid for its maintenance? Lorde examines critically the option of reconstructive surgery and the idea of "quality of life" invoked to justify it, urging women not to hide their wounds but to allow them to be visible as part of helping society come to terms with the realities of cancer.

Any attempt to list literary touchstones is, of course, doomed to incompletion and flawed by conspicuous omissions. But the above sampling, organized as it is by genre, may suggest ways of clustering literary works so as to provide competing points of view on a variety of medical topics; on medical and social history; on the relations between writing and healing; and on the intimate and intricate way the imagination informs every aspect of the life of the body, the treatment of disease, and care for the sick and dying.

Works Cited

Auden, W. H. "Musée des Beaux Arts." Reynolds and Stone 128.

Chekhov, Anton. *"Ward Number Six" and Other Stories.* Trans. Ronald Hingley. 1974. World's Classics. Oxford: Oxford UP, 1988.

Donne, John. *Devotions upon Emergent Occasions.* Ann Arbor: U of Michigan P, 1959.

Feldshuh, David. *Miss Evers' Boys.* New York: Dramatists, 1995.

Gilman, Charlotte Perkins. "The Yellow Wallpaper." *Charlotte Perkins Gilman Reader.* Ed. Ann J. Lane. New York: Pantheon, 1980. 3–19.

Hemingway, Ernest. "Indian Camp." *The Short Stories of Ernest Hemingway.* 1938. New York: Scribner's, 1966. 89–95.

Keats, John. "Ode on Melancholy." *Norton Anthology of English Literature.* Vol. 2. New York: Norton, 1974. 668.

Klass, Perri. *Other Women's Children.* New York: Ballantine, 1990.

Kramer, Larry. *The Normal Heart.* New York: New Amer. Lib., 1985.

Kushner, Tony. *Angels in America.* New York: Theatre, 1993–94.

Levertov, Denise. "Death Psalm: O Lord of Mysteries." Reynolds and Stone 233–34

Lewis, Sinclair. *Arrowsmith.* New York: Signet, 1961.

Lorde, Audre. *Cancer Journals.* Argyle: Spinsters, 1980.

Manzoni, Alessandro. *The Betrothed.* Trans. Bruce Penman. New York: Penguin, 1972.

Payer, Lynn. *Medicine and Culture: Varieties of Treatment in the United States, England, West Germany, and France.* New York: Henry Holt, 1996.

Pomerance, Bernard. *The Elephant Man.* New York: Grove Atlantic, 1987.

Reynolds, Richard, and John Stone, eds. *On Doctoring.* New York: Simon, 1995.

Sacks, Oliver. *The Man Who Mistook His Wife for a Hat.* New York: Harper Perennial, 1990.

Selzer, Richard. "Imelda." Selzer, *Letters* 21–36.

———. *Letters to a Young Doctor.* New York: Simon, 1982.

———. "Mercy." Selzer, *Letters* 70–74.

Solzhenitsyn, Aleksandr. *Cancer Ward.* Trans. Nicholas Bethell and David Burg. New York: Bantam, 1969.

Tolstoy, Leo. *"The Death of Ivan Ilych" and Other Stories.* Trans. Aylmer Maude. New York: Signet-Penguin, 1960.

Whitman, Walt. "The Wound Dresser." *Leaves of Grass.* New York: Norton, 1968. 308–11.

Williams, William Carlos. "The Use of Force." *The Doctor Stories.* Comp. Robert Coles. New York: New Directions, 1984. 56–60.

Woolf, Virginia. "On Being Ill." *"The Moment" and Other Essays.* New York: Harcourt, 1974. 9–23.

Bryon Lee Grigsby

Plague Medicine in Langland's *Piers Plowman*

For most teachers of medicine and literature, the most obvious medieval literary reference to bubonic plague occurs in Boccaccio's *Decameron*. But William Langland's *Piers Plowman*, a fourteenth-century Middle English poem found in numerous manuscripts produced between the 1360s and 1387, provides a more comprehensive approach to the effects of bubonic plague on medieval society. Unlike Boccaccio, Langland addresses the issue of the plague directly, drawing on both medical and theological beliefs. According to Michael Dols, the most important thing to remember when discussing the plague "is not the precise mechanisms contrived by men to explain contagion (which were wrong) but the fact that in the Middle Ages—whether in Christian or in Muslim society—one simply could not separate the physiological from the mental and moral process" (286). While Langland operates within a plague discourse informed by both medicine and theology, he also blames the medical and ecclesiastical communities for failing to protect the physical and moral health of society. His long allegorical poem attempts to inform readers about the plague's origin and means of transmission while criticizing the leaders of society.

The text of *Piers Plowman* exists in at least three versions, the A, B, and C texts. Most of the medical information in *Piers Plowman* is found only in C text; a recent verse translation by George Economou makes this important work accessible to a large audience.[1] Given the length of *Piers,* I recommend excerpting passus 5, 8, and 22 for classes on plague literature. I also recommend using Rosemary Horrox's *The Black Death,* which provides a broad selection of primary texts in translation.

Langland is not like the disassociated reporter who narrates "The First Day" of Boccaccio's *Decameron.* Instead, Langland actively participates in contemporary plague discourses by validating certain interpretations of the plague's origin and means of transmission. In studying some of the earliest responses to pestilence, Jon Arrizabalaga found that medieval medical authorities believed that the plague had both moral and natural origins (245). Langland supports this point. In passus 5, Reason states that the plague has a moral cause and is transmitted naturally:

> Reason preached reverently before the whole realm,
> And proved that the plague was for sin purely   *{*
> And the wind from the southwest on a Saturday evening
> Was clearly for pride and no other cause.   (114–17)[2]

Langland involves the reader in what must have been a contemporary debate about the origin of the plague: Reason "proved" that pestilence originates in sin, namely pride, thereby implying a logical conclusion exclusive of alternative origins proposed by other authors, such as earthquakes.

Although Langland establishes that the plague has a moral cause, he also appropriates some of the medical community's theories about the plague's natural means of transmission. For Langland's contemporaries, nature was not in opposition to the divine; rather, nature worked at the divinity's bidding. Consequently, it was possible for the plague both to have a divine origin and to be transmitted naturally. Mention of the southwest wind as a means of transmission is found neither in Boccaccio's frame nor in any scriptural tradition but reflects a belief of the medical community. In 1348 the Paris medical faculty described the plague's natural transmission: "The many vapours which had been corrupted at the time of the conjunction were drawn up from the earth and water, and were then mixed with the air and spread abroad by frequent gusts of wind in the wild southerly gales [. . .] and are still doing so" (Horrox 161). Langland also notes astrological portents of pestilence. For example, in passus 8 Langland conveys to the Fair Field of Folk Saturn's warning that "through floods and foul weather fruits shall fail; / Pride and pestilence shall take out many people" (348–49). The use of Saturn as a warning of pestilence is typical of both medical and literary sources. The Paris medical faculty, citing Albertus Magnus, declared the "mortality of races and the depopulation of kingdoms occur at the conjunction of Saturn and Jupiter" (Horrox 159). In Chaucer's The Knight's Tale, Saturn declares to Venus, "My looking is the father of pestilence" (1.2469).

Another aspect of medieval plague discourse is the belief in the moral responsibility of healers. Langland chastises doctors, who are responsible for the health of the body, and priests, who are responsible for the health of the soul, accusing both groups of being greedy. For example, in passus 3, Conscience declares, "Harlots and whores and also quack doctors / Ask for their fee before they have earned it" (300–01). Langland's criticism appears to be historically accurate, since medical manuals often encouraged doctors to get their fees up front.[3] Doctors' cures for the plague rarely worked and were often prescribed with regard to the patient's social standing; a wealthy patient might be prescribed a costly elixir of gold.[4] Preferential treatment of the wealthy and powerful signified the greed of the medical community to Chaucer as well.[5]

Langland believed that most illness could be cured by regimen changes rather than by medications. The clearest example of this belief occurs in passus 8 when Piers asks Hunger for "any kind of medicine" for a stomachache (267–69). Hunger responds by saying simply that Piers and his servants have overeaten (271). To be cured, they should not eat until hungry, sit too long at the table, or become lazy (272–78).

Intriguingly, the dietary regimen that Hunger advises for Piers corresponds to dietary measures that doctors prescribed to patients to avoid the plague. For example, Gentile de Foligno suggests that "if someone works moderately and leads a decorous life, he will remain untouched [by the pestilence]" (qtd. in Arrizabalaga 273). If Piers and the others follow Hunger's regimen and correct their sinful behavior, illness will be avoided and doctors will be out of work:

> [. . .] the Doctor man shall sell his fur hoods for his food
> And pledge his Calabrian cloak for his provisions
> And be glad, by my faith, to abandon his practice,
> And learn to work on the land lest livelihood fail him.
> There are many bad doctors but few true physicians;
> They prescribe men's deaths before destiny knocks.
>
> (291–96)

Langland also denounces the clergy for greedily preferring money to service. His attack focuses on two types of priests: those who take advantage of high paying civic jobs ("Prologue" 85–95)[6] and those who are unqualified to hold their positions.[7] Langland's appraisal of the effects of bubonic plague on the clergy seems historically accurate. Since mortality rates were higher among priests than among any other social group, new clerics were mass-produced and lay people were allowed to perform confession and last rites (Gottfried 62). William Courtney finds that many priests opted for chancery positions in cities, leaving vacancies in parishes that were often covered by the appointment of mediocre parsons (703–13). Because Langland associates the presence of plague with continued sin, he condemns priests for failing to provide the community with necessary moral structure. As Free Will states, "If priests do their duty well, we shall do much better" (7.122).

Much of Langland's poem is about the failure of people to live moral lives. The plague symbolizes God's wrath, twice removed. As First Mover, God controls Nature, and plagues are essentially weapons of Nature. Since Nature does God's bidding, the plague cannot be evil. In passus 22, the narrator describes the military tactics Nature uses to defend against the numerous followers of the Antichrist:

> Hoary Old Age; he was in the vanguard
> And bore the banner before Death—he claimed it his right.
> Nature came after him with many sharp sores,
> Such as poxes and plagues, and wasted many people;
> So Nature killed off many with these corruptions. (95–99)[8]

The military metaphor, as Langland uses it, develops out of a belief that those who do not submit to God's laws suffer Death's "strokes" (22.105). Langland thus portrays immorality as a confrontation between the sinner and God. Fear of God becomes manifest in a fear of punishment or a fear of disease. Like modern authors, Langland used a military metaphor to change human behavior by attempting to invoke fear.

In *The Plague*, Albert Camus writes, "Perhaps the day would come when, for the bane and the enlightening of men, [the plague] would rouse up its rats again and send them forth to die in a happy city" (308). Plague discourses describe the varied human interpretations of the meaning of plague, of what we are meant to learn from plague's visitation, of our enlightenment. From Langland and Boccaccio through Daniel Defoe to Camus, plague discourses convey both medical and social messages. From a medical perspective, plague discourses are a means to communicate information to the reader about the disease's origin and means of transmission, as well as about methods of protection. This information is usually determined by contemporary medical belief, whether the discourse advocates a physical and dietary regimen, as in *Piers Plowman*, or documents the search for a better serum, as in *The Plague*.

Unlike our medieval counterparts, we rarely contemplate the social meaning of a plague. However, plagues often realistically point to problems within a society, and plague discourses can identify these problems. For example, both Langland and Camus criticize social leaders who fail to manage the sick effectively. A parallel can be drawn to contemporary literature that condems medical and government policies regarding AIDS. Plague discourses can also identify social practices that perpetuate illness. While contemporary accounts explained the bubonic plague as God's punishment for human sin, historians have determined that two proximate causes were deforestation and overpopulation (Platt 10–12; Gottfried 22–23). While these might not be considered sins, they are societal problems. Modern-day plagues, such as AIDS or cancer, highlight problems in our society. The incidence of AIDS infections continues to increase among young people, even though most of them know the means of transmission and methods of protection. One could say that AIDS identifies a social problem: young people feel the need to use intravenous drugs and to have numerous sex partners as a way to feel accepted. Similarly, while medicine continues to develop new ways to treat cancer, few of us examine how our actions have led to a damaging environment and an increase in carcinogens.

Langland's work actively participates in at least two plague discourses. On one level, *Piers Plowman* involves the reader in the medical, theological, and social debates of the Middle Ages. Langland validates certain theories concerning the plague's origin and means of transmission. On another level, Langland's work participates in an ongoing discourse that attempts to interpret the symbolic nature of disease and to determine the reason disease is here. From Boccaccio and Langland to Camus, from bubonic plague to cancer and AIDS, we all want to know why diseases visit us; we each construct our own plague discourse.

Notes

I wish to thank Carolyn Coulson-Grigsby, Allen J. Frantzen, and Stephen J. Harris for their help with this essay.

1. Economou provides a general introduction to the C text. For a more detailed discussion, see Pearsall.
2. Citations are to Economou's verse translation and are hereafter given by passus and line number.
3. See John of Arderne 25. On the economic standing of doctors, see Rawcliffe.

4. For effectiveness of plague cures, see Gottfried 113–16. For cures related to social standing, see Arrizabalaga 285.
5. See Chaucer's description of the doctor in The General Prologue 1.441–44.
6. One reason Chaucer's Parson is deemed so pure and moral is that he does not take a civic appointment over his parish job. See The General Prologue 1.507–13.
7. Langland's references to unlearned priests are numerous. For example, Sloth is characterized as a "priest and parson passing thirty winters" (7.30) who does not know his "pater noster" (7.10). Langland also accuses the priesthood of desiring silver (16.276) and misappropriating funds (17.68–69).
8. A larger catalog of Nature's armory of ills is listed earlier in passus 22: "Nature then heard Conscience and came out of the planets / And sent forth his foragers, fevers, and fluxes, / Coughs and heart trouble, cramps and toothaches, / Colds, running sores, and filthy scabs, / Boils and tumors and burning agues; / Frenzies and foul disorders, foragers of Nature, / Had pricked and preyed upon people's skulls; / An ample legion lost their lives soon" (80–87).

Works Cited

Arrizabalaga, Jon. "Facing the Black Death: Perceptions and Reactions of University Medical Practitioners." *Practical Medicine from Salerno to the Black Death*. Ed. Luis Garcia-Ballester, Roger French, Arrizabalaga, and Andrew Cunningham. Cambridge: Cambridge UP, 1994. 237–88.

Camus, Albert. *The Plague*. Trans. Stuart Gilbert. New York: Vintage, 1975.

Chaucer, Geoffrey. *The Riverside Chaucer*. Ed. Larry D. Benson. Boston: Houghton, 1987.

Courtney, William. "The Effects of the Black Death on English Higher Education." *Speculum* 55 (1980): 696–714.

Dols, Michael W. *The Black Death in the Middle East*. Princeton: Princeton UP, 1977.

Economou, George. *William Langland's* Piers Plowman: *The C Version: A Verse Translation*. Philadelphia: U of Pennsylvania P, 1996.

Gottfried, Robert S. *The Black Death: Natural and Human Disaster in Medieval Europe*. New York: Macmillan, 1983.

Horrox, Rosemary, trans. and ed. *The Black Death*. Manchester: Manchester UP, 1994.

John of Arderne. *Treatises of Fistula in Ano and of Fistulae in Other Parts of the Body [. . .]*. Ed. D'Arcy Power. London: Early English Text Soc., 1910.

Pearsall, Derek, ed. *William Langland* Piers Plowman: *The C-Text*. Exeter: U of Exeter P, 1994.

Platt, Colin. *King Death: The Black Death and Its Aftermath in Late-Medieval England*. Toronto: Toronto UP, 1997.

Rawcliffe, Carole. "The Profits of Practice: The Wealth and Status of Medical Men in Later Medieval England." *Social History of Medicine* 1 (1988): 61–78.

Paul W. Child

Teaching Restoration and Eighteenth-Century Medical Texts as Literature

Literary scholars have long recognized the thematic influence of Restoration and eighteenth-century medical writings on canonical literature and have mined the works of medical practitioners and theorists for glosses on authors like Defoe, Swift, Richardson, Smollett, Pope, Sterne, and Johnson. While this reading of medical literature and practice is valuable because it shows that the literary artist does not live in a cultural vacuum, it nevertheless imposes what John Richetti has called a "falsifying dichotomy separating scientific and philosophical works from writing that is overtly imaginative and rhetorical" (1). Within the larger context of cultural history, in fact, such distinctions between medical and literary discourses collapse. The eighteenth century itself, whose definition of *literature* comprehended all books and all writing, did not recognize dividing lines between canonical works and "subliterary" types (Williams 185).

With respect to this historical understanding of *literature* and the guiding principle that "everything written is indeed more or less literary" (Richetti 2), we can read Restoration and eighteenth-century medical texts not as influence on imaginative works of the day or as mere background for other, canonical works but as literature itself. Medical pamphlets and epistles, clinical and theoretical works, self-help manuals, quacks' bills, and practitioners' advertisements in popular periodicals—all these can be taught side by side with the novels, poetry, plays, and essays that an instructor might offer in a survey of Restoration and eighteenth-century British literature; all invite the same critical attention to rhetorical and aesthetic features that one might devote to imaginative works.

A reading of medical texts naturally begins with a series of fundamental questions that touch on rhetorical issues: Who are the authors, and who are their target audiences? Are works addressed *ad clerum* or *ad populum*? Is medical literature bibliogenic, one work responding to or written under the influence of another? What rhetorical strategies do writers use to gain personal and professional authority? What sorts of self-characterizations do the writers make in trying to establish this authority? What appeals do they make to accepted medical theory, training, or experience? And what cultural authorities do they invoke?[1]

These are the kinds of questions we might ask about the writings of established and celebrated physicians like Richard Mead, John Arbuthnot, and George Cheyne. Such writers debate theory, therapy, and medical politics with fellow medicos, or they address the literate public, disseminating medical advice in the same spirit of popularizing learning as that which inspired contemporary periodicals like the *Spectator Papers* and the *Gentlemen's Magazine*. In their appeals to both specialized and popular audiences, these authors are as concerned with the problems of establishing authority as is the narrator of a Fielding or Richardson novel or the persona of a work like Swift's *A Modest Proposal*. Often they begin with dedicatory epistles in which they address some "great man" or "club" with other physicians.[2] Throughout their texts they make pointed appeals to accepted intellectual and scientific authorities—not only classical figures like Hippocrates, Galen, and Celsus but also more recent authorities like Harvey, Newton, and the great clinician Thomas Sydenham, the "English Hippocrates." The writers tailor their arguments, diction, and tone to their target audiences' backgrounds and understandings of medical theory and therapy, taking for granted what they can, explaining what they must. For example, in his early iatromathematical treatises, written for the "Gentlemen of the Profession" and fellow members of the Royal Society, George Cheyne confidently uses mathematical nomenclature and abstract proofs to promote his Newtonian brand of medicine. In his later regimen books, written for a popular audience, however, he dilutes his Newtonianism and is careful to gloss his terms. Writing to his printer (and patient) Samuel Richardson about the forthcoming *Essay on Regimen* (1740), Cheyne announces his intention of appending a glossary "of all the hard Words and Terms of Science for the Ease of my Readers" (*Letters* 50).

In their appeals to the authority of experience, the physicians typically include case studies. Sometimes these are mere mentions of cures, appended to a treatise to substantiate the author's claims for his treatments and theory. Sometimes they are brief abstracts interspersed throughout a text to illustrate and confirm an author's recommended procedures. In Daniel Turner's practical *Art of Surgery*, for example, 119 case studies exemplify the author's methods. And sometimes, as in Cheyne's autobiographical "The Case of the Author" or in John Woodward's history of William Rockcliff, the case histories are extended narratives (Cheyne, *Malady*; Woodward, *Select Cases*).

If the rhetorical strategies of reputable physicians like Cheyne engage our interest, those of putative quacks like Anthony Daffy and William Salmon are even more compelling, especially since their claims to authority rested largely on self-promotion. In their bids for a piece of the lucrative medical market, these practitioners published bills, pamphlets, sometimes full-length treatises. Salmon, for example, dubbed "the Ring-Leader or king of the Quacks" by one contemporary physician (Wear 314), wrote a number of medical books to establish his credentials and pitch his nostrums and *pilulae mirabiles* (miracle pills). His works (like *Collectanea Medica, the Country Physician* [1703] and *Gaza Medica* [1705]) boast impressive hybrid Latin-English titles, feature dedications to prominent medical practitioners of the day,[3] and appropriate the jargon and concomitant authority of the learned physician of the late seventeenth and early eighteenth centuries. But Salmon and other so-called empiricks, like the established writer-practitioners, were always careful not to alienate audiences with concepts and language beyond their readers' abilities. Salmon, for example, published a list of pharmaceutical receipts for the "plain Country Practicer, whose Ignorance perchance of the Learned Languages, and possibly narrowness of his Fortunes, may make him incapable of perusing or purchasing the more elaborate Works, fitted for the higher Forms" (*Collectanea Medica* ii).

Writers from the medical fringe, like the established medical writers, traded in case studies. The cases of both are fascinating pieces of rhetoric because they carry the authority of empirical evidence and at the same time cleverly manipulate logic and language: if the treatment that the writer had administered failed, he could claim that the patient was already too far gone; if the patient recovered, the writer would claim credit for the cure.

Having considered rhetorical concerns in the medical texts, we may turn to aesthetic questions. How, for example, can we characterize the styles of various medical writers, and what critical vocabulary should we use in doing so? What narrative techniques, imagery, tone, symbols, and tropes does an author use? How is a work structured and to what end? How do the various medical genres correspond to such nonmedical genres of the day as the novel, verse epistle, or spiritual autobiography? What do these correspondences tell us about contemporary definitions of *literature*? And, since rhetorical and aesthetic concerns are interdependent, how does an author use devices like plot and character for persuasive purposes?

Literary features used by both established and fringe practitioners of medicine invite our critical attention. A writer like Cheyne or Salmon who cites case histories not only plots out the story of his patient and the story of the treatment, episode by episode, but also inevitably employs methods of characterization comparable to those employed by novelists and dramatists of the day. Such storytelling features compel the same questions about narrative choices and techniques and about characterization that we ask of imaginative literature: What events do the writers choose to tell their readers? How do they organize these events? What do they leave out? What expository details do they give? What is the conflict and the climax of each narrative account? To what extent do the characters in case histories become types, especially as the practitioners attempt to make generalizations about their patients and medical therapies used? How does such character typology compare with that of a novelist like Defoe, Richardson, or Fielding?

While any number of medical works of the day invite our critical appreciation, Cheyne's *The English Malady* (1733) exemplifies the possibilities for reading a medical text in a Restoration and eighteenth-century literature class. It is a remarkable work because of its immense popularity (it went through six reissues in a scant three years); because of its centrality to contemporary issues of medical theory, therapy, and politics; and because of Cheyne's self-conscious use of features like plot, character, and imagery.

The English Malady appeared when Cheyne was in his early sixties, after he had recovered from a series of debilitating illnesses and from chronic obesity (he once weighed thirty-two stone, or 448 pounds).[4] While he wrote his earlier iatromathematical works primarily as a means of establishing intellectual authority among his peers, he addressed *The English Malady* to a popular audience, inviting his readers to diagnose and then treat their own chronic disorders, especially nervous diseases, through regimen and diet. Thus enfranchising his reader, he placed the work squarely in the middle of the debate over how much medical authority should be conferred on lay individuals and in the larger debate of where the dividing line between layperson and professional should be drawn.

How, then, does this medical treatise read as a work of literature? To begin, there are the rhetorical means by which Cheyne establishes authority with his audience: an opening dedication to Lord Bateman, Knight of the Order of Bath; copious footnotes supporting Cheyne's theory and therapy; allusions to both ancient and modern medical and scientific authorities like Hippocrates, Galen, Newton, Sydenham, and Cheyne's mentor, Archibald Pitcairn; and numerous case studies that give empirical demonstrations of Cheyne's theory and therapy. Throughout the work, Cheyne speaks in the voice of the knowledgeable, commonsensical, civic-minded (and sometimes beleaguered) physician who has won his authority through clinical observation and hard experience.

A close reading of *The English Malady* might consider features like plot and character. The iatromechanical theory that buttresses Cheyne's therapy provides a narrative account—an intelligible plot —of how the body operates in sickness. Disease and its symptoms, argues Cheyne, result from "obstructions" in the system chiefly caused by concretions of deleterious "salts" that must be dissolved and then flushed out by diaphoretics and other "deobstruent Medicines" (*New Theory* 37–39.). Because meats contain a higher concentration of the highly attractive "animal salts" that tend to accumulate in the vessels, Cheyne logically prescribes a diet of dairy products and cereals as therapy and prophylaxis against the kinds of chronic disorders caused by the accumulation of these salts. His explanation thus plots the process by which the body moves from health to sickness and back again to health.

Each of Cheyne's case studies is also plotted. In most cases, his characterizations in these histories are largely generalized, with little attempt to make anything more than mere types of his patients ("A Lady of the first Quality" or "A Gentlemen of Scotland, of an Antient and Honourable Family" [*English Malady* 267–83]), and plot is usually distilled to a simple agon of upper-class excesses and middle-class restraint. Again and again, self-indulgent, medically irresponsible patient-characters from the "Upper Orders" are cured by following a course of moderation, temperance, and common sense—in short, all the virtues Cheyne consistently associates in his treatises with the "middle Rank."

The case of "A Knight Baronet of an Antient Family" is exemplary. Having worn down his constitution with free living in London and "keeping bad Hours, in attending upon the Business of the Parliament," the baronet is afflicted by symptoms of a chronic disorder: "an habitual Diarrhoea, attended with exteme Flatulence, Lowness, Oppression, Watchfulness, and Indigestion." In short, he suffers from the English malady. Desperate, he turns to Cheyne, who puts him on a regimen of exercise and a moderate or "Trimming" diet, which includes small portions of white meat, claret, spa water, and vegetables, cereals, and milk. After a year and a half of this regimen, the baronet gradually "acquir[es] an Athletick State of Health." And Cheyne reports proudly that he "has been these twenty Years a hale, strong, fine Gentlemen, on common plain Diet, with due Temperance" (277–78). One of the persistent themes at work here, as in Cheyne's other case studies, is the fictive transformation of the upper orders by the middle class. This symbolic transformation places Cheyne in a literary tradition cultivated by contemporary novelists and dramatists like Richardson, Cibber, and Rowe, in whose works idealized middle-class characters inevitably convert or outwit their upper-class antagonists.

Aside from its narrative and thematic interests, *The English Malady* has stylistic features that warrant critical attention. Perhaps because Cheyne wrote for a popular audience and felt compelled to defend his work against the "Sneer of its being a Quack's Bill" (259), he cultivated all the best stylistic features of eighteenth-century prose elegance: parallelism, balance and caesura, antitheses, anaphora, epigram, periodic sentence structure. He also carefully manipulated patterns of imagery (a death-reanimation motif pervades the case studies, for example) to unify the work and emphasize central points, and he used figurative language (metaphors from the stage and military operations, for example) to make his more difficult ideas clear and concrete to readers who did not have his mathematical and medical background (Child 247–60).

"The Case of the Author," the autobiographical case study with which *The English Malady* culminates, invites a discussion of genre. In this history of his own illness and subsequent recovery, Cheyne invokes the language, structure, and ethos of the spiritual autobiography, in which a reflecting speaker, looking back on the apparently disconnected experiences of his past, reads "God's plot" for his life.[5] Adopting and modifying the narrative inheritance of this genre in "The Case of the Author," Cheyne traces in exhaustive and all too graphic detail the history of his illnesses and recovery. Then, in the final sentences of his narrative, he explicitly interprets the symptoms he has endured and the recovery he has enjoyed as signs of God's providence and reads his medical history as the plot for his life written by "the Author of Nature": "I shall, I hope, go on in the Method now described, and live, and I hope, die in continual Gratitude to the Best of Beings, who, by an over-ruling Providence, and as it were, by meer casual Hints, far beyond the Reach of my Penetration, has irresistably (as I should almost say, if I felt not my own Liberty) directed the great Steps of my Life and Health hitherto" (364). The reading code of spiritual autobiography having been established, the apparently disconnected and random events of Cheyne's medical history now fit coherently into the providential plot.

Medical texts like *The English Malady* and other treatises, pamphlets, and bills are the products of authors who organize and shape their materials as deliberately as the novelist or poet; address the text to an audience in a way that determines diction, tone, style, and organizing principles; make various claims to intellectual or practical authority; and carry with them certain cultural biases that determine the selection and manipulation of materials. These are the very concerns we address in reading nonmedical publications of the day, like Dryden's *Absalom and Achitophel, Religio Laici,* and *The Hind and the Panther*; Swift's *Modest Proposal* and *Gulliver's Travels*; Pope's *Dunciad*; Johnson's *Vanity of Human Wishes* and *Rasselas*; and any number of other canonical pieces. And these are the very concerns that recommend our reading medical works in a Restoration and eighteenth-century literature course.

Notes

1. Even under the time constraints of a semester, students can develop at least nodding familiarity with the ecology of Restoration and eighteenth-century practice by consulting a number of fine secondary works, including Cook's *The Trials of an Ordinary Doctor*; Holmes's *Augustan England*; Loudon's *Medical Care and the General Practitioner, 1750–1850*; Porter and Porter's *Patient's Progress*; and Wear's "Medical Practice in Late Seventeenth- and Early-Eighteenth-Century England: Continuity and Union."

2. "The method of Writing, if in your Frontispiece, you address not your

Book to some great Man," John Woodward advised would-be medical authors, tongue-in-cheek, "is to Club with some other Physicians; and thus by way of Letters, to commend each others good Practice, and so to support and make each other Famous" (*Art* 11).

3. One work is dedicated to Peter Salmon, an important practitioner of the day, but no relation whatsoever to the author. William Salmon hoped to exploit his audience's confusion over the similarity of names.

4. A Scotsman who immigrated to London at the turn of the eighteenth century armed with a medical degree from Aberdeen, Cheyne was at various times personal physician to Richardson, Pope, Beau Nash, the Walpoles, and other social and literary luminaries. He specialized in chronic ailments like gout and hypochondriasis, that complex of nervous, gastrointestinal, and psychological disorders popularly known as the English malady.

5. The most popular spiritual autobiographies of Cheyne's day were being written by Puritans and Quakers like John Bunyan and Edward Coxere, and by Daniel Defoe, whose *Robinson Crusoe* fictionalizes the usual pattern of fall and redemption. But Cheyne, an Anglican nurtured in the tradition of episcopacy, would have had the great model of Augustine's *Confessions* before him, even if he were unsympathetic or unfamiliar with the versions of the religious dissenters. (For more on reading "The Case of the Author" in this tradition, see Guerrini; Child 174–94.)

Works Cited

Cheyne, George. *The English Malady.* 1733. London: Routledge, 1990.

———. *Letters of Doctor George Cheyne to Samuel Richardson.* Ed. Charles F. Mullet. *University of Missouri Studies* 18.1 (1943): 7–132.

———. *A New Theory of Acute and Slow Continu'd Fevers [. . .] to Which Is Prefix'd an Essay concerning the Improvements of the Theory of Medicine.* 3rd ed. London: Strahan, 1722.

Child, Paul W. "Discourse and Practice in Eighteenth-Century Medical Literature: The Case of George Cheyne." Diss. U of Notre Dame, 1992.

Cook, Harold J. *The Trials of an Ordinary Doctor: Johannes Groenvelt in Seventeenth-Century London.* Baltimore: Johns Hopkins UP, 1994.

Guerrini, Anita. "Case History as Spiritual Autobiography: George Cheyne's 'Case of the Author.'" *Eighteenth-Century Life* 19.2 (1995): 18–27.

Holmes, Geoffrey. *Augustan England: Professions, State and Society, 1680–1730.* London: Allen, 1982.

Loudon, Irving. *Medical Care and the General Practitioner, 1750–1850.* Oxford: Clarendon, 1986.

Porter, Dorothy, and Roy Porter. *Patient's Progress: Doctors and Doctoring in Eighteenth-Century England.* Stanford: Stanford UP, 1989.

Richetti, John. *Philosophical Writing: Locke, Berkeley, Hume.* Cambridge: Harvard UP, 1983.

Salmon, William. *Collectanea Medica, the Country Physician; or,* A *Choice Collection of Physick: Fitted for Vulgar Use.* London: Taylor, 1703.

———. *Gaza Medica: A Set of Excellent Medicines for the Cure of Most Diseases Incident to the Bodies of Men, Women, and Children: Made and Prepared by W. Salmon, M.D., at His House near Black Friers-Stairs.* London, 1705.

Turner, Daniel. *The Art of Surgery* [. . .] *Further Illustrated with Many Singular and Rare Cases Medico-Chirurgical.* 2 vols. London: Rivington, 1722.

Wear, Andrew. "Medical Practice in Late-Seventeenth- and Early-Eighteenth-Century England: Continuity and Union." *The Medical Revolution of the Seventeenth Century.* Ed. Roger French and Wear. Cambridge: Cambridge UP, 1989. 294–320.

Williams, Raymond. *Keywords: A Vocabulary of Culture and Society.* London: Fontana, 1983.

Woodward, John. *The Art of Getting into Practice in Physick, Here at Present in London. In a Letter to That Very Ingenious and Most Learned Physician, (Lately Come to Town) Dr. Timothy Vanbustle, M.D. A.B.C., &c.* London: Peele, 1722.

———. *Select Cases, and Consultations, in Physick. By the Late Eminent John Woodward, M.D.* Ed. Peter Templeman. London: Davis, 1747.

H. Bruce Franklin

"Doctor" Frankenstein and "Scientific" Medicine

No single book offers more meaningful and complex interconnections between literature and medicine than Mary Shelley's *Frankenstein; or, The Modern Prometheus*—that "first great myth of the industrial age" (Aldiss 23). One could easily spend an enlightening semester just exploring the paths opened by this novel. Students of course know the myth—and all refer to that college dropout who created the monster as "Doctor" Frankenstein. I ask them why a novel written almost two centuries ago by someone younger than most of them should still permeate our culture. One answer is obvious: Frankenstein is the archetypal scientist, who discovers, invents, or unleashes forces that make humanity confront its own creativity in the form of awesome alien powers.

Frankenstein is a very particular kind of scientist: a man of medicine. He thus tends to embody some of the contradictions of medicine today. We have marvels of medical technology—genetic engineering, magnetic resonance imaging, organ transplants, arthroscopic surgery, in vitro fertilization, cyborg fantasies materializing as body parts are replaced, boundless promises of health and life. But we also have a disintegrating health delivery system; closed and understaffed hospitals; medical dollars and time gobbled up by endless bureaucratic paper pushing; the resurgence of supposedly archaic diseases like tuberculosis; lurking diseases like Ebola; epidemics of AIDS, drug addiction, and cancer; and the vortex of (mis)managed care. And if the individual's life *is* extended, where does it end? In the abyss of a nursing home? As an appendage to life-support machinery? Or with the mercies of a Dr. Kevorkian?

I try to defer discussion of all this obvious relevance of *Frankenstein* until after my students and I have explored, in detail, three interrelated topics: the novel's strange narrative structure, the history of medicine as a major context of the novel, and the effects of this history on Mary Shelley's life.

Although written by a woman, *Frankenstein* consists almost entirely of male voices and seems to be all about the lives of male beings. The entire novel is narrated in letters from Robert Walton, the would-be grand global explorer. Inside his narrative is that of Victor Frankenstein. And inside Frankenstein's narrative is that of his creature. Women are thus presented as the objects of male perception, desires, and fears, and the main female character's primary role is that of victim. But since the letters are all addressed to Walton's sister, Margaret Saville (whose initials happen to be those of the author), the implied listener to these male voices, though silent, is a female consciousness.

Frankenstein appeared during a crucial period in the emergence of what is called "Western," or "scientific," or "modern" medicine, as if these terms are interchangeable and as if all other systems of medicine are merely "alternative." Here we find vital connections between the narrative of the novel, so thoroughly dominated by male voices, and the history of medicine.

The swift rise of "scientific" medicine over the past two centuries looks especially spectacular because it was starting from such an abysmal level. Throughout the Middle Ages, European medicine, like that in most societies then in Asia, Africa, and the Americas, was based mainly on empirical methodology, passed on orally from generation to generation. Because the large skull of human babies often necessitates assistance in the birth process, all peoples have had to learn basic principles of obstetrics. In Europe, as elsewhere, the people who provided obstetric care were of course almost all women. Because Europe was largely agricultural, other medical tasks fell largely to village healers, usually also women. These healers reset broken bones, performed operations including abortions, provided contraceptives, and diagnosed many diseases. They assembled a massive pharmacology of herbal remedies, many still in use, including digitalis (foxglove) to treat heart disease; ergot derivatives and belladonna to accelerate or inhibit uterine contractions; and a wide assortment of painkillers, digestive aids, and anti-inflammatory agents.[1] Like most medical practitioners today, they also used incantations and rituals to promote the psychological component of their healing arts.

Because these healers were mainly women and because they excluded men from the birth scene, they posed a threat to male prerogatives. They also posed a threat to the church, which of course excluded them from the rival profession of priest, a man supposedly able to cure diseases through divine intervention. But their most direct threat was to the *profession* of medicine, reserved for a handful of men who studied at universities. The thirteenth century, when the Holy Roman Emperor Frederick II decreed that no one could practice medicine until he had been publicly approved by the masters of the University of Salerno, was also the century when the witch hunts began.

From the thirteenth through the seventeenth century, just as the all-male, university-trained medical profession was becoming hegemonic, women healers found themselves labeled as witches, tortured until they confessed that their powers came from Satan, and then hanged or burned alive. By the time the European witch hunts were over, the infrastructure of the traditional European health-care system had been shattered. In its place was a system that largely disdained empirical methods, basing itself on theory inherited from classical texts and using a variety of medical instruments derived from developing technology. What we call "scientific" medicine arose from the ruins of a female medicine that was probably more scientific than the early forms of its male successor.

By the eighteenth century, men were invading midwifery, the last preserve of female healing. (Men had a monopoly on obstetrical instruments, such as forceps, because women were legally barred from surgery.) The displacement of midwives by male physicians was deplored by Mary Wollstonecraft in her great 1792 manifesto, *A Vindication of the Rights of Woman* (148).

Five years later, Wollstonecraft chose a female midwife to attend her own delivery. The baby—the future author of *Frankenstein*—was delivered normally, but when the midwife was unable to extract the placenta, which had disintegrated, the chief obstetrician of a famous lying-in hospital was brought in. With unwashed hands, he groped for hours in her womb, almost certainly introducing puerperal fever, from which Wollstonecraft died ten days later. Not until 1843, when Dr. Oliver Wendell Holmes published *The Contagiousness of Puerperal Fever*, did Western medicine begin to comprehend why the mortality rate among women giving birth in European hospitals was between 20 and 30 percent. In 1847, Ignaz Semmelweis noted that women who gave birth at home, tended by traditional midwives, had a far lower mortality rate and that in his own hospital women attended by physicians had a death rate from puerperal fever three times higher than the rate in the division where only midwives attended. When he had doctors wash their hands before obstetrical examinations and delivery, the death rate from puerperal fever immediately plunged from nearly 20 percent to 1.3 percent (Zoltán 529).

By the early nineteenth century, university-trained professional doctors—all male—had become the main deliverers of health care in Europe, England, and America for the upper and middle classes, especially in urban settings. Most doctors had been taught to rely on what were called heroic measures: massive bleeding, huge doses of laxatives and cathartics (including calomel, a salt of mercury), emetics, and, somewhat later, opium. Holmes expressed his contempt for the medicine being practiced by his professional contemporaries when he said that if all the medicines they used were thrown into the ocean, it would be better for people and worse for fish.

One matrix for Mary Shelley's imagination was her own experience with birth and death in the medical environment of the early nineteenth century.[2] Only one of her four children lived past the age of three. Her first child, born in 1815, died after twelve days. A few days later, seventeen-year-old Mary wrote in her journal: "Dream that my little baby came to life again; that it had only been cold, and that we had rubbed it before the fire, and it had lived" (*Journals* 70). Nine months after this journal entry, Mary gave birth to her son William, the namesake of Victor Frankenstein's young brother, the monster's first victim. Within months of William's birth, Mary began writing *Frankenstein*, which she completed in May 1817 while pregnant with her second daughter, Clara. *Frankenstein* was published in January 1818. Clara died that September, at the age of one. William died the following June, at the age of three, after a highly regarded physician prescribed massive doses of calomel, gamboge, and other purgatives for worms (*Journals* 278–80). This experience with European medicine evidently influenced revisions Mary Shelley made to the 1831 edition of *Frankenstein*, which she referred to in her introduction as "my hideous progeny" (23).

Victor Frankenstein grows up with Elizabeth, a beautiful little girl whom he calls "my more than sister" (41). In the 1831 edition, Elizabeth's mother, like Mary Shelley's, "had died on giving her birth," leading to her adoption by Victor's parents (41).[3] Just as Victor is about to set off to begin his studies at the University of Ingolstadt, the first fatal event in his life occurs. Elizabeth contracts scarlet fever and is "in the greatest danger." Victor's mother insists on attending "her sick bed,—her watchful attentions triumphed over the malignity of the distemper,—Elizabeth was saved, but the consequences of this imprudence were fatal to her preserver." His mother catches the disease and dies within three days as "her medical attendants" look on helplessly (47).[4] On her deathbed, she joins the hands of Victor and Elizabeth and pledges them to marry each other. Elizabeth, thanks to the impotent medical care available, has now caused the death of both her birth mother and her adoptive mother.

It is prior to his mother's death and his study at Ingolstadt that Frankenstein, his imagination possessed by reading medieval alchemists, aspires to "banish disease from the human frame, and render man invulnerable to any but a violent death." But when he "becomes capable of bestowing animation upon lifeless matter," his goal shifts. He no longer seems concerned with either the prevention or the treatment of disease. What he now dedicates his life to is "the creation of a human being" (54–55).

At this point, I raise the gender issues at the heart of Mary Shelley's prevision of modern science. I ask the class, If Frankenstein simply wants to create a human being, wouldn't there be an easier way to go about it? They point out that this would involve having sex with Elizabeth or some other woman. So what he wants to do is create a human being all by himself, without any contact with a woman, substituting for sexual and human intercourse what he construes to be science. To make his creature, he has already cut himself off entirely from all communication with Elizabeth, whom he claims to love so passionately. Later, when his father suggests that he marry Elizabeth, Victor recoils: "[T]o me the idea of an immediate union with my Elizabeth was one of horror and dismay" (130). This is *before* the monster, a creature that has emerged from Frankenstein's mind and body, threatens, "I shall be with you on your wedding-night" (142). On the wedding night, Victor has this to say to his bride: "Oh! peace, peace, my love [. . .] this night and all will be safe: but this night is dreadful, very dreadful" (163). Then despite the obvious fact that the creature plans to kill Elizabeth, Victor sends her alone to their bridal bed while he, armed with sword and pistol, waits for the monster to attack *him*. The psychological significance of Victor's obsession had come out clearly in the dream he had the night he created his monster: "I thought I saw Elizabeth, in the bloom of health, walking in the streets of Ingolstadt. Delighted and surprised, I embraced her; but as I imprinted the first kiss on her lips, they became livid with the hue of death; her features appeared to change, and I thought that I held the corpse of my dead mother in my arms; a shroud enveloped her form, and I saw the graveworms crawling in the folds of the flannel" (58). We do not need Freud's *The Interpretation of Dreams*, published more than eight decades later, to recognize that Frankenstein's monster emerges from the unconscious depths of his masculine mind.

Disease, death, and the hubris of European medicine continued to haunt the imagination that conceived *Frankenstein*. Between the 1818 and 1831 editions, Mary Shelley brought forth one of the bleakest books in literature, *The Last Man* (1826), the first novel to imagine a disease that brings about the extinction of the human species. Entirely absent from *The Last Man* is Victor Frankenstein's boundless faith in scientific medicine.

Notes

1. Good sources for this history are Ehrenreich and English; Barstow (especially ch. 6, "From Healers into Witches"); Green; and Estes.
2. Ellen Moers provided the first extended discussion of relations between Shelley's experience with birth and *Frankenstein*. See also Bewell.
3. In the 1818 edition, Elizabeth is the niece of Frankenstein's father, who adopts her after her mother dies (at a time unspecified).
4. In the 1818 edition, Elizabeth is almost recovered when Victor's mother imprudently visits the sick chamber to see her.

Works Cited

Aldiss, Brian. *Billion Year Spree: The True History of Science Fiction*. Garden City: Doubleday, 1973.

Barstow, Anne Llewellyn. *Witchcraze: A New History of the European Witch Hunts*. San Francisco: Pandora-Harper, 1994.

Bewell, Alan. "An Issue of Monstrous Desire: *Frankenstein* and Obstetrics." *Yale Journal of Criticism* 2.1 (1988): 105–28.

Ehrenreich, Barbara, and Deirdre English. *Witches, Midwives, and Nurses: A History of Women Healers*. Old Westbury: Feminist, 1973.

Estes, Leland L. "The Medical Origins of the European Witch Craze: A Hypothesis." *Journal of Social History* 17 (1983): 271–84.

Green, Monica. "Women's Medical Practice and Health Care in Medieval Europe." *Signs* 14 (1989): 434–73.

Moers, Ellen. *Literary Women*. Garden City: Doubleday, 1976.

Shelley, Mary. *Frankenstein; or, The Modern Prometheus*. 1831. Ed. Johanna M. Smith. Boston: Bedford, 1992.

———. *The Journals of Mary Shelley, 1814–1844*. Ed. Paula R. Feldman and Diana Scott Kilvert. Oxford: Oxford UP, 1987.

————. *The Last Man*. 1826. Ed. Hugh J. Luke, Jr. Lincoln: U of Nebraska
  P, 1965.
Wollstonecraft, Mary. *A Vindication of the Rights of Woman*. New York:
  Norton, 1975.
Zoltán, Imre. "Ignaz Philipp Semmelweis." *Encyclopaedia Britannica:
  Macropaedia*. 16th ed. 1975.

Michèle M. Respaut

The Nineteenth Century's Obsession with Medicine: Flaubert's *Madame Bovary*

Gustave Flaubert's *Madame Bovary,* the narrative of a provincial housewife whose amorous and social aspirations combine with the mediocrity of her doctor-husband to produce adultery, suicide, and the destruction of a family, is the ideal beginning work for a course on literature and medicine. A masterpiece preoccupied with medicine, health, sickness, and death, it introduces concerns that are bound to recur in any course on medical themes in modern Western literature: the image of the doctor (inept or godlike); the practice, progress, and failures of doctors; worries about health problems that range from the trivial to the fatal and include female "pathologies" persistent throughout the nineteenth and twentieth centuries; depictions of the body, death, and mourning. Importantly, in this novel medicine is intimately connected both with literature and with the complex texture of human life. Devoted to the search for perfect form, Flaubert exemplifies the conflation of doctor and writer found in authors from Balzac and Zola to the present day. Flaubert's father was a celebrated physician, Flaubert's illness incapacitated Flaubert

for everything but a literary career, and the inspiration for the
novel's plot derived from the life of one of the students of Flaubert's
father — all this is summed up in a caricature of Flaubert dissecting
the corpse of Emma Bovary.[1]

Framed by the depiction of Emma's husband's childhood and
death and punctuated by the illnesses and deaths of relatives and
others, Emma's story reveals the progress of her malady: a psychosexual, familial, and societal sickness by which she will come to be
recognized as that obsessive figure, the hysterical woman. Her illness is caused and exacerbated by a number of factors: her temperament, her education and the aspirations it fosters in her, her good
but dull husband, her faithless lovers, and those who exploit her fi-
nancially or contribute to her harm in other ways (notably Homais).
Brilliantly, these factors are related to the prevailing role of medicine, which Flaubert shows to be embedded in the class and value
structures of the society depicted in his novel. Among the practitioners in the book's provincial setting, it is Charles Bovary's famous
patron, Larivière, thought by some to be an idealized portrait of
Flaubert's father, who is called on near the end of each of the novel's
three parts to attempt to cure or save Emma. He does so when she
is pregnant and despondent in Tostes, during her nearly fatal illness
after Rodolphe's betrayal, and, finally, as she dies from the arsenic
she has taken.

Charles, and perforce his wife, inhabits a degraded provincial
realm in the novel's medical and societal hierarchy. His father was a
military surgeon disgraced in a conscription scandal. Charles's medical education, at which Charles initially fails, gains for him the sec-
ond-rate degree of *officier de santé*, limiting him to low-level
medical practice. (Instituted during the Revolution and abolished in
1892, the degree did not require the equivalent of the *baccalauréat*,
limited the practitioner to a specific region, and forbade him to perform major operations except under the supervision of a regular
doctor.) Hence the reference to Charles as "the country doctor"
("le médecin de campagne"; 11) is ironic, recalling the heroic protagonist in Balzac's novel of that title. Everything about the house
where Emma finds herself after her marriage stresses mediocrity: the

uncut medical volumes, the kitchen smells in the consulting room, the patients' coughs heard in the kitchen. Charles's profession seems to invade her consciousness as well as the feminine domestic sphere that in any event she wishes to flee. Even when her husband builds up a thriving practice (and Flaubert stresses how good he is at the prudent kind of medicine he pursues), Emma cannot bear the humiliation of his having been corrected by a doctor from a slightly more prominent town. It is her depression that causes the move to Yonville, where he never achieves the same success.

Charles's lack of success is due not only to Emma's excesses but also to the illegal competition of Homais, a complex figure who is self-serving, pedantic, and frequently in error but who expresses many of the attitudes characteristic of our world regarding family, society, science, and medicine. Railing against superstition, indiscriminately in favor of science and progress (including both vaccination and such bizarre inventions as the Pulvermacher hydroelectric health belt), severely judged at the end for prostituting himself to gain his ends, Homais suggests the dubiousness of medicine that emerges from this novel. He is responsible for the book's catastrophes, providing the arsenic, about which he is later forced to invent a lie, and proposing the disastrous operation on Hippolyte's clubfoot.

The operation scene allows for much technical language, a chilling description of a gangrenous leg, and the introduction of a physician — the celebrated Canivet — from a still more prominent town. Canivet's self-presentation is boastful, but his rejection of "Parisian" inventions includes chloroform, a fact we recall when we hear the screams of Hippolyte during the amputation of his leg. At the end, when Larivière arrives too late from the provincial capital Rouen to save Emma, he excoriates Canivet for his incompetence, while Charles and Homais have again proved their ineptitude.

Larivière is described by the narrator as heroic. People respond to him as if to the "apparition of a god." He is majestically superior, belonging to the school of surgery formed by the great Bichat (1771–1802), "that generation, now extinct, of philosophical practitioners, who, cherishing their art with a fanatical love, exercised it with enthusiasm and wisdom" (233). The doctor may be godlike, but the tone of nostalgia here and the victory of Homais on the novel's closing page suggest that even the noble calling of medicine is submerged in the end by the vulgarity and mendacity of modern society.

Concerns of medicine and health pervade the alternately banal and inhumanly destructive behavior Flaubert depicts. Desire and passion, health and illness, and the outrageous pursuit of money are mingled throughout. Charles's first marriage proves deceptive on all counts: his wife, the ironically named Héloïse, is fleeced by her notary and dies, and her death is interpreted by Charles as proof of her love. Financial considerations are important again in Rouault's decision to allow his daughter's union with Charles, a relationship that begins with Rouault's broken leg and Emma's complaints about her health. Charles's success in treating patients and the discussions about health mediate subsequent events, including the invitation to la Vaubyessard and Emma's adulteries. Rodolphe brings a servant to be bled, flatters Bovary by calling him "docteur," and seduces Emma during their first ride together, having proposed this exercise to relieve her palpitations. Léon, who the narrator says would be intimidated by the wife of a "famous physician" in Paris (167), gets Emma talking about her illness and follows through with his seduction of her in the famous cab ride.

Lheureux and Guillaumin, who exploit others for money, destroying the Bovarys' wealth and contributing to the suicide of Emma, use the same tactics: complaints about health, flattery of Charles as a doctor, and exploitation of every illness to increase the family's indebtedness to them. The link between financial exploitation and medicine is explicit: Lheureux wants his money to thrive "in the doctor's care like a patient in a rest home" (153), and near the end Emma experiences the seizure of her intimate possessions as an autopsy (215). Flaubert's writing is comparable to the understanding of a great doctor, in that it does not simply describe isolated illnesses or operations. Rather, if Flaubert may be said to dissect Emma's corpse at the end, it is only after he has dissected also all the socioeconomic forces, the financial and sexual exploitations that contribute to her death.

In this light Emma Bovary may be seen as the most developed and thoroughly explained example of a figure that continues to obsess literature and psychology: the hysterical woman. Her illness begins with literature, in the romanticized reading about history and love that generates the aspirations to wealth, nobility, and passion so evident in her visit to la Vaubyessard and in her love affairs. Emma's idealized vision of "illustrious or unhappy women" (26) will be lived out in all too realistic fashion. Her education is condemned by Charles's first wife and later by Charles's mother, who uses the conventional vocabulary of *vapors* to analyze Emma's case. As a cure the mother prescribes hard work and proscribes the reading of novels. Emma's state at the end of part 1 is diagnosed by Larivière as "a nervous condition" (46) characterized by boredom, periods of torpor alternating with exaltation, paleness, palpitations, self-deprivation of food (she drinks vinegar to lose weight), and depression.

Repetition and tragic intensification mark Flaubert's unfolding of the rest of Emma's life in parts 2 and 3. Frustrated in her desire for Léon, she exhibits the classic symptoms of the hysteric: she is shattered, inert; she pants and sobs. As Tony Tanner has underscored (233–35), the story Emma's servant tells of a depressive young woman cured by marriage reveals the opposite in Emma's case: "But with me [. . .] it was after marriage that it began" (78). Her discussion with Bournisien, in which she seeks spiritual solace, is ironically interpreted by the priest in medical terms (part 2, ch. 6). Returning home, Emma angrily knocks her daughter to the ground, lies about the incident to Charles, and initiates the pattern of neglect and deceit that by the end makes her illness a family disaster. At this stage, however, the narrator explains that "the desires of the flesh, the longing for money, and the melancholy of passion all blended into one suffering" (77).

Sexual desire, emotional need, and the wish for money are evident, physically, psychologically, and materially, in the progress of Emma's illness. Lovemaking with Rodolphe provides an exaltation experienced bodily in heart rate and nerves and is accompanied by Emma's financial extravagances and exotic plans for escape with him. His betrayal produces her near suicide and prolonged illness, which are powerfully described in a passage at the end of chapter 13 of part 2. After her convalescence, the obsessive nature of her behavior with Léon in part 3 is stressed in her weekly and then more frequent visits to Rouen and in her compulsive lying. Emma's madness expresses itself in her passion for the law clerk, in her desperation as creditors close in on her, and in hysterical symptoms such as sweating, stammering, and wildly rolling eyes — behaviors that frighten Léon and cause the wet nurse Madame Rollet to think her insane.

Flaubert's description of Emma's confusion, madness, and death by suicide after the rejection of her plea for help is riveting (part 3, chs. 8 and 9), provoking sympathy for the character and self-reflection in the reader—a profound memento mori. Although in what precedes the suicide there is much that may be used in teaching this novel — the pervasive way in which medicine is embedded in the social order, particular scenes like the failed operation or Emma's earlier suicide attempt—it is undoubtedly the chapters on her death that most repay close attention. In a heroic transport, she swallows the arsenic, curiously observes her first mild symptoms, then suffers atrociously: sweating, cold, in pain, panting, convulsing, vomiting, vomiting blood. Her tongue protrudes from her mouth and then comes the final death rattle. The description of the transformations of her dead body is equally disturbing, as is the reappearance at the moment of her death of the blind beggar, who was earlier described in ghastly detail. The beggar is an occasion for Homais to demonstrate his devotion to progress and his Foucault-sounding addiction to control and power (he gets the man put away for life), but the passages on the blind man's condition illustrate the power of language to convey the corruption of the human body. Together with other motifs (the dance of death at la Vaubyessard; Madame Rollet fatefully at her spinning wheel just before the end, producing a sound that Emma confuses with the noise of Binet's lathe [224]), the blind beggar points to a universal, mythic theme

(see Goodwin, "Dance" and *Kitsch*). *Madame Bovary* is *the* novel of
literature and medicine, in which illness and death—conceived of as
psychological, familial, and societal, but ultimately physical—touch
all things.

Note

Quotations from *Madame Bovary* are from the Norton Critical Edition.

1. Remot's caricature *Flaubert disséquant Emma Bovary*, published in *La
   Parodie* in September 1869, is reproduced in the Pocket edition of
   Madame Bovary, edited by Pierre-Louis Rey. Ajac's introduction to the
   Flammarion edition of the novel discusses Maxime Du Camp's *Sou-
   venirs littéraires* on the story of Doctor Flaubert's student as well as the
   many letters in which Flaubert described the writing of *Madame Bovary* in medical terms, including terms of dissection, psychology, and
   anatomy. Selections from some of these letters are appended to the
   Norton Critical Edition of *Madame Bovary*. See also Furst; Gray.

Works Cited

Ajac, Bernard. Introduction. *Madame Bovary*. By Gustave Flaubert. Paris:
   Flammarion, 1986. 5–50.

Flaubert, Gustave. *Madame Bovary*. Trans. Paul de Man. Norton Critical
   Edition. New York: Norton, 1996.

Furst, Lilian R. "Realism and Hypertrophy: A Study of Three Medico-His-
   torical 'Cases.' " *Nineteenth-Century French Studies* 22.1–2 (1993–94):
   29–47.

Goodwin, Sarah Webster. "Emma Bovary's Dance of Death." *Novel* 19
   (1986): 197–215.

———. *Kitsch and Culture: The Dance of Death in Nineteenth-Century Literature and Graphic Arts*. New York: Garland, 1988.

Gray, Eugene F. "The Clinical View of Life: Gustave Flaubert's *Madame
   Bovary*." *Medicine and Literature*. Ed. Enid Rhodes Peschel and Edmund D. Pellegrino. New York: Watson, 1980. 81–87.

Remot, A. *Flaubert disséquant Emma Bovary*. *Madame Bovary*. By Gustave
   Flaubert. Ed. Pierre-Louis Rey. Paris: Pocket, 1990. Plate 1.

Tanner, Tony. *Adultery in the Novel: Contract and Transgression*. Baltimore:
   Johns Hopkins UP, 1979.

Vera Pohland

Kafka's Corpus: Writing Tuberculosis and Being Literature

The enigmatic writings of Franz Kafka have been subject to count-less popular and scholarly inquiries focusing on myriad aspects not only of the text but also of the author's life, mind, and body. In coming once again to these writings, this paper is predicated on two assumptions: that literature reflects and comments on the construct-edness of our world and that medicine is not independent of cultural contexts, constructions, and goals. In Kafka's era, "health was not only an ideology of national integration at a time of rapid social change, but it also could ensure national [German or Austrian] unity through a uniform life style" (Weindling 1). Contemporary images and ideas about disease, especially tuberculosis, are signifi-cant in understanding Kafka's work. Through disease and otherness, his writings explore an understanding of self that does not conform to the rational and scientifically ordered bourgeois society of his time but, rather, transgresses it.

Tuberculosis has inspired fears and romantic fantasies through-out the ages (Pohland 144–54). Up through the nineteenth century, those affected often died in their youth and were frequently considered to be physically beautified by the marks of the disease. Consumption was thus perceived as a signature of heightened spirit, sexuality, and individualization, even genius (Waksman 14–47; Moorman vii–xxxiv). These positive perceptions of consumption began to give way in the first few decades of the twentieth century as German (and European) health politics and public images of virility, honor, strength, and health came to define civic virtue and social value. Medical literature and public health crusades for hygiene exercised powerful social control in the ways they characterized disease and disability (Weindling 19). In an environment influenced by authoritarian hygienic and dietetic therapies, theories of heredity, and social Darwinism and eugenics, this control led to ever-increasing stigmatization of the tubercular. The shift from a positive to a negative image of tuberculosis is illustrated by the physician K. E. Ranke's adoption of syphilis as a model to describe tuberculosis, in 1917 (Burke 64). This representation suggests not only a new scientific perception of the path of the disease but also a shift toward understanding health as a social virtue and disease as a public threat.[1]

Kafka contracted tuberculosis in this period of shifting paradigms. Cultural values were also shifting from an emphasis on personal liberties, humanitarianism, and autonomy toward conformity and subordination to authoritarian national politics and social programs. Medicine and science reflected these changes in developing tensions between treatment of the sick and the interests of society. This ambiguity in the medical and cultural context of early-twentieth-century western Europe is of crucial importance in understanding both the ambivalence toward disease in Kafka's work and the way Kafka appropriated disease as a transgressive agent.

Born in 1883, Kafka was a health-conscious vegetarian who loathed his body. He exercised regularly and spent most of his vacations in spas and sanatoriums long before he became seriously ill. In 1917, he suffered a hemorrhage, and his doctor diagnosed tuberculosis of the lungs. In 1920, having survived a deadly wave of influenza that killed many tubercular patients, Kafka was still hopeful that he could recover. But from 1922 on, the disease took its toll, and at the end of 1923, tuberculosis of the larynx was diagnosed. He died at the age of forty-one, in June 1924.

As a lawyer, Kafka worked during the day and wrote at night, often in an eruptive, dreamlike state, although he was very deliberate in his art. This lifestyle produced chronic insomnia, and his frequent writing blocks caused headache and neurasthenic symptoms. Though he aspired to a respectable, normal life as a bourgeois married man and father, he was obsessive in his need to write and convinced that his passion for writing required the kind of solitary existence tuberculosis seemed to make available. Thus he experienced his tuberculosis in its initial stages as "more like a guardian angel than a devil" (*Letters to Friends* 144). Above all, he struggled with his identity as a German-writing Czech Jew, whose obsession was to *be* literature: "I have no literary interests, but am made of literature, I am nothing else, and cannot be anything else" (*Letters to Felice* 304).

As much as his enigmatic texts, the author has been the object of numerous pathobiographical and psychobiographical investigations.[2] Some characterize him as hypersensitive and hypochondriac, as neurotic, oedipal, suffering from the loss of the mother to the world of the father, and burdened with an inferiority complex. Some see him as a latent homosexual, autoerotic and masochistic. His writing has been considered obsessive and a compensation for guilt. Kafka's own characterization of his tuberculosis as mental illness reflected psychosomatic notions about sickness: "I am spiritually ill. My lung disease is nothing but an overflowing of my spiritual disease" (*Letters to Milena* 22).[3] John S. White views Kafka's tuberculosis as an outcome of the psychic conflicts Kafka experienced in the oedipal struggle with his father and as an expression of oral, cannibalistic autoaggression. Sander L. Gilman traces Kafka's illness to negative representations of the male Jewish body and "the illnesses of the Jews" that Kafka could not escape (26–29).

Obviously, Kafka's biography and psyche influenced his art, most notably his belief that literature was his destiny; the literature Kafka produced transformed reality into an independent, expansive, and significant complexity all its own. In his created world, disease is more than a metaphor. Illness, especially tuberculosis, reflects his time and is a subtext in his fiction.

Kafka departed from the bourgeois attitudes of his day in never believing the body to be an unproblematic presence or a stable entity whose perceptions he could rely on. He was highly conscious of the cultural constructedness, transformations, and deformations of the body as well as of language. He deeply explored both in his writing, where he sought to give language the stability he never possessed. His comment about "The Judgment," that "the story came out of me like a real birth, covered with filth and slime," manifests his ideal of writing as the "complete opening of body and soul" as well as his repudiation of the boundaries between body and text (*Diaries* 214, 213). Language used to describe bodily sickness must be especially stable, because the infirm body seeks stabilization in it. Furthermore, the flow of language is therapeutic, relieving psychic pressure and emotional trauma. So Kafka wrote in 1904 that "a book must be the axe for the frozen sea inside us" (*Letters to Friends* 16).

Human beings, animals, machines, and mechanical devices are the main actors in Kafka's stories. A man becomes a giant insect; an ape acts like a human; balls, tops, and buckets behave like intelligent beings; mice sing; dogs do research; dead people travel. Kafka's world is full of challenges to our realistic and logical conceptions of the world. In a number of his stories, these challenges are mediated through bodily disease, wounds, and scars. The differentiating marks of illness and injury serve to interrogate paradigms of social interaction and in some cases constitute complex subtexts.

Wounds have cultural, social, and even historical meaning for Kafka, as the following four stories show. "The Metamorphosis" depicts a sudden and unexpected change of bodily identity and the struggle to master the changed body. It is also a story about a family that tries to come to terms with a deviant family member. The sudden transformation of Gregor Samsa's body into a giant insect challenges the social self-formations of the Samsa family, whose members put all their efforts into stabilizing their threatened bourgeois identity—an identity rooted in clearly defined norms of health and disease. For Gregor, the metamorphosis is only the start of a

process of physiological and psychological degeneration. His transformed body is not a vessel for self-fulfillment or enhanced spirituality; rather, its symbolic space is occupied by nothing but
repugnance. Three wounds inflicted by his family—two physical
wounds by his father and a psychic injury by his sister—hasten Gregor's decline. These wounds limit his mobility, deprive him of his
humanness, and lead to his death. His body wastes away, at the end
becoming "completely flat and dry" (*Stories* 137). The wounds are
symbols—social stigmata marking his displacement outside family
and human society.

"A Report to an Academy" is in many ways a reverse of Gregor
Samsa's story, presenting human-inflicted wounds and suffering as
catalysts for the transformation of an ape into an intelligent being.
Two gunshot wounds, visible in a red scar in the ape's face and a scar
below the hips (possibly a sign of castration), as well as the imprints
of the bars of the cage on his flesh, are the marks that disclose to the
ape the only possible way out of his imprisonment: "I had to stop
being an ape. A fine, clear train of thought, which I must have constructed somehow with my belly" (*Stories* 253). The turning point
in the life of the ape is thus caused not by a rational decision but by
a resolution effected by and through his body. The ape's transformation into a human being is depicted not only as progress, as integration into human society, but also as the loss of animality, nature,
and freedom.

In "The Penal Colony," torturous inscriptions on the body of a
criminal cause injuries that are intended to be the inscribed judgment that represents truth. It is through the wounds on his body,
not through his eyes, that the convict has to read his judgment. But
the machine breaks, fails to produce the inscription, and turns the
body into nothing but a bloody corpse: "[N]o sign was visible of the
promised redemption" (*Stories* 166). It is not the attempt to master the body that Kafka explores here, as he did in "The Metamorphosis"; rather, he examines the reasons for mastering the body.
Institutionalized wounding through torture cannot produce meaning; enlightenment cannot be induced through imposed bodily
suffering.

In "A Country Doctor," Kafka does entertain the idea that wounds bear meaning. The wound of a young patient is a symbol, "open as a surface mine to the daylight" (*Stories* 223). But even for the specialist, the doctor, the wound remains unreadable. Because the country doctor is obsessed with a domestic drama, imagining rape and castration, he can read only his own inner crisis into the wound. The story interrogates the traditional role of the country doctor as well as the symbolic meaning and value of the wound. The doctor is variously represented as magician, hygienist, intellectual, quack, diagnostician, and scientist. He arrives like a magician with unearthly horses, criticizes the air in the sickroom as would a hygienist, asks to see the patient and unpacks his instruments like a competent practitioner. The doctor distances himself from the patient's father, believing himself to be intellectually and socially superior to the father, while the mother cajoles the doctor to the bed as if he were a quack. The doctor's first diagnosis exemplifies standard health norms: he reflects on his role as a district doctor serving the poor and on the enormous gap between the easiness of writing prescriptions and the difficulty of understanding people. His willingness "to admit conditionally that the boy might be ill after all" (223) derives from concern for the family as his audience, not for the patient. Finally he examines the boy and discovers the wound. At this point he turns into the scientist who describes the object of inspection precisely but in a detached fashion. The boy asks, "Will you save me?" (224) and the doctor responds with yet another reflection on his profession.

Kafka judges harshly this doctor who sees the malady instead of the sick person and who reads his own malaise into his patient's sickness: in the end, the doctor loses his profession, his home, and even his attachment to reality. Fleeing the physicality of his patient's body, the doctor finds himself in a surrealistic landscape, "naked, exposed to the frost of this most unhappy of ages" (225). Previous reflections about possible roles he might perform as a medical doctor culminate in a complaint: "A false alarm on the night bell once answered—it cannot be made good, not ever"(225). The night bell can be interpreted not only as a call from his patient but also as the profession's call for scientism and political and economic efficiency, which Kafka sees as the "frost of this most unhappy of ages."

In "The Penal Colony," the wounded body must decipher the unwritable text of justice; in "A Country Doctor," the wound carries the unread text of suffering. In an earlier era the diseased, consumptive, or wounded body was held to be of higher value than the healthy one because of its proximity to the soul and thus to transcendent values. Kafka draws on these notions to deconstruct them yet leaves untouched the metaphorical potential of wound or illness. The idea of the wound as inscription of a transcendental message in "The Penal Colony" is undercut by the outcome of the story. In "The Country Doctor," the notion of the wound as an open text easily read by the specialist is disproved. In both cases the body resists interpretation and makes its very vulnerability a secret text that can be neither written over nor misread.

In these four stories, wounds can be interpreted as marks of difference. Wounds reveal and intensify the body's pain, but they also appear as a force for change and thus reflect the way that individual suffering is often subordinated to "higher" social and cultural goals. These stories investigate the utilization of suffering in the name of the moral development of humankind. The wound in Kafka's fiction has substantial meaning, but Kafka's critical interrogation generates that meaning with each reading. The wound becomes an open, significant, and readable text only when not written over with subjective concerns or collective interests.

If wound symbolism is linked to event and picture, disease symbolism seems to be connected to process and narration. In *The Trial* and "The Vulture," disease functions as subtext, directing the narrative structure and shaping the reader's interpretation of the story. *The Trial* characterizes both a powerful lawyer and the vulnerable protagonist, K., by disease symptoms. In my reading of the novel, tuberculosis is the subtext. Approximating an allegory (the German title *Der Process* also connotes the course of an illness), the disease and its course are used by the author to comment on existential and social afflictions by inscrutable powers.

In the modern era the legal and medical professions have largely defined bourgeois normality and abnormality, making precise, legal, and clinical distinctions between guilt and innocence, between disease and health. In this story, a disease process becomes evident through Kafka's use of terms appropriate to legal processes. A case of consumption follows a path similar to K.'s trial: the infiltration of foreign subjects into one's private world; sudden apprehension; unpredictability of the course of events; powerless specialists and bureaucrats; a feverish search for recovery; periods of remission and exacerbation, restlessness and nervousness; symptoms such as coughing, shortness of breath, fever, and fainting; and finally the hands of the executor at the throat (laryngeal tuberculosis). In this light, *The Trial* explores the reaction of an individual unprepared for a life event, whether it is a despotic trial or an incurable disease; the novel depicts his struggle to cope with a destructive course of events that he cannot influence, in a sociocultural context that seems to have its own destination and be devoid of any meaning.

In contrast, the subtext of "The Vulture," also an allegory of the path of disease, seems to claim that tuberculosis can be personally meaningful despite its destructiveness. The vulture's animality is uncontrollable, vicious, and parasitic. Like tuberculosis, it occupies and consumes the body, yet provides its victim a final orgasmic hemorrhage. This culminating experience seems to be worth all the preceding pain. Self-fulfillment and metaphysical gain through suffering are romantic notions familiar through the ages. Not only are the vulture and the victim united in death but it is the victim's blood that drowns them both, just as death ends the life of a parasitic pathogen. The agent freeing the flow of blood—for the artist, the freeing of "[t]he tremendous world I have in my head" (*Diaries* 222)—is tuberculosis.[4]

Kafka inquires into the wounded, diseased, and declining body and its creative or destructive force, and his investigation of the conditions of culture and society at the same time stabilizes his passionate motivation as a writer. He wrote about tuberculosis before experiencing it. In 1917, he accepted his first hemorrhage as an event that determined the future direction of his life. From 1921 on, he felt more and more the destructive and debilitating power of the disease. But he had already laid out in his works a paradigm of meaning that enabled him to come to terms with his illness. The consumption of the body he accepted as the agent for the passion of writing.

Notes

1. This attitude is evident in books that connect tuberculosis and "immoral habits" (Lukas).
2. The *Kafka-Handbuch* (Binder 2:802–07) lists numerous biographical, psychological, and psychoanalytic studies on Kafka up to 1979; Gilman lists them up to 1994 (286–88, 304, 312). Gray lists general bibliographies and reference works.
3. He also wrote: "Sometimes it seems to me that my brain and lung came to an agreement without my knowledge" (*Letters to Friends* 138). Similar statements may be found in his *Letters to Friends* (137, 140, 144, 149, 151, 154); in *Diaries* (338, 339, 392, 393); in *Letters to Felice* (545–47); and in *Letters to Milena* (5–7, 10, 216).
4. James Mish'alani also reads the vulture as Kafka's tuberculosis and interprets the body of the text as the text of Kafka's own body.

Works Cited

Binder, Hartmut, ed. *Kafka-Handbuch in zwei Bänden*. Stuttgart: Kröner, 1979.

Burke, Richard M. *An Historical Chronology of Tuberculosis*. 2nd ed. Springfield: Thomas, 1955.

Gilman, Sander L. *Franz Kafka, the Jewish Patient*. New York: Routledge, 1995.

Gray, Richard T., ed. *Approaches to Teaching Kafka's Short Fiction*. New York: MLA, 1995.

Kafka, Franz. *The Complete Stories*. Ed. Nahum N. Glatzer. Trans. Willa Muir and Edwin Muir. New York: Schocken, 1971.

———. *The Diaries, 1910–1923*. Ed. Max Brod. Trans. Joseph Kresh, Martin Greenberg, with cooperation of Hannah Arendt. New York: Schocken, 1988.

———. *Letters to Felice*. Ed. Erich Heller and Jürgern Bom. Trans. James Stern and Elisabeth Duckworth. New York: Schocken, 1988.

———. *Letters to Friends, Family, and Editors*. Trans. Richard Winston and Clara Winston. New York: Schocken, 1977.

———. *Letters to Milena*. Trans. Philip Boehm. New York: Schocken, 1990.

———. *The Trial*. Introd. George Steiner. Trans. Willa Muir and Edwin Muir. Rev. trans. E. M. Butler. New York: Schocken, 1995.

Lukas, Clarence A. *Tuberculosis and Diseases Caused by Immoral or Intemperate Habits*. Indianapolis: Bookwalter, 1920.

Mish'alani, James K. "Kafka: Text's Body, Body's Text." *Philosophy and Literature* 10 (1986): 54–64.

Moorman, Lewis J. *Tuberculosis and Genius*. Chicago: U of Chicago P, 1940.

Pohland, Vera. "From Positive Stigma to Negative Stigma: A Shift of Literary and Medical Representation of Consumption in German Culture." *Disease and Medicine in Modern German Cultures*. Ed. Rudolf Käser and Pohland. Ithaca: Western Societies Program, Cornell U, 1990. 144–68.

Waksman, Selman A. *The Conquest of Tuberculosis*. Berkeley: U of California P, 1964.

Weindling, Paul. *Health, Race, and German Politics between National Unification and Nazism, 1870–1945*. Cambridge: Cambridge UP, 1989.

White, John S. "Psyche and Tuberculosis: The Libido Organization of Franz Kafka." *Psychoanalytic Study of Society* 4 (1967): 185–251.

Laura Otis

The Tigers of Wrath: Mann's *Death in Venice* as Myth and Medicine

While reading Robert Koch's articles on germ theory, I made a startling discovery. In 1884, Koch described the Ganges delta, the area he envisioned as the origin of cholera, as follows: "Luxuriant vegetation and abundant animal life have arisen in this uninhabited area. This area is shunned by humans, not only because of floods and tigers, but principally because of the pernicious fever that befalls everyone who remains there even for a short time" (166). The passage seemed familiar to me, and, turning to *Death in Venice* (1911), I compared Thomas Mann's description with Koch's: "His desire acquired vision. [. . .] He saw, saw a landscape, a tropical swamp under a vaporous sky, moist, luxuriant, and monstrous, a sort of primitive wilderness [. . .] saw the eyes of a lurking tiger sparkle between the gnarled stems of a bamboo thicket; and felt his heart pound with horror and mysterious desire" (5).[1] Both writers, one a bacteriologist who wrote no fiction, the other a novelist who never studied science beyond the high school level, use the word *üppig* ("luxuriant") to convey what they perceive as a dangerous overabundance of life, and both specifically refer to tigers. What might this mean?

Mann's *Death in Venice* has been praised as a work of genius for its ability to describe sexuality and disease on realistic, psychological, and mythological levels simultaneously (Gronicka; Luke; Reed).[2] Besides re-creating the invasion of Europe by a foreign god, it describes the literal, physical action of a real pathology. Often it is taught in conjunction with Plato's *Phaedrus*, Euripides's *The Bacchae*, and Nietzsche's *The Birth of Tragedy*, texts on which it builds. At the same time, *Death in Venice* incorporates contemporaneous medical discourse and at moments owes as much to Koch as it does to Plato or Nietzsche. Koch's writing, like Euripides's or Nietzsche's, is a strand from which Mann has woven his story, a strand that will lead students into his text and help them consider how stories are made. Until now, this bacteriological dimension of Mann's story has remained largely unexplored. Presenting students with Koch's scientific article on cholera while they are reading *Death in Venice* has proved extremely valuable to me as a way to study how the most highly esteemed scientific and literary texts deal with the same cultural fears and rely on the same metaphors and images. The juxtaposition suggests that Koch's article, like *Death in Venice*, is a story that has been made.

Koch and Mann may be using the same metaphor because the culture of European imperialism offered its language and mythology to artists and scientists alike. In the late nineteenth century, bacteriological discoveries provided Europeans with a new focus for long-standing colonialist fears. The fear of native reprisal merged with the fear of native microbes, which threatened to colonize Europe as Europeans had colonized Africa and Asia (Latour; Arata).[3] In Koch's and Mann's descriptions the tiger becomes what Stephen Arata has called "imperial ideology mirrored back as a kind of monstrosity" (634); the violent beast waiting to attack, studying its prey, represents both the imperial conquest and the repressed desires of European invaders.

Koch discovered the tuberculosis bacillus in 1882 and became a hero of the German empire in 1884 with his triumphant journey to

India and identification of the comma bacillus that causes cholera. His bacteriological discoveries and the hygiene plans they inspired quickly became a matter of national pride (Brock 167; Genschorek 115). Between 1896 and 1906, he represented the *Reich* on numerous missions both in Germany's new African colonies and at home, seeking the bacteria that caused diseases and trying to stop their spread. Because the government promoted Koch's achievements as evidence of German superiority in science, his activities received great attention in the press, so that Mann need not have gone to scientific journals to learn about the latest developments in bacteriology.[4] Examining newspaper articles from 1892, one sees that the comparisons Mann would make in 1911 were already being made by writers around him. One journalist wrote: "The *Fleete* [waterways] in Hamburg are worse than the canals in Venice, and Venice, too, is a preferred city of pestilences and all diseases" *(Kleiner Journal* 30 Aug. 1892).[5]

Mann's notes for *Death in Venice* reveal a genuine interest in the comma bacillus, its spread, and its action in the body. Although there is no proof that Mann read Koch's article, his notes on cholera's spread from India to Europe follow Koch's 1884 account so closely that Mann must have been working either with the original report or with a journalistic synopsis of it. Mann mentions that microscopic examination of the intestines of cholera victims uncovers "numerous bacteria, among them the specific causative organisms" (Reed, *Thomas Mann* 109, my trans.).[6] The bacteria move from one person to another, he notes, either by direct contact or through contaminated water, so that those who distributed food presented a particular danger: "[I]f there is a vegetable salesman or a milk saleswoman among those taken ill then comma bacilli can infect the wares" (*Death* 87).

Frequently Mann's versions of Koch's theories provide ironic echoes of newspaper accounts.[7] By comparing Mann's description of how one catches a disease with descriptions by Koch and contemporary journalists, students can discuss how—if at all—creative writing may be distinguished from "objective" writing. By looking for differences, they can begin to consider what irony and fiction *are*. The degrees of freedom available in fictional writing, particularly the opportunity to develop ironic resonances, allow creative writers to question cultural and scientific assumptions even as they use the same words employed by scientists and journalists. Mann's story encourages readers to rethink a fundamental principle of germ theory and colonialism: that cholera—and the rage, violence, and decay associated with it—is a foreign disease, with its "homeland" in Asia.[8]

Mann emphasizes the disturbing closeness of Europe and Asia, of Venice and India, by using the same word to describe each. *Üppig,* connoting an exotic, overgrown luxuriance, recurs throughout the story, tying Aschenbach's initial vision not just to Koch's description of the Ganges delta but also to the Italian city, the beckoning of death, and the nature of art. Mann's choice of the tiger as symbol also links his text to Koch's but invites readers to interpret this symbol on multiple levels. Native to India, known for its stealth and the ferocity of its attacks, the tiger suggested to Europeans of 1911 the oppressed colonials and foreign bacteria lying in wait in jungles, ready to devour them not just in the colonies but even on European soil. Mann's two descriptions of the tiger express the anxiety of the imperial age, that of being watched and studied by a hungry and ultimately more powerful life-form. The inevitable attack is all the more deadly because Aschenbach's "European soul" has suppressed and denied the stalker—the tiger, the microbe, the choleric native, or, more likely, the internal threat of his own libido—for so long (*Death* 5). Aschenbach, who planned to travel "not quite all the way to the tigers," finds that the tiger comes to him (*Death* 6).

Even as the tiger suggests India, the "homeland" of cholera, its appearance makes Aschenbach's demise mythological. According to Greek mythology, the tiger was a sacred animal to Dionysus; Zeus once sent a tiger to help Dionysus cross the Tigris River in his journey from East to West (Bell 254; Krotkoff 448; Parkes 78). In *The Birth of Tragedy* Nietzsche invites his readers, "[P]ut on wreaths of ivy, put the thyrsus into your hand, and do not be surprised when tigers and panthers lie down, fawning, at your feet. [. . .] You shall accompany the Dionysian pageant from India to Greece" (124). Besides suggesting a tiger, Mann's description of cholera's movement to Europe echoes Euripides's account of Dionysus's journey to Greece, particularly in Mann's phrase "shown its grim mask" (*Death* 54) and in the reference to Persia (see Dierks 22–29; Parkes 77–78). Mann's reference to Dionysus in his notes as "a foreigner invading from without by force" indicates that from the outset he conceived of the bacterium and the god as analogous conceptions of an extrinsic, penetrating force (Dierks 208; my trans.).[9]

The belief that Dionysus and the wild, libidinal impulses associated with him come from Asia and the belief that cholera has a homeland in the Ganges delta can be read as two incarnations of the same idea: the conviction that evil or destructive forces must originate outside the self. But even as Mann's tale of disease incorporates Koch's vision of cholera as a foreign, invasive force and interweaves that vision with a mythological Dionysian invasion, *Death in Venice* presents the chaos, luxuriance, and wrath associated with cholera as intrinsic to its German protagonist. With the words "desire acquired vision," Mann introduces a psychological landscape in which the Ganges delta—which Aschenbach, Mann, and Koch have never actually seen—epitomizes "horror and mysterious desire" projected onto it by the German mind (Mann, *Death* 5; see Cadieux 59; Krotkoff 448). Mann's story mocks the assumption that sexual drives or foreign peoples can be controlled and excluded from one's definition of self.

While Koch and Mann use the same animal to depict the origin of a disease, Mann's story is much more than a fictional adaptation of a scientific idea. His writing, unlike Koch's, encourages readers to question the ideology on which it builds. In providing this cultural and scientific context in the classroom, teachers should avoid implying that the bacteriology explains the story, gives it its meaning. I have found that this impression of explanation tempts students from all fields, and one way to undermine it is to ask why Koch takes the trouble, in an otherwise straightforward article tying a disease to a particular microorganism, to describe cholera's homeland in such a vivid way. Why mention the tigers?

Koch's determination to conquer an "Asian" disease by traveling to its geographical source can be compared to contemporary attempts to pinpoint the origin of AIDS or Ebola in Africa, as depicted in Richard Preston's *Hot Zone*. The quest for the origin of a disease might be an attempt to attribute blame, yet from an epidemiological standpoint such a search could yield information that saves lives. Students can discuss how practical and humanitarian concerns and cultural prejudices merge in decisions about how best to spend money to understand and defeat epidemics.

In an undergraduate course on literature and medicine, *Death in Venice* and Koch's writing can provide a valuable opportunity to create dialogue between students of literature, trained to analyze the "form" of texts, and science students who will be heading for the laboratory right after class, trained to read for "content." Koch's and Mann's tigers provide powerful evidence that narratives we read for style and narratives we read for content incorporate the same images and ideas. Should we therefore read all texts the same way? Encouraging students to discuss the similarities between texts classified as literary and texts classified as scientific can lead students to question the ways in which they themselves are classified as readers and scholars.

Notes

1. I prefer Clayton Koelb's translation of *Death in Venice* because it is direct and literal and brings out the strongly sexual implications of Mann's phrasing. For a more thorough analysis of Mann's and Koch's representations of cholera, including comparisons of the original German texts, please see my study *Membranes*.

2. In a letter to Carl Maria Weber in 1920, Mann refers to "the *naturalistic* attitude of my generation, which is so alien to you younger writers: it forced me to see the 'case' as *also* pathological and to allow this motif (climacteric) to interweave iridescently with the symbolic theme" (*Death* 203).

3. The German colonial drive in the mid 1880s coincided with the heyday of bacteriological discoveries, and German colonialists quickly found that unicellular natives provided a much greater threat to their occupation than did human ones. It is particularly interesting, in this light, to compare *Death in Venice* with Joseph Conrad's *Heart of Darkness*, another text of the same period that explores the relation between the jungle and the "European soul" (Mann, *Death* 5; see McIntyre; Vidan).

4. In August 1892, a cholera outbreak in Hamburg killed thousands in

just a few weeks, attracting international attention. The government sent Koch to investigate, and the national press provided widespread coverage, offering a great variety of preventive measures. It is impossible that the seventeen-year-old Mann, then finishing school in nearby Lübeck, could have failed to hear of the outbreak.

5. This statement and the one in note 7 about the 1892 cholera epidemic are taken from the Zeitungsausschnittsammlung 3006, Rudolf Virchow Nachlaß, Archiv der Berlin Brandenburgische Akademie der Wissenschaften, Berlin. The statements are from articles that have no titles or authors, and the translation is mine.

6. Koelb's translation, "countless bacteria, among them those that carry the specific virus" (Mann, *Death* 84), is misleading, since the bacteria do not carry a virus; they themselves produce the toxin that causes the disease.

7. Mann's choice of overripe strawberries as the vehicle through which the cholera penetrates Aschenbach reveals the author's determination to make the story work both on realistic and mythological levels. The *Leipziger Zeitung* had warned that "one must take care with raw fruits and vegetables, which often, unfortunately, are eaten when still unripe" (26 Aug. 1892). While the blackened corpse of "a woman who sold vegetables" makes the infection plausible, according to contemporary scientific findings, the "overripe and soft" fruit, suggesting an eroticism past its prime, implies that Aschenbach dies as much from his own fermenting libido as from a foreign disease (Mann, *Death* 54, 60).

8. In positing the agents of infectious diseases as living organisms, bacteriologists believed that each species of bacteria must have a *Heimat* ("homeland"), a native habitat.

9. The original German, "ein Fremder, von draußen gewaltsam Eindringender"—literally, "a foreigner pushing violently inward from without"—has strongly sexual connotations and suggests that Aschenbach —and, by association, Europe—is being raped by the foreign force. In the nineteenth century, both bourgeois scientists and politicians defined the individual as a distinct, bounded, independent, self-willed, and responsible social unit (Goldberg 9). Bacteria, associated with other continents and other people, threatened to penetrate these boundaries. The collapse of the boundaries, brought on either by hygienic or moral laxness, would leave the self open to foreign forces of all kinds. *Death in Venice* depicts just such a collapse. More accurately, the story depicts Aschenbach's discovery that belief in self-defining barriers is merely a comforting illusion. The imagery of piercing and violation becomes most vivid in Aschenbach's dream, when the protective boundaries he has maintained all his life fall to pieces. The Dionysian experience, literally "a mixing with no regard for borders" ("eine grenzenlose Vermischung"), mocks the very ideas of boundaries and individual independence demanded by the new science (Mann,

Der Tod 90; my trans.). Koelb's translation, "an unfettered rite of copulation" (Mann, *Death* 57), does justice to the powerful sexuality of Mann's passage but detracts from the possibility of multiple readings by focusing on only one type of mingling.

Works Cited

Arata, Stephen D. "The Occidental Tourist: *Dracula* and the Anxiety of Reverse Colonization." *Victorian Studies* 33 (1990): 621–45.

Bell, Robert E. *A Dictionary of Classical Mythology: Symbols, Attributes, and Associations.* Santa Barbara; Oxford: ABC-CLIO, 1982.

Brock, Thomas D. *Robert Koch: A Life in Medicine and Bacteriology.* Madison: Science Tech; Berlin: Springer, 1988.

Cadieux, André. "The Jungle of Dionysus: The Self in Mann and Nietzsche." *Philosophy and Literature* 3 (1979): 53–63.

Dierks, Manfred. *Studien zu Mythos und Pathologie bei Thomas Mann.* Bern: Francke, 1972.

Genschorek, Wolfgang. *Robert Koch: Selbstloser Kampf gegen Seuchen und Infektionskrankheiten.* Leipzig: Hirzel, 1985.

Goldberg, Ann. "Reshaping the Self: Religion, Medicine, and Madness in *Vormärz* Germany." Unpublished essay, 1995.

Gronicka, André von. " 'Myth plus Psychology': A Style Analysis of *Death in Venice.*" Mann, *Death* 115–30.

Koch, Robert. *Essays of Robert Koch.* Trans. K. Codell Carter. Contributions in Medical Studies 20. New York: Greenwood, 1987.

Krotkoff, Hertha. "Zur Symbolik in Thomas Mann's *Tod in Venedig.*" *Modern Language Notes* 82 (1967): 445–53.

Latour, Bruno. *The Pasteurization of France.* Trans. Alan Sheridan and John Law. Cambridge: Harvard UP, 1988.

Luke, David. "Thomas Mann's 'Iridescent Interweaving.' " Mann, *Death* 195–207.

Mann, Thomas. *Death in Venice.* Ed. and trans. Clayton Koelb. New York: Norton, 1994.

———. Der Tod in Venedig *und andere Erzählungen.* Frankfurt: Fischer, 1989.

McIntyre, Allan J. "Psychology and Symbol: Correspondences between *Heart of Darkness* and *Death in Venice.*" *Hartford Studies in Literature* 7 (1975): 216–35.

Nietzsche, Friedrich. *The Birth of Tragedy.* Trans. Walter Kaufmann. New York: Vintage-Random, 1967.

Otis, Laura. *Membranes: Metaphors of Invasion in Nineteenth-Century Literature, Science, and Politics.* Baltimore: Johns Hopkins UP, 1998.

Parkes, Ford B. "The Image of the Tiger in Thomas Mann's *Tod in Venedig.*" *Studies in Twentieth-Century Literature* 3 (1978): 73–82.

Preston, Richard. *The Hot Zone.* New York: Random, 1994.

Reed, T. J. "The Art of Ambivalence." Mann, *Death* 150–78.

————. *Thomas Mann:* Der Tod in Venedig: *Text, Materialen, Kommentar.* München: Hanser, 1983.

Vidan, Ivo. "Conrad and Thomas Mann." *Contexts for Conrad.* Ed. Keith Carabine, Owen Knowles, and Wieslaw Krajka. Boulder: Eastern European Monographs; New York: Columbia UP, 1993.

Michelle Bollard Toby

"There Is Something Wrong about the Fellow": Willa Cather's "Paul's Case"

Celebrated as a popular, realist writer throughout the twentieth century, recently Willa Cather has been rediscovered by feminist critics, who identify in her work a subtext that directly challenges the more conservative, dominant narrative. In her 1905 short story "Paul's Case," that hidden subtext is Paul's suspect, indeed "pathological," sexuality. "Paul's Case" puts the reader into the role of an investigative physician who must carefully track and interpret Paul's symptoms in order to arrive at a plausible explanation for Paul's abnormality. The reader-investigator, finally unable to reach a satisfactory diagnosis, is forced to question the repressive white middle-class ideology against which Paul's difference asserts itself, for Paul's unspeakable illness can be interpreted only in relation to the ideals of normality that define it as illness. "Paul's Case" is set in the early years of the twentieth century, when psychological and medical explanations of human behavior were supplanting moral or religious ones.[1] Ultimately, however, Cather's story illuminates the limitations of any one interpretive approach to Paul's trouble; instead, the story impresses on the reader the historical contingency of our various models of interpretation and the cultural authority those models wield.

Although it opens with Paul before his judges as he attempts to "account for his various misdemeanors" (102), "Paul's Case" is approached from a medical model as easily as from a legal model. The legitimacy of reading the story as a psychomedical case study is suggested by the subtitle: "A Study in Temperament." Readers will quickly note that Paul's temperament is an artistic one and that Paul's moralistic teachers consider this artistic sensibility pathological. The teachers are incensed by the boy's manner, largely because it seems to defy interpretation. When asked to articulate their charges against him, they do so with "such rancor and aggrievedness as evinced that this was not a usual case." They list "disorder" and "impertinence" among the charges, and yet each feels that it is "scarcely possible to put into words the real cause of the trouble" (102).

The story begins with a presentation of Paul's various symptoms, all of which have to do with how Paul deviates from prescribed gender roles. He is physically unusual, "very thin, with high, cramped shoulders and a narrow chest" while "[h]is eyes [are] remarkable for a certain hysterical brilliancy, and he continually [uses] them in a conscious, theatrical sort of way, particularly offensive in a boy." Above all, Paul's teachers are bothered by "a sort of hysterically defiant manner of the boy's" (102). Paul's symptoms are described in physical terms — "twitching" and "trembling" — and suggest his extreme nervousness and discomfort. Indeed, Paul himself seems intent upon keeping his "disorder" a secret, for he is "always glancing about him, seeming to feel that people might be watching him and trying to detect something" (103).

In most cases, students are rather quick to arrive at a preliminary diagnosis of Paul's trouble: he is homosexual. This conclusion is supported by Paul's love of beauty and passion for the theater, especially opera, and his rather glamorous style of dress: "[H]is clothes were a trifle out-grown and the tan velvet on the collar of his open overcoat was frayed and worn; but for all that there was something

of the dandy about him, and he wore an opal pin in his neatly knot-
ted black four-in-hand" (102). Most significant is Paul's telltale
signature: the "scandalous" red carnation that he flaunts in his but-
tonhole in a rather Wildean fashion, a detail repeatedly emphasized in the text (103). That Paul chooses a red carnation is
underscored later in the text, when some neighbors joke "about
the suspicious colour" of a red lemonade pitcher that Paul's sisters
always use for entertaining (109).[2] Clearly red is intended to signal
illicit desire and raises eyebrows in this extremely puritanical mid-
western town. The suggestiveness of the term *dandy* and the allu-
sion to Oscar Wilde often have to be clarified for students; such
details acquire special significance only when brought together
and decoded.[3]

The emphasis on Paul's inability to conform to socially defined
gender roles opens the way for classroom discussion about how
medical discourse in the early years of the twentieth century began
to consider sexual deviance as within its domain rather than within
the domain of religion or the law. Throughout the story the various
discourses—medical, legal, and religious—compete with and blur
into one another, suggesting the complex ways in which homosexual identity emerged historically at that time.[4]

Once students consider the possibility that Paul's trouble is
linked to a repressed homosexuality, the story provides a rich starting
point for a complex exploration of the relation between medicine and
art, between interpreters and the subjects of their interpretation, between tellers and listeners. At first, students tend to assume that
their diagnosis of Paul as homosexual solves the mystery of the text
and renders any further analysis unnecessary; they seem to have an
"Ah, well that explains it then" response. I welcome this response,
in that it provides a way to have students examine the assumptions
they bring to the interpretive act we call diagnosis and to examine
the implications of using the language of medicine metaphorically. A
reading that decodes Cather's story to find a repressed undertext
provides merely one possible interpretation among many. At the
same time, this reading usefully demonstrates to students that interpretation itself is an exercise of power, an exercise that can have con-

sequences ranging from the subtle to the violent. Rather than allow students to rest with their initial diagnosis, the teacher should require them to go back through the text and trace the currents of desire as the narrative speaks the language of its unfolding drama. This exercise leads to fascinating questions about the relation between literature and medicine. For example, students begin to ask themselves exactly why and how Paul's difference is pathologized and why the narrative drives the reader on in quest of a suitable diagnosis. Why do both literature and medicine tend to posit a secret that needs to be discovered, divulged, and interpreted? How do both discourses transmit and produce power, but also undermine and expose it? And why do we tend to assume that the truth of one model transcends the truth of another, whether it is the "objective" truth of scientific discourse that is valorized, for example, or the "sacred" truth of art?

Most notably, the story challenges students to be sensitive to the limitations of their interpretive models and to how those models are determined by history and class. Paul's father hopes that Paul might be cured through the example of a young man in the neighborhood who, like Paul, "had been a trifle dissipated" but who was able to "curb his appetites" by entering the business world, marrying, and having four children (109). As students read Paul as a rebel against the repressive white middle-class ideology of Cordelia Street, it is useful to remind them that the medical profession itself grew out of this class and reflects its values. Paul's condition becomes diagnosable against the heterosexual model of normality and the biological determinism that model supports. As George Chauncey, Jr., notes, at the turn of the century "medical theory tied men and women's gender characteristics so closely to their respective biological sexes that a somatic explanation had to be found for those people who threatened to contradict their theory by appearing to be one sex while assuming the gender role of the so-called 'opposite sex' " (130–31).[5] When Cather wrote "Paul's Case" in 1905, it was not yet clear that the emerging medical discourse on sexuality would eventually result in positive alternative models of sexual identity. While Paul is made extremely uncomfortable by the pictures of George Washington and John Calvin that preside over his bed, we can imagine that he would be as unsettled by representations of medical authority as he is by national and religious iconography.

The diagnosis of Paul's homosexuality thus can be read more precisely as a response to the demand that his difference be accounted for than as a correct interpretation of the story. Ironically, the very symptoms that make Paul's otherness legible can also be read as the result of his having to repress his difference in a society that finds difference intolerable. This repression is coded in the text through the many references to masking and hiding. Paul's flamboyance is an attempt to cover his secret through an elaborate disguise that only makes the secret more recognizable.[6] While he makes "not the least effort to conceal" his contempt for his teachers, he is at the same time always lying to overcome friction with teachers, neighbors, and especially his father (102). Paul finds the "delicious excitement" of Carnegie Hall "the only thing that could be called living at all" (106), but upon returning home after such "orgies of living, he [experiences] all the physical depression which follows a debauch" (107). So afraid is he of meeting his father on the stairs, he chooses instead to creep through a lower window of the house and hide in the basement until morning. Wondering what excuse he might give in the morning, he decides to tell his father that he "had no car fare, and it was raining so hard he [went] home with one of the boys and stayed all night" (108). Here the text speaks Paul's secret desire; he tells his truth through lying, just as the elaborate details of his jovial masquerade—his red carnation, opal pin, and velvet collar—become read as the symptoms of his disorder.

It is not enough to diagnose Paul; we must also allow ourselves to empathize with him, feeling his anguish through a careful process of listening to his story as it emerges. Some students are likely to be bothered that they find themselves blaming Paul for his inability to cope. Indeed, the text is not particularly sympathetic to Paul. As in William Carlos Williams's *Doctor Stories,* Cather presents doctor-readers with ethical dilemmas that revolve around their emotional investment in the text and the possibility that they may not like or be able to identify with the principal character. Similarly, teachers may feel justifiably uncomfortable teaching a story that encourages them to read homosexuality in terms of a medical model of pathology, even as it forces them to question that model. They should emphasize the difference between reading Paul and reading Paul within the larger context of the narrative that presents his case. Students can then begin to shift their analysis from Paul as a unique individual to the dominant culture that makes his behavior the symptom of an underlying disease. That is, if read in the cultural context in which the story was written and set, how does the story encourage us to apply the interpretation of Paul as sick and how much room does the story leave us to question that interpretation? The working thesis I propose to students is that we are encouraged to read Paul's "disorder" as a pathologized homosexuality, precisely so that we will question our investment in that interpretive strategy. While diagnosing Paul can leave us with a strong sense of satisfaction regarding our ability to order and explain experience, a more careful reading turns to an examination instead of the ways our desire to explain, classify, and diagnose produces an interpretation that can either shore up or dismantle normalizing conceptualizations of human sexuality.

Ultimately, "Paul's Case" asks students to consider the dangers of medicalizing homosexuality (or art, for that matter), encouraging them to examine the boundaries of their discipline and how those boundaries are culturally determined. Having become invested in an interpretation of the story that focuses on the decoding of Paul's homosexuality, students can then be asked to consider equally plausible alternative readings: the story is really about adolescent identity crisis, really critiques materialism, really presents the plight of the modern artist, and so on. The relation between aesthetics and sexuality is particularly intriguing: Paul's suspected homosexuality might be dismissed in favor of the idea that he is simply a frustrated artist. Being an artist and being a homosexual might be seen as conditions equally pathological and equally capable of generating hostility. By recognizing the competing claims of a number of different readings, students are forced to see that the act of interpretation often tells us more about ourselves than about the object of our investigation. This insight is valuable for students of both medicine and literature as they learn their various arts of interpretation.

Notes

1. Michel Foucault's *The History of Sexuality* is an excellent text to teach along with "Paul's Case," in that *History* traces the emergence over the last three centuries of various discourses that functioned to produce the truth of sexuality as the key to modern identity. At work here was a need "to pronounce a discourse on sex that would not derive from morality alone but from rationality as well" (24). In the nineteenth century, Foucault suggests, the medical establishment was at the forefront of this discursive drive. Psychomedical models, I would assert, achieved an almost unquestioned hegemony in the twentieth century.

2. Though Oscar Wilde and his friends were famous for wearing green carnations to signal homosexuality, Cather's use of both the color red and the flower imagery throughout the story has been read as a coded reference to homosexual desire. Judith Butler argues that the "stray flower in Cather's stories becomes a motif that engages the conventions of the dandy" (160). In a biography of Wilde, Richard Ellmann notes Wilde's predilection for scarlet and related tints — "vermilion was a word that Wilde liked to draw out lingeringly" (4).

3. Cather's public disparagement of homosexuality as unnatural, especially given the extent to which her fiction has been read in terms of a repressed homosexual politics, is an interesting starting point for inquiry into current debates about homosexual coding in literature. "Paul's Case" was written in 1905, ten years after Wilde's trial of 1895. Cather was deeply affected by the event and wrote at least two essays in which she publicly denounced Wilde's "infamy" (*Kingdom* 392). My thanks to Sharon Delaubenfels, who made the argument at the 1995 Willa Cather conference that Cather may have written "Paul's Case" as a way to pay homage to Wilde, whom in her earlier writing she had judged harshly.

4. Although the obscenity trial of Radclyffe Hall occurs after Cather's publication of "Paul's Case," it is useful to familiarize students with the trial's impact on contemporary writers. Sonja Ruehl discusses how writers began to appropriate medical models of inversion in order to create positions of authority from which to speak.

5. Chauncey is quite useful for providing students with some background on the changing medical discourse about homosexuality at the turn of the century.

6. A useful text to teach alongside this story is Sedgwick's essay "Epistemology of the Closet."

Works Cited

Butler, Judith. "'Dangerous Crossing': Willa Cather's Masculine Names." *Bodies That Matter.* New York: Routledge, 1993. 143–66.

Cather, Willa. *The Kingdom of Art.* Ed. Bernice Slote. Lincoln: U of Nebraska P, 1966.

———. "Paul's Case: A Study in Temperament." *The Troll Garden*. Ed. James Woodress. Lincoln: U of Nebraska P, 1983. 102–21.

Chauncey, George, Jr. "From Sexual Inversion to Homosexuality: Medicine and the Changing Conceptualization of Female Deviance." *Salmagundi* 58–59 (1982–83): 114–46.

Delaubenfels, Sharon. " 'Paul's Case': Willa Cather's Homage to Oscar Wilde." Sixth International Willa Cather Seminar. Quebec City. 24 June–1 July 1995.

Ellmann, Richard. *Oscar Wilde*. New York: Knopf, 1988.

Foucault, Michel. *The History of Sexuality: Volume 1: An Introduction*. New York: Vintage, 1980.

Ruehl, Sonja. "Inverts and Experts: Radclyffe Hall and the Lesbian Identity." *Feminist Criticism and Social Change*. Ed. Judith Newton and Deborah Rosefelt. New York: Methuen, 1985. 165–79.

Sedgwick, Eve Kosofsky. "Epistemology of the Closet." *The Lesbian and Gay Studies Reader*. Ed. Henry Abelove, Michèle Aina Barale, and David M. Halperin. New York: Routledge, 1993. 45–61.

Williams, William Carlos. *The Doctor Stories*. Comp. Robert Coles. New York: New Directions, 1984.

Kristin Lindgren

Birthing Death: Sharon Olds's *The Father* and the Poetics of the Body

In *The Father*, a sequence of fifty-two poems, Sharon Olds chronicles her father's illness and death from cancer and her experience of caring for and mourning him. By placing her father's dying body at the center of these poems, Olds insists that the reader confront the concrete and often repellent physical details that accompany disease and death. Her unflinching descriptions of body fluids and bodily processes — descriptions that many readers find uncomfortable — transgress literary and cultural codes that have worked to distance and aestheticize the dying body. The detailed renderings of bodily suffering at times resemble clinical observation, but they are suffused with the complex emotions of a daughter; they demand intimate engagement, not distanced assessment. Enacting what Alicia Ostriker has called "the imperative of intimacy," Olds employs motifs of "mutuality, continuity, connection, touch" (Ostriker 166) to depict the slow process of the father's dying and the ways in which the daughter is implicated in this process. In doing so, Olds challenges cultural, clinical, and literary discourses that have represented the dying body primarily as an object of inquiry or contemplation.

Replacing a discourse of distance with one of engagement and intimacy, Olds violates not only the conventions that have shaped how we talk about death but also those that have governed how daughters talk about their fathers. She frequently draws on metaphors of maternity and sexuality, the most prominent themes of her earlier work, to represent the relationship between father and daughter. By employing these metaphors, Olds depicts the daughter's experience of her father's dying as one of profound bodily connection, potentially as intimate as sex and motherhood. The poems in which the daughter figures herself as mother to her dying father suggest not simply a reversal of roles; they suggest a more fundamental challenge to the boundaries between self and other. Pregnancy involves the literal redrawing of the body's boundaries, the incorporation of another within the self; caring for a child requires the redefinition of both psychic and corporeal boundaries. Likewise, Olds's use of sexual metaphor challenges the corporeal limits that define one subject as distinct from another. The erotic, for Olds, dissolves boundaries between bodies, between subject and object, between the healthy and the diseased—indeed, between any categories that operate to draw distinctions and maintain separateness. In these poems she represents disease and death as experiences that, instead of reinforcing distance, open up a space in which boundaries can be challenged and renegotiated.

A reader familiar with Olds's previous work will come to this volume with a sense of the father as mythically powerful. As Suzanne Matson has observed of her earlier poems, "Olds [. . .] addresses a personal father, but his specter becomes so gargantuan in her own memory—the only available medium for re-collecting him—that he becomes mythic" (35). In *The Father,* Olds demythologizes this personal father; even when she employs biblical or mythological language, she depicts her father as insistently material and particular. The physical changes that mark his movement toward death enable the daughter to recognize both his materiality and her own. Out of this recognition, she forges a new relationship based on mutuality. Reflecting on her earlier view of him, she writes: "I had / always known him as an object in the world / of objects because he would not speak, / sometimes, for a week" (14). These poems record a daughter's reconception of her father; he is no longer a mythic figure or an objectified, inarticulate body, he is an embodied subject.[1]

Olds's representation of the act of dying reflects her recognition both of the father's embodiment and of his subjectivity. Throughout the sequence, she depicts death as akin to other bodily acts: work, sex, birth. In the first poem in the book, "The Waiting," she somewhat humorously figures death as a daily job: "By then, he knew he was dying, / he seemed to approach it as a job to be done / which he knew how to do. He got up early / for the graveyard shift" (3). Rejecting the notion of dying as a process that lacks agency or subjectivity, Olds invests the father's act of waiting—for death, for his daughter—with the agency and dignity of work. In a later poem, "The Present Moment," she recognizes the exertion, the solitary accomplishment, inherent in dying as well as her own enabling role: "I stay beside him, like someone in a rowboat / staying abreast of a Channel swimmer, / you are not allowed to touch them, their limbs / glow, faintly, in the night water" (20). Yet in most of these poems, the father's dying is not a solitary act: it implicates the bodies and emotions of his wife; of the nurses, interns, and ministers who inhabit the margins of the poems; and especially of his daughter.

Olds repeatedly invokes metaphors of pregnancy and birth to signify both the daughter's bodily involvement in her father's dying and the radical revision of their relationship that occurs through this process. In "Nullipara," the daughter casts herself as an expectant mother, holding his body within hers after his death. In "The Pulling," her father is traveling toward death through the birth canal, her own:

> [. . .] my father
> moves, hour by hour, head-first,
> toward death, I sense every inch of him moving
> through me toward it, the way each child
> moved, slowly, down through my body.   (6)

In these poems the father is no longer a mythic other against whom the daughter defines herself; here the images of pregnancy and childbirth enable her figurally to reincorporate her father into herself, producing a split or doubled subjectivity that redefines their relation. Olds inverts the figure of pregnancy in "Last Acts," saying "I want / to be in him, as I was once inside him, / riding in his balls the day before he cast me—" (21). And in the poem "Death," the daughter imagines that death will make possible a reparative coupling: "[A]nd when he died I wanted him to rise up / into me or me to climb down / into his body, we were like two baskets / ripped at the sides which could now be woven together" (41). These figures, as I read them, signify not simply a nostalgic fantasy of bodily reunion or a primarily erotic union but also a struggle to renegotiate the terms of identity. The transgression or blurring of corporeal boundaries that occurs again and again in these poems marks both the impulse to merge bodies and selves and the desire to achieve a more fluid and intersubjective relationship.

The metaphors of incorporation and connection that Olds employs in *The Father* suggest that the process of her father's dying enables the daughter to reclaim his body, which she had often feared and hated, as intimately connected to her own. When the father displays his wasted body for his daughter's inspection in "The Lifting," she emphasizes their similarity:

> Right away
> I saw how much his hips are like mine,
> the long, white angles, and then
> how much his pelvis is shaped like my daughter's,
> a chambered whelk shell hollowed out.   (15)

Olds registers the attendant danger of overidentification in a description of the extreme weight loss that accompanies a chronic flu: "I am flirting with my father, / his cadaver the only body this thin / I have seen—I am walking around like his corpse / risen up and moving again" (65). Even in this poem, though, their separate subjectivity is clear, as they laugh together about her becoming his shadowy double. In the stunning final poem in the collection, "My

Father Speaks to Me from the Dead," the father, more articulate in
death than in life, reciprocates the verbal attention she has lavished
on his body by reciting a litany of her body parts. He tells her what
he loves about her body, and in so doing he too blurs the boundaries
between himself, his daughter, and his granddaughter:

> I love your our my legs, they are so
> long because they are yours and mine
> both [. . . . .]
> Of course I love
> your breasts—did you see me looking up
> from within your daughter's face, as she nursed?
> [. . . . .]
> and your womb, it is a heaven to me,
> I lie on its soft hills and gaze up
> at its rosy vault.   (78–79)

Olds's claim is not the more conventional one that her father will
live on after death in these poems but that he will live on in his
daughter's body, housed not only in the long legs they share but
also in her womb.

The process of the father's death engenders, for the speaker of
these poems, both a newly conceived father and a newly constituted
self. It also gives rise to reflections on the nature of death. *The
Father* extends the genre of literary accounts of illness and death,
a genre that Anne Hunsaker Hawkins has called "pathography."
Hawkins suggests that recent pathographies about dying create
meaning from fragments of cultural and religious myth (97). Like
the narratives Hawkins analyzes, Olds's sequence of poems constructs meaning from fragments. But in *The Father* these fragments
are seldom those of religious or ideological belief; instead, they are
fragmented images of the body. Olds rhetorically dissects the father's body, focusing on the changes wrought by disease and death
on individual parts—eyes, tongue, skin, hair. While depicting his
body in fragments, however, the daughter resists the actual fragmentation of his body. In "The Dead Body," speaking of his crema-
tion, she insists:

> I wanted this man
> burned whole, don't

let me see that arm on anyone in
Redwood City tomorrow, don't take that
tongue in transplant or that unwilling eye. (39)

The integrity of the body is crucial here, because in her view there is
no transcendent soul that survives it. The body is coterminous with
the soul. Its fragmentation in the poems enables the daughter to reconstruct it, to make it whole, on her own terms.

In *The Father* there is no religious or moral framework through
which to perceive and make sense of death; there is only the embodied self's transmutation to pure matter. In "Death and Morality,"
Olds removes the process of dying from the moral universe and
places it squarely in the realm of immanent, somatic experience:

> This
> is the world where sex lives, the world
> of the nerves, the world without church,
> we kiss him in it, we stroke back his gummed
> hair [. . .] one
> on either side, we wipe the flow of
> saliva like ivory clay from the side of his mouth. (9)

She finds meaning in these intimate acts of care, and in the material
reality of the body, rather than in any interpretive system. In
"Psalm," the daughter rejects the hospital chaplain's reading of a
psalm as detached and inappropriate, but she affirms the power of
touch: "I had never / held his feet before, we had hardly / touched
since the nights he had walked the floor at my arrival" (30). The
charged intimacy she discovers at the end of her father's life is linked
once again to the physical bond between parent and child at the beginning of life. Throughout this volume, Olds enacts a poetics of
radical intimacy in which touch is the central act. Rather than distance herself or the reader from the process of dying, she presents
unapologetically the details of the father's suffering and the daughter's care. Both the literal acts of touch that she recounts and the
metaphors of bodily connection that structure many of these poems
work to break down and redefine the distinctions between two bodies, two subjects. For Olds, meaning is firmly grounded in the material body and in the intimate connections it enables.

Note

1. In an excellent article on *The Father*, Laura Tanner makes a similar argument by tracing the dynamics of the gaze in these poems. While my reading of some of the poems differs from hers, I am generally indebted to Tanner's article.

Works Cited

Hawkins, Anne Hunsaker. *Reconstructing Illness: Studies in Pathography.* West Lafayette: Purdue UP, 1993.

Matson, Suzanne. "Talking to Our Father: The Political and Mythical Appropriations of Adrienne Rich and Sharon Olds." *American Poetry Review* 18.6 (1989): 35–41.

Olds, Sharon. *The Father.* New York: Knopf, 1992.

Ostriker, Alicia Suskin. *Stealing the Language: The Emergence of Women's Poetry in America.* Boston: Beacon, 1986.

Tanner, Laura E. "Death-watch: Terminal Illness and the Gaze in Sharon Olds's *The Father*." *Mosaic* 29.1 (1996): 103–21.

Paul Delaney

The Hospital Poetry of U. A. Fanthorpe

Unable to reconcile her experience behind a hospital receptionist's desk with the way she would like to treat the poor and afflicted, U. A. Fanthorpe asks, in a poem titled "Clerical Error":

> What must I do when Job and his daughters
>
> Cram into my office where they are not allowed,
> When I am typing medical reports against the clock [. . .]?
>> (*Neck-Verse* 15)

Fanthorpe, the first woman to be nominated for the post of Oxford Professor of Poetry, began to write poetry while working in a hospital.[1] After taking an Oxford degree, she had begun a teaching career at a preparatory school, the Cheltenham Ladies' College, where she served for sixteen years and eventually became head of the English department. Then, she says, she became "a middle-aged dropout" (qtd. in Hendry). At forty-one, she gave up her academic post to spend two years doing clerical work at temp jobs before finding herself employed as a hospital receptionist. It was not until after she quit teaching, left academe, and was working in a hospital that—as she describes it —"poetry struck" ("Slow Learner" 67).

Drawing on her lengthy stay as a hospital patient while an undergraduate, Fanthorpe writes about the experience of being in the hospital with a keen sense of it as a world apart. Being admitted to the hospital seems to involve crossing not merely a threshold but a gangplank. In "After Visiting Hours," visitors are shore creatures who can only briefly accompany those who are now seaborne:

> Like gulls they are still calling—
> *I'll come again Tuesday. Our Dad*
> *Sends his love.* They diminish, are gone.
> Their world has received them,
>
> As our world confirms us. Their debris
> Is tidied into vases, lockers, minds.
> We become pulses; mouthpieces
> Of thermometers and bowels. (*Selected Poems* 17)

Fanthorpe dramatizes the disorienting effect of being in the hospital, of sensing that "our world" is separated by a gulf from those who from "their world" can only send their love. While aware that it is dehumanizing to "become pulses" and "mouthpieces / Of thermometers," the speaker implies that such vital signs are, at least for this voyage, vital. Visitors only bring "debris." The patients are in the hospital because they are ill, and on this strange voyage there is something comforting about being able to "relax / Into illness." But the experience is so distancing, it assumes an exotic quality:

> Now the bed-bound rehearse
> Their repertoire of movements,
> The dressing-gowned shuffle, clutching
> Their glass bodies.
>
> Now siren voices whisper
> From headphones, and vagrant
> Doctors appear, wreathed in stethoscopes
> Like South Sea dancers.

All's well, all's quiet as the great
Ark noses her way into night,
Caulked, battened, blessed for her trip,
And behind, the gulls crying.   (17)

Whereas visitors are described with such clichés as "our nearest and dearest," the patients with "their glass bodies" are not only fragile creatures but also artists who need to "rehearse / Their repertoire." Referring to doctors and nurses as South Sea dancers and sirens may suggest that the SS *Hospital* has reached deep water both mythologically and geographically. Still, Fanthorpe's benedictory conclusion is that "all's well" and the "ark" is "blessed."

However, Fanthorpe's experience as a patient scarcely prepared her for what she would encounter when she began work in a neuropsychiatric hospital. "From my receptionist's glass dugout I watched a world I hadn't imagined," Fanthorpe says, "of the epileptic, the depressed, the obsessed, the brain-damaged, the violent, the helpless" ("Slow Learner" 67). In that charged environment, poetry offered a means "to bear witness" ("Interview" 70). "I can't help the patients," she told Diana Hendry, "I don't have the training of the doctor, nurse or specialist. I am simply there as a human being, and sometimes I feel a great need to do something about it—and that explodes into a poem."

Fanthorpe says what first moved her to poetry was anger: "I can pinpoint the day and the moment that actually did it—noticing the hierarchy; the devout approach of the nurses to the doctors, the devout approach of the doctors to themselves. I was in charge of the outpatients, and no-one thought they were important" (qtd. in Bensley and Kazantzis 18). The poem that exploded was "For Saint Peter":

I have a good deal of sympathy for you, mate,
Because I reckon that, like me, you deal with the outpatients.

Now the inpatients are easy, they're cowed by the nurses
(In your case, the angels) and they know what's what in the
        set-up.

> They know about God (in my case Dr Snow) and all His little
>   fads,
> And if there's any trouble with them, you can easily scare them
>   rigid
>
> Just by mentioning His name. But outpatients are different.
> They bring their kids with them, for one thing, and that creates
>   a wrong atmosphere.
>
> They have shopping baskets and buses to catch. They cry, or
>   knit,
> Or fall on the floor in convulsions. In fact, Saint Peter,
>
> If you know what I mean, they haven't yet learned
> How to be reverent.   (*Selected Poems* 11)

Addressing Saint Peter ingratiatingly as "mate," the speaker assumes that she and the keeper of heaven's gate share an intimacy of understanding that stands over against the outpatients and all their ilk. The speaker emphasizes the third-person pronoun to indicate the gulf between an implicit *us* and the derisively explicit *them*: "*They* bring *their* kids with *them*, [. . .] *They* have shopping baskets [. . .] *They* cry" (emphasis added). The sardonic litany concludes with the speaker's confiding to Saint Peter: "they haven't yet learned / How to be reverent." What the speaker wants is for "them" to revere the hospital and respond with obeisance to "our" system. What the speaker misses but the poet sees is that the only offense of the outpatients is that they have their own lives to live. Contrary to the speaker's dismissive attitude, the poem evokes sympathy and respect for the outpatients.

"For Saint Peter" also provides access to the mind-set of one who serves as an institutional functionary. The speaker here is Fanthorpe herself—or at least the speaker sits at Fanthorpe's desk. The impetus for the poem may have been anger at misplaced piety in the cosmos of the clinic. But in comparing her day job to the task of Saint Peter, Fanthorpe may also be reminding herself of what her attitude toward outpatients should be, confessing how wide of the mark her disgruntlement sometimes is, and acknowledging her oneness with those who are perceived as being difficult. Complaining about annoying people, the speaker proves to be genuinely annoying. Thinking she is one of *us*, the speaker must strike Saint Peter as one of *them*. But the ironies do not stop there. If from Saint Peter's perspective the inpatients are the souls in heaven, then the irritating outpatients might be taken to include all the rest of us. Frequently Fanthorpe's poetry lets us hear the voice of the other, lets us savor just how odd or annoying or inept the other is. We hear what is ungrammatical or strange or offensive in the way "those people" talk or behave. With the skill of a satirist, Fanthorpe invites us to smile at a pompous or petty or inarticulate voice. But while we are chortling at them, Fanthorpe offers an oblique ray of light that reveals we've been peering through a window that turns out to be a mirror. We realize with a start that the voice we have been laughing at sounds remarkably like our own. But the effect of her poetry is not so much to satirize "us" as to invite a compassionate recognition of our oneness with "them."

After writing out of her own experience as a receptionist, Fanthorpe began to imagine her way into the experience of the outpatients. She found that one thing she could do was to listen attentively to patients and seek to apprehend experience as they see it and say it. She says that when she is "thinking about something that wants to be written, one of the ways that it comes best is to think of the actual syntax, the vocabulary, the intonation people use that distinguish them from other people" (Pitt 12). We hear that concentration on a particular voice in such poems as "Casehistory: Julie (encephalitis)." Julie, trying to come to terms with her limitations, says:

> If I been rude, I apologize.
> I lost me memory
> 'Cos I had the flu, didn't I?
> I thought it was 'cos our dad died, see.
> But it was 'cos I had the flu. (*Selected Poems* 12)

In such ungrammatical awkwardness Fanthorpe finds a voice worthy of poetry. Asked if she goes "straight for the emotions of the reader," Fanthorpe says she does not think of it that way. In fact, she was writing such poems long before there was any prospect of publication. "Like most poets I began with a long experience of silence, as far as people reading me was concerned," Fanthorpe says. "What I do think about is trying to get to that arcane and peculiar subject, the truth. So the ways I have of writing are those that seem to me to be the most likely to reach into that truth" (Pitt 12). The truth she reaches into in her hospital poems has to do with the human worth of the marginalized.

"I feel the need to rectify, to correct the balance if I feel things are unfair," Fanthorpe says. "If I have any objectives, it's to bear witness, to say, 'I have seen this, and no one else was there looking at that precise moment'; especially perhaps on behalf of the dispossessed." Much of her poetry explores the border between what is expressed and what remains inexpressible. Some of her most moving poems grow out of her empathetic attempt to speak out the experience of those who are prevented from speaking for themselves. "I'm particularly involved with people *who have no voice*," she says. "I'm not carrying on a 'campaign' on their behalf but this is the theme I recognise as having a call on me: people at the edges of things" ("Interview" 70–71).

"Casehistory: Alison (head injury)" functions more as an internal monologue in which Fanthorpe conjectures what the thoughts and feelings of Alison might be instead of attempting to re-create her syntax:

(*She looks at her photograph*)

I would like to have known
My husband's wife, my mother's only daughter.
A bright girl she was.

Enmeshed in comforting
Fat, I wonder at her delicate angles.
Her autocratic knee

Like a Degas dancer's
Adjusts to the observer with airy poise,
That now lugs me upstairs

Hardly. Her face, broken
By nothing sharper than smiles, holds in its smiles
What I have forgotten.

She knows my father's dead,
And grieves for it, and smiles. She has digested
Mourning. Her smile shows it.

I, who need reminding
Every morning, shall never get over what
I do not remember.

Consistency matters.
I should like to keep faith with her lack of faith,
But forget her reasons.

Proud of this younger self,
I assert her achievements, her A levels,
Her job with a future.

Poor clever girl! I know,
For all my damaged brain, something she doesn't:
I am her future.

A bright girl she was.   (*Selected Poems* 14–15)

Fanthorpe gives a voice to Alison and speaks out something of what Alison might think or feel. The poem treats Alison's suffering—both physical and emotional—with dignity. That she cannot remember that her father is dead but needs to be reminded of it each morning does not diminish the reality of her grief. Indeed, Alison's grief is all the more painful because it is forever fresh. The poem leaves us with the sense that even in her damaged state, Alison is worthy of being treated with respect and seriousness.

But, Fanthorpe is also clearly aware of how the pressures of work in an institutionalized setting can impinge on the way patients are treated. Hospital patients who know the rules, observes Fanthorpe wryly, grasp not only "the printed ones / In the *Guide for Patients* about why we prefer / No smoking" but also "the real ones, like the precise quota / Of servility each doctor expects" (*Selected Poems* 94). In that poem, ironically titled "Patients," the ones most in need of treatment are neither the inpatients nor the out-

patients but the caregivers. Fanthorpe cites nurses who are "fatally /
Addicted to idleness and tea"; a lustful psychiatrist; and a distressed,
babbling director. But she implicitly includes herself among the un-
official patients when she asks, "What can be done for us, / The undiagnosed?" She seems to imply that what distinguishes caregivers
from patients is not so much the presence of health as the absence of
a diagnosis. There are many ways—emotionally, psychologically,
spiritually—to be unhealthy. And Fanthorpe, somewhat like the
American writer Flannery O'Connor, is keenly aware of what is
grotesque about those who are "normal."

Fanthorpe confesses her culpability more pointedly in the autobiographical poem "Clerical Error." Any mistake Fanthorpe made as
a typist could be dismissed as clerical error. The phrase points to a
mistake easily corrected, a typo, a momentary lapse devoid of moral
implications. But as an apostrophe implicitly addressed to Christ,
"Clerical Error" puts the clerk's errors in a larger context:

> My raiment stinks of the poor and the afflicted,
> Of those whom healers, in a parody of you,
> Have called back to mimic life.
>
> I understand they are yours, and concern
> All of us. But I am paid to do other things.
> What must I do when Job and his daughters
>
> Cram into my office where they are not allowed,
> When I am typing medical reports against the clock,
> When they mop and mow at me, seeking comfort?
>
> I can tell you what I do. I address them as *love*
> (Which is an insult), and say in a special soothing voice
> (Which fools no one), *Go to the nurses, Judith,*
>
> *Judith, the nurses are looking for you* (which is a lie).
> How, Sir, am I to reconcile this with your clear
> Instructions on dealing with the afflicted
> And the poor? I do not seek to justify
> My jobdescription. I did not write it,
> But I volunteered to live by its commandments.
>
> (*Neck-Verse* 15)

The speaker acknowledges that actions she is impelled to take to fulfill the obligations of her job cannot be reconciled with what she knows is right. She acutely feels the tension between her "jobdescription" and what she has come to recognize as a vocation. She neither defends her actions nor reconciles the demands of the workplace with her recognition of what is right.

Instead, she acknowledges the tension. In her poems Fanthorpe identifies with different populations, giving a voice to inpatients and outpatients, to those willing to "relax / Into illness" and those who restlessly worry over their symptoms, to caregivers harried by having too many people around, and to patients on deathbeds who face their solitary struggle largely uncared for. She understands what it is to be a functionary of an institution and feels the force of ethical obligations that may be at odds with institutional imperatives. Her awareness of her own incapacities and awkwardnesses enables her to enter empathetically into others' experience. Her poetry is wry, accessible, sharply observed but deeply compassionate. Fanthorpe's readers encounter in her poetry something of the complexity and challenge of responding to other persons as persons, and something of the pain of recognizing the competing claims of Job and the job.

Note

1. All six volumes of poetry by Fanthorpe—*Side Effects* (1978), *Standing To* (1982), *Voices Off* (1984), *A Watching Brief* (1987), *Neck-Verse* (1992), and *Safe as Houses* (1995)—were originally published in England by Peterloo Poets. The best one-volume introduction to her hospital poetry is *Selected Poems* (1986), a selection from her first three books (now out of print). First published in hardback by Peterloo Poets and in paperback by Penguin Books, *Selected Poems* remains available—in the United Kingdom only—from Penguin. *A Watching Brief* and *Neck-Verse* are available from Peterloo Poets (2 Kelly Gardens, Calstock, Cornwall, PL18 9SA, UK). *Safe as Houses* was published by Peterloo Poets and by Story Line Press, Brownsville, Oregon, and is the only volume by Fanthorpe in print in the United States. Peterloo Poets hopes to bring out a collected edition of Fanthorpe's poetry. On the Internet, all her books in print are available from Blackwell's (http://bookshop.blackwell.co.uk) or from BOL (www.uk.bol.com). Most of her poetry is available at the Internet

Bookshop (http://www.bookshop.co.uk) or at Waterstone's (http://www.waterstones.co.uk). *Safe as Houses* is also available from Amazon.com (http://www.amazon.com). All quotations in this essay are used with permission of the poet.

Works Cited

Bensley, Connie, and Judith Kazantzis. "Dropping Out and Standing To: An Interview with U. A. Fanthorpe." *The Pen: Broadsheet of the English Centre of International P.E.N.* 20 (1986): 18–19.

Fanthorpe, U. A. "Interview with U. A. Fanthorpe." Wainwright 69–75.

———. *Neck-Verse*. Calstock, Eng.: Peterloo Poets, 1995.

———. *Safe as Houses*. Calstock, Eng.: Peterloo Poets; Brownsville: Story Line, 1995.

———. *Selected Poems*. London: Penguin, 1986.

———. "Slow Learner." Wainwright 66–68.

———. *Voices Off.* Calstock, Eng.: Peterloo Poets, 1984

Hendry, Diana. "Watchwords from the Wards." *Gloucestershire and Avon Life* Aug. 1979: 65.

Pitt, Angela. "Face to Face: A Conversation between U. A. Fanthorpe and Angela Pitt." *English Review* 4.4 (1994): 10–14.

Wainwright, Eddie. *Taking Stock: A First Study of the Poetry of U. A. Fanthorpe*. Calstock, Eng.: Peterloo Poets, 1995.

Deborah R. Grayson

Health and Healing in the Works of Three African American Women Writers

In both fiction and nonfiction writing, African American women writers address the importance of maintaining a sense of spiritual wholeness and good health, a sense that the day-to-day stress of economic and psychological oppression frequently threatens to erase. In teaching African American literature and medicine, I explore with my students the reciprocal relations among African American literature, medicine, public health, and medical ethics. In particular, by focusing on the writings of African American women about healthcare issues, I hope to foster a critical consciousness of those issues among students. In my classes, which are primarily made up of literature, science, premed, nursing, and public health majors, we focus on how medicine and medical practice have an influence on, and are influenced by, social, cultural, political, and economic contexts. The study of literature is one way to pull together these diverse views and examine how they relate to medicine. Literary analysis represents one way to approach and begin to understand the complex relations between medicine and human experiences.

In this essay I discuss the work of two contemporary African American women writers, Gloria Naylor and Charlotte Watson Sherman, and how their fiction invites the kinds of questions my course is designed to raise. I then discuss the work of a third writer, the health-and-science editor Linda Villarosa, and her nonfiction writing on black women's health and healing.[1] I argue that each of the texts described in this essay is effective in the medical humanities classroom because of the ways each examines the social, historical, and contemporary contexts of African American women as health-care workers and as health-care clients.

In her novel *Bailey's Cafe*, Gloria Naylor extends the boundaries of institutional medicine to include the mystical and magical healing powers of people and places found in everyday life. As with all her novels, a central theme is that health and healing can and often do occur outside the protocols of scientific medicine. For Naylor, love and care of family and friends as well as community connection are as important as, if not more important than, any method scientific medicine might provide to heal and make whole the abused and injured.

Naylor presents a series of personal narratives, mostly from women, that reveal the almost unbearable sadness, pain, and suffering they endure as a result of neglect, physical and sexual abuse, and the lack of respect they receive from others and have for themselves.[2] The gallery of characters presented in *Bailey's Cafe* are Sadie, a woman who since childhood so desperately wanted her mother's love and approval that she would do anything for it, even become a prostitute; Eve, who is cast out of her godfather's house because he fears her developing sexuality and growth into womanhood; Esther, whose violent hatred of men comes as a result of her brother's selling her into sexual slavery at the age of twelve; Mariam (Mary), a mentally retarded Ethiopian Jewish adolescent who is turned away by her community when she mysteriously becomes pregnant (her pregnancy occurs despite her claim that "no man has ever touched me" [145] and the fact that her mother saw to it that Mary underwent the ritual of having her labia sewn shut); Miss Maple, a black man with a PhD in statistics who struggles to find a definition of manhood that counters the demoralizing and dehumanizing model of black manhood in jim crow America; Peaches (Mary Too), who is objectified by, paralyzed by, and eventually frees herself from her own physical beauty by slashing her face; and finally Jesse Bell (pun intended), who is penalized for loving men and women and loses herself in heroin addiction.

Naylor connects embodied symptoms of illness with the complex relation between illness and its social and cultural contexts. In the novel, the social ills of racism and sexism are directly connected to illness that is both mental and physical. Suggesting that illness is directly related to society and community, she constructs a vision of a community-based and community-centered model of health care that works in conjunction with, and is perhaps more far-reaching than, institutional medicine. Through its literary representation of such issues as sexual abuse, the objectification of women, religious and sexual persecution, and tensions among ethnic and cultural groups, Naylor's book is useful in articulating the medical-ethical issues these problems raise.

Charlotte Watson Sherman's novel *Touch* also examines themes of spiritual wholeness and the healing power of community—particularly the power of a community of women to restore the physical and emotional well-being of black women. Rayna Sargent, a thirty-five-year-old artist who supports herself by working as a crisis counselor in a hospital, learns that she is HIV-positive. She finds out that she became infected at the very moment she was beginning to build relationships with women friends and with Theodore, her new partner. Ironically, as a counselor involved in healing people through speaking and active listening, she is afraid to speak and listen when it comes to her own healing. Instead, she turns away from her circle of friends and family, seeking isolation.

Her fear of connection with anyone or anything but her art causes Rayna to shut down completely when she finds out that she is HIV-positive. Afraid to touch anyone or even to tell anyone that she has HIV, she is afraid of the very things that could help her in her attempts to live with the disease. When eventually she allows herself to trust her family and friends enough to tell them she is infected, she discovers that they are able to help her cope with her fear. The novel, one of the few portrayals of a black woman living with HIV, uses touch as a metaphor for healing.[3] In the novel, touch is an anointing, a means of passing on love and of staying connected to self and to others. In classroom discussion, *Touch* usually generates heated discussion among students on such topics as informed consent, whether women with HIV have the right to bear children, and whether HIV testing should be compulsory for pregnant women.

Body and Soul, a volume edited by Linda Villarosa, highlights all the themes and concepts of *Bailey's Cafe* and *Touch.* A project of the National Black Women's Health Project (NBWHP), this anthology provides a combination of historical data, personal narrative, and health-advocacy information geared specifically toward black women in order to eradicate what NBWHP founder Byllye Avery describes as a "conspiracy of silence" of black women regarding their health concerns (7). Like Naylor's and Sherman's novels, *Body and Soul* focuses on the importance of communities of women empowering themselves through education and self-help. A central tenet of *Body and Soul* and of the black women's health movement in general is the use of lay health workers and other community resources to educate and empower black women and their families about health issues. The anthology facilitates this empowerment by suggesting ways to translate the discouraging statistics on black women's health into something that is more meaningful to black women. Instead of focusing on what black women are dying from, the book suggests ways to talk about what black women are trying to live with.

In *Body and Soul,* good health is presented as something more than the "mere absence of disease" (xi). According to Villarosa, good health is also about self-esteem, feeling worthy of feeling good. Good health is about power, having a sense of how our bodies function and should feel and knowing what to do when we don't function or feel well; about intuition, following our inner voices regarding what we should know and do about our health; and about overcoming silence and speaking about our bodies and their sexuality (xvi-xvii).

Divided into six parts, *Body and Soul* provides detailed analyses and statistics on topics ranging from the body weight and image of black women to combating violence and environmental racism. It is a useful core text to use in the medical humanities classroom, because it provides a strong history and analysis of the health concerns of black women. At the end of each chapter is a list of resource centers, organizations, and books and articles for further study. The anthology provides a good point of departure for classroom discussions and research projects related to the health of black women.

All three books discussed here help students read and evaluate literature and medicine while focusing specifically on how an analysis of race, gender, and class adds another dimension to that evaluation.

Notes

1. Though I prefer to capitalize the word *black,* it is lowercased here following MLA style.
2. Students are often curious about what they see as Naylor's overwhelmingly negative portrayal of black women's health issues. In response to this, I talk about the dismal health conditions actual black women face. I then return our focus to the novel, to talk about the possible solutions Naylor gives us to heal the health problems of black women. I suggest that despite her negative portrayal of black women's health conditions, she leaves her characters and her readers with hope. Her discussion of the importance of the community in combating social and physical ills is one example of providing hope.
3. Pearl Cleage recently published a novel whose protagonist is a young black female infected with HIV.

Works Cited

Avery, Byllye. "Breathing Life into Ourselves: The Evolution of the National Black Women's Health Project." *The Black Woman's Health Book: Speaking for Ourselves.* Ed. Evelyn C. White. Expanded ed. Seattle: Seal, 1994. 4–10.

Cleage, Pearl. *What Looks like Crazy on an Ordinary Day.* New York: Avon, 1997.

Naylor, Gloria. *Bailey's Cafe.* New York: Vintage, 1992.

Sherman, Charlotte Watson. *Touch.* New York: Harper, 1995.

Villarosa, Linda, ed. *Body and Soul: The Black Woman's Guide to Physical Health and Emotional Well-Being.* New York: Harper, 1994.

G. Thomas Couser

Critical Conditions: Teaching Illness Narrative

Although what Anne Hunsaker Hawkins asserted a few years ago may still be true, that "pathography is a genre that awaits its master-pieces" (159), there are two powerful reasons for teaching at least one illness narrative, preferably autobiographical, in any course on literature and medicine. The first is that such narratives provide a unique literary perspective on medicine—the written testimony of the person who is ill. The second is that the genre has flourished so dramatically in the last two decades as to be a cultural phenomenon worth exploring in its own right.

Though not without predecessors, contemporary illness narra-tive constitutes a distinctive form of life writing, a large body of texts only beginning to be studied and appreciated. The best guide to ill-ness narratives is the extensive annotated bibliography in Hawkins's *Reconstructing Illness*. Hawkins assesses the quality of each narrative and indicates the illness it chronicles and the major themes, meta-phors, and myths it invokes—for example, journey, rebirth, battle, and athletic challenge.[1] Because the recent flood of illness narratives has produced many texts of high literary caliber, ranging (alphabetically) from Stewart Alsop's *Stay of Execution* to Paul Zweig's *Departures*, one need not look far for well-written testimony. My goal here is not to establish a canon; rather, I focus my suggestions on two books that are distinguished in conception and execution: Emmanuel Dreuilhe's *Mortal Embrace* (1988), an AIDS narrative, and Christina Middlebrook's *Seeing the Crab: A Memoir of Dying* (1996), a breast cancer narrative. In suggesting ways of approaching these narratives, I hope to facilitate the teaching of other narratives that may prove more suitable in particular courses—or that are yet to be written.

Books like Dreuilhe's and Middlebrook's are worth teaching in part because they actively contest the marginalization of illness and the denial of death in American culture. An illuminating preliminary approach to the texts, then, is to ask students to gather examples from popular culture of the background against which illness narrative can be seen as counterdiscursive. As Verlyn Klinkenborg has noted,

> When you contract a disease, you contract the world of that disease, and that world is what threatens self-definition. In this, as in so much else, AIDS has reminded us of things that were on the verge of being forgotten. It has distanced us from the medical optimism of the nineteen-fifties and sixties and reasserted the fact that no sickness—and certainly no epidemic—comes without its myths, which can be every bit as damaging as the sickness itself. (78)

Given the subjects of these two texts, an obvious but worthwhile strategy with both is to assign Susan Sontag on illness metaphors and ask how Dreuilhe and Middlebrook address the problem of the mystification and stigmatization of their conditions. Sontag's example is particularly interesting since, as she acknowledged in *AIDS and Its Metaphors*, her earlier book *Illness as Metaphor* was provoked by her experience with breast cancer, which brought home to her the outrageous way in which cancer metaphors can exacerbate the suffering of the ill (*AIDS* 12). Instead of writing the narrative of her illness in *Illness as Metaphor*, she launched a direct discursive attack on illness metaphor with all the force of her powerful intellect. In *AIDS and Its Metaphors*, she shifted her position slightly but significantly. Rather than condemn all metaphors, she acknowledged that some are less insidious than others. Recognizing that abstaining entirely from metaphors is neither possible nor desirable, she urged that they be "exposed, criticized, belabored, used up" (94).[2]

Mortal Embrace is particularly ingenious in challenging the prevailing metaphors of HIV-AIDS (and stereotypes of gay men). Far from eschewing metaphor or explicitly deconstructing it, Dreuilhe appropriates the very metaphor that Sontag declares herself "most eager to see retired" (94)—the military metaphor—and puts it to his own subversive purposes.[3] That Middlebrook's *Seeing the Crab* also plays with the trope of illness as combat, the patient as foot soldier, provides a good opportunity to explore the gender implications of this trope.

One can then move to discussion of more general issues, especially that of the construction of illness in narrative. In addition to providing gripping tales of life-threatening conditions, illness narrative offers a special opportunity to explore the means by which nature or biology is given cultural expression and form. Whatever texts are assigned, students will benefit from having the apparently simple relation between illness and narrative—you get sick, you get better, you write your story—problematized. Indeed, a useful pedagogical technique is to ask students to write a short narrative of an illness they have experienced or witnessed before they read the assigned texts. These narratives need not be shared (or graded); they can serve rather as a source of data. Students' illness narratives can provide an immediate context for discussion of the published accounts. The experience of attempting illness narrative may also suggest to students the role of narrative conventions in enabling, and constraining, such writing.

Students may sharpen their sense of the ethics and dynamics of illness narrative by asking the same questions of their own narratives as of the published ones: Which illness is narrated? Is it acute or chronic? Is the narrative autobiographical or biographical? What role is played by physicians? To what extent does the course of the illness (or of treatment protocols) determine the shape of the narrative? Does the narrative have a comic plot (i.e., the protagonist is better off at the end than at the beginning)? How does the narrative achieve closure or resolution? What sorts of other stories, if any, get grafted onto illness plots? Is the narrative exclusively or primarily a story of illness, or is illness a pretext for writing autobiography? How does the text represent the relation between body and psyche or soul?

Since the generic illness narrative title is, in effect, "One Person's Triumph over X," there is some question as to whether the story of a chronic or terminal illness can be told. Both *Seeing the Crab* and *Mortal Embrace* demonstrate that the story can be told, but both do so by deviating from or revising generic conventions. Each is quite innovative within its subgenre. *Seeing the Crab* begins with the frank admission that its author is doomed; she has undergone a bone marrow transplant that bought her some time but will not, she insists, save her life. Given this premise, the book raises interesting questions about the relation of narrative time to historical time and to personal time, or "life time." Students may be encouraged to consider how Middlebrook's handling of narrative—including overall structure, pace, and style—reflects the sense of living on borrowed time.

While readable and engaging, this book explores territory where few have gone before; it exposes the decorousness and sanitization of most illness narratives (including *Mortal Embrace*). It is challenging precisely because a comic resolution seems unavailable and because it violates the powerful taboo against the discussion of one's impending death. (Kübler-Ross's *On Death and Dying* provides a paradigm against which Middlebrook's narrative may be read.)

In contrast to narratives of breast cancer, which are almost always autobiographical, most narratives of HIV-AIDS are posthumous stories about gay men written by survivors—family members (parents, siblings, even children) or partners. The reasons for and implications of this difference are worth exploring. *Mortal Embrace* is one of the very few autobiographical accounts of AIDS.[4] Dreuilhe's book is not an illness narrative in the narrow sense but a series of essays that may be read independently of one another. The choice of the essay form is worth attention. Students should be asked to think about the implications of pure narrative, with its reliance on plot and chronology, for the representation of an illness like AIDS, which, at least until recently, was assumed to be invariably fatal.

From a discussion of these characteristics of genre, one can move to still more general concerns, which may resonate with the larger concerns and themes of the course. Arthur W. Frank has suggested in *The Wounded Storyteller* that illness narratives are postcolonial discourse insofar as they express the impulse of those marginalized by illness to witness their conditions in their own terms —a hypothesis that may instructively be tested on *Mortal Embrace* and *Seeing the Crab*.[5] One source of illness narratives is patients' sense that the language and practice of traditional medicine translate their concerns into somewhat alien terms and detach the body from its life context. (For a helpful account of the medical genres to which personal narrative can be contrasted, see Hunter's *Doctors' Stories*.) This observation is not to deny that Western medicine is for the most part effective and benign; as Frank points out, one of the historical factors behind the contemporary proliferation of illness narratives is that more people are surviving conditions that would once have been fatal. But biomedical discourse is not adequate to express the lived experience of illness or to infuse it with meaning. The more serious an illness, the more it demands to be interpreted as a life event, and Western medicine does not concern itself with that demand. Illness narrative is often a way, then, of reclaiming one's story, of re-siting one's illness in the context of one's whole life. Exploring this more general aspect of the narratives helps to root them in a broad cultural-historical context and to encourage reflection on the implications of the medicalization of contemporary American culture.

A multidimensional approach that moves from student-generated texts through exemplary published narratives and collateral secondary sources should enable students to ask, and answer, significant questions about the motives and meanings of illness narrative. The approach should also give students insight into at least one way in which the medical becomes literary: how pathology becomes autopathography and even—when bad things happen to good writers —autobiography; how, and why, the story of a patient's disease becomes the story of a person's life.

Notes

1. Three books are especially useful in contextualizing and approaching illness narrative. Hawkins's work offers the best introduction and overview. Frank's *The Wounded Storyteller: Body, Illness, and Ethics* is especially good on the context, motives, and ethical implications of illness narrative (not necessarily literary). My own *Recovering Bodies: Illness, Disability, and Life Writing* focuses on the poetics and politics of narratives of two illnesses in particular, breast cancer and HIV-AIDS.

2. In addition to Sontag's work, anthologies edited by Crimp and by Feldman provide useful collateral reading on HIV-AIDS; Kahane provides a useful account of the myths of breast cancer (10).

3. In many ways, Lorde's *The Cancer Journals* is analogous: a series of essays that directly challenges the sexist and heterosexist discourse of breast cancer. Lorde could therefore be taught in place of Dreuilhe, in a similar manner. Precisely because of the similarities between their books, however, *The Cancer Journals* would not make a good companion text to *Mortal Embrace;* hence my recommendation of Middlebrook as a breast cancer narrative.

4. If time permits, one might read Dreuilhe's account against a family narrative like Wiltshire's *Seasons of Grief and Grace* or an account by a surviving partner, like Monette's *Borrowed Time.*

5. Of all forms of marginalization, the most universal—those caused by illness and disability—have been the least discussed in the academy. Teaching narratives of illness and disability is, among other things, a way to address this imbalance.

Works Cited

Alsop, Stewart. *Stay of Execution.* Philadelphia: Lippincott, 1973.

Couser, G. Thomas. *Recovering Bodies: Illness, Disability, and Life Writing.* Madison: U of Wisconsin P, 1997.

Crimp, Douglas, ed. *AIDS: Cultural Analysis / Cultural Activism.* Cambridge: MIT P, 1988.

Dreuilhe, Emmanuel. *Mortal Embrace: Living with AIDS.* Trans. Linda Coverdale. New York: Hill, 1988.

Feldman, Douglas A., ed. *Culture and AIDS.* New York: Praeger, 1990.

Frank, Arthur W. *The Wounded Storyteller: Body, Illness, and Ethics.* Chicago: U of Chicago P, 1995.

Hawkins, Anne Hunsaker. *Reconstructing Illness: Studies in Pathography.* 1993. Rev. ed. West Lafayette: Purdue UP, 1998.

Hunter, Kathryn Montgomery. *Doctors' Stories: The Narrative Structure of Medical Knowledge.* Princeton: Princeton UP, 1991.

Kahane, Deborah Hobler. *No Less a Woman: Ten Women Shatter the Myths about Breast Cancer.* New York: Prentice, 1990.

Klinkenborg, Verlyn. "Dangerous Diagnoses." Rev. of *Living in the Shadow of Death,* by Sheila M. Rothman, and *Silent Travelers,* by Alan M. Krant. *New Yorker* 18 July 1994: 78–80.

Kübler-Ross, Elisabeth. *On Death and Dying.* New York: Macmillan, 1969.

Lorde, Audre. *The Cancer Journals.* Argyle: Spinsters Ink, 1980.

Middlebrook, Christina. *Seeing the Crab: A Memoir of Dying.* New York: Basic, 1996.

Monette, Paul. *Borrowed Time: An AIDS Memoir.* New York: Harcourt, 1988.

Sontag, Susan. *AIDS and Its Metaphors.* New York: Farrar, 1989.

———. *Illness as Metaphor.* New York: Farrar, 1978.

Wiltshire, Susan Ford. *Seasons of Grief and Grace: A Sister's Story of AIDS.* Nashville: Vanderbilt UP, 1994.

Zweig, Paul. *Departures.* New York: Harper, 1986.

Elizabeth Homan and Sidney Homan

"Dancing in Very Narrow Spaces": Pinter's *A Kind of Alaska* in Performance

Using plays in a course on humanities and medicine is hardly unique. There are numerous eligible candidates: George Bernard Shaw's *The Doctor's Dilemma*, where a physician's moral distaste for a patient conflicts with the physician's professional oath; Scott McPherson's *Marvin's Room*, with its sardonic portrait of the sick and the elderly; Brian Clark's *Whose Life Is It Anyway?* whose paralyzed central character refuses medical treatment. Stage comedies often provide a perspective unencumbered with dogma: Molière satirizes the medical establishment in *A Flea in Her Ear* and *The Doctor in Spite of Himself*; Norman Barasch's *Send Me No Flowers* involves the diagnosis of terminal illness overheard by the wrong patient.

Harold Pinter's *A Kind of Alaska* provides an especially complex example of a play about medicine because of the play's roots in real life. Based on Dr. Oliver Sacks's factual account of an epidemic of encephalitis lethargica that swept through Europe and the United States at the beginning of the twentieth century (Pinter 3), it chronicles the awakening of a middle-aged woman named Deborah, who, twenty-nine years earlier, at the age of sixteen, fell victim to the unusual sleeping sickness and "just stopped" (21). Her sister, Pauline, and her doctor (who is also her brother-in-law), Hornby, are the only family members who have remained loyal through her debilitating illness, and it is this triangular relationship that fuels the dramatic action of the play.

Pinter's Deborah describes her coma in this fashion: "I've been dancing in very narrow spaces. Kept stubbing my toes and bumping my head. Like Alice" (24). This provides an apt metaphor for the process of analyzing a play, finding one's way into it—whether as actor, director, or audience member—and negotiating the precarious and very narrow spaces that join the literary text to the performance text to turn drama into theater.

W. B. Worthen observes that "text and performance have long seemed to compete for legitimacy as a means for representing drama." If the dramatic texts are stable, "organically coherent systems," then performance occupies some peripheral space subordinate to or in the service of this system (442). Conversely, to distinguish itself from literary criticism, performance criticism would argue that theater invokes meanings only suggested, indeed sometimes not even present, in a play's written text, because a stage enactment takes place in space and time, is physical (sets, costumes, lighting), has a language beyond that on the page (characters' inner feelings, the characters' histories as devised by the actors), and requires the presence of an audience for its reception and ratification. The semiotician Patrice Pavis offers the term *performance text* as an interpretation or metatext mediating between enactment and the playwright's written word (136). Clearly, in Pinter's play, Sacks's actual case history of Rose R. (the real patient reflected in Pinter's Deborah) adds a third possible text.

Using plays as theatrical case histories has advantages. Unlike that sprawling, infinite life offstage, the play's world, albeit illusory, is finite, complete; we can grasp that world in its entirety during the stage's "two hours' traffic" (*Romeo and Juliet*, Prologue). Moreover, the play is safe: for every measure of Aristotelian fear we experience, there is an equal measure of pity allowing us to distance ourselves from the story. As an object of discussion, therefore, *A Kind of Alaska* admits a host of topics: the relationship between physician and patient, the double-edged sword of the patient's awakening, the complications of the physician's becoming a member of the family, the patient's special and to some degree unfathomable experience.

Still, to consider the play only as a case history ignores that more inclusive performance text of which Pavis speaks and the medium that Pinter used for translating Rose's history. When Deborah awakens from her thirty-years' sleep, her "temporary habitation in a kind of Alaska" (34), she is faced with the details of a reality with which she is unfamiliar but from which she must construct herself anew. Likewise, scholars or teachers approaching a dramatic work must learn to maneuver—to dance, if you will—among the play's various texts without stubbing their toes or bumping their head on any of them.

Having students stage the play in class and take on the roles of Deborah, Hornby, and Pauline has the advantage of allowing them to consider the three characters from the inside, because students, in enacting a character, must devise (to use two terms dear to actors) both an *object* for the character (what the character is after, the character's agenda, the character's conscious as well as unconscious desires) and a *subtext* (all those unvoiced things we say to ourselves that influence but are not fully replicated in actual discourse with others). *Subtext* also means the character's history prior to the start of the play: the life, as fashioned by the actor during rehearsals, that affects the character's behavior on stage. To this character the student also brings real-life experiences, or at least real-life observations.

Staging *A Kind of Alaska* in class hardly precludes class discussion. Indeed, discussion of the overview of the play and its issues has affinities with what in the theater is called the director's concept, the individual interpretation the director envisions before becoming engaged with the technical staff and before meeting, even before casting, the actors. But unlike straight discussion—which is by definition after the fact, reflective, and abstract—this theatrical approach treats the play as happening, evolving, as something specific and human.

Consider the following dialogue between Hornby and Deborah, where he tries to define her transition to consciousness:

Hornby. You have been asleep for twenty-nine years.
[*Silence.*]
Deborah. You mean I'm dead?
Hornby. No.
Deborah. I don't feel dead.
Hornby. You're not.
Deborah. But you mean I've been dead?
Hornby. If you had been dead you wouldn't be alive now.
Deborah. Are you sure?

Rehearsing this passage, students might want to consider how and why Hornby struggles with *asleep* and *alive* and why he is torn between being the loving brother-in-law and the accurate physician. A silence rather than the more common Pinter pause intervenes between his first line and Deborah's response: what is she thinking, planning during this time? How satisfying is his "If you had been dead," given her response, "Are you sure?" Who is winning this scene (winning in the actor's sense)? Normally, the physician would have the upper hand, yet Deborah's simple but probing questions unsettle Hornby. To the physicians or future physicians acting the part of Hornby, the passage has implications for their real-life practice, as Hornby's inadequate euphemism "asleep" is challenged by his patient. Knowing she is anxious to get a clear definition of her state—ironically, something that she has experienced internally and that he can define only from observations of her outward appearance—he has to deal with her fear that she has been dead. His semi-comic logic—that if she were dead, she wouldn't be here, "alive now"—is again challenged when Deborah raises the more profound question of what defines life. For physicians, future physicians, or any health-care workers, this exchange—indeed the entire play—exposes the conflict inherent when a fellow human in a professional role deals with a patient whose illness, albeit physical in origin, has deeply emotional, not to mention philosophical, ramifications.

Hornby and Pauline, who have married during the period of Deborah's coma, have the following interchange:

Hornby. I didn't call you. [*Pauline regards him.*] Well, all right. Speak to her.
Pauline. What shall I say?
Hornby. Just talk to her.
Pauline. Doesn't it matter what I say?
Hornby. No.
Pauline. I can't do her harm.
Hornby. No.
Pauline. Shall I tell her lies or the truth?
Hornby. Both.

Consider these questions. What kind of marriage do they have? What is Hornby's attitude toward his wife? Has his love, even his envy, of her sister (in her coma she experienced a rich, fantastic world denied him) affected that marriage? How should this interchange be blocked? To what degree does Hornby or Pauline or both, by their movements, try to avoid Deborah's overhearing them? What is Pauline's subtext after Hornby's first line during the stage direction that she "regards him"? What does she say to herself that will influence her facial expression, any gesture, perhaps even stage movement? What is Hornby's object in his final line, "Both"? For the student who plans to enter the medical field, the passage raises two larger real-life issues: To what degree should or—better yet—can a member of a patient's family be involved in the treatment? Do recovering patients have the right to know the complete facts of their condition, if so knowing might prove too unsettling; and (a corollary question)—does the physician alone, the expert, have the right to make this determination?

Through performance students can enter the mind of the character, as they conceive that mind, in a way denied to conventional discussion. Teachers do not necessarily need experience in the theater; there is something to be said for their learning along with their students, bringing to the rehearsals their more extensive experience. In a humanities and medicine class, albeit within those safe confines of the stage's illusory world, *A Kind of Alaska* can become a case history *experienced*.

For medical students such empathy is inseparable from self-knowledge or, at the very least, from an understanding of the health-care professional's art of interacting with patients. Actors speak of connecting with one another onstage, of being alert to the vocal rhythms, the nuances of tone and volume, the pauses, the gestures, the physical position of a fellow actor. Thus, playing Hornby as he deals with his patient, Deborah, can provide students with a mirror to a doctor's bedside manner. The interns and physicians who watched the production of *A Kind of Alaska*, which inaugurated the Arts in Medicine Program at Shands Teaching Hospital on the University of Florida campus in 1990,[1] later took part in an acting workshop with the play's director. In that workship, they played themselves about to tell a patient (played by a professional actor) news about the patient's condition that was worse than what the patient was expecting. The point of the exercise was to bring an actor's awareness, and technique, to the meeting. How do you enter the room? How close do you sit to the patient? How do you break the difficult news? How do you deliver your text? What gestures do you use? Once the patient knows the truth, do you touch the patient, comfort the patient? How do you leave the patient? The exercise reflected, in miniature, Hornby's dilemma in Pinter's play. Thinking of themselves as actors allowed the physicians to see from a theatrical perspective an event that happens all too often in real life and to bring an actor's skill to a difficult situation. The conflict between play as text and play as performance, or between real life and the illusory stage world, therefore became a productive combination.

Note

1. This production was directed by Sidney Homan, whose daughter, Elizabeth Homan, first got him interested in Pinter. Hence their present collaboration.

Works Cited

Pavis, Patrice. "Towards the Semiology of the Mise en Scène." Trans. Susan Melrose. *Languages of the Stage: Essays on the Semiology of Theatre.* New York: PAJ, 1982. 133–59.

Pinter, Harold. *A Kind of Alaska. Other Places.* New York: Grove, 1983. 2–40.

Worthen, W. B. "Deeper Meanings and Theatrical Technique: The Rhetoric of Performance Criticism." *Shakespeare Quarterly* 40 (1989): 442–48.

Part III

Literature in Medical Education and Medical Practice

Kathryn Montgomery

Sherlock Holmes and Clinical Reasoning

Clinical judgment is the quintessential skill of a good physician, but exactly what it is and how to develop and sustain it are not well established. Experience is vital; firsthand experience is best, but next best is the vicarious experience of reflecting on the cases of others. Case presentation, formal and informal, occupies much of clinical education. This essay describes a five-week (ten-hour) seminar at Northwestern University Medical School that pairs Arthur Conan Doyle's Sherlock Holmes stories with analytic studies of diagnostic reasoning. Clinical analogues abound in the stories: Holmes's reliance on retrospective narrative hypotheses, the importance of reading signs (the boon of a pathognomonic sign, the disappointment of a red herring), the value of a good history, the judicious use of tests, the preference for ruling out rather than ruling in, the use of maxims, and the claim to be engaged in a deductive science.

A detective story, like a doctor's story, is an ur-narrative: the rational reconstruction of what has happened so that a reliably accurate account of the event can be given, an account that will explain the past and direct the future. Dr. Watson, the clerk of Sherlock Holmes's records, presents Holmes's cases as medical cases are presented: beginning with the sufferer's account of the evil for which he or she seeks help, a chief complaint augmented by Holmes's close and often unexpected questioning. A physical examination follows —house calls! Signs are investigated, tests sometimes performed. In the process Holmes pieces together the likeliest narrative explanation of the puzzling event, an explanation that will make sense of even the unlikeliest signs. This retrospective task requires observational and interpretive skills and a wealth of accumulated experience, actual and vicarious, stored as remembered cases. Holmes's narrative taxonomy of crime prompts his questions, inspires his speculative imagination, shapes his interpretation. From time to time Holmes offers procedural hints to the official police or utters one of the maxims that guide his expert judgment. That these maxims conflict and that he describes his method as both science and deduction only render his practice more like the clinical reasoning that was Arthur Conan Doyle's model.

The seminar Sherlock Holmes and Clinical Reasoning is part of a required course for second-year medical students, Patient, Physician, and Society. The seminar is limited to a dozen students, all of whom are well advanced in their physical diagnosis course. In addition to doing the paired readings each week, students contract to learn more about a related area of inquiry—logic, narrative theory, cognitive studies, epistemology—and report on their reading or research. It is a busy hour and fifty minutes.

The first week, "Clinical Semiotics: Reading the Signs," begins where Arthur Conan Doyle and his narrator John Watson, MD, began, with *A Study in Scarlet*. This novella introduces both Watson and his readers to Sherlock Holmes and poses two mysteries. The first, the Lauriston Garden Murder, occupies Holmes. The second occupies Watson: What does his strange new flatmate do for a living? Holmes keeps peculiar hours, has odd interests, knows nothing of Copernican cosmology, but has at his fingertips the details of every notable crime for the last century. Watson is baffled until he ridicules

an anonymous essay left lying around the flat. It concerns the interpretation of signs, and Holmes reveals that he is its author: "I am a
consulting detective—if you know what that means" (15).

Holmes's skill in reading signs is highlighted by the parallel
reading, "The Bedside Sherlock Holmes," a masterpiece of clinical
semiotics by Faith Fitzgerald and Lawrence M. Tierney, Jr. As a catalog of clinical signs, the essay bulges with detail: the recently let-out
belt, unevenly worn shoe heels, a blanched bare ring finger, sights
and smells that provide clues to expeditious diagnosis and treatment.
Other clinical parallels in *A Study in Scarlet*—Holmes's taxonomy
of cases, his contradictory maxims, the retrospective construction
of a plot with variants that are ruled in or out, and Watson's beginning attempts to emulate the master in his own narrative—are
marked for discussion in subsequent weeks. Students also notice
the resemblance between the Utah section of the novella, a copi-
ously detailed etiology of the present murders, and the histories of
present illness that cause their own first clinical write-ups to burst at
the seams.

Week 2, "The Method: Discerning Plot, Making the Diagnosis," focuses on Holmes's interpretive, narrative procedure. Peter
Brooks's brilliant analysis of Doyle's "The Musgrave Ritual" has
made this story required reading. Reginald Musgrave's butler has
disappeared after his master finds him studying the ritual memorized
by Musgrave heirs since the mid-seventeenth century. Soon after,
the fiery Welsh maid, who had broken off with the butler not long
before, also disappears. Holmes focuses on the ritual, and its interpretation is the story's plot. On the grounds of the Musgrave estate,
Holmes plots out the villain's plot, arriving, like him, at the plot of
ground that holds the family's ancient legacy, the crown jewels entrusted to them by Charles I.

The parallel reading is a section of Alvan Feinstein's classic *Clinical Judgment,* which describes the interpretive practices that characterize diagnostic reasoning. During this second week, students may
report on related topics—such as C. S. Peirce's concept of abduc-
tion, Umberto Eco's *The Name of the Rose,* or National Public

Radio's diagnostic tour de force *Car Talk*—or return to topics that properly belong to the beginning week: chapter 3 of Voltaire's *Zadig* or Thomas Sebeok's work in semiotics.

Readings for week 3, "Clinical Reasoning: The Review of Systems and Rule-Outs," are Doyle's "The Adventure of the Priory School" and Jerome P. Kassirer and G. Anthony Gorry's early investigation of expert reasoning, "Clinical Problem Solving: A Behavioral Analysis." The kidnapping mystery offers a vivid demonstration of Holmes's thorough investigation of signs, of his imaginative production of alternative hypotheses, and of his choices among them. Signs generate hypotheses; hypotheses prompt a search for signs that will confirm or eliminate them. A bicycle is missing. Might the young heir and the villain have gone by the road? No, for the innkeeper's wife was ill, and someone watched the road all night for the doctor's arrival. (Can this informant be trusted? This is a "zebra" to be ignored until Holmes and Watson have finished the obvious: scouring the countryside in the opposite direction for clues.) The extended sequence of reviewing and ruling out that constitutes the action ultimately demands that a temporarily stumped Holmes sit down to think—and discover the final essential clue: hoofprints, cattle prints, with no cattle in sight.

The narrative demands of competing hypotheses are also traced in Kassirer and Gorry's investigation of the clinical reasoning of two groups of experts, nephrologists and cardiologists, asked to diagnose a patient whose kidneys have shut down. The nephrologists, working with a brief and fully detailed taxonomy of kidney disease, establish the diagnosis of aspirin-induced kidney failure quickly, with only a few key questions and no review of systems. Taking longer, asking many more questions, the cardiologists nevertheless reach the same diagnosis. The patient has suffered headaches for years. What did she take for them? How much aspirin? Aha! For this section, students may report on other research in clinical reasoning and expert knowledge, such as that by Arthur Elstein, Lee Shulman, and Sarah Sprafka; Georges Bordage and Madeleine Lemieux; Geoffrey Norman; Herbert Dreyfus and Stuart Dreyfus; and Patricia Benner.

Week 4's topic is "Narrative Knowledge: Imagination and the

Construction of the Plot." The Holmes story is "Silver Blaze," a mystery characterized, as Holmes remarks, less by the need for new clues than by the proper understanding of what is already known. To that end, Holmes, wearing his flap-eared traveling cap (for the only time), turns to Watson and says, "At least I have a grip of the essential facts of the case. I shall enumerate them to you, for nothing clears up a case so much as stating it to another person" (456–57). By the time they reach the scene of the crime, Holmes is occupied with gathering evidence that only he knows to look for. A few pointed questions supply a pertinent negative: the dog didn't bark in the night. It is the confirmatory detail in Watson's account of Holmes's invention and testing of the narrative that will at once identify the murderer and lead the detective to the missing race-horse. Along with this story, we read my "Knowledge in Medicine" (Hunter), which argues for the existence and efficacy of narrative in clinical knowing. Students may report on research in cognitive psychology, the epistemology of psychotherapy, or the effort in the field of artificial intelligence to model a narrative rationality.

The topic for the final week is "Watson's Method: Making a Case." Throughout the stories Holmes describes his method with fair accuracy as a narrative one. Yet he always characterizes this method as "deduction" and "science." It is, of course, neither. Like so much else, he shares this misrepresentation of his considerable rational skill with the physicians who were Doyle's models. "The Copper Beeches" not only exhibits Holmes's usual rational strategies but also includes an especially egregious instance of his scientific hubris. "You have perhaps erred," he tells Watson, whose cases proceed from effect to cause, as good case narrative should, "[. . .] instead of confining yourself to the task of placing upon record that severe reasoning from cause to effect which is really the only notable feature about the thing" (430). Such dull, short, textbook abstractions have their uses, of course, but Watson's case narrative is best for teaching and reminding clinicians of the subtleties of their actual rational process.

Marsden S. Blois's explication of the distinction between scientific and clinical reasoning, "Medicine and the Nature of Vertical

Reasoning," reinforces the point that clinical reasoning is not positivist science but a much more complicated, counterbalanced application of scientific knowledge and clinical judgment to the unfolding circumstances of the present case. For this section, students might report on work in the epistemology of practice by Barney Glaser and Anselm Strauss and by Donald Schön and on the potential relevance of chaos theory.

The seminar's objectives are easily met. Students readily understand and describe the reasoning used by Sherlock Holmes; they are critically aware of its resemblance to clinical reasoning. Its differences—how Holmes cheats, and the patently readable social world he inhabits—are identified. They gain some familiarity with theories of cognitive psychology, artificial intelligence, and the philosophy of knowledge—especially as these disciplines critique *science* as a synonym for rationality. Above all, students have a chance at the beginning of their clinical careers to reflect on rational method as their chief tool and to enjoy classics of that most modern of genres, the detective story.

Works Cited

Benner, Patricia. *From Novice to Expert: Excellence and Power in Clinical Nursing Practice.* Reading: Addison, 1984.

Blois, Marsden S. "Medicine and the Nature of Vertical Reasoning." *New England Journal of Medicine* 318 (1988): 847–51.

Bordage, Georges, and Madeleine Lemieux. "Semantic Structures and Diagnostic Thinking of Experts and Novices." *Academic Medicine* 66 (1990): 570–72.

Brooks, Peter. *Reading for the Plot: Design and Intention in Narrative.* New York: Vintage, 1984.

Doyle, Arthur Conan. "The Adventure of the Priory School." Doyle, *Holmes* 744–72.

———. "The Copper Beeches." Doyle, *Holmes* 429–52.

———. "The Musgrave Ritual." Doyle, *Holmes* 527–44.

———. *Sherlock Holmes: The Complete Novels and Stories.* Vol. 1. New York: Bantam, 1986.

———. "Silver Blaze." Doyle, *Holmes* 455–77.

———. *A Study in Scarlet.* Doyle, *Holmes* 3–103.

Dreyfus, Herbert L., and Stuart E. Dreyfus. "From Socrates to Expert Systems: The Limits of Calculative Rationality." *Interpretive Social Sciences:*

A Second Look. Ed. Paul Rabinow and William M. Sullivan. Berkeley: U of California P, 1987. 327–50.

Elstein, Arthur S., Lee S. Shulman, and Sarah A. Sprafka. *Medical Problem Solving: An Analysis of Clinical Reasoning.* Cambridge: Harvard UP, 1978.

Feinstein, Alvan. *Clinical Judgment.* Baltimore: Williams, 1967.

Fitzgerald, Faith T., and Lawrence M. Tierney, Jr. "The Bedside Sherlock Holmes." *Western Journal of Medicine* 137 (1982): 169–75.

Glaser, Barney G., and Anselm L. Strauss. *The Discovery of Grounded Theory.* Chicago: Aldine, 1967.

Hunter, Kathryn Montgomery. "Knowledge in Medicine." *Doctors' Stories: The Narrative Structure of Medical Knowledge.* Princeton: Princeton UP, 1991. 5–26.

Kassirer, Jerome P., and G. Anthony Gorry. "Clinical Problem Solving: A Behavioral Analysis." *Annals of Internal Medicine* 89 (1978): 245–55.

Norman, Geoffrey R. "The Non-analytical Basis of Clinical Reasoning." Presented to the case-based reasoning group in the Department of Computer Science, University of Chicago, December 1994.

Schön, Donald A. *The Reflective Practitioner: How Professionals Think in Action.* New York: Basic, 1983.

Cortney Davis

Nurses' Poetry: Expanding the Literature and Medicine Canon

The growing field of literature and medicine is opening a horizon in medical studies, but in that opening a valuable resource may be overlooked: the writing of registered nurses. Nurses' poetry is often not included in the arts-medicine canon or in courses on literature and medicine. Students only occasionally study literature written by nurses, while writing by and about physicians is utilized to provide important, sometimes essential, insights into patient-caregiver interactions, ethical dilemmas, and other sensitive issues in patient care. But physicians' narratives tell only part of the health-care story. Nurses' poetry provides a complementary emotional and professional perspective on medical situations.

A survey of both nurses' and physicians' poetry shows that what nurses write about their work is sometimes different from what physicians report about theirs. What nurses reveal also differs dramatically from what the culture (through books, TV, and movies) tells us about nursing, yet it is often these media representations that shape public perceptions. Ask new medical students what the word *nurse* conjures, and, depending on their age, they might mention Florence Nightingale; Carol Hathaway, head nurse on the popular TV show *ER;* Hana, the self-sacrificing nurse in Michael Ondaatje's *The English Patient;* or Loretta Swit's classic character Hot Lips from *M*A*S*H.* The students might not mention certain other images of nurse: the willing, white-stockinged student nurses of pornographic films or the battle-ax bullies like Nurse Ratched in Ken Kesey's *One Flew over the Cuckoo's Nest* and Sairy Gamp in Charles Dickens's *Martin Chuzzlewit.*[1] These archetypes—nurse as great mother, nurse as ambiguous sexual provider, nurse as old hag or evil death-tender—may be tempered only if health-care students consider what has been said and written about nursing, then read what nurses say about themselves.

A careful study of nurses' poetry will also modify the belief that the nurse's statement about patient care is less significant and authoritative than the doctor's. But, one might ask, what *do* nurses have to say? Nurses tend patients; they don't battle disease and death on the front lines, as doctors do. Nurses carry out orders; they less often make the life-and-death decisions that physicians do. It is exactly these differences that nurses recognize and honor in their poetry.

Fortunately, some excellent volumes of nurses' poems have been published, although their number is still small in comparison with that of the collections by physicians. An anthology of nurses' writing, *Between the Heartbeats* (Davis and Schaefer), was published in 1995, five years after Belle Waring's *Refuge* and Theodore Deppe's *Children of the Air,* two volumes that contained few poems specifically about the author's nursing but nevertheless served to break the silence. Recently, four useful collections have been added to the poetry available by nurses: a second book by Deppe (*The Wanderer King*) and by Waring (*Dark Blonde*) and first full-length collections by me (*Details of Flesh*) and by Judy Schaefer (*Harvesting the Dew*). Several chapbooks of nurses' poetry are available from small presses (Bernichon; Bryner; Davis, *Body Flute;* Masson; Mercer; Sievers).

Nurses write creatively about their work for many of the same reasons physicians do: to make sense of illness and death; to enter the patient's narrative and try to see through the patient's eyes; and to acknowledge that, suffering or healthy, we all fear dependency and decay. Yet nurses' writing can differ from physicians' in specific, significant ways.

Nurses' poems frequently focus on individual patients, particularly on the minute physical details of their bodies, rather than on disease or the conquest of illness. Such close observation is part of the dailiness of nursing, permitting nurses a poetic vocabulary that utilizes sensual imagery replete with sounds, smells, sights, and especially touch. Physicians' poems may more often evoke intellectual struggles, the clinical grappling with illness or death, and the burdens of decision making. Doctors, not involved in the same way nurses are with the intimate physical care of patients, use the body as metaphor differently. My poem "The Body Flute" begins:

> I go on loving the flesh
> after you die.
> I close your eyes
> bathe your bruised limbs
> press down the edges of tape
> sealing your dry wounds.
>
> I walk with you to the morgue
> and pillow your head
> against the metal drawer. To me
> this is your final resting place. (*Details* 65)

In writing this poem, I remembered the way I moved my hands up and down the length of this patient's body as I washed, suctioned, turned, catheterized, and cleaned him—an intimate vigil not usually performed by physicians. The image of a nurse bending over her patient as she tends his last hours persists; the body becomes a metaphor, the source of my music not only as a nurse but also as a poet. As nurses do, I accompany the patient to the morgue, finding power not in the fight against death but in my ability to stay with the patient, to go with him hand in hand, to soften his way and not look away from the physical details of dying.

Like other nurses, I have studied a dying patient's body many times in order to remember that individual—to honor his or her life, to acknowledge the private and significant final moment that I was privileged to share. At the conclusion of "The Body Flute," the patient dies when he is alone with me:

> Your last glance, your last
> sensation of touch,
> your breath
>
> I inhale, incorporating you
> into memory,
> your body,
>
> silvery and still on the bed,
> your lips fluttering into blue.

At the moment of a patient's death, the nurse—tender of the flesh—becomes guardian of memory as well.[2]

This same intense physicality is evident in many nurses' poems, among them Amy Haddad's "Dehiscence," in which a nurse catalogs the failure of a patient's body:

> Holes appear on your threadbare abdomen.
> Tunnels develop and connect bowel, liver, pancreas.
> Enzymes ooze out and digest your skin,
> no matter how hard we try to stem the flow.
> (Davis and Schaefer 86)

Nurses are present at the bedside and must struggle, day and night, with the rebellion of the flesh—the result of the disease process or of a medical or surgical intervention. Nurses comfort their patients physically, since they are, as Haddad says, "helpless in the face of your tragedy."

> Since I cannot bear your suffering,
> since the truth is too horrible to grasp,
> since I can offer you nothing else,
> I clean you up.
> I wash your face,
> brush your teeth,

> comb your hair,
> turn you gently on your side.

In other authors' poems, we read about how nurses stroke a patient's hair or skin,[3] how they are splattered with blood and vomitus,[4] how they tend open wounds and slather ointment over burned skin.[5]

Because they are powerless to fight disease in the same way physicians do, nurses often identify with their patients. Indeed, some report feeling that they merge with their patients, experiencing the same fears and physical sensations. This lends a vulnerability to nurses' poetry that echoes the patient's. In Janet Bernichon's poem "Why Not Me," the nurse stands outside the ICU looking in at her patient, a young drug addict:

> He was my son's age and was dying,
> separated from us by a glass partition
> and the modern medical miracle—
> life support. A respirator
> marked time in the slow wait.
> His mother had her back to me
> in her vigil. She enclosed his hand,
> the flesh of her flesh, in hers
> as if the tight hold
> could keep him from slipping away. (Davis and Schaefer 17)

Although the nurse is physically outside this scene, she identifies with both the patient and the patient's mother. The poem closes with the reflection of the nurse superimposed on the image of mother and child.

> In the window, my reflection
> stood within this tangle of tubes
> and someone else's child.
> I whispered, "I'm sorry,"
> then I leaned my head against the glass and closed my eyes.

In my poem "Becoming the Patient," I imagine that a nurse might actually slip inside a patient's body in order to truly know what he experiences. Nevertheless the patient's body remains a land of "unfamiliar places" (*Details* 50). As intimately as a nurse might tend a patient, the nurse is ultimately an outsider; therefore the relationship between nurse and patient is often forged through emotional as well as physical channels.

Nurses, like physicians, often write about the intuitive and empathic relationships they develop with patients and their families, kinships that allow room for magic, spirituality, and myth. Taught to be accurate observers, nurses frequently rely not only on what they see, touch, and know but also on what they feel. The best nurse-poets craft their poems with both myriad sensual details and a rich, intuitive underbelly.

Poems such as Dana Schuster's "NICU" and Jeanne Bryner's "Blue Lace Socks" (Davis and Schaefer 176, 32) are based on the instinctual connection with patients that many nurses testify to having. The connection may be spiritual as well. At the conclusion of a poem by Bryner, "What Nurses Do: The Marriage of Suffering and Healing," a nurse baptizes a dying man:

> The paper cup was blue, I asked a blessing
> For the tap water and did it, water fell
> Soft as a kiss to his forehead.
>
> And so I kept the devil far away
> And let the wife cry into my shoulder
> For a long time after
> For a long time after.

Waring's "From the Diary of a Clinic Nurse, Poland, 1945" is also an excellent illustration of a unique nurse-patient relationship. In Waring's prose poem, a nurse cares for a feral child discovered in the wild and now studied by linguists and physicians. The nurse, when the doctors aren't looking, lies on the floor with her patient and tries to coax the girl to speak.

> Alone with the child, I lay down to bare my neck like a dog surrendering, and for the first time she crouched near enough to sniff me. Then the neurologist barged in and, finding us on the floor like that, had a jealous snit. The grunting little academic—he wants her for research, but first he must examine her—and this she won't permit.

> I gave her an orange whirligig, I swear I heard her laugh: a
> hoarse, exotic yelp.
>   *Muh,* I said, *Marie.*

At the poem's end, the nurse reveals that she too is scared; like this
child, she has heard the howling of the "maternal wolves," a
metaphor suggesting both love and danger (Davis and Schaefer
196).

This frightening aspect of caregiving—the commingling of
healing and hurting—is often addressed in nurses' poetry. Touch is
the nurses' domain, yet that nurses cause pain in the name of cure is
recognized by patients and reflected in such nurse-as-bad-mother
figures as Nurse Ratched. In the beginning of "The Body Flute,"
this realization is articulated in a stark listing of nursing's double-
edged identities that evokes the hurting-loving mother.

> I am the nurse
> of childhood's sounds in the night,
> nurse of the washrag's sting
> nurse of needle and sleep
> nurse of lotion and hands on skin
> nurse of sheets and nightmares
> nurse of the flashlight's beam at 3 a.m.

The repetition of the word *nurse,* the drumlike occurrence of stresses
and sounds, and the association of safe words (*washrag, sleep, lotion,
sheets*) with words that carry a more frightening connotation (*sting,
needle, hands on skin, nightmares*) acknowledge the darker side of
caregiving.

Psychiatric nurse Deppe, particularly in his poem "Gloria," addresses the violent or damaging elements inherent in nursing:

> Three years ago
> patients slept in beds we'd pulled to the hall
> the night Gloria approached. As wind battered glass,
> I played gin with a pianist from East Hartford—
>
> we might have been old friends, sitting up late
> in some all-night café, though I was the one
> that day who found his hidden syringe.

Watching from the wire-and-glass window, we worried
for our families, but when I pointed out the snowplows
brought to roads of pine boughs and debris—

those blue sparks the steel plow struck from blacktop—
he sensed my love of storms, turned to me, half-smiling,
asked how much damage it would take to really satisfy me.

(*Children* 67)

In her poem "The Tea-Master 3–11 Shift" from *Harvesting the Dew*, Schaefer's nurse-narrator coaxes a dying patient to drink some iced tea, recognizing the intermingling of pain and comfort but arriving, with the patient, at a place of rest and healing:

I tell you I know it hurts
try to hold you in the nest of my arms
and remind you again to swallow
We both smile as if we had caught
the same allusive feather at the same time
We recall how the birds returned to Capistrano
We know we need to trust something
You swallow and relax into the temporary nest
of my arms and your unmade bed   (26)

The characteristics that inform nurses' poems—a physicality evidenced by sensual imagery, a vulnerability that comes from identifying with the patient rather than fighting the patient's disease, the recognition of an intuitive connection with the patient, and the acknowledgment of the duplicities inherent in caregiving—may also serve to impart a poignant honesty to nurses' creative writing. This honesty is composed equally of nurses' powerlessness in the face of illness and the raw, clear-eyed relating of what nurses do and see.

Nurses' poetry might be thought of as fulfilling the function of a "counterstory," described by philosopher Hilde Lindemann Nelson as "one that contributes to the moral self-definition of its teller by undermining a dominant story, undoing it and retelling it in such a way as to invite new interpretations and conclusions." Nelson continues: "Counterstories can be told anywhere, but particularly when told within chosen communities, they permit their tellers to reenter, as full citizens, the communities of place whose goods have been only imperfectly available to its marginalized members" (23). Plying their art at the bedside or walking darkened halls at night, nurses come to know things, amazing and controversial stories they can speak of only in poems.

Nursing's literary voices, like the voices of physicians, are instructive for students and practicing professionals alike. Read and taught alongside poetry by physicians and patients, nurses' poetry may complement physicians' and patients' insights on medicine in valuable and irreplaceable ways. Nurses' poems reveal, often eloquently, what occurs between patient and nurse in the intimate, fragile, and profound moments they share—a time and space necessarily different from that shared by patient and physician but equally important to our understanding of caregiving.

Notes

1. For an excellent commentary about these and other myths, see Fiedler.
2. See also my poem "The Nurse's Pockets" (Davis and Schaefer 48).
3. See "Butterfly" by Bryner (Davis and Schaefer 33); "This Happened" by Davis (Davis and Schaefer 52).
4. See "Rhythms" by Bethany Schroeder (Davis and Schaefer 168); "Night Nurse" by Davis (*Details* 43).
5. See "The Demonstration" by Dawn Ramm, "A Story" by Richard Callin, and "White Flame before the Long Black Wall" by Madeleine Mysko (Davis and Schaefer 146, 38, 137).

Works Cited

Bernichon, Janet. *Part of the Scenery.* New York: God's Bar, 1995.

Bryner, Jeanne. *Breathless.* Kent: Kent State UP, 1996.

———. "What Nurses Do: The Marriage of Suffering and Healing." *Annals of Internal Medicine* 127 (1997): 162.

Davis, Cortney. *The Body Flute.* Easthampton: Adastra, 1994.

———. *Details of Flesh.* Corvallis: Calyx, 1997.

Davis, Cortney, and Judy Schaefer, eds. *Between the Heartbeats: Poetry and Prose by Nurses.* Iowa City: U of Iowa P, 1995.

Deppe, Theodore. *Children of the Air.* Cambridge: Alice James, 1990.

———. *The Wanderer King.* Farmington: Alice James, 1996.

Fiedler, Leslie. "Images of the Nurse in Fiction and Popular Culture." *Literature and Medicine.* 2 (1983): 79–90.

Masson, Veneta. *Just Who*. Washington: Crossroad Health Ministry, 1993.

Mercer, Lianne Elizabeth. *No Limits but Light*. San Antonio: Chile Verde, 1994.

Nelson, Hilde Lindemann. "Resistance and Insubordination." *Hypatia* 10.2 (1995): 23–40.

Schaefer, Judy. *Harvesting the Dew: A Literary Nurse Bears Witness to Pain*. Long Branch: Vista, 1997.

Sievers, Kelly. *Making Room*. Waldport: Alsi, 1995.

Waring, Belle. *Dark Blonde*. Louisville: Sarabande, 1997.

———. *Refuge*. Pittsburgh: U of Pittsburgh P, 1990.

LaVera M. Crawley

Literature and the Irony of Medical Science

I recall, as a sophomore medical student in pathology, holding a dissected heart and being told to examine its ragged edges of torn tendinous bands and to memorize them as the lesion of a ruptured chorda tendineae. Handling the cold, gray, formaldehyde-preserved specimen produced no particular effect in me at the time other than intellectual curiosity, or perhaps a bit of academic anxiety. The goal of the exercise, I presume, was to demonstrate the pathological sequela of mitral valve prolapse, and that was the extent of what my classmates and I were told to look for, to examine, and to learn. What we were not told to see in the specimen held in our hands was the story of how it came to be an object for our education. We were not told, prior to our examination, that this very heart had once beaten in a student who had walked the halls of that same medical education institution, had sat in the same classrooms, and had shared our aspiration of becoming a physician. Later, we learned the student's story: some two years earlier, he had suffered sudden cardiac death while playing intramural basketball in the gymnasium across the street from the basic-science building. His autopsy revealed the above-mentioned lesion. His family, perhaps hoping to realize at least some vestige of an unfulfilled dream, donated his body to the university.

The Grand Irony

When I reflect back on how we proceeded with the once living specimen with such detachment, I am moved to ask: How could we, as professionals involved with the most intimate processes of life, have become so estranged from a heart still very much alive in the story that it contained? This "estrangement of the familiar" (Rowe 32)[1] repeated in many anatomy, pathology, and other basic-science classrooms, illustrates a grand irony in the metanarrative of medical science. In its quest for factual truth, the underlying epistemological framework of scientific medicine (positivism, objectivism, determinism, mechanism, and individualism) sets aside as irrelevant those qualities that provide life with texture, meaning, fullness, and purpose. Medical science proceeds as if culture, history, social status, relationships, personal desires, aspirations, creativity, and other intangible values have no bearing at all on its assigned task (Gordon 23–33). Through the lens of the natural sciences (physics and biology), biomedicine constructs a narrative about human existence as purely physical, reducible to the level of dead matter, organic and inorganic, that organizes itself through complex interactions into hierarchical structures. This concept is represented by the disciplines of anatomy, physiology, biochemistry, and pathology — the cornerstones of basic medical science education.

The story's irony is reinforced by a medical education process that has thought it necessary to depersonalize the human body in order to teach basic sciences to medical students (Cassell 17). The emphasis on science in the first years of medical school has created a curriculum that makes science central in importance and puts it outside the context of other disciplines. Eric Cassell suggests that this bias is reflected by the emphasis on science in exams and by faculty and departmental status within the academy (19). Add to this equation medical students who as premeds were enormously competitive and almost exclusively concerned with academic performance and who are conditioned to perform successfully on exams, and the result is a selective focus on the scientific, factual content of courses.

Reform efforts in medicine, such as George Engel's biopsychosocial model and the relationship-centered models for medical education (Tresolini), acknowledge the need to repersonalize medicine to produce compassionate, empathic physicians who will apply the knowledge of medical science to living situations. Courses in the medical humanities can serve this goal.

At first glance, the curricular conflicts that exist between science and the humanities raise a singularly important question: Can the goals of humanities in medical education be met not outside of and in competition with anatomy, physiology, biochemistry, pathology, and the like but, rather, within basic medical science education? Even more profound questions challenge the epistemological irony that lies at the heart of medical science.

What fallacy do we commit in constructing the metanarrative of medicine from the foundations of a lifeless life science? The story of my sophomore pathology encounter dramatized a sort of deconstructive aporia, where the logic of the metanarrative of science unraveled in the face of the startling reality of a human loss.

What might have been learned in that pathology lab about the significance of so violent and lethal a tendinous rupture if the visual discourse with the specimen we held had been accompanied by the narrative discourse of the life event? Michel Foucault reminds us of the sovereignty of the clinical gaze, "the eye that knows and decides, the eye that governs" (88–105). Could we not expand the visual fields that we create for students as they engage with the specimens of human life, so that their gaze can serve a fuller purpose? If, as Elaine Scarry states in *Literature and the Body*, "users of language regulate the degree to which language describes or discards the material world" (xiv), would not a thicker description of a multitextured lived experience in our articulation of science make visibile the human qualities of life?

Reflection on these questions points again to the potential of the literary and visual arts to create a context of verisimilitude for an objective science. What we need is not a medical humanities in isolation. The humanities must stand coterminously with science to enable the student's gaze and the student's understanding of life's dramas to counter the irony of an inanimate science of life. We need a transdisciplinary collaboration between the medical humanities and the science curriculum that starts in the basic-science classroom.

Model Course: A Humanistic Approach to Pathology

Traditional course work in pathology, which offers instruction in the underlying causes, mechanisms, structural sequelae, and functional consequences of disease processes, lends itself ideally to complementarity in the medical curriculum. Situated between the basic biomedical sciences and clinical training, the pathology curriculum provides an excellent metaphoric and pedagogical opportunity to redress the epistemological irony of medicine. The etymological sense of *pathology* is "the study of suffering." The word, sharing the same root as *empathy* and *sympathy,* can remind us to remain engaged with the most human aspects of illness, pathos, even as we focus our gaze toward the structural manifestations of disease. Being both a highly visual specialty (relying on gross and microscopic materials for illustrative purposes) and an interpretive discipline (whereby signs at the molecular, microbiological, or morphological level are translated into diagnoses), pathology is amenable to an analytic framework informed by such humanities disciplines as semiotics, narrative, literature, and literary theory.

The syllabus of a model curriculum in humanistic pathology might describe the course as an introduction to the study of the etiology, pathogenesis, and clinical significance, as well as the symbolic and semantic perspectives, of disease and illness in the human patient. The course would not only strive to have students master general pathology principles but also highlight those skills gained from the humanities that may assist in repersonalizing the discipline. The information for this course would be derived from specialty texts, such as the classic *Robbins Pathologic Basis of Disease* (Cotran,

Kumar, and Robbins), from laboratory specimens, and from selected works of visual art and literarature. As the standard pathology curriculum is designed to train students to see and interpret, introductory lectures or demonstrations on visual and narrative discourse that orient students to the semiotic nature of pathology would be critical. The various backgrounds in art or literary theory that students bring to the course would be balanced through the introduction of short, simple-to-understand articles that summarize the theoretical and analytic foundations for the use of literature and art in medicine.

John Nessa's summary of medical semiotics is a good example. As he suggests, we engage in teaching semiotics when we train medical students to interpret a holly-leaf-shaped or sickle-shaped object on a peripheral blood smear as sickle-cell anemia, or a torn fingerlike band of muscle as the sequela of a cardiac event (363–64). Semiotics is the study of the interpretation and meaning assigned to referent objects, both material and linguistic (Burnum). An object becomes a sign when it denotes an underlying reality (Colapietro 69–70). Thus, a deformed red blood cell may denote a deoxygenated mutated hemoglobin molecule (HbS). Signs can also be connotative, that is, they can signify some secondary level of meaning, and it is here that narrative can play a role. The distorted red cell we see not only refers to an abnormal hemoglobin state but also can connote a sickle-cell crisis event, suggesting a story of suffering and a lifetime of chronic, agonizing pain faced, perhaps, by an African American child.

A semiotic and narrative inquiry reveals the highly interpretive and subjective nature of what we may otherwise hold as purely objective. The goal of the humanities is not to dispute whether or not an object is a sickled red blood cell or a ruptured chorda tendineae, but in the interpretive process of assigning meaning to objects a curricular focus on semiotics and narrative representation may enhance the student's ability to reflect and think critically. Thus may the science of pathology be animated. Such inquiry, introduced early in the model course and reinforced throughout, can provide the thick descriptions that restore biomedicine to its place within the larger human context.

A pedagogical example of this thicker context is illustrated in a sample course module of valvular heart disease (see table). The structured activities for this course, like those for many pathology courses offered in medical schools, would take place in large-group lectures, smaller clinical correlation discussion groups, and laboratory sessions. This same format would accommodate the integration of the two disciplines. The course would be taught by a faculty team that represents both fields, and each field would provide context for the other, alternating as foreground and background.

Large-group lectures would continue to emphasize traditional pathology topics—in this case, congenital and acquired stenotic and regurgitant disorders of the mitral and aortic valves. But alongside appropriate chapters in the Robbins text, required preparatory readings would include narratives or other literary works that have relevance to the topic. These narratives would be referred to by the pathology instructor during lectures to illustrate the embodied meaning of valvular heart disease. In a lecture on aortic valve disease, for example, the teacher might reference John Stone's pedagogical story "The Long House Call." The narrative follows Stone's twenty-year medical relationship with the graceful and elderly Mrs. Corrigan, providing a "living seminar in aortic valve disease." His narrative simultaneously details the pathological progression of this particular lesion alongside the progress of cardiac technology and is a useful model of a relationship-centered science offering "breathing proof that to study [humanistically] and know one patient well is often better than studying a hundred patients less thoroughly" (37).

Narratives also provide excellent discussion material for later exploration in small-group clinical correlation sections. Traditional courses use these sessions to discuss case narratives, which are presented as heuristic devices for developing clinical reasoning. The following case is an example.

> A fifteen-year-old girl presents with chest pain, fever, joint pain and swelling, rash, and "strange jerking movements," according to her mother. On exam she has a friction rub. What is the most likely diagnosis? What pathogenetic sequence could account for the chest pain and friction rub?

What are possible long-term sequelae for this patient? What is the most important long-term treatment strategy for this patient?

This case illustrates the classic signs and symptoms of rheumatic fever. The kinds of clinical questions raised in case examples are designed to guide students toward an understanding of the pathogenesis associated with a given condition—in this case, the post-infectious immunologic sequelae in rheumatic heart disease. Questions that focus on the chest signs and symptoms are intended to point the student's gaze toward the effects of disseminated inflammatory lesions in the heart, namely, carditis. As rheumatic fever carries an attendant risk of recurrent disease reactivation, the case points to the long-term use of antibiotics in patients as an important therapeutic strategy.

This last important clinical detail is brought to life in Robert Coles's account of accompanying William Carlos Williams on a house call (111–15). As a medical student following Williams, Coles encountered a case similar to the one above—a fifteen-year-old girl with a history of rheumatic fever who might have been having a relapse of pneumonia. The characters and setting in this narrative suggest that the girl was from an immigrant, perhaps uneducated, economically depressed household. On her mother's recommendation, she prematurely discontinued antibiotics and became sicker. In his interaction with the patient and her family, Williams was indignant with the girl's mother, revealing his impatience at her ignorance of basic infectious disease processes. Expanding the small-group discussion case to include a thicker narrative such as Coles's gives students further opportunity to integrate their basic-science understanding of a disease with its clinical and social meaning.

The format of small-group discussions allows students to apply basic literary concepts introduced early in the course. Approaching cases or narratives from perspectives offered by literary and critical theory, Rita Charon and her coauthors suggest, increases students' ability to reflect critically. For example, the teacher can offer a critical-theory reading of the Coles story to raise two points: the significance of power dynamics in the doctor-patient relationship (how might Williams's anger toward the mother have been detrimental to the case, discouraging the adequate use of antibiotics?) and the clinical relevance of socioeconomic factors (rheumatic disease is often seen among those in poverty).

By applying another literary approach, reader-response theory, the teacher can directly invite the students' personal involvement in a case. This theory recognizes the importance of the reader in creating meaning (Sorum 552–53). In engaging the Coles narrative, students might experience some resonance with the lived experience and might empathize with the values, hopes, and fears of the story's characters. Or they might feel some dissonance. This approach provides an opportunity for students to bring themselves to the discussion and to be active players in case narratives rather than merely passive observers.

Assignments for small-group discussions provide an ideal opportunity for students to write their own stories or compositions. The goal here is not the development of literary technique. The students' subjectivity, expressed in their writings, is worth exploring and may serve to balance the more traditional, objective approach. For example, writing about the literal and metaphoric heart while studying valvular heart disease can engage students in reflection, the outcome of which may be cathartic or may open to students a deeper meaning of heartfulness (Jones; Woodcock). At a minimum, these activities affirm the importance of students' own humanity in their practice of medicine. This affirmation is in turn invaluable to their developing skills as empathic, reflective clinicians.

The teaching activities in laboratory sessions can further this reflective process. Various microscopic, gross, or digitized cardiac specimens that depict lesions to be studied can be accompanied by fictional or actual accounts of individuals who may have lived or died with such disorders. These pathographies would serve to enlarge the student's gaze to hold both the denoted biomedical disease state and its embodied human meaning. Another useful laboratory activity would be for the teacher to ask students to come up with metaphors for concepts such as stiffened or weakened valves and to ask them what understanding emerges as they study the pathology specimens through that figurative lens. Engaging students in these metaphoric and storying activities might also help them retain information contextually.

———

In summary, references to literary and visual arts begin in the large lecture classes, serving as background to the basic-science content. Small-group clinical correlation discussions and laboratory exercises are enhanced by a humanities perspective that makes a place for the students' subjective experience in the context of mastering objective facts. If this approach is done well, the subjective-objective dichotomy in the case discussions and lab activities will essentially disappear.

Such a course requires a high degree of collaboration between faculty members in the sciences and faculty members in the humanities. Humanities materials must be tightly matched to the pathology subject matter and, in order to meet the pedagogical goals of recontextualizing medical science, must be not only of good quality and highly engaging but also discernibly relevant to the scientific course content. This model also assumes interdepartmental cooperation. Faculty members must commit fully to the transdisciplinary nature of the endeavor, working closely and constantly as a team and modeling integration through the design of the syllabus, in course dialogues, in shared department resources, and in student evaluation.

Until the required standardized national exams begin to reflect a shared science-humanities discourse, students may continue to weigh the science content over the humanities—understandably so. The inclusion of literary works on examinations in such a model course may offer a challenge to the implicit curriculum of test taking. This proposed course in no way suggests that we compromise the rigor of scholarship of either the humanities or science. After all, we seek to develop students who do more than perform well on written exams. We are here to engage their hearts—to cultivate their relationship to the humanity that they will serve. I call for a partnership of humanities and literature *in* medicine to begin to unravel the grand irony of our medical science. The response to this call, through an integrated, transdisciplinary curriculum, may restore the living human, in all its fullness, meaning, and purpose, to the heart of biomedicine.

Humanistic Pathology: Sample Course Module

Week 4: Valvular Heart Disease: Disorders of the Aortic and Mitral Valves

---

Lecture (Mon.-Tues.)
Objectives: To understand the etiology, pathogenesis, clinical significance, and humanistic context of those disorders involving the aortic and mitral valves of the heart
Required readings:
1. *Robbins,* ch. 12, pp. 543–57
2. John Stone, "The Long House Call"

Lab (Mon.-Tues.)
Objective: Specimens have been chosen for this module to illustrate valvular disturbances that occur as a result of stenosis (failure to open) or regurgitation (failure to close).

Required: View assigned lab specimens (gross and microscopic, located in lab or digitized online) along with accompanying pathographies.

Optional assignment: Identify literary or visual metaphors for stenotic or regurgitant processes. Post entries online or discuss in small-group session.

Small Group (Thurs.-Fri.)
Objective: Critical analysis of assigned cases in relation to clinical content and humanistic context
Required readings:
1. Case narratives
2. Robert Coles, *The Call of Stories,* pp. 111–15
Assignments:
Thursday: Problem-oriented case-based discussion
Friday: Student mini-essays on the meaning of valvular diseases

Note

1. The "*ostranenie* or strategic 'estrangement of the familiar' " deemed by the Russian formalists to be "essential to literary language" (Rowe 32) is similar to the subject-object alienation that is posited by medical epistemology and that is essential to the goals of science.

Works Cited

Burnum, John F. "Medical Diagnosis through Semiotics: Giving Meaning to the Sign." *Annals of Internal Medicine* 119 (1993): 939–43.

Cassell, Eric J. *The Place of Humanities in Medicine.* Hastings-on-Hudson: Hastings Center Inst. of Soc., Ethics, and the Life Sciences, 1984.

Charon, Rita, et al. "Literature and Medicine: Contributions to Clinical Practice." *Annals of Internal Medicine* 122 (1995): 599–606.

Clarke, Bruce, and Wendell Aycock, eds. *The Body and the Text: Comparative Essays in Literature and Medicine.* Studies in Comp. Lit. 22. Lubbock: Texas Tech UP, 1990.

Colapietro, Vincent. *Glossary of Semiotics.* New York: Paragon, 1993.

Coles, Robert. *The Call of Stories: Teaching and the Moral Imagination.* Boston: Houghton, 1989.

Cotran, Ramzi S., Vinay Kumar, and Stanley L. Robbins. *Robbins Pathologic Basis of Disease.* 5th ed. Philadelphia: Saunders, 1994.

Engel, George. "The Need for a New Medical Model: A Challenge for Biomedicine." *Science* 196 (1977): 129–36.

Foucault, Michel. *The Birth of the Clinic: An Archaeology of Medical Perception.* Trans. A. M. Sheridan Smith. New York: Vintage, 1994.

Gordon, Deborah. "Tenacious Assumptions in Western Medicine." *Biomedicine Examined.* Ed. Margaret Lock and Gordon. Boston: Kluwer Academic, 1988. 19–56.

Jones, Anne Hudson. "Literature and Medicine: Traditions and Innovations." Clarke and Aycock 11–24.

Nessa, John. "About Signs and Symptoms: Can Semiotics Expand the View of Clinical Medicine?" *Theoretical Medicine* 17 (1996): 363–77.

Rowe, John Carlos. "Structure." *Critical Terms of Literary Study.* Ed. Frank Lentricchia and Thomas McLaughlin. Chicago: U of Chicago P, 1995. 23–38.

Scarry, Elaine. Introduction. *Literature and the Body: Essays on Populations and Persons.* Ed. Scarry. Baltimore: Johns Hopkins UP, 1988. vii–xxvii.

Sorum, Paul C. "Patient as Author, Physician as Critic: Insights from Contemporary Literary Theory." *Archives of Family Medicine* 3 (1994): 549–56.

Stone, John. "The Long House Call." *In the Country of Hearts: Journeys in the Art of Medicine.* New York: Delacourt, 1990. 29–37.

Tresolini, Carol P. *Health Professions Education and Relationship-Centered Care.* San Francisco: Pew Health Professions Commission, 1994.

Woodcock, John. "Teaching Literature and Medicine: Theoretical, Curricular, and Classroom Perspectives." Clarke and Aycock 41–54.

Douglas Robert Reifler

"Poor Yorick": Reflections on Gross Anatomy

Medical training radically alters the perspective of its participants, particularly their outlook on human illness and death. The student's transition from a nonmedical perspective to a professional medical perspective is an important function of medical education. The nature of this transition is difficult to define and is rarely acknowledged overtly in the medical curriculum. The transition is accomplished, at least in part, by a variety of compelling training rituals that bring the trainees to medical vantage points. Among the earliest training—or initiation—rituals is gross anatomy, in which new medical students are exposed to graphic details of naked, dead, diseased, and mutilated human bodies, typically in a straightforward way.

In gross anatomy, medical students feel a tension between viewing the cadavers as people who once lived and viewing them primarily as biological specimens. The sociologist Frederic Hafferty has described the cadaver as "ambiguous man," whose nature students are challenged to conceptualize when given a dissonant blend of human and inhuman components (98–112). To conduct the dissection and successfully complete what would be, if taken out of context, a ghastly and ghoulish process, students generally learn to emphasize the biological details. A variety of devices reinforces an emotionally disengaged perspective — the immense task of learning the names of thousands of body parts, the fact that these names are mainly obscure scientific Greek and Latin terms, matter-of-fact demonstrations by faculty members and assistants, and graveyard humor (Finkelstein; Lief and Fox). Yet, even for the majority of students who learn to disengage, the dilemma of coping with the human side of death remains.

The graveyard scene in *Hamlet* (5.1.1–217) succinctly dramatizes this dilemma and the shift in perspective that occurs with graphic and continued exposure to dead bodies. This scene is both very funny, demonstrating detachment and graveyard humor in its finest form, and filled with somber irony, illustrating a sensitive and thoughtful glimpse at death. It begins with two grave diggers, lower-class buffoons who are identified as clowns; they speculate briefly on why Ophelia's death was not ruled a suicide (i.e., because of class privilege), then tease each other, joking, singing about time and the ravages of age, and tossing skulls around as they dig her grave. Hamlet and Horatio happen upon the scene.

Hamlet. Has this fellow no feeling of his business? 'a sings in grave-making.
Horatio. Custom hath made it in him a property of easiness.
Hamlet. 'Tis e'en so, the hand of little employment hath the daintier sense. (65–70)

The grave-digger clowns continue singing merrily as they unearth skulls, and Hamlet goes into a reverie imagining the skulls' human origins. He is struck by ironies in life and death — that the skull could sing once, whereas the grave digger is singing now; that we all assume the same humble state in death despite any loftiness life may provide in the form of wealth and nobility. Hamlet speculates on how the parchment deeds of a "great buyer of land" (104) might not fit into the box that contains the buyer's remains. When the First Clown identifies one of the skulls as that of the king's jester, Yorick, the most widely misquoted segment of the scene ensues. The point of this segment is, of course, not that Hamlet knew Yorick well but rather that Hamlet is looking at the rotten skull of someone he actually knew. The scene finishes as Hamlet takes another existential plunge and Horatio, ever the voice of sense and reason, tries to bring him back to a more ordinary perspective.

Hamlet. To what base uses we may return, Horatio! Why may not imagination trace the noble dust of Alexander, till 'a find it stopping a bunghole?
Horatio. 'Twere to consider too curiously, to consider so. (202–06)

The grave diggers' and Hamlet's responses to the graveyard represent extremes of light detachment and somber sensitivity. Medical students' perspectives in gross anatomy lab typically reflect both positions in degrees that vary over time. Although it is no "little employment" to complete the prerequisites for medical school, most medical students arrive in gross anatomy with little or no concrete exposure to the stark realities of death and dead bodies. As a result, their pre–gross anatomy perspective on these issues tends to be daintier, more like Hamlet's. After a few weeks in the dissection lab, however, medical students can often understand why the grave digger clowns sing and throw body parts, and it is easier for the students to identify with the clowns' disengaged and cavalier attitude.

In pedagogical terms, people at all levels of medical training can find parallels between this scene and their own medical experiences. I have used it most often at Northwestern University Medical School with first-year medical students in a literature-and-writing elective called Reflections on Gross Anatomy (Reifler). This six-week seminar for eight to twelve students has met weekly during the winter of the students' first year, concurrent with gross anatomy. Beginning in 1996, its scope was expanded to include a gross anatomy writing assignment for the entire first-year class. The graveyard scene works just as well to start discussions among junior medical students who are facing the deaths of the first patients they take care of on the wards, internal medicine residents who regularly deal with patients' deaths, and attending physicians who are out of the fray of training but may be wondering how they became emotionally disengaged in the process.

Normally I ask four members of a small discussion group to volunteer to read the four parts: Hamlet, First Clown, Horatio, and Second Clown. The sixteenth-century text is much more accessible to modern medical audiences if they have a written copy in front of them while they read or listen to it read aloud. After clarifying what is actually happening in the scene, I usually ask participants to identify any parallel experiences they have had in medical training. For larger groups, such as an entire medical school class, I sometimes show Kenneth Branagh's 1996 *Hamlet,* the only major commercial film version that preserves the full dialogue of the scene.

Discussions have typically focused on the impact of medical training on the trainees. Some students express active worries that medical training will make them callous. Others, less concerned about this effect, tend to see less value in discussing *Hamlet.* Still others worry that they will not become callous enough and will instead feel emotionally overwhelmed in practicing medicine. Reading this scene often prompts students to speculate on circumstances in medicine where detachment is useful and perhaps necessary either for decisive action, as when one is handling emergencies or performing surgeries, or to avoid personal overload, as when one is coping with patients' disasters and deaths. We discuss the role of graveyard humor as an appropriate and understandable adaptation to duress but an adaptation that quickly becomes grotesque when it oversteps certain boundaries. The graveyard scene also leads students to discuss the problem of shifting out of detachment to make effective connections with people, particularly patients and their families, who have not had the students' experiences and do not share the students' professional view. I suggest that students pay attention to narrative aspects of their interactions with others—to voice, context, and perspective. I ask them how the clowns could communicate more appropriately with Hamlet and remind them that their own initial reactions to gross anatomy might help them to imagine what their patients feel.

I also prompt students to consider the impact that medical

training will have on their personal lives. Even first-year medical students are often called on to lend medical wisdom when someone they know is ill. How does having learned medical detachment affect them when as sons, daughters, brothers, sisters, and friends they need to cope with a major illness or death? I have told them, for example, that my grief was hindered when my sister died. Her physicians were animated in showing me the abnormalities of her CT scans, and my attention gravitated toward the medical details. The medical perspective became an anesthetizing defense against a stark personal situation that deserved a very different kind of attention.

Regarding Yorick, most people do not have in a lifetime the eerie experience of viewing a dead body fragment of someone they knew. But with a little imagination, medical students in a gross anatomy course can put themselves in Hamlet's position. They can turn back the clock in their minds and imagine their cadavers as people who once lived, the way Hamlet remembers Yorick. Indeed, medical students and practicing physicians, later in training, are often called on to examine the autopsy findings of patients they knew in life, raising the same potential for revulsion, horror, and intrigue that Hamlet faces with Yorick's skull. I try to persuade students that it is professionally acceptable to maintain some of these reactions and not to repress their dismay at every gory detail they encounter.

To enhance the impact of reading this scene, I ask first-year medical students to write a brief story based on their experiences in the anatomy lab. For example, "Describe on sensory, cognitive, and emotional levels the first incision into your cadaver," or, "Write an autobiographical sketch of your cadaver's life (in the cadaver's words); base your details on physical evidence." They then bring their stories to class, and those who are willing read them aloud. When I have given these writing assignments to an entire class of 176 students, the small-group discussions have been led by ethics-course faculty members, some of whom are physicians and some of whom are humanities professors. My emphasis on writing reflects the concern that the transition from a nonmedical to a medical perspective typically occurs amid a blur of factual information, pressure to perform and achieve, and dramatic exposures to human circumstances. Writing slows down the clock and allows each person to make sense of the whirlwind in his or her own terms.

Whether students read *Hamlet* or write their own gross anatomy stories, the goal is the same: to dramatize the radical shift in perspective on illness, death, and the human body that medical students undergo as they enter the medical profession. The grave digger clowns' perspective is important and useful in medicine. It also tends to hinder communication with anyone who shares Hamlet's perspective, and it is a personal hazard of the medical profession. Few, if any other, literary passages so clearly spell out this particular dilemma of being a physician.

Works Cited

Finkelstein, Peter. "Studies in the Anatomy Laboratory: A Portrait of Individual and Collective Defense." *Inside Doctoring: Stages and Outcomes in the Professional Development of Physicians.* Ed. R. H. Coombs, D. S. May, and G. W. Small. New York: Praeger, 1986. 22–42.

Hafferty, Frederic W. *Into the Valley: Death and the Socialization of Medical Students.* New Haven: Yale UP, 1991.

Lief, Harold I., and Renée C. Fox. "Training for 'Detached Concern' in Medical Students." *The Psychological Basis of Medical Practice.* Ed. Lief, V. F. Lief, and N. R. Lief. New York: Harper, 1963. 12–35.

Reifler, Douglas R. "'I Actually Don't Mind the Bone Saw': Narratives of Gross Anatomy." *Literature and Medicine* 15 (1996): 183–99.

Shakespeare, William. *The Riverside Shakespeare.* Ed. G. Blakemore Evans et al. Boston: Houghton, 1974.

Joseph Cady

In Brief: A Literature Seminar in Clinical Medical Education

Among my more unusual offerings in literature and medicine at the University of Rochester Medical School were brief seminars in the medicine, pediatrics, and psychiatry clerkships during the third year, when it is famously difficult for medical humanities to find time in the curriculum as students start clinical work. I summarize here my hour-and-a-half pediatrics seminar as an example of my immersive approach in all three clerkships, where I brought in short readings pertinent to each and engaged students with them through discussion. We read two poems by physician-authors about their medical work with children: William Carlos Williams's "The Birth" (based on an experience early in his practice but not written until the 1950s and not published in book form until 1984)[1] and Robert Bridges's "On a Dead Child" (1880).

An ultimately celebratory poem about assisting at a home birth and about women's distinct ability to bear children, "The Birth" is also a genial critique of the physician's traditional role, which it represents through the symbol of the mask ("I [. . .] smiled to myself quietly / behind my mask" [40–44]). The poem shows Williams departing from that role both as speaker and character. He starts by talking in technical medical terms ("A 40 odd year old Para 10" [1]) and ends in outright enthusiasm and admiration, adopting his Italian patient's vernacular ("Madonna! / 13½ pounds! / Not a man among us / can have equaled / that" [51–55]); he takes surprising linguistic turns, inserting the line "I am a feminist" in the midst of the birth scene (45); he assumes a democratic relationship with the patient ("we had been working all night long" [6]); and, when he falls asleep during a lull in the procedure and then has to improvise an intervention with a sheet, he calls himself "stupid / not to have thought of that earlier" (31–32). None of these presumed irregularities, however, blocks the event's (and the poem's) final happy outcome.

In "On A Dead Child," which takes place in a hospital and is his only poem based on his medical experience, Bridges openly mourns the "disaster" of the child-patient's death that has just occurred (22). In the central action, the corpse's hand grasps Bridges's in an automatic reflex as he arranges the body. Shocked by this reminder of the child's "trust" in him in life (16) and, it is implied, weighed down by a sense of failure, futility, and guilt, Bridges goes on to deny the existence of a compensating afterlife ("A world, do I think, that rights the disaster of this? / The vision of which I miss" [22–23]) and ends with a despairing assertion of humanity's isolation and helplessness in the face of death ("in the dark, / Unwilling, alone we embark, / And the things we have seen and have known and have heard of, fail us" [26–28]).

In all my Rochester courses, which spanned the entire curriculum and also included resident and faculty education, I focused on the recurring concerns I saw in literature about medicine itself, particularly its critiques of the medical tendency to live "only in theory" (Chekhov 49) and, relatedly, of medical detachment and "abstraction" (Camus 127–28). In contrast, I worked to instill in my students the steadfast "attention" to self and to the patient's experience that is also a major theme of literature about medicine (Camus 253). There were at least four phenomena I wanted my students to attend to in the pediatrics clerkship seminar. The first was the acts of attention in the poems themselves—the features of these physician-writers' lives and work that their readers were asked to think about, especially the presence of the emotional and irregular amid the professedly impersonal and technical. The second was any aspects of the students' experiences during the clerkship that the poems may have evoked. The third was the way the materials illustrated the poles of pediatrics as a specialty, with Williams's poem demonstrating pediatrics' reputation as a chiefly happy practice and Bridges's poem demonstrating its darker side, where clinicians have to face and learn to cope with what is usually the most devastating kind of death. The fourth was the way the poems embodied the "unmasking" that I saw as one of the genre-defining activities of literature about medicine, in which physician-authors characteristically remove the official doctor mask and speak their profession's customary unspeakables (e.g., joy, "stupidity," grief, depression).

In the class itself, I was able to cover my first two concerns chiefly by discussion; I usually just summarized the second two didactically at appropriate moments. After handing out the poems, I began by briefly identifying each writer and describing my four areas of concern in the seminar (though without proposing any theses about them). Then I worked to involve the students immediately by having volunteers read the poems aloud (we considered each poem separately before discussing them together). Next I asked a leading question based on one of the students' core learning experiences in the third year: "This year you're being taught how to write about medicine and illness in a certain accepted way" (that is, the patient's chart, the clinical case presentation). "What do you think about this poem as an example of a physician's writing about a medical experience? Anything different or similar about it?"

On good days, this question was enough to launch students into a discussion that eventually focused on most of the features above (e.g., "Well, first of all, the personal perspective. You wouldn't say 'I' in a chart."). But I did not hesitate to steer the discussion if, for example, students missed Williams's "feminist" or "mask" references; I might prod them with questions like "Is there anything that surprises or puzzles you here?" or "What do you think he means by his 'mask'?" Some of the most illuminating discussion occurred when we went beyond the manifest differences between Williams's poem and Bridges's to talk about the similarities: for example, both men were physicians with limited or no control over a natural process, physicians expressing intense feeling.

It was usually after our discussion of the poems that I made my point about their relation to pediatrics as a specialty. Usually the students discussed their clerkship experiences after this, though at the start of the class I would invite students to bring them up at any point. Here the students usually were sparked more by Bridges's poem than by Williams's, and the discussion could get powerfully emotional; they talked not only about patients' deaths but also about their own private losses, and it was often impossible to reach an easy, bright closure. I hoped that at least a partial sense of resolution might be provided at the end, which I saved for making my point about the "unmasking" that seems to occur in all literature about medicine. The point possibly carried more force at this juncture than it would have earlier in the seminar, since in the personal discussion that had just occurred, students may have themselves "unmasked" in a way that paralleled my thesis about literature and medicine.

Even if our limited time permitted only partial exploration of the seminar's issues, the mere act of raising them offered the students two unusual opportunities, for which they often thanked me afterward. The first was the chance to discuss anything at all, given the passivity of much learning in medical education. The second was the opportunity to address the intensely emotional dimension of medicine, which they said was rarely acknowledged elsewhere in their clinical training. The seminar's most immediate value to a pediatrics clerkship was its materials' graphic reflection of clinical actuality—the poems' portraits of two physicians at peak moments in the medical care of children. But what seemed to make the seminar memorable was the combination of that focus and the chance to discuss the inner life of medicine, the silenced subject in clinical education that often becomes only more unspeakable in medical practice.

Note

1. I use the version of "The Birth" in Robert Coles's edition of Williams's *The Doctor Stories*, not the inferior version later included in Williams's *Collected Poems* (1988). Quotations in this essay are from the Coles edition. I was cheating somewhat in using the poem in a pediatrics seminar, since in technical medical terms birth is an event in obstetrics/gynecology. But pediatricians often attend births, and Williams himself was chiefly a pediatrician.

Works Cited

Bridges, Robert. "On a Dead Child." *The Norton Anthology of Modern Poetry*. Ed. Richard Ellmann and Robert O'Clair. New York: Norton, 1973. 88–89.

Camus, Albert. *The Plague*. Trans. Stuart Gilbert. 1948. Vintage Int. ed. New York: Vintage, 1991.

Chekhov, Anton. *"Ward Number Six" and Other Stories*. Trans. Ronald Hingley. 1974. World's Classics. Oxford: Oxford UP, 1988.

Williams, William Carlos. "The Birth." *The Doctor Stories*. Comp. Robert Coles. New York: New Directions, 1984. 127–28.

Jonathan M. Metzl

Signifying Medication in Thom Jones's "Superman, My Son"

Medications are frequently presented in medical education in a fixed and denotative manner. In pharmacology courses, for example, students are responsible for digesting massive amounts of information concerning every aspect of a medication's profile, ranging from its half-life to its mechanism of action to its clinical indications. These and other details are often given as facts to be memorized and then reproduced on fill-in-the-bubble, multiple-choice examinations. In the process students learn to master "the latest, most authoritative drug information possible," to quote the *Physicians' Desk Reference* (1). Lithium alters sodium transport in nerve and muscle cells and effects a shift toward intraneuronal metabolism of catecholamines. The volume of distribution of Mefloquine is approximately 20 1/kg; the in vivo half-life is from .36 to 2 hours. Such an approach is thought an adequate apprenticeship for a career in which these students will be asked to make the diagnosis, write the appropriate prescription, and move on to the next patient's room. Little attention, if any, is paid to the complexities that can arise when these

338

treatments are considered as symbols rather than as hard-and-fast facts.

And yet a consideration of the symbolic functions of a medication can be as important to understanding its clinical efficacy as memorizing its membrane-stabilizing properties or its hypothesized elimination half-life. When approached as theoretical symbols rather than as physiological absolutes, medications can be understood to carry messages that are both highly connotative and varied and that are often quite difficult to quantify scientifically. A symbolic approach allows students to consider important topics not often broached in pharmacology courses. These topics range from the unspoken psychological messages of nurturance that are at play when doctors prescribe medications for patients to the larger social and commodified messages these medications stealthily invoke. In such interactions the information presented in the pharmacology course is complicated, and at times effaced, by the many cultural roles medications can play—often before they are ever prescribed. When medications are considered as symbols, the study of pharmacology may ultimately yield the uncertainty of possibilities rather than the certainty of answers.

But how is it possible to discuss such multiplicity of choice within a system of medical education that often rewards only multiple choice? And where in the discursive certainty that pervades medical education is it possible to acknowledge the often rote precision needed for an understanding—and, finally, for the prescribing—of pharmacology, while at the same time constructively undermining this precision in the search for a different kind of medical knowledge? One answer is the literature and medicine course, where the mechanisms of interaction among medicine, literature, and literary theory can both affirm the importance of what is presented as medical information and concomitantly encourage the consideration that this information must at times be deconstructed in the pursuit of other kinds of understanding.

When discussing medications, a theory-based presentation of Thom Jones's short story "Superman, My Son" can both acknowledge traditional approaches to pharmacology and simultaneously question the systems that pharmacology represents. "Superman, My Son" tells the story of the Blane family, reunited on the day after Walter's most recent manic episode. The narrative is given from the perspective of Wilhelm, the aging patriarch of the Blane family and founder of the Shoprite Food Value Emporium. Both institutions, the family and the business, are in a state of decline: Shoprite has fallen on hard times, and the members of the infertile Blane family have fallen prey to a variety of mental and physical ailments. Wilhelm is a post-traumatized and now shocked victim of armed robbery. Walter, Wilhelm's only son, suffers from bipolar disorder. Zona, Walter's wife, is sterile and a chain-smoker. And Freddy, Wilhelm's nephew, appears to have contracted malaria. For their maladies the characters of "Superman, My Son" have been prescribed numerous medications, the side effects of which pharmacologically astute readers will readily identify. Walter's extreme thirst, for example, is more than likely caused by lithium. Freddy's insomnia is a common side effect of Mefloquine.

But the complex narrative allows for readings in which these medications play roles unexplainable solely by clinical indications or side effects. Explanations based on approaches ranging from psychoanalysis to Marxist theory to postmodernism can help students think of medications not only as facts but also as symbols. For example, medications can be presented psychoanalytically, as what D. W. Winnicott calls transitional objects, a child's first "not me" possession in the transition from dependency to autonomy. Children react to the terrifying process of weaning by locating an external object and imbuing it with meaning. Transitional objects act as developmental metonyms, small parts that stand in for, and ultimately replace, larger relationships. Often these objects are associated with oral gratification. A thumb or the corner of a worn blanket stands in for a mother's breast. The pleasures of oral gratification are thought to endure in adult life, where objects like cigarettes and even medications are laden with the reassuring allusions to an earlier safety.

"Superman, My Son" is full of such symbols. All the characters are at some point in the story defined by what they put into their mouth. Zona is calmed by cigarettes and explains that "I like them too much" (35); Freddy is calmed by coffee with Nutra-Sweet; Walter's descent from mania is marked by his request for a diet soda. Medications, however, offer the greatest reassurance. When Freddy reads the entry for Eskalith from the *Physicians' Desk Reference,* he exclaims, "Why, it sounds great. We could all do with some" (40). Eskalith's symbolic connection to the calm of an earlier state is proved soon thereafter, when Walter takes the medication and subsequently descends the stairs to rejoin (or normalize) the family.

Students may point out that the medications in the story are not generic objects unconsciously chosen by the characters but, instead, specific brand names. This realization can lead to a discussion of how brand names function as commodities in the story. These commodities—much like transitional objects—have undergone a transformation from denotative objects of everyday use to connotative symbols of desire, from use value to exchange value. In the process, they become imbued with a larger meaning. Describing the theft of his watch, Wilhelm realizes that an employee has stolen his Patek Phillipe. Later in the story, a new car is described as a Corvair. In this brand-name-obsessed landscape, medications function as the most widely known and most powerful commodities, able to determine symptoms, actions, and ultimately subjectivities in addition to treating them. Walter's physical appearance, for example, is dictated by Eskalith ("the psoriasis is because of the pills"), his sexuality by Prozac ("Five times a day!"), and his behavior by Tegretol and Xanax (33). Walter eventually explains that "the pills have started to work" and to control his actions (43). In a discussion it can be pointed out that the medications themselves never appear in the narrative. Instead—and much like a fetishized commodity—their labor is assumed, and their mechanism of action is represented not by the laborer (the pills) but by the copyrighted product of their labor. Does the medical establishment, students may be asked, place similar faith in brand names, given an economy in which pharmaceutical representatives are frequent visitors to doctors' offices and AMA-endorsed advertisements for medications appear in many popular magazines?

Seeing the power of the commodity in the economy of the story may lead students to reconsider the traditional relationship between prescriber and prescribed. When Walter's sexual potency is pointed out (ironically) to be the result not of his desire but of the brand name Prozac and when he attributes his actions solely to Tegretol, medications come to represent postmodern symbols of a new, chemical subjectivity. In such an approach, the patient autonomy that clinical master narratives often seek as an end point of treatment may be constructively questioned, while the notion of a uniform mechanism of action may be presented as impossible in a postmodern culture. The epistemology of Winnicott's object relations (which promises a generalized transition from dependence to autonomy) or of pharmacology (which promises a generalized freedom from symptoms) is replaced by the ontology of the barren local narrative of the Blanes. In other words, characters who in a modern or psychoanalytic context would be thought to control medication through acts of volition—buying it, taking it, or even prescribing it—are in a postmodern reading powerless and even colonized by that medication.

The character Freddy can be presented pedagogically as the most salient example of the fractured master subject. He is a physician who went to Africa to heal the natives. But he returns not as the authoritative master of medication described in the *Physicians' Desk Reference*. Instead, "a whiter shade of pale" (25), he demonstrates how physicians, too, can be deconstructed in a postmodern world. His actions, he explains, are not the result of his agency or control; rather, he has become a helpless supplicant to the tools of his trade. "'Am I talking too fast?' Freddy didn't wait for an answer. 'I am now and was then all whacked out on Mefloquine. I was not really lucid" (30).

The goal in a classroom discussion of "Superman, My Son" should not be to force students to choose which theoretical model is the correct one; the goal should be to raise the possibility that when we think about the complex symbols of medications, selecting the right answer might mean answering the wrong question. Instead of choosing one interpretation or one source of information, students should begin to realize that when seeking an integrated understanding of the many factors at play in the act of prescribing medication, alternative models can be employed simultaneously. Thinking through theoretical approaches, in contradistinction to the more comfortable practice of memorizing, may ultimately reveal broader mechanisms of action than those found in the *Physicians' Desk Reference*.

The presentation of multiple interpretations calls into question the authority that the act of memorization asks students of medicine to assume. Medical training is increasingly driven by the certainty of laboratory values and high-tech scans, often at the expense of interpersonal interactions. By constructively raising open-ended questions rather than demanding immediate responses, medical humanities courses offer one of the few sites where medical students may feel free to explore the possibilities of not knowing or not needing to select a definitive answer. Students in these courses must be challenged to rethink the implications of the treatments they are being asked to master. In discussions that allow such a dynamic to occur, the drive for mastery can be combined—if only momentarily —by a far less certain and yet ultimately more well-rounded consideration of the ambiguity inherent in the kinetics of pharmacology. Such ambiguity leads to a deeper understanding of the dynamics of the clinical interactions between doctor and patient and to a consideration of the many cultural interactions that result when patient and prescription leave the doctor's office and enter a much larger, if less predictable, volume of distribution.

Works Cited

Jones, Thom. "Superman, My Son." *Cold Snap*. Boston: Little, 1995. 18–46.

Physicians' Desk Reference. 51st ed. Oradell: Medical Economics, 1997.

Winnicott, D. W. "Transitional Objects and Transitional Phenomena." *Through Paediatrics to Psycho-analysis*. New York: Basic, 1975. 229–42.

Rhonda L. Soricelli and David H. Flood

(Un)Professional Relationships in the Gendered Maze of Medicine

As women claim an ever-increasing presence in medicine, it is not surprising that a growing body of literature attempts to address gender politics in the medical establishment. Numerous studies document the demographics of sexual harassment between physician and patient as well as in professional, collegial relationships. Others focus primarily on the power dynamics that invariably influence physician-patient and teacher-learner interactions (e.g., see Phillips and Schneider; Nora; Gabbard and Nadelson; Gordon, Labby, and Levinson). While an occasional essay such as Eliza Shin's witty discussion of the "Victim-Valkyrie spectrum" enlightens and enlivens the topic (71), few formal studies have attempted to analyze the more subtle components of gendered behavior that contribute to these situations. Indeed, limited by confusion over basic terminology, poor response rates, and reliance on self-reported, retrospective data (Nora S115), questionnaire-based approaches are unlikely to uncover the complexities of gender socialization and role conflict inherent in encounters between doctors and patients and among members of the medical community. How, then, can we best probe the deeper layers of these issues?

To answer this question, we begin with a brief summary of our joint, interdisciplinary approach to researching and teaching the medical humanities in general. For more than a decade we have shared a rich working relationship, female clinician and male professor of English literature, bringing to whatever discussion is at hand our different backgrounds, experiences, and perspectives. We have explored gender issues in medicine in multiple settings, from courses and seminars for medical students at all levels of training to workshops for family-medicine residents and internal-medicine faculty members. By juxtaposing analyses in the traditional medical literature with literary portrayals of gendered relationships between physicians and patients as well as among physicians themselves, we have found that we create a powerful instructional tool. Even when students cannot read in advance of class, a brief summary of the text at hand with role-playing that uses dialogue drawn from the text will usually stimulate active discussion.

Like many other educators, we have found that the student body has changed significantly in the past ten years. Today's students come to class well equipped with the basic jargon of gender stereotypes, sexual harassment, power dynamics, and stress in the training environment. They have heard about gendered styles of communication and boundary crossings. Most endorse the popular understanding of male as objective, task-oriented; female as nurturant, empathic, but also as victim in need of empowerment. But these concepts, in general, have been embraced without true understanding of their meaning, without consideration of the specific culture of medicine, without subjective engagement with the issues. The literary sources we share with our students bring to the discussion of previously objectified, formalized concepts a contextual richness not only of the medical scene but also of the gender dynamics that affect us all. While portrayals of the physician-patient relationship help generate much-needed dialogue about medicine's gendered dimensions, those readings that illuminate physician-colleague interactions lead to the most lively and revealing discussions with both students and mature physicians. And perhaps our team approach with our own gendered voices helps open doors to dialogue that might otherwise remain closed.

Authored respectively by a male physician, a well-known female writer, and a female physician, the three stories we have selected for this essay provide vivid images of the power of gender to shape, to strengthen, to corrupt, even to corrode collegial relationships in medicine. Furthermore, while our medical audiences have been consistently receptive to these stories, we believe the stories have great potential for the professions in general.

When first published in 1978, Samuel Shem's satirical portrayal of the medical profession in *The House of God* was considered an outrage.[1] But the book has endured and continues to be both popular and instructive at multiple levels. Through the retrospective gaze of the "handsome and tall" Roy Basch (53), we romp at times and stumble mostly through an internship year largely bereft of human feeling or effective role models. We meet Roy's fellow interns, who learn, as he does, to survive through "the sexualization of the ternship" (120) if they don't commit suicide or have a psychotic break first. Jo, Roy's senior resident and the only female physician in the book, is portrayed as the House of God's "most ruthless and competitive resident. [. . .] A short, trim woman with clipped black hair, a jutting jaw, and dark circles under her eyes"—a "victim of success" (99–100), who has rejected her feminine role and learned to "outman" the men. Class discussion quickly identifies the fact that while much has changed in medicine over the last twenty years, Jo's stereotypical character still speaks loudly to today's medical environment, where gender bias and discrimination continue to demand that women perform at a higher level than men. And we are not surprised, sadly, that it is from a gendered construct of male power that Roy and his peers dare to challenge Jo's authority, partly by flaunting their sexual prowess with the nurses and housemaids: "Our trump card with Jo could always be sex" (122).

When Roy does identify role models for himself, they are flawed. The Fat Man truly cares for patients, even though his gross appetite for food and his cynicism toward the system initially sicken

Roy. We come to realize that in presenting Fats as an essentially sex-less character, Shem has made it safe for our protagonist to bare his soul to him and to shed tears in his arms. In Pinkus, an almost-forty cardiologist, Roy sees "a legend, fanatic in his personal and profes-sional life [. . .] rarely [leaving] the House [. . .] night after night, prowling the corridors, in the guise of following up consults on car-diac patients" (324). Blind to the fact that Pinkus is essentially Jo in male attire, Roy embraces his ideals so strongly that he literally runs, not walks, in Pinkus's shoes (a pair of hand-me-down sneakers). Pinkus is "patient, helpful, courteous, ready to produce an article" (324), so much like Jo, but without that defensive edge we see in her and must at least consider as a compensatory response to the gendered assumptions within which she is trapped.

Roy and his colleagues are painted with such strongly gendered strokes that at first reading students do not see in these characters any nurturing, empathic, "feminine" traits. Roy can and does com-fort a twenty-three-year-old rape victim with a compassionate sense "that part of her had died" (246). While cradling the dying Dr. Sanders in his arms, Roy cries "[i]n silence, so as not to scare him" and then refuses to ask for a postmortem because he "loved him too much to see his body ripped apart" (176, 178). Even the Fat Man, a "hero overcome," sheds "fat wet tears of desperation and loss" (313) over what the House has done to Potts, an intern who has committed suicide—and to himself. We are left to wonder, however, how Jo's colleagues would have reacted had she been the one to weep.

In Joyce Carol Oates's "Psychiatric Services," three physicians play out a complex drama of sexual aggression in the outpatient clinic. Jenny Hamilton, a resident in psychiatry, must try to care for fellow house officer Saul Zimmerman as he grapples with paranoid delusions and suicidal ideation in response to the stress of medical training. While Dr. Zimmerman constantly tests the boundaries of their relationship as professional colleagues, Dr. Hamilton struggles to cope with the new dynamics of colleague-as-patient, receiving lit-tle support from her supervisor. Students and mature physicians alike initially leap to defend the harassed female physician. When we point out, however, that it is she who first crosses the professional line by slipping into a gendered role, the tone of the discussion dramatically changes. At the beginning of the story, Zimmerman fantasizes about committing murder. Hamilton responds, "I'm a woman" (385), implying that women do not consider such things, seeking refuge in her purely female persona. When he telephones her late at night, she says, "It's all right. It doesn't matter" (388). Later, when he pushes to visit her at home, she uses his first name and suggests, "Saul, please, we could talk in the first-floor cafeteria, at the back, I'll wait for you there at noon" (395). We speculate that Jenny Hamilton, held hostage by the gender-role socialization of women that implies greater empathy, sensitivity, and intuition in the medical setting, simply cannot find a proper professional balance between caring and detachment.

She must also contend with Dr. Culloch, a veritable Supervisor from Hell. Equally ill-equipped to deal constructively with issues of gender because of his own deeply embedded sexist ideology, Dr. Culloch continually belittles her and forces her to see her involvement with her patient as fundamentally sexual:

> "Love-play on both sides. Totally unconscious, totally charming. Do you see it now, rationally?"
> "I . . . I didn't see it at the time, but now . . . now . . . you're probably right."
> "Probably?"
> "You're right." (400)

While trying to clarify an essential issue in psychiatry, he accuses her of exercising "gross maternal power" (398) over her patient and of attempting to castrate him. Dr. Culloch suggests that Jenny is trying to become not a God to her patient—that is a masculine image—but a Venus. He further reveals his own confused expectations of women in medicine, and his own gendered frailties, by insisting that Jenny acknowledge a sexual level of interaction in even their teacher-learner relationship: "[D]on't sit like that, as if you're ashamed of your body, why be ashamed? . . . you're attractive, you know it, your physical being is most attractive and *it* senses that power whether you do or not, Dr. Hamilton . . . right?" (398).

It would seem that the aging Dr. Culloch feeds his personal need for male power and control at the expense of humiliating Jenny and destroying her self-confidence. When we note, however, that he admiringly regards her as "an adventuresome young woman, not a lily, a wilting fawning creature" (396), we must at least question if we have, instead, been witness to a terribly distorted attempt by him to empower the physician within her. In the end, though we come to see Jenny as primarily the victim of sexual harassment and psychological abuse within the complex relationships of her training environment, we still must consider to what extent she plays a complicit role in confusing the boundaries between professional and gendered self.

In every class of students we have encountered, at least one woman volunteers an anecdote of a senior male in the medical hierarchy who propositions a younger female. Other women report the classic denigration of the successful female physician: "She slept her way to the top." It is in this context that Susan Onthank Mates, a practicing physician, dares us to see as implausible[2] the sexual encounter between Chief of Medicine Helen van Horne and the golden-skinned, "goof-off" medical student Michael Smith, in her story "The Good Doctor" (32). Dr. van Horne is a fifty-year-old self-described spinster who has just returned from Africa to reenter the world of academic medicine on the strength of her description of Tanzanian mountain fever and isolation of the culprit virus. Again we witness the complex play of professional role in constant tension with gendered self, not only through the eyes of Helen but also through the actions of the medical chief resident Diana Figueroa. Helen envies Diana her apparent fulfilment of her gender role as wife and therefore as potential mother, oblivious to the disenchantment Diana feels toward her partner, a would-be lawyer: "'One of us does work part-time [. . . w]hen he works at all.' [Diana] laughed. 'Men,' she said" (31). While Helen is jealous of the lecherous attention paid to the young physician by senior men in the medical academy, Diana increasingly looks to the lonely, sexually frustrated, introspective, dry, but professionally successful older woman as mentor and role model, even adopting the same ponytail hairstyle.

Throughout the story, we are well aware of the rising sexual tension between Helen and Michael Smith: "'If you don't work, I will fail you, don't think I won't,' she told him. But he glanced at her breasts and her nipples hardened" (35). We also see Helen's revulsion at her own behavior: "You are a fifty-year-old woman [. . . y]ou are inappropriate. You are disgusting" (35). Glen O. Gabbard has suggested that when a female clinician crosses sexual boundaries with a male patient it is, in part, due to an unconscious desire to "rescue" an otherwise decent man, to influence him to "give up his wayward tendencies" (Skelly, "Crossings" 18).[3] In class we hypothesize that the same may be true for relationships between a female teacher and a male learner, a codependent bond being forged between the two. (Similar forces might have contributed to Diana's choice of husband.) So when "the dean would not remove Michael Smith, [and] Helen decided she would make him into a doctor" (37), perhaps for her the die was cast.

In the crashing finale of "The Good Doctor," Diana has abandoned her husband in her quest for true fulfillment of professional self, and Helen is contemplating suicide, having compromised the deep conviction she expressed earlier to Diana: "When you are a teacher, [. . .] you must be careful about personal relationships. There is the issue of abuse of power" (34). We are left, however, with a disturbing sense that Michael Smith is the real sexual predator here, and artful manipulator of grades, rather than victim of a power dynamic that results in boundary crossing between teacher and student. And ultimately, even more disquieting is Helen's final resolution of the situation within a previously rejected and traditionally male model of behavior, which she now validates. Echoing Diana's earlier sentiments, "'The men,' she [says] firmly, to herself, 'do it all the time' " (41).

Readers identify, perhaps too readily and at first too superficially with Shem's stereotypical personalities in *The House of God*. In contrast, Oates and Mates demand a different level of engagement with their characters, forcing us to explore the multiple layers of male-female interaction in their stories. But the centrality of gender in medical settings and the power of role models to shape younger physicians in both positive and negative ways are overarching themes in each narrative. Regardless of the gendered preconceptions (and, perhaps, agendas) that each author surely brings to the works at hand, these stories argue for change in the cultural environment of medicine. Through the kind of dialogue and discussion generated in the classroom setting, we have the potential to free both men and women from sexual stereotypes, to celebrate both feminine and masculine virtues, and to help all members of the medical establishment in the struggle to find an appropriate professional voice. Finally, if we acknowledge that the institution of medicine not only reflects social values but also has the power to influence social mores, then from a pedagogical standpoint the medical context provides, for all students, valuable insights on the effects of gender in the broader world of professional relationships.

Notes

1. For a more in-depth discussion, see Hunter's essay on *The House of God*.
2. Michaelson in fact questioned the plausibility of "The Good Doctor" in her review of Mates's collection of the same name.
3. For a discussion of the perspectives of Gabbard and others on the topic, see Skelly, "Fruit" and "Crossings."

Works Cited

Gabbard, Glen O., and Carol Nadelson. "Professional Boundaries in the Physician-Patient Relationship." *Journal of the American Medical Association* 273 (1995): 1445–49.

Gordon, Geoffrey H., Daniel Labby, and Wendy Levinson. "Sex and the Teacher-Learner Relationship in Medicine." *Journal of General Internal Medicine* 7 (1992): 443–47.

Hunter, Kathryn Montgomery. "The Satiric Image: Healers in *The House of God*." *Literature and Medicine* 2 (1985): 135–47.

Mates, Susan Onthank. "The Good Doctor." *The Good Doctor*. John Simmons Short Fiction Award Ser. Iowa City: U of Iowa P, 1994. 30–41.

Michaelson, Ellen. Rev. of *The Good Doctor*, by Susan Onthank Mates. *Literature and Medicine* 14 (1995): 273–77.

Nora, Lois Margaret. "Sexual Harassment in Medical Education: A Review of the Literature with Comments from the Law." *Academic Medicine* 71 (Jan. supp., 1996): S113–18.

Oates, Joyce Carol. "Psychiatric Services." *The Goddess and Other Women*. New York: Vanguard, 1974. 384–401.

Phillips, Susan P., and Margaret S. Schneider. "Sexual Harassment of Female Doctors by Patients." *New England Journal of Medicine* 329 (1993): 1936–39.

Shem, Samuel. *The House of God.* 1978. New York: Dell, 1981.

Shin, Eliza S. "Of Locker Rooms and Labor Pains." *Annals of Internal Medicine* 123 (1995): 71–72.

Skelly, Flora Johnson. "Boundary Crossings." *American Medical News* 5 July 1993: 11–14.

———. "Forbidden Fruit." *American Medical News* 28 June 1993: 15–20.

Anne Hunsaker Hawkins

"Read Two Chapters and Call Me in the Morning": Teaching Literature to Physicians

In their daily work physicians encounter people undergoing some of the most profound of human experiences—sickness and disability, death, birth—and the turbulent emotions that attend them. Literature that deals with fundamental aspects of human experience can help physicians negotiate those deep waters of human need, grief, and suffering; it can also help them voice their often unarticulated responses to their work. Literature can give them a vehicle, as it were, to explore all these things. A literature course offers the physician an acquaintance with another discipline that, like medicine, deals with character, relationships between characters, story, interpretation, and major life issues.

I have offered seminars in literature for faculty physicians at the Pennsylvania State University College of Medicine over the past seven years. The physicians in my seminars appreciate difficult and challenging texts, whether ancient or modern. When asked about their preferences, they have been, unfortunately, lukewarm toward poetry and uniformly negative toward writings by physicians about medical practice. Given these preferences, I use readings, such as ancient Greek tragedy and epic, that do not directly concern medicine but that richly engage issues of value and meaning that physicians confront in their work. The ancient texts work well, partly because of their unfamiliarity and remoteness and partly because they embody perspectives and values that have shaped Western intellectual discourse for centuries.

Seminars in literature for physicians work best if the number of participants is kept to no more than twelve or thirteen and if the instructor prepares and hands out written materials about each text. Notes on author, genre, and the text itself as well as carefully prepared study questions help introduce physicians to a new work and prepare them to discuss it in the seminar. Such materials also function as levelers in a group of people with varied backgrounds in literature and literary analysis. Finding a time is difficult: care must be taken to choose an hour when most participants can attend most often. The seminar schedule will vary with the length and difficulty of texts: meeting once a month permits participants to complete long works and think more deeply about what they have read; meeting twice a month enhances the cohesiveness of the group. Humanities courses for practicing physicians rarely involve pay for the instructor or formal credit for the student. But there are benefits in such teaching: the instructor gains a unique insider's view of the medical profession with all its stresses, frustrations, and triumphs; and there is the sheer pleasure of sharing literature one loves and of helping participants sharpen their reading skills. In the future, humanities courses may be incorporated more frequently into continuing medical education programs, and their instructors may be remunerated.

I have taught seminars in which the readings were individual and independent texts, seminars centering on one long text, and seminars organized around a theme. One seminar was intended to present participants with works from varied cultures and different genres—texts calling for a range of analytic approaches. The relevance of the readings to medicine was sometimes direct, as when Sophocles dramatizes the anguish of the diseased Philoctetes, or when Henry James in "The Middle Years" writes of a doctor and his dying patient, or when Harriet Doerr defamiliarizes the North American perspectives on life and death in *Stones for Ibarra*. More often, their relevance was oblique, as in Robert Frost's exploration of the psychology of bereavement in "Home Burial" or James Joyce's use of epiphanies in "Araby" and "The Dead" to diagnose Dublin's moral paralysis.

Another seminar focused only on Homer's *Iliad*. We read the poem carefully and in depth, attending to such matters of form as epic simile, geometric pattern, and formulaic descriptions of death in battle, as well as to such matters of content as the function of the divinities and the themes of honor *(tīmé)* and wrath *(mênis)*. Suggested supplemental readings included Simone Weil's The Iliad; *or, The Poem of Force* and Jonathan Shay's *Achilles in Vietnam*. Homer's ancient epic proved surprisingly relevant to issues confronting patients and physicians in today's world. At first it seemed a poem about a war from long ago and far away. Gradually participants began to see that the battle Homer describes is not so much a historical event as a constant and universal aspect of the human condition. Topics that emerged over and over in discussion were the way the Homeric divinities personify forces that still shape or destroy human life, the struggle to achieve power and excellence, the conflict between social code and individual moral insight, the confrontation with suffering and death, and the meaning of heroism— all themes as real and relevant to a modern medical center as they were centuries ago at Troy. Interestingly, it was in this seminar that physicians talked most directly about their experience with patients.

A third seminar, which I discuss in more detail, was intended to address not only aspects of physicians' work with patients but also their response to managed care and to the resultant corporatization of academic medicine. In The Individual, the Community, and the Powers That Be, participants explored literary works from different periods and cultures that deal with the confrontation between individual people and the overwhelming forces that direct and sometimes persecute or victimize them. Readings included the Book of Job, Aeschylus's *Prometheus Bound*, Vergil's *Aeneid,* and Camus's

The Plague, followed by modern (and shorter) works selected by instructor and participants that seemed relevant to the course theme.[1] Participants discussed such recurring topics as destiny and fate, suffering, the relation between individual and community, and human responses to coercive power—responses ranging from patience and obedience to visionary apprehensions of renewal and regeneration to challenge, resistance, or revolt. Participants were encouraged to examine these themes in the context of the contemporary world— of medicine especially—where the conflict between the individual and the powers that be is recognizable in everyday encounters with bureaucratic and institutional structures, large economic forces, and the politics of money and power.

I introduced the Book of Job as an amalgam of works by different authors and periods and as a text in the tradition of the Hebrew lament, which is exemplified in Psalms. The psalmist regularly assumes that the good are rewarded and the evil are punished in this life (e.g., Ps. 69, 71, 73, 74), and this is also the assumption of Job's comforters. A good way to begin a discussion of Job—a story familiar to everyone but a text that few have actually read—is to ask seminar participants about the discrepancy between their received sense of the story and the written text. Invariably two points are raised: their bafflement and discomfort with the preliminary legend of the wager between God and Satan, which often seems to be omitted from popular versions and which infinitely complicates the story; and the contrast between the Bible's fiery Job, who comes close to cursing God, and the pallid and patiently suffering servant as presented in synagogue and church lessons who endures all and still believes. Both points are related to the problem of theodicy so central to the Book of Job. If God is both powerful and just, why do the righteous—and the innocent—suffer?

The wager between God and Satan undercuts any simple idea of divine justice. Why for the sake of a wager should a just God consent to Satan's proposal of testing a man by causing him to suffer? Or is the wager more a metaphysical symbol than a simple and rather meaningless bet? Job maintains his innocence throughout, crying, "I will speak in the anguish of my spirit / I will complain in the bitterness of my soul" (7.11), even demanding that God appear and talk with him (13.22). In the Psalms, outcry is followed only by the psalmist's idea of God's expected response; but here God actually replies to Job. Do God's magnificent speeches about deep time and vast space really answer Job? Is the theophany itself a kind of answer? Such questions provoke—and deserve—extended and animated discussion. One issue that the instructor can bring up (if seminar participants do not) is the legitimacy of lament. Perhaps the fact that God *does* respond to Job's laments suggests that Job is somehow en-titled to engage God in challenging and even intimate dialogue. Lament and outcry are thus ratified as a necessary—even a religious —act, and the mystery of human suffering is placed in the context of the grandeur of creation.

How do these problems relate to participants' own life experi-ences? In the culture of medicine, is there a response to suffering that doctors expect of themselves and of patients and their families —such as acceptance, or even stoicism? What ways of dealing with suffering seem most tolerated (and best rewarded) in a hospital en-vironment? Many physicians have witnessed the struggle of patients and families to reconcile their religious faith with the fact of suffer-ing. Job never swerves from the belief that God is both just and good, though he does not hold back in expressing his pain and in asking why God permits it. The Book of Job may not answer the question of why the innocent suffer, but it does seem at least to af-firm our right to give voice to our suffering, even to the point of calling God to account for it.

Participants next read Aeschylus's *Prometheus Bound,* a play so similar in ways to the Book of Job that some scholars have thought that Aeschylus was familiar with the story (see "Book of Job"). Teaching this play successfully requires notes on Greek tragedy, on the relation of *Prometheus Bound* to the lost plays of the original tril-ogy, and on mythological background relevant to the play and its characters. To give physicians a sense of the formal elements of the genre, I include materials on Aristotle's theory of tragedy, emphasiz-ing the recognition, reversal, and scene of suffering, but I am careful to point out that the *Poetics* postdates fifth-century Greek tragedy and that Aristotle thus derived these concepts from the plays them-selves. A description of the structure of Greek tragedy—prologue, choral odes, episodes, and so on—is desirable, if time permits. Given the ethical dimensions of medicine, physicians are interested to hear that tragedy served as a major source of moral learning for Greek audiences.[2] Emphasizing the ethical aspects of *Prometheus Bound* proves useful when participants read and discuss *The Plague*.

Because *Prometheus Bound* is much less familiar than Job, dis-cussion can be inhibited at first. It helps to focus on the opening scene, in which the god Hephaestus, spurred on by Might and Vio-lence, chains Prometheus to the rock. Beginning in this way shows how general discussion of issues raised by the play can be grounded in specific passages in the text. The first line of the play, with its ref-erence to the "world's limits," deserves special attention, since this is a play about limits and going beyond them. Prometheus has gone beyond the limits set by Zeus. Is this his crime or his heroism—or both? Which character is more constrained: Prometheus, chained to the rock, or Hephaestus, forced to perform an action he believes is wrong? Prometheus remains silent while he is being chained; his si-lence renders even more striking his powerful opening speech with its long open lines, its inclusion of chanting and song, its imagery of abundance, motion, light, even laughter—as he summons the ele-ments to witness his suffering. What are the differences and similar-ities between lament in Job and in *Prometheus Bound*? Prometheus's lament calls on a much wider reality—nature, the elements, the whole range of being—of which gods and Titans are only a part. Al-though Zeus has power over all this, he does not dictate or control its meaning as does Yahweh. But Prometheus, like Job, appeals to a cosmic order that is moral: creation is outraged by Prometheus's suffering and Zeus's tyranny.

There are further contrasts and likenesses between the Book of Job and *Prometheus Bound*: the relationship of Prometheus to Zeus (who are both divine) as opposed to that of the human Job to God/Satan; the parallel between Oceanus, Io, and Hermes in *Prometheus Bound* and the comforters in the Book of Job; the final posture adopted by Prometheus as opposed to that of Job. Job and

Prometheus respond differently to punishment they consider unjust: Job cries out and protests, then repents; Prometheus defies Zeus, even though he knows he will incur further punishment for his defiance. Job is vindicated and rewarded by God, but Prometheus is plunged into the abyss by thunderbolts from Zeus. The ultimate reconciliation of god and Titan occurs only in the distant future of the myth and the lost ending of the trilogy.

The powers that be are easily identified in the Book of Job—but what of *Prometheus Bound*? Since Prometheus is a god, must he too not be considered a power? What forces or values do Prometheus and Zeus represent? What is the function of the Io episode? Both Prometheus and Io suffer; both are victims, Io of Zeus's love, Prometheus of Zeus's hate. How does Prometheus help Io? Does Io help Prometheus? He represents contrasting attitudes: on the one hand, love and service to humankind; on the other, resistance and rebellion against divine oppression. What place do service, altruism, and generosity have in our society and, specifically, in medicine? Are they rewarded? What values does society rank higher than these? What can be seen as forces of oppression? Of course the instructor will need to pick and choose among the many topics suggested by this play, but one that should not be omitted is the developing role of the Chorus, whose final decision to stay with Prometheus is a moral choice that seems crucial to any interpretation of the play.

In Vergil's *Aeneid*, the powers that be are a blend of the divine and the historical. The *Aeneid* is a poem about societal and personal change and the cost of those changes. It seems an especially relevant text in an era when our social policies about health care are undergoing such radical alteration. Carefully prepared study questions prove helpful, as with the other readings, in bringing readers into dialogue with the text. Participants will also benefit from a brief introduction to aspects of Roman history that pertain to the poem (e.g., Caesar Augustus and the transition from republic to empire; Antony and Cleopatra).

I teach the *Aeneid* in two seminar sessions, since there is a natural division between the first six and the last six books. Fruitful topics for discussion especially relevant to physicians include the need for self-reflection and self-scrutiny, both in dealing with harm done to others and in establishing priorities and setting goals for the future (Aeneas's descent into the underworld); the function of nostalgia and the tendency—so evident in current medicine—to idealize the past (the Arcadian interlude); the hard necessity of renouncing one's desires and disciplining one's inclinations in the interest of achieving a goal (abandoning Dido; fighting Turnus); the attitude toward women reflected in the poet's ambivalence about erotic love (Helen, Dido, Amata) and in the depiction of mad, destructive females (Dido, Juno, Allecto)—a theme especially significant for academic medicine.

My seminar participants are usually puzzled at first by Aeneas, who seems, they say, so passive and so unheroic. To ground discussion in the text, we look at Aeneas's first speech, in which he laments having survived the Trojan War (1.133–43). At the very beginning of the poem, the hero's special task is established: to identify not with the Trojan Aeneas of the past but with the Roman Aeneas of the future; to move toward a dimly perceived destiny that will be no simple reenactment of the past but something totally new. This aspect of his character is emphasized by his response to the fighting when Troy falls: his instinct is to rush into battle and die nobly, and he must repeatedly be deflected from doing this (2.38, 49, 52, 55). Sympathy for Aeneas will emerge as discussion focuses on his suffering and his losses (a person important to Aeneas dies in each of the first six books), and the sense of him as unheroic will yield to a sense of his human lifelikeness.

In a sense, the *Aeneid* is a tragedy of success: Aeneas achieves his goal but at enormous cost. Physicians can identify with this pattern. Any analysis of Aeneas's gains and losses introduces the central controversy among scholars as to Vergil's overall purpose in the *Aeneid*: Is it to glorify Caesar Augustus and *Romanitas* or to point to the suffering and loss underlying the glory of Augustus and of Rome? In other words, does Vergil ask us to celebrate Aeneas's heroic feats? Or does he ask, given the suffering they cause, that we judge whether they were worth it? A useful exercise here is to ask participants to define the dominant values in the epic and think about how they might conflict. The list might include, on the one hand, loyalty to the past, perseverance in reaching a future goal, the sense of duty, and heroic and even historical achievement and, on the other, a sense of humanity and tenderness, reason, restraint, generosity, and a tragic awareness of the moral ambiguity in human acts and choices.

Discussion of the *Aeneid* will be enriched by allusions to other texts in the seminar. As his epithet suggests, "pius Aeneas" is dutiful: how does he compare with Job and Prometheus in his response to the powers that rule his world? Venus and Juno are deities opposed in Vergil's epic: how might they be contrasted with God and Satan in the Book of Job? How do all three texts configure human suffering? Seminar participants are intrigued with the notion that in both *Prometheus Bound* and the *Aeneid*, suffering is somehow connected to civilization, change, growth, and achievement.

When I teach *The Plague*, I give students little more preparatory information than facts about Albert Camus (his chronic tuberculosis, his political activism) and the polysemous nature of this novel. Besides the historical analogy to the Nazi occupation and the French Resistance, participants should be alerted to the text's openness to other more general and more existential interpretations.

Inevitably, discussion about *The Plague* at some point turns to the roles of the various characters and the dominant values that each one represents and lives by. For example, the journalist Rambert, somewhat like Aeneas, must choose between personal happiness and duty to a higher goal. He chooses duty: why? Rieux and Tarrou are paired figures. Rieux's ideal is "being a man" (231); Tarrou's is becoming a saint. Why is the first ideal harder? Physicians are especially interested in Dr. Rieux and his attitude toward his work. They are impressed with the fact that he—speaking perhaps for Camus—eschews the idea of heroism, claiming that he is only doing his job, acting out of common decency. If there must be a hero, declares Rieux, it is the insignificant minor official Grand, who dedicates himself to fighting the plague while retaining his regular job—and his passion for writing. Readers sometimes claim that Camus has no sense of humor, but surely Grand, the minor official who is always rewriting the first sentence of his ultraromantic novel, is an ironic self-portrait of Camus himself.

Father Paneloux is especially interesting, because his ideas about suffering recall those of the Psalms and the Book of Job. In his first sermon, Paneloux, like Job's comforters, interprets the plague as punishment for human sinfulness; in the second sermon, like Job, he argues that God is inscrutable and we must accept suffering, "trusting in the divine goodness, even as to the deaths of little children," because it is God's will (205). But in its actual depiction of a child's agonizing death, *The Plague* goes beyond the Book of Job. This is a terrible episode, one meant to call into question all the pretty conventions surrounding the death of children in nineteenth-century novels. Camus's stance toward the powers that be (as well as his position vis-à-vis theodicy) is embodied in Rieux's response to the child's death: "Until my dying day I shall refuse to love a scheme of things in which children are put to torture" (197). His is a Promethean stance of revolt and active resistance.

It is important in teaching this text to concretize moral issues. *The Plague* is ethical fiction: it helps us examine our values and priorities, then urges us to act in a way that reflects those things we care about most. Camus suggests that complying with conventional behavior and institutional policies that we ought to resist makes us unconscious collaborators. Physicians today are finding themselves suddenly caught up in a transformation of health-care policy in which serving the needs of the ill and the dying is subordinated to economic interests. Academic medicine, too, is being transformed as it succumbs to corporatization. How ought physicians respond to these changes? The various texts in this course explore possible answers to this question, but the answer implicit throughout *The Plague* is the most drastic and direct: the healer must resist plague in all its forms, for institutional, professional, and societal disorders are as epidemic as any that affect the body or the mind.

Notes

1. Some of the other texts were Franz Kafka's *The Castle,* André Malraux's *Man's Fate,* Toni Morrison's *The Bluest Eye,* and Zora Neale Hurston's *Their Eyes Were Watching God.*
2. For a discussion of the ethical dimensions of Greek tragedy, see Nussbaum.

Works Cited

Aeschylus. *Prometheus Bound. The Complete Greek Tragedies: Aeschylus II.* Rev. trans. David Grene. 2nd ed. Ed. Grene and Richmond Lattimore. Chicago: U of Chicago P, 1956. 139–80.

Book of Job. Bible. King James Version.

"Book of Job." *The Interpreter's Dictionary of the Bible.* Vol. 2. Ed. George A. Buttrick. New York: Abington, 1962. 911–25.

Camus, Albert. *The Plague.* Trans. Stuart Gilbert. New York: Random–Modern Lib., 1948.

Doerr, Harriet. *Stones for Ibarra.* New York: Viking, 1978.

Frost, Robert. "Home Burial." *The Poems of Robert Frost.* New York: Random, 1946. 59–63.

Homer. *The Iliad.* Trans. Richmond Lattimore. Chicago: U of Chicago P, 1951.

Hurston, Zora Neale. *Their Eyes Were Watching God.* New York: Harper, 1937.

James, Henry. "The Middle Years." *"The Figure in the Carpet" and Other Stories.* New York: Penguin, 1986. 233–58.

Joyce, James. "Araby." *Dubliners.* New York: Penguin, 1992. 21–28.

——— ."The Dead." *Dubliners.* New York: Penguin, 1992. 175–225.

Kafka, Franz. *The Castle.* Trans. Willa Muir and Edwin Muir. New York: Penguin, 1930.

Malraux, André. *Man's Fate.* Trans. Haakon M. Chevalier. New York: Modern Library, 1934.

Morrison, Toni. *The Bluest Eye.* New York: Holt, Rinehart, 1970.

Nussbaum, Martha C. *The Fragility of Goodness.* Cambridge: Cambridge UP, 1986.

Shay, Jonathan. *Achilles in Vietnam.* New York: Simon, 1994.

Vergil. *The Aeneid.* Trans. Allen Mandelbaum. New York: Bantam, 1971.

Weil, Simone. The Iliad; *or, The Poem of Force.* Trans. Mary McCarthy. Wallingford: Pendle Hill, 1956.

Part IV

Resources for Teachers and Scholars in Literature and Medicine

General Bibliographies

"Bibliography: Relations of Literature and Science." Entry on medicine. *Configurations*. Spring issues.

Literature and Medicine: An Annotated Bibliography. Ed. Joanne Trautmann and Carol Pollard. Rev. ed. Pittsburgh: U of Pittsburgh P, 1982.

Literature, Arts, and Medicine Database. Ed. Felice Aull. New York Univ. School of Medicine. <http://endeavor.med.nyu.edu/lit-med/lit-med-db/topview. html>. See page 368, this volume.

Journals

Academic Medicine. Ed. Addeane S. Caelleigh. Washington: Assn. of Amer. Medical Colls. See the special feature "Medicine and the Arts," ed. Lisa Dittrich.

Configurations: A Journal of Literature, Science, and Technology. Ed. Wilda Anderson, James Bono, and Kenneth J. Knoespel. Society for Literature and Science. Baltimore: Johns Hopkins UP.

Journal of Medical Humanities. Ed. Delese Wear. Northeastern Ohio Univs. Coll. of Medicine. New York: Human Sciences.

Literature and Medicine. Ed. Suzanne Poirier. Baltimore: Johns Hopkins UP.

Medical Humanities Review. Ed. Ronald A. Carson and Thomas H. Murray. Galveston: U of Texas Medical Branch.

Mosaic: A Journal for the Interdisciplinary Study of Literature. Ed. Evelyn J. Hinz. Winnipeg: U of Manitoba.

Perspectives in Biology and Medicine. Ed. Richard L. Landau and Robert Perlman. Chicago: U of Chicago P.

Pharos. Ed. Robert J. Glasser. Menlo Park: Alpha Omega Alpha Honor Medical Soc.

Anthologies of Primary Sources

Belli, Angela, ed. *Blood and Bone: Poems by Physicians*. Iowa City: U of Iowa P, 1998.

Davis, Cortney, and Judy Schaefer, eds. *Between the Heartbeats: Poetry and Prose by Nurses*. Iowa City: U of Iowa P, 1995.

Donley, Carol, Martin Kohn, and Delese Wear, eds. *Literature and Aging: An Anthology*. Kent: Kent State UP, 1992.

Donley, Carol, and Sheryl Buckley, eds. *The Tyranny of the Normal: An Anthology*. Kent: Kent State UP, 1996.

Downie, R. S., ed. *The Healing Arts*. Oxford: Oxford UP, 1994.

Enright, D. J., ed. *The Oxford Book of Death*. Oxford: Oxford UP, 1983.

Mukand, John, ed. *Articulations: The Body and Illness in Poetry*. Iowa City: U of Iowa P, 1994.

——, ed. *Vital Lines: Contemporary Fiction about Medicine*. New York: St. Martin's, 1990.

Reynolds, Robert, and John Stone, eds. *On Doctoring: Stories, Poems, Essays*. New York: Simon, 1991.

Secundy, Marian Gray, ed. *Trials, Tribulations, and Celebrations: African-American Perspectives on Health, Illness, Aging, and Loss*. Yarmouth: Intercultural, 1992.

Walker, Sue B., and Rosaly D. Roffman, eds. *Life on the Line: Selections on Words and Healing*. Mobile: Negative Capability, 1992.

Online Resources at New York University School of Medicine

Felice Aull

To facilitate and promote the use of literature in medical education, medical training, and scholarship in the medical humanities, a collaborative, multi-institutional project was initiated in 1993. Scholars and educators in the field were recruited as editor-annotators to create a continually expanding, dynamic, globally accessible resource of relevant literary works. The result of that initiative is the *Medical Humanities* World Wide Web site at New York University School of Medicine, available without charge at http://endeavor.med.nyu.edu/lit-med/medhum.html. Resources at the Web site include the *Literature, Arts, and Medicine Database;* medical humanities course syllabi; the medical humanities directory; and archives of the literature and medicine discussion group.

Literature, Arts, and Medicine Database

The Literature, Arts, and Medicine Database is a multimedia annotated resource of fiction, poetry, prose, art, and film. It is written by scholars who use these media to teach in the health-care professions and in preprofessional settings. The annotations include discussion of how the works are relevant to medicine and how they are being—or potentially could be—used in teaching. Because the database is expanded and revised bimonthly, it maintains its relevance to contemporary issues in medicine and in society. Currently, the database comprises more than twelve hundred annotations. Wherever possible, links have been made to online literary texts, to audio recordings of authors' readings, and to art works. Biographical information about each author or artist is also available.

Annotations can be accessed by more than one hundred keywords or topics, formulated by the editors. Examples are acculturation, doctor-patient relationship, domestic violence, empathy, illness narrative/pathology, literary theory, medical ethics, family relationships, human worth, physician experience, and women's health. Access through several other categories—ethnicity and gender of authors, for example—is also possible. In addition, the entire database and its literature, art, and film subsections can be searched for any word or phrase of interest. Extensive cross-links between annotations facilitate use of the database. Also available is a book version of this resource, *Literature, Arts, and Medicine Database,* edited by Felice Aull (New York: New York U School of Medicine, 1996).

Medical Humanities Course Syllabi

Syllabi of courses and programs in the medical humanities are posted in full to the Web site. Syllabi can be accessed by course topics, including literature and medicine, or by institution. Many courses posted to the site use literature extensively.

Medical Humanities Directory

The Web site includes a directory that lists medical humanities programs and faculty members in North American medical schools. Included are addresses, phone and fax numbers, and, wherever possible, e-mail addresses, Web site addresses, areas of interest, elective course titles, and special projects.

Archives of the Literature and Medicine Discussion Group

Archived at the Web site are all the messages of an e-mail discussion group, Lit-Med, which is administered at New York University School of Medicine. Messages can be accessed chronologically, by subject, by message "thread," or by sender. Lit-Med is an unmonitored e-mail discussion group, a resource available to anyone with an interest in the field of literature and medicine or related areas. To become a subscriber, send an e-mail message that includes the word *subscribe* to lit-med-request@popmail.med.nyu.edu. Subscribers can e-mail the discussion group at lit-med@popmail.med.nyu.edu.

Inquiries about the Web site, the e-mail discussion group, or the book version of the annotated bibliography should be made to Felice Aull (212 263–5401; aullf0l@popmail.med.nyu.edu).

Centers and Societies

Center for Literature, Medicine, and the Health Care Professions

The Center for Literature, Medicine, and the Health Care Professions, located in Hiram, Ohio, is a collaborative project of Hiram College and Northeastern Ohio Universities College of Medicine. The center has received two NEH grants for Institutes for Humanities and Medicine (1988–89 and 1991–92) and since then has sponsored annual summer seminars in narrative bioethics. These seminars attract health-care professionals, theologians, philosophers, and literary scholars interested in interdisciplinary issues in humanities and medicine, especially narrative approaches to bioethics. The center has also produced two anthologies, *Literature and Aging* (Kent: Kent State UP, 1992) and *The Tyranny of the Normal* (Kent: Kent State UP, 1996), and is working on a third. Center faculty members teach several interdisciplinary courses in literature and medicine and sponsor workshops led by writers who are also health-care professionals. For more information, write to Carol Donley, Center for Literature, Medicine, and the Health Care Professions, Hiram College, Hiram, OH 44234.

American Society of Bioethics and Humanities (formerly the Society for Health and Human Values)

The American Society of Bioethics and Humanities (ASBH) is an interdisciplinary organization dedicated to the advancement of healthcare related teaching and scholarship in the humanities. The ASBH sponsers an annual fall meeting that includes panel discussions, informal workshops, presentations of peer-reviewed papers, and other scholarly formats. The topics covered reflect the diversity of the membership and the variety of ethical problems facing clinical practice and teaching. Papers and workshops in literature and medicine are a part of the general program. For information write to ASBH, PO Box 468, Des Plaines, IL 60016-0468.

Society for Literature and Science

The Society for Literature and Science (SLS) fosters the multidisciplinary study of relations among literature and language, the arts, science, medicine, and technology. SLS holds an annual convention for scholars from different disciplines whose work focuses on the intersection between literature and any area of science, technology, engineering, or medicine. SLS publishes *Configurations* three times a year and a newsletter, *Decodings*, twice a year. For information write to Carol Colatrella, School of Literature, Communication, and Culture, Georgia Institute of Technology, Atlanta, GA 30332-0165.

Selective Bibliography of Secondary Sources in Literature and Medicine

Brody, Howard. *Stories of Sickness.* New Haven: Yale UP, 1972.

Charon, Rita, Joanne Trautmann Banks, Julia Connelly, Anne Hunsaker Hawkins, Kathryn Montgomery Hunter, Anne Hudson Jones, Martha Montello, and Suzanne Poirier. "Literature and Medicine: Contributions to Clinical Practice." *Annals of Internal Medicine* 122 (1995): 599–606.

Clarke, Bruce, and Wendell Aycock, eds. *The Body and the Text: Comparative Essays in Literature and Medicine.* Studies in Compar. Lit. 22. Lubbock: Texas Tech UP, 1990.

Coles, Robert. *The Call of Stories: Teaching and the Moral Imagination.* Boston: Houghton, 1989.

Couser, G. Thomas. *Recovering Bodies: Illness, Disability, and Life Writing.* Madison: U of Wisconsin P, 1997.

Foucault, Michel. *The Birth of the Clinic: An Archaeology of Medical Perception.* Trans. A. M. Sheridan Smith. New York: Vintage, 1994.

Frank, Arthur. *The Wounded Storyteller: Body, Illness, and Ethics.* Chicago: U of Chicago P, 1995.

Furst, Lilian R. *Between Doctors and Patients: The Changing Balance of Power.* Charlottesville: UP of Virginia, 1998.

Gilman, Sander L. *Disease and Representation: Images of Illness from Madness to AIDS.* Ithaca: Cornell UP, 1988.

Gossin, Pamela, ed. *Encyclopedia of Literature and Science.* Westport: Greenwood, 2000.

Hawkins, Anne Hunsaker. *Reconstructing Illness: Studies in Pathography.* 2nd ed. West Lafayette: Purdue UP, 1999.

Hunter, Kathryn Montgomery. *Doctors' Stories: The Narrative Structure of Medical Knowledge.* Princeton: Princeton UP, 1991.

Hunter, Kathryn Montgomery, Rita Charon, and John L. Coulehan. "The Study of Literature in Medical Education." *Academic Medicine* 70 (1995): 787–94.

Meyers, Jeffrey. *Disease and the Novel, 1880–1960.* New York: St. Martin's, 1985.

Morris, David B. *The Culture of Pain.* Berkeley: U of California P, 1991.

———. *Illness and Culture in the Postmodern Age.* Berkeley: U of California P, 1998.

Payer, Lynn. *Medicine and Culture: Varieties of Treatment in the United States, England, West Germany, and France.* New York: Penguin, 1989.

Sontag, Susan. *AIDS and Its Metaphors.* New York: Farrar, 1989.

———. *Illness as Metaphor.* New York: Vintage, 1979.

Selective Bibliography of Primary and Secondary Sources in the History of Medicine

Dieter J. Boxmann, Paul W. Child,
Bryon Lee Grigsby, Monica Maillet

General

Ackerknecht, Erwin H. *A Short History of Medicine*. Baltimore: Johns Hopkins UP, 1968.

Bullough, Vern L. *The Development of Medicine as a Profession*. New York: Hafner, 1966.

Bynum, W. F., and Roy Porter. *Companion Encyclopedia of the History of Medicine*. 2 vols. London: Routledge, 1993.

Clendening, Logan, ed. *Source Book of Medical History*. New York: Dover, 1942.

Conrad, Lawrence, Michael Neve, Vivian Nutton, Roy Porter, and Andrew Wear. *The Western Medical Tradition, 800 BC to AD 1800*. Cambridge: Cambridge UP, 1995.

Gilman, Sander L. *Disease and Representation: Images of Illness from Madness to AIDS*. Ithaca: Cornell UP, 1988.

Karlen, Arno. *Man and Microbes: Diseases and Plagues in History and Modern Times*. New York: Putnam, 1995.

Loudon, Irving, ed. *Western Medicine*. Oxford: Oxford UP, 1997.

Magner, Lois N. *A History of Medicine*. New York: Dekker, 1992.

Nutton, Vivian. *From Democedes to Harvey: Studies in the History of Medicine*. London: Variorium, 1988.

Pastore, Judith Laurence, ed. *Confronting AIDS through Literature: The Responsibilities of Representation*. Urbana: U of Illinois P, 1993.

Porter, Roy, ed. *The Cambridge Illustrated History of Medicine*. Cambridge: Cambridge UP, 1996.

———. *The Greatest Benefit to Mankind: A Medical History of Humanity*. New York: Norton, 1998.

Quetel, Claude. *History of Syphilis*. Trans. Judith Braddock and Brian Pike. Baltimore: Johns Hopkins UP, 1990.

Ranger, Terence, and Paul Slack, eds. *Epidemics and Ideas: Essays on the Historical Perception of Pestilence*. Cambridge: Cambridge UP, 1992.

Sigerist, Henry. *Civilization and Disease*. Ithaca: Cornell UP, 1943. College Park: McGrath, 1970.

Starr, Paul. *The Social Transformation of American Medicine*. New York: Basic, 1982.

Watts, Sheldon. *Epidemics and History: Disease, Power, and Imperialism*. New Haven: Yale UP, 1997.

Wear, Andrew, ed. *Medicine in Society: Historical Essays*. Cambridge: Cambridge UP, 1992.

Classical

Primary Texts

Aristotle. *Generation of Animals*. Trans. A. L. Peck. Cambridge: Loeb Classical Lib., 1953.

———. *History of Animals*. Vols. 1–3. Trans. A. L. Peck. Vols. 4–6. Trans. and ed. D. M. Balme. 6 vols. London: Loeb Classical Lib., 1965–70.

———. *Parts of Animals*. Trans. A. L. Peck. Cambridge: Loeb Classical Lib., 1937.

Brock, Arthur J. *Greek Medicine, Being Extracts Illustrative of Medical Writers from Hippocrates to Galen*. New York: Dutton, 1929.

Edelstein, Emma J., and Ludwig Edelstein, eds. *Asclepius: A Collection and Interpretation of the Testimonies*. Baltimore: Johns Hopkins UP, 1998.

Galen. *The Doctrines of Hippocrates and Plato*. 2nd ed. Berlin: Akademie, 1981.

———. *On the Natural Faculties*. Trans. A. W. Brock. Cambridge: Cambridge UP, 1985.

———. *On the Therapeutic Method*. Trans. R. J. Hankinson. Oxford: Clarendon, 1991.

———. *On the Usefulness of the Parts of the Body*. Trans. Margaret Tallmadge May. Ithaca: Cornell UP, 1968.

———. *Selected Works*. Trans. P. N. Singer. Oxford: Oxford UP, 1997.

———. *Three Treatises on the Nature of Science*. Trans. Richard Walzer and Michael Frede. Indianapolis: Hackett, 1985.

Hippocrates. *The Aphorisms of Hippocrates: With a Translation into Latin and English*. Birmingham: Classics of Medicine, 1982.

———. *La consultation*. Paris: Herman, 1986.

———. *Hippocratic Writings*. Ed. G. E. R. Lloyd. Trans. J. Chadwick et al. Harmondsworth: Penguin, 1978.

Soranus of Ephesus. *Gynecology*. Trans. Owsei Temkin. Baltimore: Johns Hopkins UP, 1956.

Staden, Heinrich von, ed. and trans. *Herophilus: The Art of Medicine in Early Alexandria*. Cambridge: Cambridge UP, 1989.

Secondary Texts

Amundsen, Darrel W. *Medicine, Society, and Faith in the Ancient and Medieval Worlds*. Baltimore: Johns Hopkins UP, 1996.

Edelstein, Ludwig. *Ancient Medicine: Selected Papers of Ludwig Edelstein*. Ed. Owsei Temkin and C. Lilian Temkin. Baltimore: Johns Hopkins UP, 1976.

Entralgo, Pedro Lain. *The Therapy of the Word in Classical Antiquity*. Ed. and trans. L. J. Rather and John M. Sharp. New Haven: Yale UP, 1970.

Grmek, Mirko D. *Diseases in the Ancient Greek World*. Trans. Mireille Muellner and Leonard Muellner. Baltimore: Johns Hopkins UP, 1989.

Jackson, Ralph. *Doctors and Disease in the Roman Empire*. Norman: U of Oklahoma P, 1988.

Jones, W. H. S. *Philosophy and Medicine in Ancient Greece*. Baltimore: Johns Hopkins UP, 1946.

Lloyd, G. E. R. *Early Greek Science: Thales to Aristotle*. London: Chatto, 1970. New York: Norton, 1974.

———. *Greek Science after Aristotle*. London: Chatto, 1973.

———. *Science, Folklore, and Ideology: Studies in the Life Sciences in Ancient Greece*. Cambridge: Cambridge UP, 1983.

Longrigg, James N. *Greek Rational Medicine: Philosophy and Medicine from Alcmaeon to the Alexandrians*. London: Routledge, 1993.

———. "Philosophy and Medicine: Some Early Interactions." *Harvard Studies in Classical Philology* 67 (1963): 147–75.

———. "Presocratic Philosophy and Hippocratic Medicine." *History of Science* 27 (1989): 1–39.

———. "Superlative Achievement and Comparative Neglect: Medical Science and Modern Historical Research." *History of Science* 19 (1981): 155–200.

Miller, H. W. "A Medical Theory of Cognition." *Transactions of the American Philological Association* 83 (1952): 168–83.

———. "Techne and Discovery in *On Ancient Medicine*." *Transactions of the American Philological Association* 86 (1955): 51–62.

Nutton, Vivian, ed. *Galen: Problems and Prospects*. London: Wellcome Inst. for the Hist. of Medicine, 1981.

Oliver, J. R. "Greek Medicine and Its Relation to Greek Civilization." *Bulletin of the History of Medicine* 2 (1935): 623–38.

Phillips, Eustace D. *Aspects of Greek Medicine*. New York: St. Martin's, 1973. Philadelphia: Charles, 1987.

Simon, Bennett. *Mind and Madness in Ancient Greece: The Classical Roots of Modern Psychiatry*. Ithaca: Cornell UP, 1978.

Smith, Wesley D. *The Hippocratic Tradition*. Ithaca: Cornell UP, 1979.

Taylor, Henry. *Greek Biology and Medicine*. Boston: Jones, 1922.

Temkin, Owsei. *"Double Face of Janus" and Other Essays in the History of Medicine*. Baltimore: Johns Hopkins UP, 1977.

———. *Galenism: Rise and Decline of a Medical Philosophy*. Ithaca: Cornell UP, 1973.

Temkin, Owsei, and C. L. Temkin. "Experiment and Experience in Hellenistic Medicine." *Bulletin of the Institute of Classical Studies* 22 (1975): 178–99.

Medieval and Renaissance

Primary Texts

Aretaeus. *The Extant Works of Aretaeus, the Cappadocian*. Ed. and trans. Francis Adams. Boston: Milford, 1972.

Avicenna [Ibn Sina]. *A Treatise on the* Canon of Medicine *of Avicenna*. Trans. O. Cameron Gruner. New York: Kelley, 1970.

Benivieni, Antonio. *On Some Hidden and Miraculous Causes of Diseases and Cures*. 1507. Trans. Charles Singer. Springfield: Thomas, 1954.

Bright, Timothy. *A Treatise of Melancholie*. London, 1586.

Bullein, William. *A Dialogue against the Feuer Pestilence*. Ed. Mark W. Bullen and A. H. Auden. London: Early English Text Soc., 1888.

Burton, Robert. *The Anatomy of Melancholy*. Ed. Floyd Dell and Paul Jordan-Smith. New York: Tudor, 1927. East Lansing: Michigan State UP, 1965.

Chauliac, Guy de. *The* Cyrurgie *of Guy de Chauliac*. Ed. Margaret S. Ogden. London: Early English Text Soc., 1971.

——. *The Middle English Translation of Guy de Chauliac's* Anatomy. Ed. Bjorn Wallner. Lund: Gleerup, 1964.

Cockayne, T. O. *Leechdoms, Wortcunning and Starcraft of Early England: Being a Collection of Documents*. London, 1864–65. London: Holland, 1961.

Cogliati Arano, Luisa. *The Medieval Health Handbook Tacuinum Sanitatis*. Trans. Oscar Ratti and Adele Westbrook. New York: Braziller, 1976.

Culpeper, Nicholas. *A New Method of Physick*. London, 1654.

Fleischhacker, Robert V., ed. *Lanfrank's "Science of Cirurgie."* London: Early English Text Soc., 1894.

Getz, Marie Faye, ed. *Healing and Society in Medieval England: A Middle English Translation of the Pharmaceutical Writings of Gilbertus Anglicus*. Madison: U of Wisconsin P, 1991.

Grant, Edward, ed. *A Source Book in Medieval Science*. Cambridge: Harvard UP, 1974.

Grattan, John Henry Grafton. *Anglo-Saxon Magic and Medicine: Illustrated Specially from the Semi-Pagan Text "Lacnunga."* London: Oxford UP, 1952.

Henslow, G., ed. *Medical Works of the Fourteenth Century*. New York: Franklin, 1972.

Horrox, Rosemary, trans. and ed. *The Black Death*. Manchester: Manchester UP, 1994.

John of Arderne. *Treatises of Fistula in Ano and of Fistulae in Other Parts of the Body [. . .]* . Ed. D'Arcy Power. London: Early English Text Soc., 1910.

Jordon, Edward. *A Briefe Discourse of a Disease Called the Suffocation of the Mother*. London, 1603.

Kibre, Pearl, ed. *Hippocrates Latinus: Repertorium of Hippocratic Writings in the Latin Middle Ages.* New York: Fordham UP, 1985.

O'Malley, Charles D., and J. B. Saunders, eds. *Leonardo da Vinci on the Human Body.* New York: Schuman, 1952.

Paracelsus. *Four Treatises of Theophrastus von Hohenheim called Paracelsus.* Ed. Henry Sigerist et al. Baltimore: Johns Hopkins UP, 1996.

———. *Paracelsus: Selected Writings.* Ed. Jolande Jacobi. Trans. Norbert Guterman. Princeton: Princeton UP, 1988.

Paré, Ambrosie. *Ten Books of Surgery.* Trans. R. W. Linker and N. Womack. Athens: U of Georgia P, 1969.

Rawcliffe, Carole. *Sources for the History of Medicine in Late Medieval England.* Kalamazoo: Medieval Inst., 1995.

Raynalde, Thomas. *The Byrth of Mankynde, Otherwyse Named the Womans Booke.* London: Watkins, 1598.

Singer, Charles, trans. and ed. "A Thirteenth Century Clinical Description of Leprosy." *Journal of the History of Medicine* 4 (1948): 237–39.

Wright, Cyril Ernest, ed. *Bald's* Leechbook. Baltimore: Johns Hopkins UP, 1955.

Secondary Texts

Amundsen, Darrel W. *Medicine, Society, and Faith in the Ancient and Medieval Worlds.* London: Johns Hopkins UP, 1996.

Arrizabalaga, Jon, John Henderson, and Roger French. *The Great Pox: The French Disease in Renaissance Europe.* New Haven: Yale UP, 1997.

Bloch, Marc. *The Royal Touch: Monarchy and Miracles in France and England.* Trans. J. E. Anderson. New York: Dorset, 1961.

Bonser, Wilfred. *The Medical Background of Anglo-Saxon England: A Study in History, Psychology, and Folklore.* London: Wellcome Hist. Medical Lib., 1963.

Brody, Saul. *The Disease of the Soul: Leprosy in Medieval Literature.* Ithaca: Cornell UP, 1974.

Caden, Joan. *Meanings of Sex Difference in the Middle Ages: Medicine, Science, and Culture.* Cambridge: Cambridge UP, 1993.

Cameron, M. L. *Anglo-Saxon Medicine.* Cambridge: Cambridge UP, 1993.

Campbell, Sheila, Bert Hall, and David Klausner, eds. *Health, Disease, and Healing in Medieval Culture.* New York: St. Martin's, 1992.

Curry, Walter Clyde. *Chaucer and the Medieval Sciences.* New York: Barnes, 1960.

Debus, Allen G. *The Chemical Philosophy: Paracelsian Science and Medicine in the Sixteenth and Seventeenth Centuries.* New York: Science Hist., 1977.

Eccles, Audrey. *Obstetrics and Gynaecology in Tudor and Stuart England.* Kent: Kent State UP, 1982.

Funkenstein, Amos. *Theology and the Scientific Imagination: From the Middle Ages to the Seventeenth Century*. Princeton: Princeton UP, 1986.

García-Ballester, Luis, Roger French, Jon Arrizabalaga, and Andrew Cunningham, eds. *Practical Medicine from Salerno to the Black Death*. Cambridge: Cambridge UP, 1994.

Gottfried, Robert S. *The Black Death: Natural and Human Disaster in Medieval Europe*. New York: Macmillan, 1983.

Hoeniger, F. David. *Medicine and Shakespeare in the English Renaissance*. Newark: U of Delaware P, 1992.

Hunt, Tony. *Popular Medicine in Thirteenth-Century England*. Cambridge: Brewer, 1990.

Jacquart, Danielle, and Claude Thomasset. *Sexuality and Medicine in the Middle Ages*. Trans. Matthew Adamson. Princeton: Princeton UP, 1988.

Kealey, Edward J. *Medieval Medicus: A Social History of Anglo-Norman Medicine*. Baltimore: Johns Hopkins UP, 1981.

Leavy, Barbara Fass. *To Blight with Plague: Studies in a Literary Theme*. New York: New York UP, 1992.

Lindberg, David C. *The Beginnings of Western Science*. Chicago: U of Chicago P, 1992.

MacDonald, Michael. *Mystical Bedlam: Madness, Anxiety and Healing in Seventeenth-Century England*. Cambridge: Cambridge UP, 1981.

Maclean, Ian. *The Renaissance Notion of Women: A Study in the Fortunes of Scholasticism and Medical Science in European Intellectual Life*. Cambridge: Cambridge UP, 1980.

Marland, Hillary, ed. *The Art of Midwifery: Early Modern Midwives in Europe*. London: Routledge, 1993.

McNeill, John T. "Medicine and Sin as Prescribed in the Penitentials." *Church History* 1 (1932): 14–26.

Miller, Timothy. *The Birth of the Hospital in the Byzantine Empire*. Baltimore: Johns Hopkins UP, 1997.

Pagel, Walter. *Paracelsus: An Introduction to Philosophical Medicine in the Era of the Renaissance*. Basel: Karger, 1958.

Platt, Colin. *King Death: The Black Death and Its Aftermath in Late-Medieval England*. Toronto: U of Toronto P, 1997.

Pouchelle, Marie-Christine. *The Body and Surgery in the Middle Ages*. Trans. Rosemary Morris. New Brunswick: Rutgers UP, 1990.

Prescott, Elizabeth. *The English Medieval Hospital, 1050–1640*. London: Seaby, 1992.

Rawcliffe, Carole. *Medicine and Society in Later Medieval England*. Phoenix Mill: Sutton, 1997.

Richards, Peter. *The Medieval Leper*. New York: Barnes, 1977.

Riddle, John M. *Contraception and Abortion from the Ancient World to the Renaissance*. Cambridge: Harvard UP, 1992.

Sawday, Jonathan. *The Body Emblazoned: Dissection and the Human Body in Renaissance Culture*. London: Routledge, 1995.

Schleissner, Margaret R., ed. *Manuscript Sources of Medieval Medicine: A Book of Essays*. New York: Garland, 1995.

Siraisi, Nancy G. *Avicenna in Renaissance Italy*. Princeton: Princeton UP, 1987.

―――. *Medieval and Early Renaissance Medicine: An Introduction to Knowledge and Practice*. Chicago: U of Chicago P, 1990.

Talbot, Charles H. *Medical Practitioners in Medieval England: A Biographical Register*. London: Wellcome Hist. Medical Lib., 1965.

―――. *Medicine in Medieval England*. New York: Elsevier, 1967.

Temkin, Owsei. *Galenism: Rise and Decline of a Medical Philosophy*. Ithaca: Cornell UP, 1973.

―――. *Hippocrates in a World of Pagans and Christians*. Baltimore: Johns Hopkins UP, 1991.

Watts, Sheldon. *Epidemics and History: Disease, Power, and Imperialism*. New Haven: Yale UP, 1997.

Wear, Andrew, Roger French, and Ian Lonie, eds. *The Medical Renaissance of the Sixteenth Century*. Cambridge: Cambridge UP, 1985.

Webster, C., ed. *Health, Medicine and Mortality in the Sixteenth Century*. Cambridge: Cambridge UP, 1979.

Seventeenth and Eighteenth Centuries

Primary Texts

Arbuthnot, John. *An Essay Concerning the Effects of Air on Human Bodies*. London: Tonson, 1733.

―――. *An Essay Concerning the Nature of Ailments and the Choice of Them, according to the Different Constitutions of Human Bodies*. London: Tonson, 1731.

Archer, John. *Every Man His Own Doctor*. 2nd ed. London, 1673.

Buchan, William. *Domestic Medicine; or, A Treatise on the Prevention and Cure of Diseases by Regimen and Simple Medicines*. 2nd ed. London: Strahan, 1772.

Chambers, Ephraim. *Cyclopaedia; or, An Universal Dictionary of Arts and Sciences*. 5th ed. 2 vols. London: Midwinter, 1741–43.

Cheyne, George. *The English Malady*. London: Strahan; Bath: Leake, 1733.

―――. *An Essay of Health and Long Life*. London: Strahan; Bath: Leake, 1724.

―――. *An Essay on Regimen*. London: Rivington; Bath: Leake, 1740.

―――. *A New Theory of Acute and Slow Continu'd Fevers [. . .] To Which Is Prefix'd an Essay concerning the Improvements of the Theory of Medicine*. 3rd ed. London: Strahan, 1722.

―――. *Observations concerning the Nature and Due Method of Treating the Gout*. London: Strahan, 1720.

Cockburn, William. *Account of the Nature, Causes, Symptoms, and Cure of the Distempers That Are Incident to Sea-Faring People*. 2nd ed. London: Strahan, 1706.

Freind, John. *Emmenologia*. Trans. Thomas Dale. London: Cox, 1729.

―――. *The History of Physick from the Time of Galen to the Beginning of the*

Sixteenth Century, Chiefly in Regard to Practice, in a Discourse Written to Dr. Mead. 2 vols. London: Walthoe, 1725–26.

Garth, Sir Samuel. *The Dispensary.* London, 1699. Delmar: Scholars', 1975.

Goodall, Charles. *The College of Physicians Vindicated, and the True State of Physick in This Nation Faithfully Represented.* London: Kettilby, 1676.

———. *The Royal College of Physicians of London.* London: Kettilby, 1684.

Gregory, John. *Lectures on the Duties and Qualifications of a Physician.* London: Strahan, 1772.

Hancocke, John. *Febrifugum Magnum; or, Common Water the Best Cure for Fevers, and Probably for the Plague.* 2nd ed. London: Halsey, 1723.

Harvey, Gideon. *The Accomplisht Physician, the Honest Apothecary, and the Skilful Chyrurgeon Detecting Their Necessary Connection and Dependence, on Each Other; Withall a Discovery of the Frauds of the Quacking Empiric, the Praescribing Surgeon, and the Practicing Apothecary.* London, 1670.

James, Robert. *A Medicinal Dictionary.* 3 vols. London: Osborne, 1743–45.

Keill, James. *An Account of Animal Secretion, the Quantity of Blood in the Humane Body, and Muscular Motion.* London: Strahan, 1708.

———. *The Anatomy of the Humane Body Abridg'd.* London: Keblewhite, 1698.

Knight, Thomas. *Reflections upon Catholicons; or, Universal Remedies.* London: Osborne, 1749.

A Letter from an Apothecary in London, to His Friend in the Country; Concerning the Present Practice of Physick, in Regard to Empiricks, Empirical Methods of Cure, and Nostrums. London: Cooper, 1752.

A Letter from the Facetious Dr. Andrew Tripe at Bath. To His Loving Brother the Profound Greshamite. London: Morphew, 1719.

Lind, James. *A Treatise on the Scurvy.* London: Millar, 1753.

Mead, Richard. *Dissertatio de Imperio Solis ac Lunae in Corpora Humana, et Morbis inde Oriundi.* Amsterdam: Gefser, 1739.

———. *A Mechanical Account of Poisons.* London: South, 1702.

Medicina Flagellata; or, The Doctor Scarify'd. Laying Open the Vices of the Faculty, the Insignificancy of a Great Part of Their Materia Medica, with Certain Rules to Discover the True Physician from the Empirick, and the Useful Medicine from the Noxious and Trading Physick. London: Bateman, 1721.

Merret, Christopher. *A Letter concerning the Present State of Physick, and the Regulation of the Practice of It in This Kingdom. Written to a Doctor Here in London.* London: Martyn, 1665.

Natural Sagacity the Principal Secret, If Not the Whole in Physick; All Learning without This, Being in Effect Nothing. Which Is Contrary to the Assertion of a Pamphlet, Lately Published Call'd One Physician Is as Good as t'Other. London: Cooper, 1742.

Pitcairne, Archibald. *Elementa Medicinae.* London: Innys, 1717.

———. *The Philosophical and Mathematical Elements of Physic.* Trans. John Quincy. London: Bell, 1718. 2nd ed. London, 1745.

———. *The Whole Works of Dr. Archibald Pitcairn; Wherein Are Discovered the True Foundation and Principles of the Art of Physic. With Cases and Observations, upon Most Distempers and Medicines.* Trans. George Sewell and J. T. Desaguliers. London: Curll, 1715. 2nd ed. London: Pemberton, 1727.

Quincy, John. *Lexicon Physico-Medicum; or, A New Physical Dictionary.* London: Bell, 1719.

———. *Pharmacopoeia Officinalis and Extemporanea; or, A Complete English Dispensatory.* 8th ed. London: Osborn, 1730.

Salmon, William. *Collectanea Medica, the Country Physician; or, A Choice Collection of Physick: Fitted for Vulgar Use.* London: Taylor, 1703.

Stukeley, William. *Of the Spleen, Its Description and History, Uses and Diseases, Particularly the Vapors, with Their Remedy.* London, 1722.

Sydenham, Thomas. *Dr. Thomas Sydenham (1624–1689): His Life and Original Writings.* Berkeley: U of California P, 1966.

———. *The Works of Thomas Sydenham.* Trans. R. G. Latham. 2 vols. London: Sydenham Soc., 1848–50.

Turner, Daniel. *The Art of Surgery [. . .] Further Illustrated with Many Singular and Rare Cases Medico-Chirurgical.* 2 vols. London: Rivington, 1722.

———. *The Drop and Pill of Mr. Ward Consider'd [. . .] in an Epistle to Dr. James Jurin.* London: Clarke, 1735.

———. *The Modern Quack; or, Medicinal Imposter.* 2nd ed. London: Warner, 1724.

———. *Siphylis: A Practical Dissertation on the Venereal Disease.* London: Wilkin, 1737.

Wesley, John. *Primitive Physick; or, An Easy and Natural Method of Curing Most Diseases.* London: Trye, 1747.

Woodward, John. *The Art of Getting into Practice in Physick, Here at Present in London. In a Letter to That Very Ingenious and Most Learned Physician, (Lately Come to Town) Dr. Timothy Vanbustle, M.D. A.B.C., &c.* London: Peele, 1722.

———. *Select Cases, and Consultations, in Physick. By the Late Eminent John Woodward, M.D.* Ed. Peter Templeman. London: Davis, 1747.

———. *The State of Physick: And of Diseases.* London: Horne, 1718.

Secondary Texts

Allen, Phyllis. "Medical Education in Seventeenth Century England." *Journal of the History of Medicine* 1 (1946): 115–43.

Beier, Lucinda McCray. *Sufferers and Healers: The Experience of Illness in Seventeenth-Century England.* London: Routledge, 1987.

Bynum, W. F. "Health, Disease and Medical Care." *The Ferment of Knowl-*

edge. Ed. George S. Rousseau and Roy Porter. Cambridge: Cambridge UP, 1980. 211–54.

Bynum, W. F., and Roy Porter, eds. *Medical Fringe and Medical Orthodoxy, 1750–1850*. London: Croom, 1986.

———, eds. *William Hunter and the Eighteenth-Century Medical World*. Cambridge: Cambridge UP, 1985.

Clark, George N. *A History of the Royal College of Physicians of London*. 3 vols. Oxford: Clarendon, 1964–72.

Cook, Harold J. *The Decline of the Old Medical Regime in Stuart London*. Ithaca: Cornell UP, 1986.

———. *The Trials of an Ordinary Doctor: Johannes Groenvelt in Seventeenth-Century London*. Baltimore: Johns Hopkins UP, 1994.

Cunningham, Andrew, and Roger French, eds. *The Medical Enlightenment of the Eighteenth Century*. Cambridge: Cambridge UP, 1990.

Fissell, Mary Elizabeth. *Patients, Power, and the Poor in Eighteenth-Century Bristol*. Cambridge: Cambridge UP, 1991.

Fox, Christopher, ed. *Psychology and Literature in the Eighteenth Century*. New York: AMS, 1987.

Frank, Robert G. *Harvey and the Oxford Physiologists: Scientific Ideas and Social Interaction*. Berkeley: U of California P, 1980.

French, Roger, and Andrew Wear, ed. *The Medical Revolution of the Seventeenth Century*. Cambridge: Cambridge UP, 1989.

Holmes, Geoffrey. *Augustan England: Professions, State and Society, 1680–1730*. London: Allen, 1982.

Jewson, Nicholas. "Medical Knowledge and the Patronage System in Eighteenth-Century England." *Sociology* 8 (1974): 369–85.

King, Lester. *The Medical World of the Eighteenth Century*. Chicago: U of Chicago P, 1958.

Lawrence, Susan Co. *Charitable Knowledge: Hospital Pupils and Practitioners in Eighteenth-Century London*. Cambridge: Cambridge UP, 1996.

LeFanu, W. R. "The Lost Half-Century in English Medicine, 1700–1750." *Bulletin of the History of Medicine* 46 (1972): 319–48.

Porter, Dorothy, and Roy Porter. *In Sickness and in Health: The British Experience, 1650–1850*. London: Fourth Estate, 1988.

———. *Patient's Progress: Doctors and Doctoring in Eighteenth-Century England*. Stanford: Stanford UP, 1989.

Porter, Roy. *Disease, Medicine, and Society in England, 1550–1860*. London: Macmillan, 1987.

———. "Lay Medical Knowledge in the Eighteenth Century: The *Gentleman's Magazine*." *Medical History* 29 (1985): 138–68.

———, ed. *Patients and Practitioners: Lay Perceptions of Medicine in Preindustrial Society*. Cambridge: Cambridge UP, 1985.

Risse, Guenter B. "Medicine in the Age of Enlightenment." *Medicine in Society: Historical Essays*. Ed. Andrew Wear. Cambridge: Cambridge UP, 1992. 149–95.

Roberts, Marie Mulvey, and Roy Porter, eds. *Literature and Medicine during the Eighteenth Century*. London: Routledge, 1993.

Rousseau, G. S. *Enlightenment Borders: Pre- and Post-modern Discourse, Medical and Scientific*. Manchester: Manchester UP, 1991.

———. "'Sowing the Wind and Reaping the Whirlwind': Aspects of Change in Eighteenth Century Medicine." *Studies in Change and Revolution: Aspects of English Intellectual History, 1640–1800*. Ed. Paul J. Korshin. London: Scolar, 1972. 129–59.

Waddington, Ivan. *The Medical Profession in the Industrial Revolution*. Dublin: Gill, 1984.

Webster, Charles. *The Great Instauration: Science, Medicine and Reform, 1626–1660*. London: Duckworth, 1975.

Wiltshire, John. *Samuel Johnson in the Medical World: The Doctor and the Patient*. Cambridge: Cambridge UP, 1991.

Nineteenth Century and Early Twentieth Century

See the extensive bibliographies in Lilian R. Furst's *Between Doctors and Patients: The Changing Balance of Power* (Charlottesville: UP of Virginia, 1998) and Roy Porter's *The Greatest Benefit to Mankind: A Medical History of Humanity* (New York: Norton, 1998).

Notes on Contributors

Felice Aull, PhD, is associate professor of physiology and neuro-science at New York University School of Medicine, where she teaches an elective in literature and medicine, organizes the Litera-ture, Arts, and Medicine Speakers Series, and heads a literature and medicine discussion group. She is the founder of the *Literature, Arts, and Medicine Database* and a member of the advisory group for the Humanities in Medicine Program at the New York Academy of Medicine. She is a candidate for the MA in the Draper Program in Humanities and Social Thought at New York University.

Dieter J. Boxmann is instructor of communication at the Univer-sity of Minnesota, Duluth, and at Kirkwood Community College, Iowa. After more than ten years as a practicing registered nurse in emergency and critical-care departments of inner-city hospitals in New York, Oakland, and San Francisco, he is now finishing a disser-tation entitled "The Rhetoric of Medical Practice." He is also working on two articles: "CAT Scanner Rhetoric and the Anatomy of Medical Perception" and "Don't Worry, Be Happy and Other Moral Directives in Self-Help Ads and Products."

Stephanie P. Browner, PhD, is assistant professor in the Department of English and Theater at Berea College. Her recent publications include articles on the discovery of ether, in *American Quarterly*, and on literature and medicine, forthcoming in *Texas Studies in Language and Literature*. She is a consulting editor for *Whitman, Dickinson, and Teaching American Literature with New Technologies*, an Internet project funded by the United States Department of Education, and she is finishing a manuscript on representations of medicine in literature in the United States during the second half of the nineteenth century.

Sheryl Buckley, MD, is medical director of Rockside Surgical Center in Independence, Ohio. She recently completed her master's in administrative medicine at the University of Wisconsin, Madison. For several years, she has taught medical ethics and team-taught the What's Normal? course in the Weekend College Program at Hiram College. With Carol Donley, she is editor of *The Tyranny of the Normal* (Kent State UP, 1996) and a forthcoming anthology on literature and mental disabilities. She has participated in the summer seminar on narrative bioethics at Hiram College and has chaired the ethics committee at a regional hospital.

Joseph Cady, PhD, taught medical humanities for ten years at the University of Rochester Medical School, where he was awarded the Harry L. Segal Prize for Excellence in Third-Year Teaching and elected by the students to Alpha Omega Alpha, the national medical honor society. He is currently visiting professor of literature and medicine at the University of Utah Medical School. Recent essays appear in *Desire and Discipline: Sex and Sexuality in the Premodern West* (U of Toronto P, 1996), *The Gay and Lesbian Literary Heritage* (Henry Holt, 1995), and *Writing AIDS* (Columbia UP, 1993).

Rita Charon, MD, PhD, is associate professor of clinical medicine at the College of Physicians and Surgeons of Columbia University, where she is the director of the program in humanities and medicine. A practicing general internist, she directs medical student education in medical interviewing, the patient-physician relationship, and the humanities. She has lectured and published widely on narrative ethics, narrative knowledge in medicine, doctor-patient relationships, feminist reader-response theory, and the late novels of Henry James. She is on the editorial boards of six journals and has held leadership positions in the Society for Health and Human Values, the Association of American Medical Colleges, and the American College of Physicians. She received her doctorate from the Department of English at Columbia University.

Paul W. Child, who holds a PhD from the University of Notre Dame, is associate professor of English at Sam Houston State University, where he teaches courses in Restoration and eighteenth-century literature and in the classical tradition. His publications include "'Platonick Love' by George Cheyne," in the *Scriblerian*.

G. Thomas Couser, PhD, is professor of English at Hofstra University. He has published extensively on autobiography; his work includes three books — *American Autobiography: The Prophetic Mode* (U of Massachusetts P, 1979), *Altered Egos: Authority in American Autobiography* (Oxford UP, 1989), and *Recovering Bodies: Illness, Disability and Life Writing* (U of Wisconsin P, 1997) — as well as a collection of essays edited with Joseph Fichtelberg, *True Relations: Essays on Autobiography and the Postmodern* (Greenwood, 1998). He teaches a wide range of courses in American literature, including Native American literature and life writing. His current research focuses on ethical issues in life writing, especially in the representation of people with disabilities.

LaVera M. Crawley, MD, is a Soros Faculty Scholar and research fellow at the Center for Biomedical Ethics at Stanford University School of Medicine. She is a former associate professor at the

California Institute of Integral Studies and has practiced family medicine for the Indian Health Service on the Navajo reservation in Arizona, where she served as the local director of prenatal services. Her articles and workshops have focused on the functions of narrative in education, medicine, and new medical paradigms.

Cortney Davis, MA, APRN, is a nurse practitioner at Danbury Hospital in Danbury, Connecticut. Her publications include *Details of Flesh* (Calyx, 1997) and *The Body Flute* (Adastra, 1994). She is coeditor of an anthology, *Between the Heartbeats* (U of Iowa P, 1995). She has published poems, articles, and fiction in various journals and teaches creative writing workshops for nurses and physicians. Currently she is completing a collection of essays on women's health. She was a visiting poet at Northeastern Ohio Universities College of Medicine in 1998, and she is on the editorial board of the *Journal of Medical Humanities.*

Paul Delaney, PhD, is professor of English at Westmont College. He is editor of *Tom Stoppard in Conversation* (U of Michigan P, 1994) and the author of *Tom Stoppard: The Moral Vision of the Major Plays* (Macmillan; St. Martin's, 1990). His recent articles include one on U. A. Fanthorpe in *Christianity and Literature.* He teaches courses in contemporary drama and poetry, Shakespeare, Irish literature, and Faulkner. He is currently editing a collection of interviews with the Irish playwright Brian Friel, to be published as *Brian Friel in Conversation* by the University of Michigan Press.

Carol Donley, PhD, is professor of English and codirector of the Center for Literature, Medicine, and the Health Care Professions at Hiram College. Her publications include *Einstein as Myth and Muse,* with Alan Friedman (Cambridge UP, 1985); *Literature and Aging: An Anthology,* with Martin Kohn and Delese Wear (Kent State UP, 1993); and *The Tyranny of the Normal: An Anthology,* with Sheryl Buckley (Kent State UP, 1996). Donley is completing work with Sheryl Buckley on another anthology focusing on literature and mental illness and mental disabilities. She teaches several literature and medicine courses, including narrative bioethics. In 1998 she earned an MA in bioethics from Case Western Reserve University School of Medicine. She has codirected two NEH Institutes in Humanities and Medicine and has helped establish the annual summer seminar in narrative bioethics held at Hiram College.

Martin Donohoe, MD, is assistant professor of medicine and senior scholar at the Center for Ethics in Health Care, Oregon Health Sciences University. His publications include studies of anti-diabetic drugs and swallowing disorders, quality of care, referral practices, and other public health topics. He is the author of "Perspectives of Physician-Authors Lewis Thomas and Samuel Shem on the Art of Medicine and the Training of Doctors," in the *American Medical Writers Association Journal.* He has expanded his course into a month-long elective for senior medical students and has developed an ethics, humanities, and social justice curriculum for internal medicine residents. He also lectures on the health consequences of environmental degradation and on the pharmaceutical and tobacco industries.

David H. Flood, PhD, is professor at the School of Health Professions and director of the Division of Arts and Social Sciences at MCP Hahnemann University. He has coauthored with Rhonda Soricelli articles for *Literature and Medicine,* including an analysis of physician narrative voice in the medical case history and an original script for a play about literary physicians in professional crisis, as well as commentaries on medicine and the arts for *Academic Medicine.* He has also written on blood and transfusion in *Dracula* and on H. Ryder Haggard's role in the nineteenth-century antivaccination controversy. He is currently working on the role of the medical thriller in shaping popular perceptions of medical science and ethics.

H. Bruce Franklin, PhD, is a cultural historian and the author or editor of seventeen books and more than two hundred articles. He is currently the John Cotton Dana Professor of English and American Studies at Rutgers University, Newark. His many publications include *War Stars: The Superweapon and the American Imagination* (Oxford, 1988), *Future Perfect: American Science Fiction of the Nineteenth Century* (Rutgers UP, 1995), and *M.I.A.; or, Mythmaking in America* (Rutgers UP, 1993).

Lilian R. Furst, PhD, is Marcel Bataillon Professor of Comparative Literature at the University of North Carolina, Chapel Hill. Among her numerous publications on intersections between medical history and literature are "Realistic Pathologies and Romantic Psychosomatics in Thomas Mann's *Buddenbrooks*," in *Romanticism and Beyond: A Festschrift for John F. Fetzer* (Lang, 1996); *Between Doctors and Patients: The Changing Balance of Power* (UP of Virginia, 1998); and "'You Have Sprained Your Brain': Margaret Cleaves's Autobiography of a Neurasthene," in *Nineteenth-Century Prose*. She is also the author of *"Just Talk": Narratives of Psychotherapy* (UP of Kentucky, 1999), and she is completing an anthology for classroom use on nineteenth-century literature and medicine.

Deborah R. Grayson, PhD, is assistant professor in the school of literature, communication, and culture at the Georgia Institute of Technology. Her recent publications include "Mediating Intimacy: Black Surrogate Mothers and the Law," in *Critical Inquiry*, and "Necessity Was the Midwife to Our Politics: Black Women's Health Activism, 1980–1996," in *Still Lifting, Still Climbing: Contemporary African American Women's Activism* (New York UP, 1999). She is guest editor of a special issue of *Camera Obscura* on black women, spectatorship, and visual culture, which includes her essay, "Is It Fake? Black Women's Hair as Spectacle and Spectacular." She teaches African American literature and literary theory, cultural studies of health and science, and feminist studies.

Bryon Lee Grigsby is a PhD candidate at Loyola University, Chicago, and an instructor of English at Eastern Connecticut State University. He is working on a dissertation entitled "'The Doctour maketh this descriptioun': Describing the Unification of Medicine,

Theology, and Literature in Medieval Culture." His publications include "The Social Position of the Surgeon in London, 1350–1450," in *Essays in Medieval Studies*, and "Medical Misconceptions," in *Misconceptions about the Middle Ages: An Electronic Book* (http://bede.net).

Anne Hunsaker Hawkins, PhD, is associate professor of humanities at the Pennsylvania State University College of Medicine. She is the author of *Archetypes of Conversion* (Assoc. UP, 1985) and *Reconstructing Illness: A Study in Pathography* (Purdue UP, 1993; 2nd ed. 1999) as well as coeditor of an issue of *Literature and Medicine* on the medical case history (1992), an issue of the *Journal of Medicine and Philosophy* on literature and medical ethics (1996), and *Time to Go: Three Plays on Death and Dying, with Commentary on End-of-Life Issues* (U of Pennsylvania P, 1995). She is currently working on a book about pediatric AIDS patients and their caregivers in a tertiary-care medical center.

Elizabeth Homan, PhD, is an assistant professor of theater at Texas Tech University. As an actor and director as well as a scholar, she strives to find the delicate balance between dramatic theory and practice. She has presented papers at such national conferences as the Association for Theatre in Higher Education and MLA and hopes to publish portions of her dissertation, "Cultural Contexts and the American Classical Canon: Contemporary Approaches to Performing Tennessee Williams's *A Streetcar Named Desire*," as a series of articles on the twentieth-century American dramatic canon.

Sidney Homan, PhD, is professor of English and artist in residence in the Arts in Medicine Program at Shands Teaching Hospital, University of Florida. He has published several books and over sixty articles and reviews on Shakespeare and modern theater as well as articles on arts and medicine. He has edited three collections of essays on aspects of Shakespeare's work. For four years he directed Theatre Strike Force, an improvisation company that played in hospitals, prisons, and other venues. He is currently working on a book on the function of arts in medicine and on two autobiographical collections of short stories.

Kristin Lindgren teaches in the English department at Haverford College. She is currently completing her dissertation, a study of gender and the construction of illness in nineteenth-century women's fiction and autobiography. Her research and teaching interests include Victorian literature and culture, contemporary poetry, and the literature of illness and disability.

Monica Maillet teaches in the Medical Ethics and Humanities Program at Northwestern University; her seminars have focused on a range of topics from Health and Cultural Difference to Medicine and *Macbeth*. She is a PhD candidate in theater at Northwestern University, where she is writing a dissertation on gender and modes of knowing in Aeschylus and Shakespeare.

Jan Marta, MD, PhD, is assistant professor of psychiatry and research associate in the Psychoanalytic Thought Program at the University of Toronto. Her fifteen articles, in English and in French, include "Lacan and Post-structuralism," in the *American Journal of Psychoanalysis;* "Whose Consent Is It Anyway? A Poststructuralist Configuration of the Person in Medical Decision Making," in *Theoretical Medicine;* and "Signifiants de l'identité ortho-(a)gonale: Vers une nouvelle semiotique de la subjectivité," in *Semiotica.*

Marilyn Chandler McEntyre, PhD, is chair of the English department at Westmont College, where she teaches a range of courses in poetry and fiction as well as literature and medicine to undergraduates. She serves on the boards of *Literature and Medicine;* the online *Literature, Arts, and Medicine Database;* and the Center for Medicine, Humanities, and Law in Berkeley. She offers occasional workshops on topics in literature and medicine to physicians and other health-care workers as well as to various interest groups. Her writing includes articles on literature and medicine in *Academic Medicine,*

Perspectives in Biology and Medicine, Literature and Medicine, Medical Humanities Review, and other professional journals. She also serves as associate editor of the *Santa Barbara Review,* a literary journal, and writes poetry and essays.

Jonathan M. Metzl, MD, is senior lecturer in the women's studies program and the Department of Psychiatry and is codirector of the Rackham Interdisciplinary Institute at the University of Michigan, Ann Arbor. Recent publications include "Psychotherapy, Managed Care and the Economy of Interaction: A Narrative Approach to Managed Mental Health Care," in *American Journal of Psychotherapy;* "Trauma, Listening, and 'A Way You'll Never Be,'" in *Medical Humanities Review;* and "Managed Care and Mental Health: An Oxymoron of Ethics," in *Jefferson Journal of Psychiatry.* He currently teaches a course on the interactions of biological psychiatry and American popular culture and has lectured widely on the applications of literature and literary theory in medical education. His soon to be completed PhD dissertation project examines representations of psychotropic medications in American fiction, media, and advertising.

Kathryn Montgomery, PhD, is professor of medical ethics and humanities, professor of medicine, and director of the Medical Ethics and Humanities Program at Northwestern University Medical School. She is the author of *Doctors' Stories: The Narrative Structure of Medical Knowledge* (Princeton UP, 1991) and of many articles on literature and medicine. Fascinated by the curious process that turns students of science into physicians, she is currently attempting to describe the development of clinical judgment.

Laura Otis, PhD, is associate professor of English at Hofstra University. Her recent publications include *Membranes: Metaphors of Invasion in Nineteenth-Century Literature, Science, and Politics* (Johns Hopkins UP, 1998); *Organic Memory: History and the Body in the Late Nineteenth and Early Twentieth Centuries* (U of Nebraska P,

1994); "The Empire Bites Back: Sherlock Holmes as an Imperial Immune System," in *Studies in Twentieth-Century Literature*; and "The Language of Infection: Disease and Identity in Schnitzler's *Reigen*," in *Germanic Review*. She is now writing a third book, *Networking*, which will explore representations of communications networks in nineteenth-century biology and literature. She draws on training in biochemistry and neuroscience to bring the discourses of literature and science into dialogue in her teaching and writing.

Vera Pohland, PhD, is assistant professor of German at Hobart and William Smith Colleges. Her publications include *Das Sanatorium als literarischer Ort* (Lang, 1984); "From Positive-Stigma to Negative-Stigma: A Shift of the Literary and Medical Representation of Consumption in German Culture," in *Disease and Medicine in Modern German Cultures* (Center for Intl. Studies, Cornell U, 1990); and "Die andere Seite der Krankheit: Epilepsie als Fiktion: Zu Alfred Kubins Roman *Die andere Seite*," in *Die Rampe: Hefte für Literatur*. She has coauthored "Der Wichser: Edgar Hilsenrath: Schreiben über den Holocaust, Identität und Sexualität," in *Der Deutschunterricht*, and coedited *Disease and Medicine in Modern German Cultures*.

Suzanne Poirier, PhD, is professor of literature and medical education at the University of Illinois College of Medicine, Chicago, where she has taught literature to health professions students since 1980. She is editor (with Timothy F. Murphy) of *Writing AIDS: Gay Literature, Language, and Analysis* (Columbia UP, 1993), author of *Chicago's War against Syphilis, 1937-1940: The Times, the "Trib," and the Clap Doctor* (U of Illinois P, 1995), and editor of the journal *Literature and Medicine*.

Kendrick W. Prewitt, PhD, is assistant professor of English at the University of the Ozarks. He has taught courses in literature and medicine in the Department of Social Medicine at the University of North Carolina, Chapel Hill, and at Washington University Medical

School. His recent publications include "Gabriel Harvey and the Practice of Method," in *Studies in English Literature, 1500–1900*.

Douglas Robert Reifler, MD, is assistant professor of medicine and medical ethics and humanities at Northwestern University Medical School. His publications include " 'I Actually Don't Mind the Bone Saw': Narratives of Gross Anatomy," in *Literature and Medicine,* and "Early Patient Encounters: Second-Year Student Narratives of Initiation into Clinical Medicine," in *Pharos.* His current research and teaching focus on creative writing in medical education, medical professionalization, and mental disorders in primary care. His students' stories have been published in the *Journal of the American Medical Association, Annals of Internal Medicine, Pharos,* and *Medical Encounter.* He is collecting an anthology of stories from various stages of training.

Michèle M. Respaut, PhD, is professor and chair of French at Wellesley College, where she teaches an interdisciplinary course on literature and medicine. She has written on major works of French fiction from the seventeenth to the twentieth centuries. She is a participant in the NEH project Text and Teachers: The Interdisciplinary Challenge, which involves collaborative courses on literature and medicine designed by both high school teachers and faculty members at Wellesley College, Brown University, Smith College, and the University of Massachusetts, Amherst. Her current research focuses on representations of children in mourning.

Iliana Alexandra Semmler, PhD, is lecturer emerita at the State University of New York, Albany, where she teaches a class in literature and medicine. Her recent publications include commentaries on *White Noise,* by Don DeLillo, and *Patrimony,* by Philip Roth, both in *Academic Medicine,* and an article entitled "Ebola Goes Pop: The Filovirus from Literature into Film," in *Literature and Medicine.* She recently reviewed Richard Selzer's *The Doctor Stories* (in *Medical Humanities Review*) and is currently editing his journals. She also teaches courses on William Carlos Williams and the twentieth-century American novel.

Rhonda L. Soricelli, MB, BS, who holds a bachelor of medicine and a bachelor of surgery from the University of Sydney, draws on an extensive background in private-practice nephrology and internal medicine and more than a decade of teaching clinical ethics and medical humanities at MCP Hahnemann University. She has coauthored with David Flood articles for *Literature and Medicine* (including an analysis of physician narrative voice in the medical case history and a script for a play about physicians in professional crisis) and commentaries on medicine and the arts for *Academic Medicine*. She teaches about home care, gender issues in medicine, and the experience of illness revealed by the visual arts. She is exploring uses of theater in educating professional and lay audiences about aging and end-of-life decision making.

Lois S. Spatz, PhD, is professor of English at the University of Missouri, Kansas City. Her publications include three books on Greek myth and drama and several articles that bring together literature and medicine, including "Six Women: Reflections on Pregnancy, Abortion, and the Uses of Poetry," in *College English*. In addition to the course Writing, Healing, and the Humanities, she teaches one entitled Doctors and Literature.

Michelle Bollard Toby, PhD, recently completed her doctorate at the University of California, Irvine, specializing in Anglo-American modernism with emphasis on literature and medicine and gender studies. Her dissertation is entitled "Healing Visions: Women, Modernism, and the Ailing Body." Her paper "From Bridal Bier to Death Bed: Woolf's Rejection of the Beautiful Death" appeared in *Virginia Woolf and Her Influences: Selected Papers from the Seventh Annual Conference on Virginia Woolf* (Pace UP, 1998). She teaches at the University of California, Irvine.

Kathleen Welch, PhD, teaches English, adult education, and medical humanities at the University of Missouri, Kansas City. Her publications include "Narrative Writing: The Forgotten Tool," in the *Medical Humanities Newsletter*, and "Student/TA/Professor Relations in a Social Studies Education Course," in *Research in the Teaching of English*. She has spoken at a variety of educational and medical forums on the uses of writing in medical education.

Elizabeth M. Willingham, PhD, is assistant professor in the Department of Modern Foreign Languages at Baylor University. Her work in literature and medicine includes a paper on the relations between science and the humanities and analyses of *One Flew over the Cuckoo's Nest*, *Like Water for Chocolate*, and Katherine Anne Porter's "The Grave." She has three books in progress: one on *Like Water for Chocolate*, one on a long poem of Robert Browning, and one on Christopher Columbus's Barcelona Letter.

Janice L. Willms, MD, PhD, is a lecturer in the College of Creative Studies at the University of California, Santa Barbara. Her recent publications include "Alienation and Imagination: The Literature of Exclusion," in *Annals of Internal Medicine*, and several short essays in *Academic Medicine* on medical themes in literature. She authored two medical textbooks, in 1994 and 1996. She is currently working on a history of Saint Patrick Hospital in Missoula, Montana, and compiling clinical vignettes for a volume stressing the problems generated by the medical-education system in the United States.

Index